ARCHI-
TECTURE
AND SUR-
REALISM

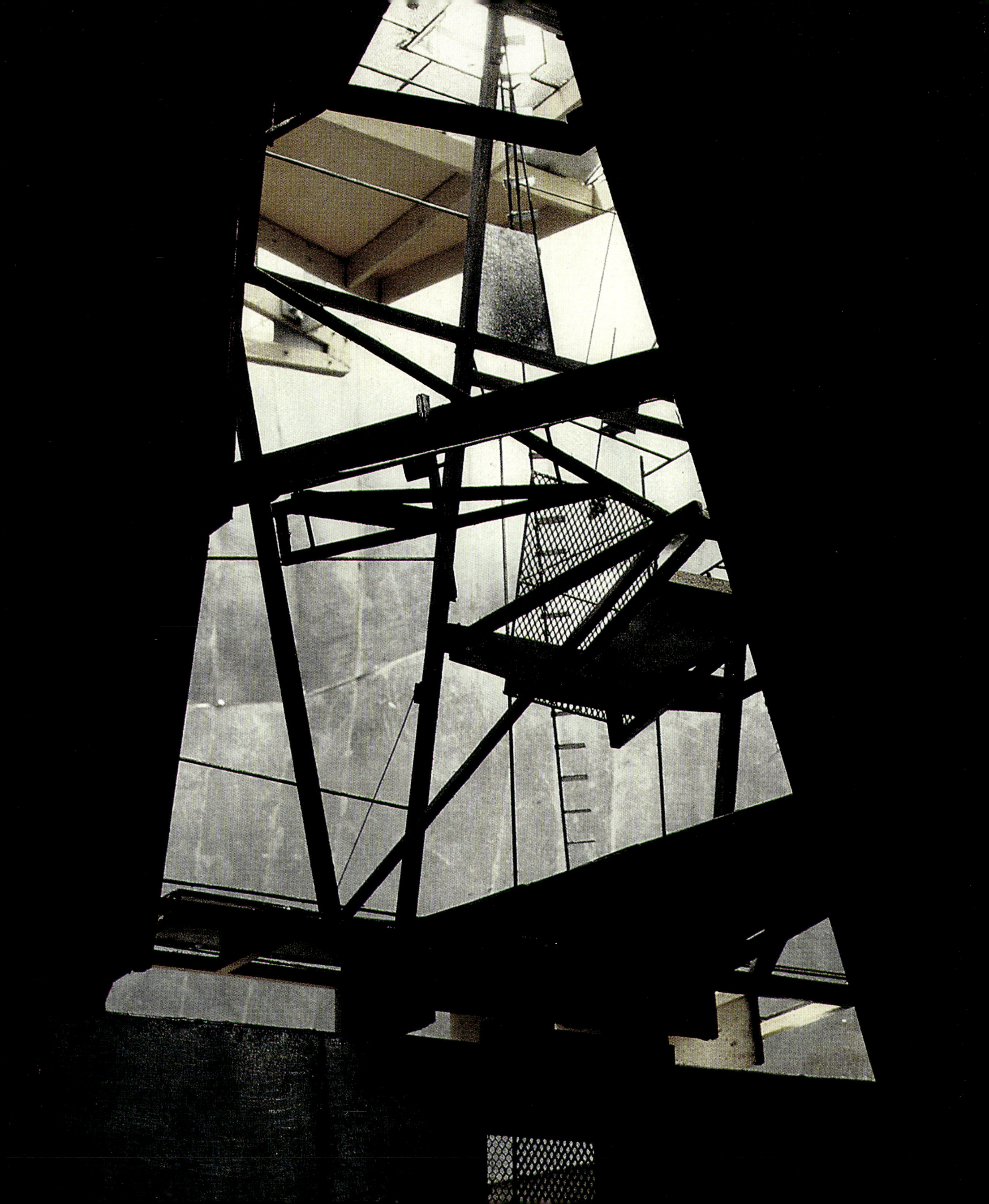

ARCHITECTURE AND SURREALISM

A BLISTERING ROMANCE

Thames & Hudson

With 199 illustrations

NEIL SPILLER

Page 2
Lebbeus Woods • Solohouse
1988–89

First published in the United Kingdom in 2016
by **Thames & Hudson Ltd**, 181A High Holborn,
London WC1V 7QX

Architecture and Surrealism: A Blistering Romance

Designed by **Barnbrook**

British Library Cataloguing-in-Publication Data
A catalogue record for this book is available
from the British Library

ISBN 978-0-500-34320-3

Printed and bound in China by Imago

CONTENTS

The bones are gently cradled below the surface of the table like a landscape, like an excavation, like an archaeological dig. The table is set. Sitting at the table waiting to eat, we look back in time. Mother's meals. The flesh that is not there becomes mother's flesh. The flesh she prepares for dinner is made emphatically present. Life and mortality, the miracle inside us, the fundamental sacrifice is made beautiful, comic and creepy.

Natalija Subotincic, 'Incarnate Tendencies: An Architecture of Culinary Refuse', 2004[1]

He is fair as...the chance meeting on a dissecting table of a sewing machine and an umbrella!

Comte de Lautréamont, The Songs of Maldoror, 1868–69

THE ARCHITECTURE, CITIES AND JUNGLES OF SURREALISM

INTRODUCTION

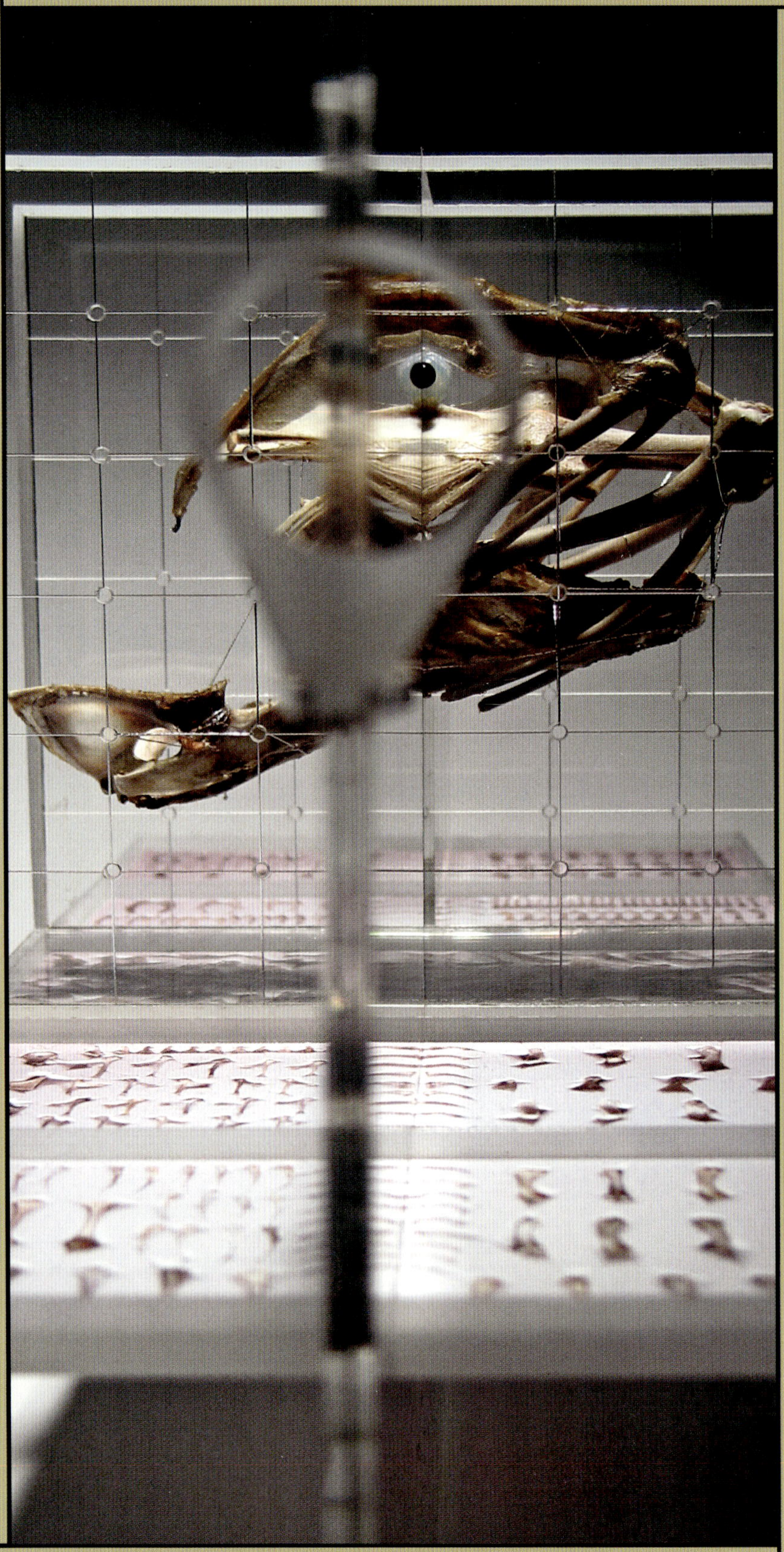

←

Natalija Subotincic

Incarnate Tendencies:

An Architecture of Culinary Refuse

2007

This book is an exploration and celebration of the spatial and visual possibilities where architecture has met, and continues to meet, Surrealism.

This interaction between architecture and Surrealism has a long and interesting history, and is now enjoying a renewed vitality invigorated by the profound technological changes currently influencing leading-edge architectural designers. In this technological and digital tumult, the protocols, concepts and otherworldliness of Surrealism often seem more appropriate precedents than the tired dogmas and limited palette of architectural Modernism.

We live in a world where a duvet can blog, where guns can be manufactured using a desktop 3D printer, where modified scanner drones can be used to grab buckets of 'big data' about sites they survey. We can create augmented reality storms. Such spatial opportunities and conditions are all surreally architectural, and an understanding of Surrealism can help today's architects deal with these and the many other new possibilities available to them.

We can now create personal and public reflexive environments that exist both virtually and actually. We can choreograph their sensitivity, their scale, their biological, mechanical and ecological interactions, how we observe them, how they observe us, how they recognize us and how they fully accommodate our spatial and visceral desires. We are able to seamlessly hybridize materials, expanding the traditional palette of materials in many previously unimaginable ways. Soon we will be able to conceive of buildings and their sites as agile, and maybe create sustainable architectures that utilize synthetic biologies. We might be able to grow architecture.

In charting the development and evolution of surreal architectural ideas, the aim of this book is to illustrate how they are being put to use by contemporary architects in extraordinary ways.

The Origins of Surrealism

The term 'Surrealism' was first coined in May 1917 by the French poet and playwright Guillaume Apollinaire in his programme text for the ballet *Parade* – a collaboration between choreographer Léonide Massine, Jean Cocteau and Pablo Picasso, with music by Erik Satie scored for machinery such as propellers, sirens and typewriters. Apollinaire wrote that this collaboration of artists of all sorts had 'given rise, in *Parade*, to a kind of Surrealism. In my view this is just the first of many manifestations of the New Spirit abroad.... We expect it to bring about profound changes in our arts and manners through universal joyfulness.'[3] It should be mentioned that in French '*sur*' means 'on top', so to be 'surreal' is to be on top of the real – another dimension.

However, strange portents could be felt in the half-century before Surrealism knew its name, the origins

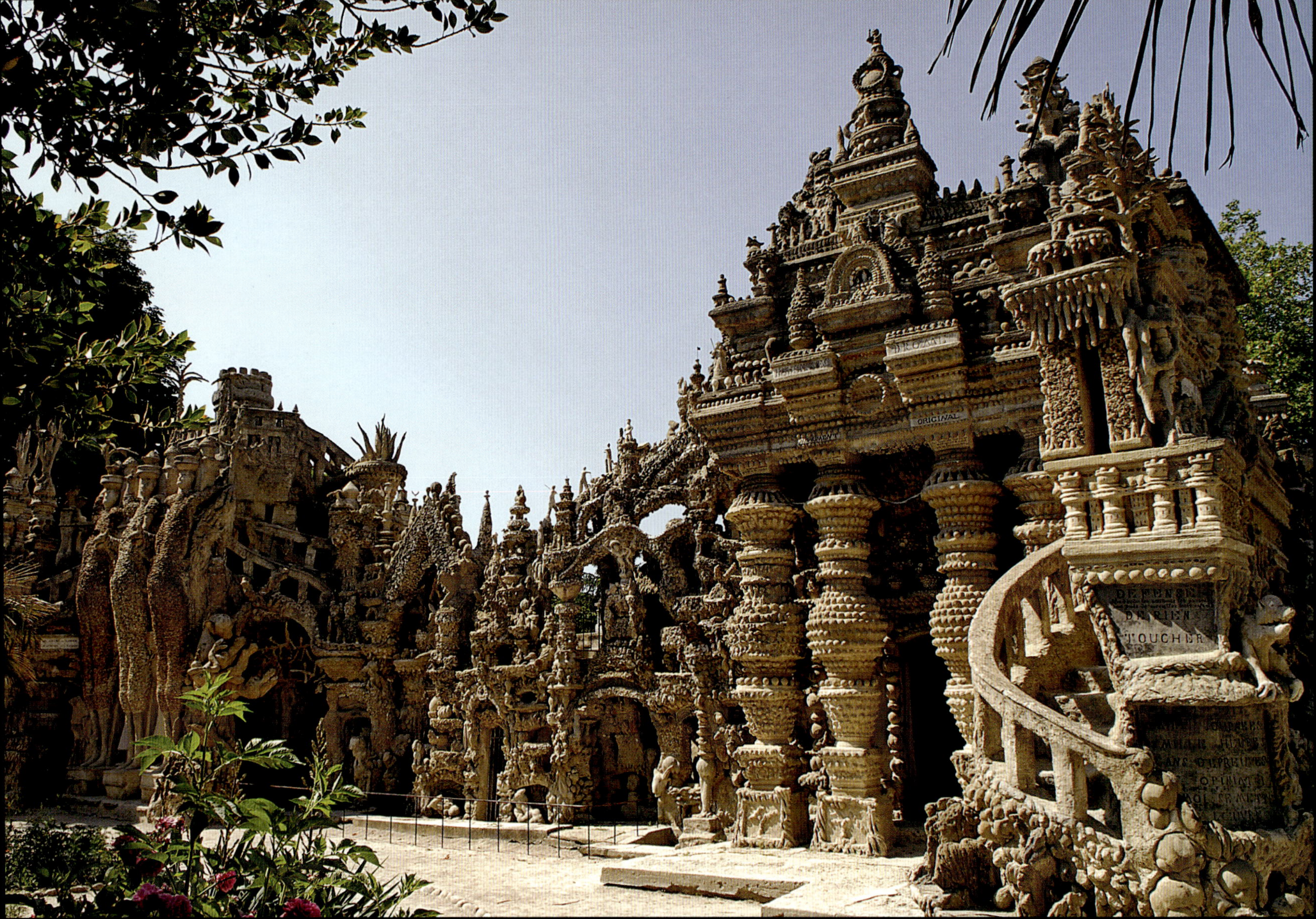
ORIGINAL
DEFENSE
DE RIEN
TOUCHER

←

Palais Idéal du Facteur Cheval

(Postman Cheval's Ideal Palace)

Hauterives, Drôme, France

1879–1912

of which were mostly literary; for example, the French poet Charles Baudelaire's *Les Fleurs du Mal* (1857) and the Comte de Lautréamont's *Les Chants de Maldoror* (1868–69).[4] It was in the 1920s that Surrealism first started to respond to the visual arts, initially to the work of Giorgio de Chirico, Max Ernst and others, engaging with their representations of buildings, architectural interiors and cities, and casting architecture as an active backdrop to Surrealist obsessions.

An important architectural precedent for the aspirations of the Surrealists was French postman Ferdinand Cheval's Palais Idéal at Hauterives in southeastern France. Cheval began the construction of his magical palace in 1879, using the stones he collected on his rounds. Taking thirty-three years to build, it became his life's work. More of a sculpture than a building, it is mostly exterior, the inside being only large enough to store the wheelbarrow in which he gathered his stones. A mix of all kinds of stylistic preoccupations, it is a warped cacophony of grottoes, pockets, statues, columns and protusions. Its disregard for the protocols and culture of its time, and any rules of composition, endeared it to the Surrealists, and its unbridled imagination and ambition struck a chord with the Surrealist sensibility. Its juxtaposition of the mutually strange and at odds enchanted them as they searched for examples of the 'marvellous'. The French writer and poet André Breton, in particular, was eloquent (for instance, in his famed Prague lecture, delivered on 29 March 1935, on the 'Surrealist Situation of the Object') in his defence of it as Surrealist architecture. Cheval – outsider, idiot savant and maker of homages to stony found objects – thus became assimilated into the Surrealist architectural canon, one of its first architectonic precursors and a Surrealist weapon against the evolving architectural Modernism that they so despised.

After splitting from the Dadaists, Breton formed an embryonic Surrealist group of mainly writers, including Paul Eluard, Louis Aragon and Philippe Soupault, and wrote the *Manifeste du surréalisme* (1924). The manifesto evoked the unbound creativity of children, the symbolism of Freudian dream interpretation and the importance of automatic writing, and sought to establish Surrealism as a new 'vice'. Breton's own Surrealist pantheon of precedents is instructive, and he claims a number of individuals as Surrealist in their peculiarities in his manifesto, including Charles Baudelaire (his morality), Arthur Rimbaud (the manner in which he lived), Stéphane Mallarmé, Saint-Pol-Roux (his symbolism), Jacques Vaché (a key collaborator of Breton's) and Raymond Roussel (his storytelling).[5] To this list he added the names of the alchemic magi Ramon Llull and Nicolas Flamel. Llull and Flamel had dedicated their lives to the alchemic opus, which, with its emphasis on the transmutation of mind and material from the lowly to the profound, proved to be a major inspiration for the Surrealists and continues to be so in contemporary architecture.

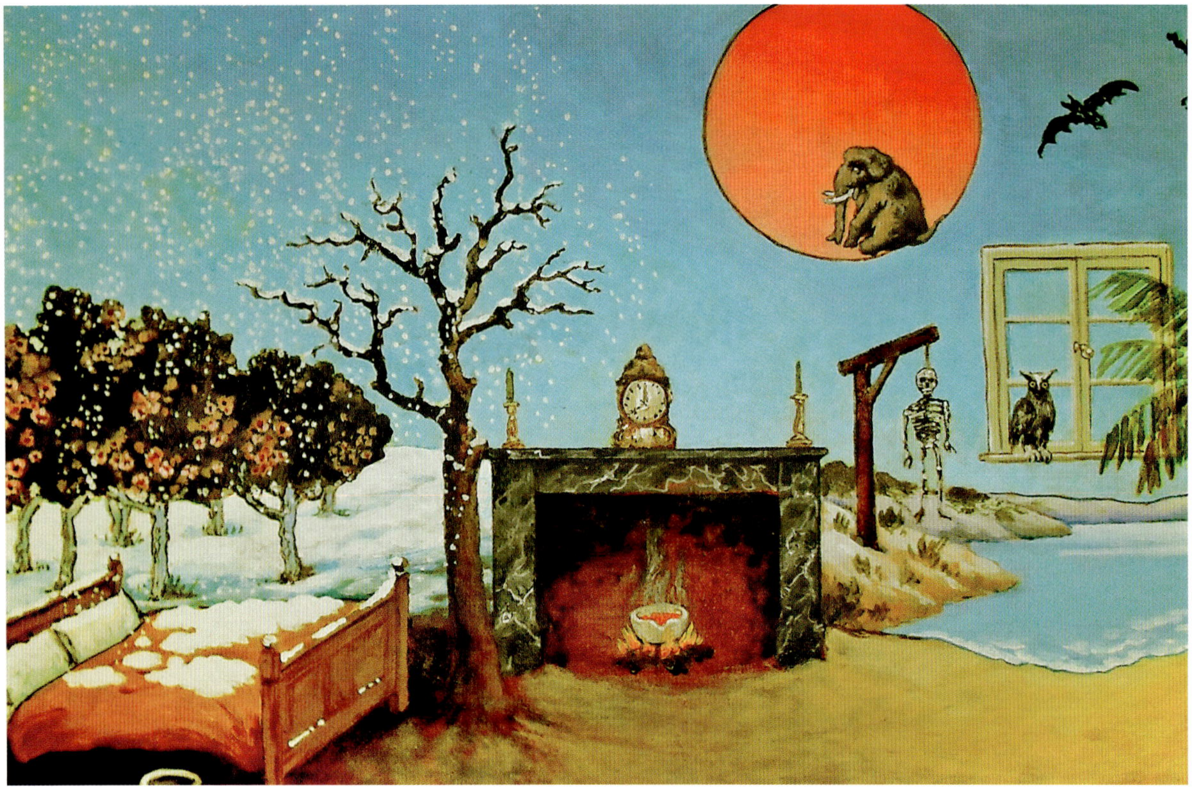

A Wormhole of Contradictions

On 10 December 1896, the French Symbolist writer Alfred Jarry premiered his play *Ubu Roi* (King Ubu) at the Théâtre de l'Oeuvre in Paris. In both literature and theatre, the play resonates to this day with its seemingly illogical structure, its obscene references and wordplay that oscillates between sound poetry and childlike jibes. The play's infamous opening word '*Merdre*' (the French word for 'shit', with an extra 'r') set the tone and caused a near riot. While the play itself ridicules the pomposity of humankind with its portrayals of vanity, dishonesty, vulgarity and selfishness, the highly original and disarming backdrop against which the whole production was set was also a questioning of the conventions of theatrical scenery and artistic protocols. One forgets that it was painted nearly twenty years before Apollinaire made public the word 'Surrealism', and more than ten years before De Chirico commenced his Metaphysical works.

This painted backdrop was an essay in simultaneity, of differing realities occupying the same space at the same time. This seamless blending creates a carnival of allusions where we are at once at home, in strange lands, tempted by the snake, hot, cold, dead, alive, asleep and awake, where the chamber pot and cooking vessel remind us of our bodies, their metabolism and continuous river of fundament. This is a landscape that is timeless, but timed; it was painted swiftly, presumably to Jarry's instructions, by a group of painters including Pierre Bonnard and Henri de Toulouse-Lautrec. The oppositional vistas and ambiences and their reconciliation within an enigmatic multidimensional image is one of the key works of proto-Surrealism and a genesis of the surreal take on domesticity. Space and time are unstable, continually breaking down, and geography is unreliable and transient. The backdrop is an apt illustration of Breton's polemic statement from his second *Manifeste du surréalisme* (1930), three decades or so later, in which he claimed that there is a particular point in a person's mind at which contradictions, such as life and death, the real and the imaginary, future and past, the conversable and the non-conversable, are no longer seen as irreconcilable.[6]

Alongside the creation of Pere Ubu (the main protagonist of *Ubu Roi* and his 'Ubu' cycle of plays), Jarry is best known for his later book, *Exploits and Opinions of Doctor Faustroll, 'Pataphysician* (published posthumously in 1911) and his invention of the poetic and pseudo-science of 'Pataphysics. Canadian experimental poet Christian Bök more recently defined its modus operandi of composition and poetic juxtaposition as being governed by three declensions:

← **Alastair Brotchie**
Reconstruction of the backdrop for the first production of Ubu Roi **(Théâtre de l'Oeuvre, Paris, 1896)**
2010

'anamalos' (the principle of variance), 'syzygia' (the principle of alliance) and 'clinamen' (the principle of deviance) – the last of which Jarry used in *Exploits* to describe a system's ability to swerve.[7] In short, Jarry believed that the ubiquitous laws of physics are a great disservice to humanity; they neither celebrate, respect nor predict the spectacular, exceptional nature and particularity of events in human existence. Jarry's world, like that of the Surrealists who followed him, was a world of one-offs, of marvellous occurrences and ideas provoked by objects in close association or intimate juxtaposition – a kind of conceptual reconciliation of opposites.

Pinning Down the Effervescence of Ideas

The strange juxtaposition of iconic objects, closely packed and displayed, as a means of garnering innovative creative and intellectual insights was pursued vigorously by Sigmund Freud and Breton within their most intimate environments. Architect and academic Natalija Subotincic has conducted a detailed analysis of Freud's consulting rooms at Berggasse 19 in Vienna, and those at his subsequent address of 20 Maresfield Gardens in London, charting the position of his 2,300 objects, seeing through their eyes, experiencing and recording their vistas and cones of vision. She writes of Freud: 'His texts were full of images of spatial constructions described through words. The occasional diagram and drawing he would also include to clarify or represent something specifically within these texts, further revealed his efforts in this regard.' These texts and images allowed her to easily locate herself 'within his ideas much like a physical construction or landmark allows one to locate oneself in a space or place'.[8]

↓ **Freud's consulting room showing the entry to his study beyond, Berggasse 19, Vienna**
1938

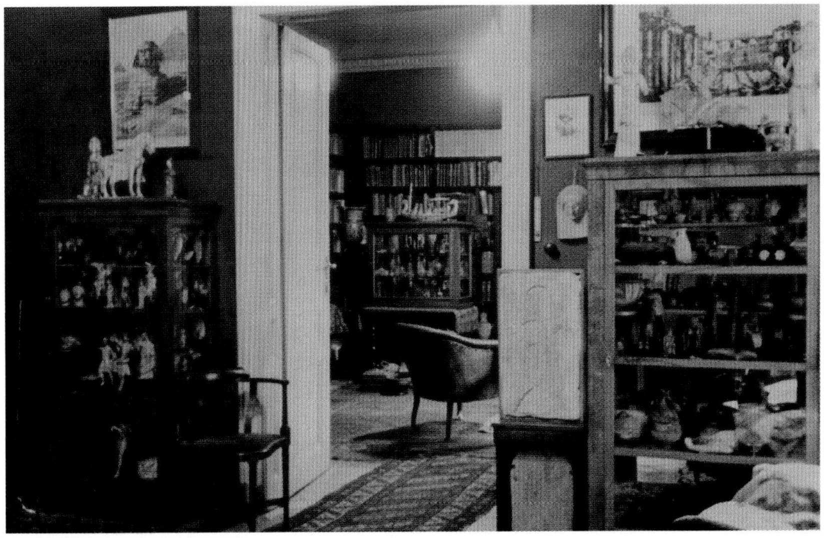

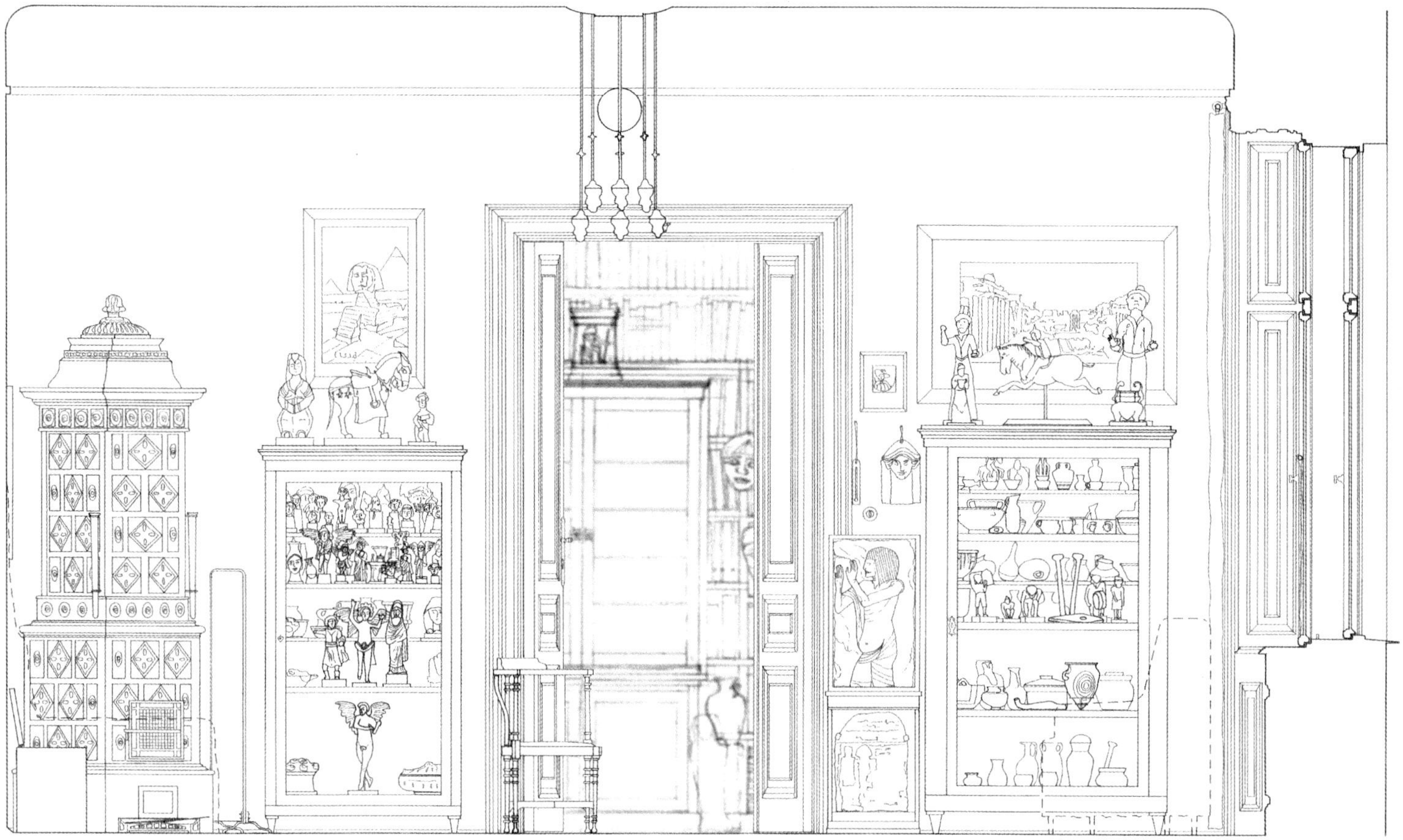

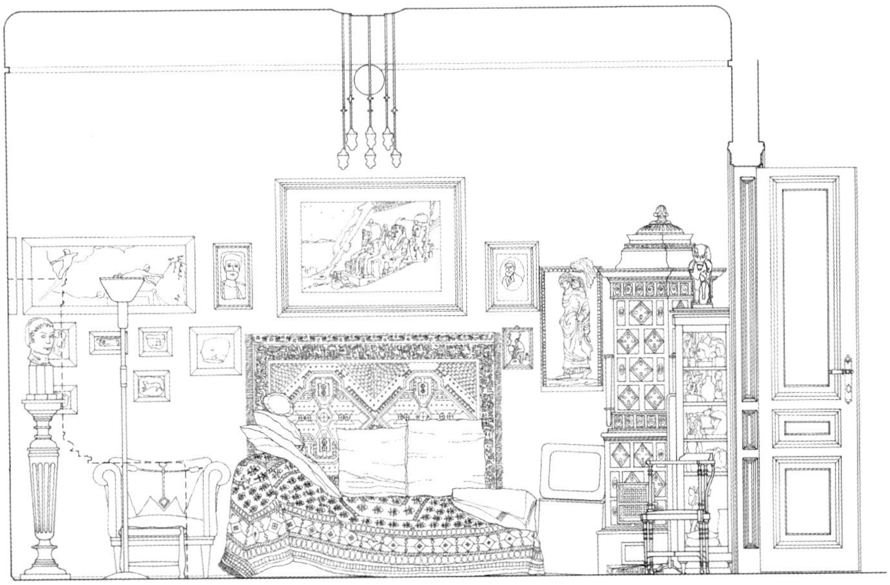

←↑→ **Natalija Subotincic**

Architecture of

Sigmund Freud's Cabinet

Berggasse 19, Vienna

1998

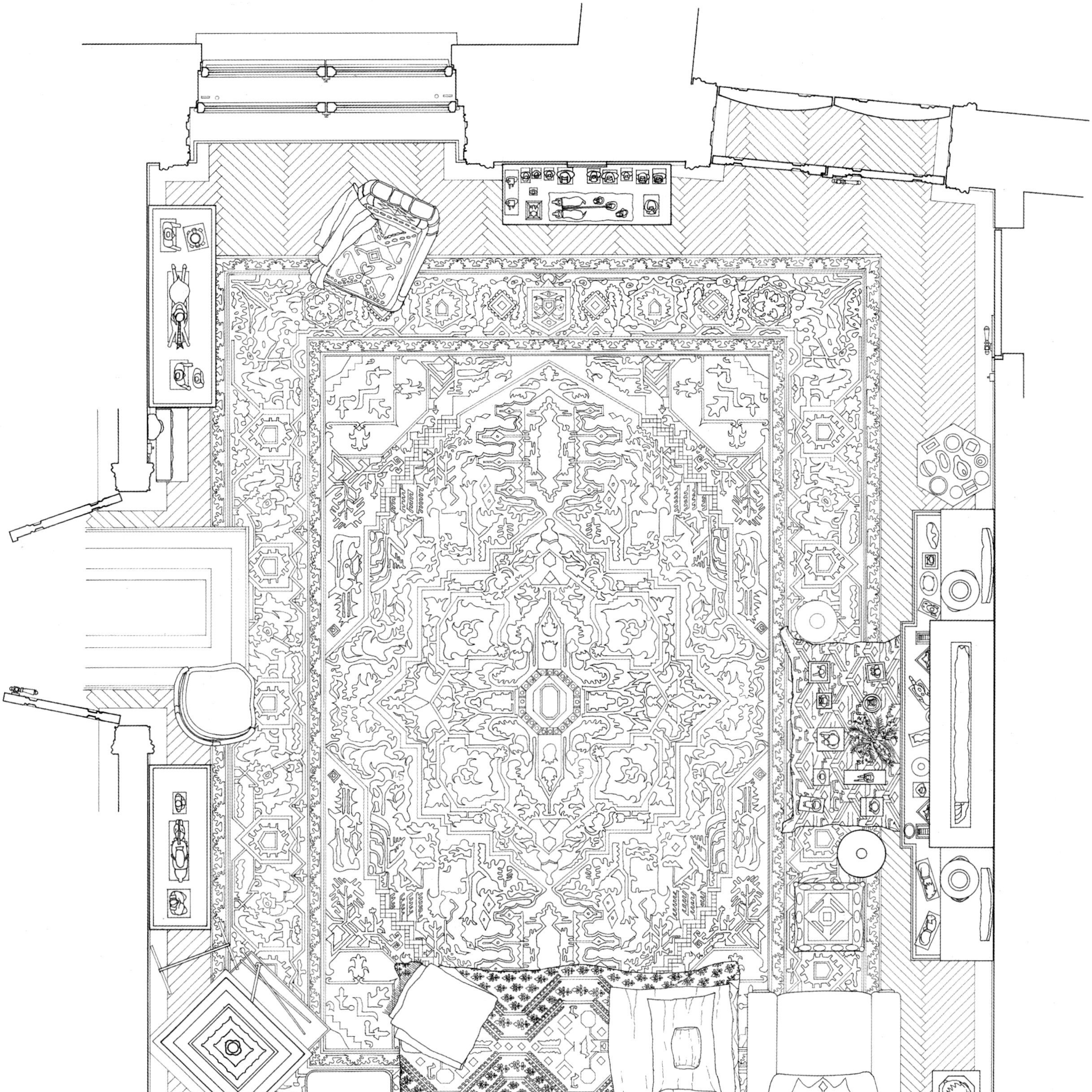

15 THE ARCHITECTURE, CITIES AND JUNGLES OF SURREALISM

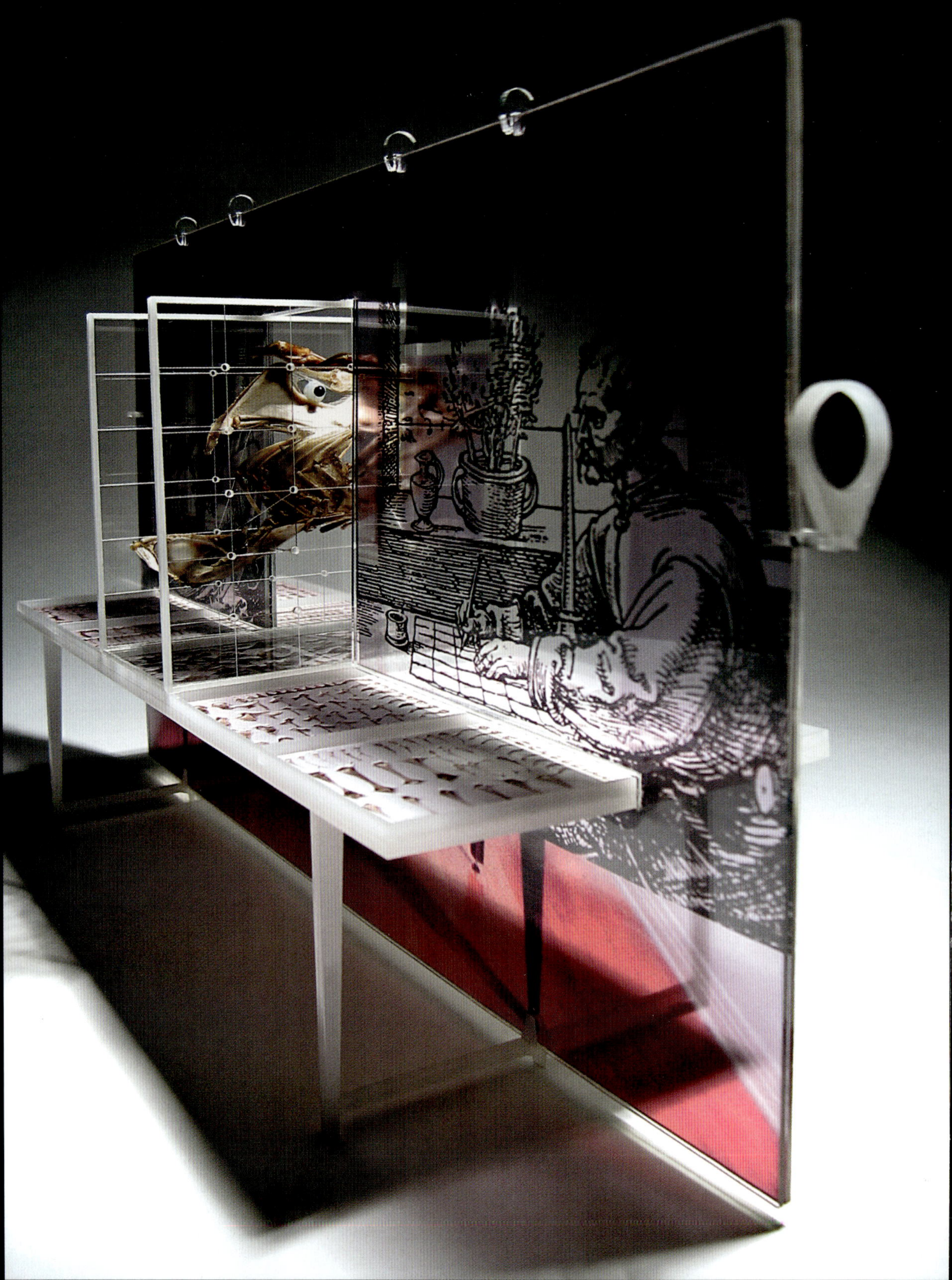

← **Natalija Subotincic**
Incarnate Tendencies: An Architecture of Culinary Refuse
2007

↓ **Natalija Subotincic**
Incarnate Tendencies: An Architecture of Culinary Refuse
1996

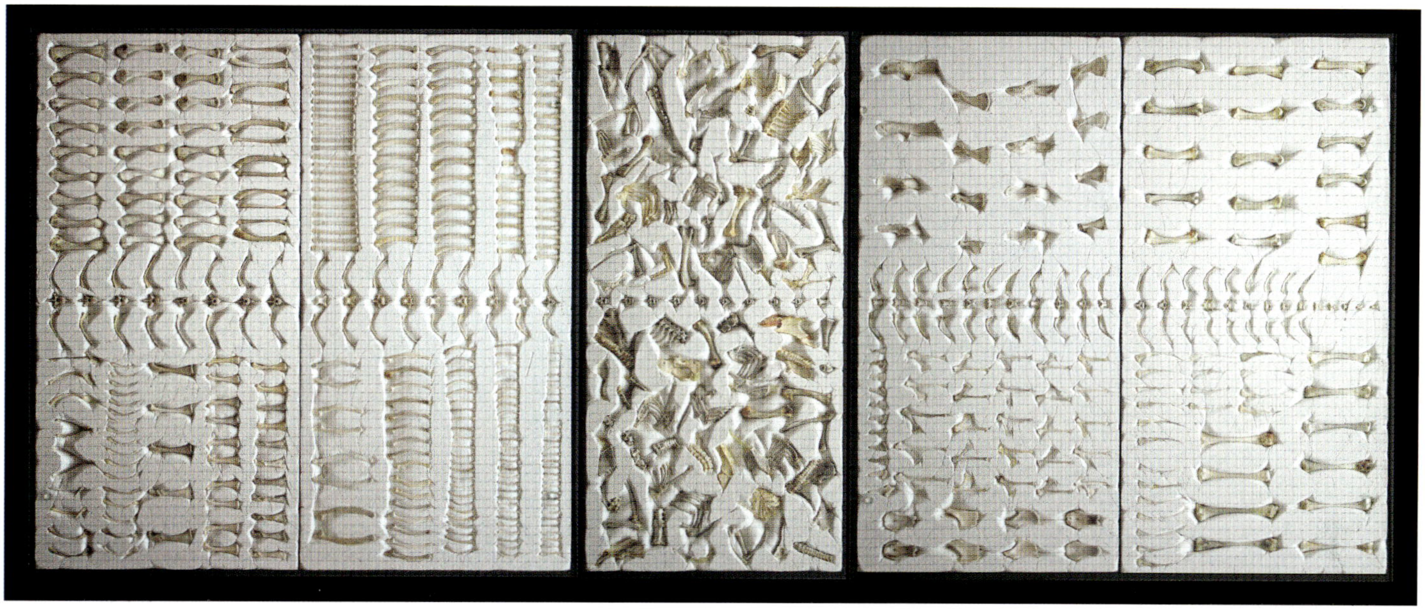

The act of archaeologically surveying, drawing and 'holding' objects in the mind, and using the pencil/pen as a way of embedding them there, is a much underrated skill in contemporary architectural production, reliant as it is on computer-aided design that is often soulless and lacking in materiality. Once the surveying part of Subotincic's exploration of Freud's rooms and objects was completed, she could creatively speculate about adjacencies, semiotics and points of view, a stage that manifests itself in her paintings and text. The work also then flits across time and space, to contemporary Winnipeg, from one domestic setting of the twentieth century to another in the twenty-first, and across her chicken-bone-encrusted dining table. Boundaries are blurred and the personally subjective intertwines with the objective.

Subotincic then transcribes an imaginary, one-sided conversation with Freud:

> Is it possible that your complete oeuvre – the writings and rooms – will ultimately bear the fullest expression of the conflict and union, your oscillation, between the life and death instinct? For as I know you know, many thoughts cannot be uttered through words, but require alternate forms to assert their presence. Architecture is often about realizing this kind of presence. I know you realized this, for why would you have so carefully collected and arranged these rooms for so many years…[9]

Subotincic's *Incarnate Tendencies: An Architecture of Culinary Refuse*, a chicken bone table, made from the bones she has saved and prepared from her family meals, is a homage to her own nurturing domestic environment, her motherhood and the meat that sustains it all. The project presents a back-and-forth 'free association' between Subotincic and Freud across the table, illuminating a discursive space that describes and Freudianly analyses notions of food and woman. In so doing Subotincic turns the subconscious 'eye' of Surrealism back on one of its fundamental inspirations.

In his first *Manifeste du surréalisme*, Breton expounded the virtues of Freud's theories of dream analysis as a key reference for the evolving practices of Surrealism, believing that in the future the seemingly opposed states of reality and dreams would be reconciled, emerging as a total reality, or Surreality.[10] Breton visited Freud in Vienna in 1921, and so was well aware of his consulting rooms and their strange populations of mnemonic objects. Incidentally, Breton moved

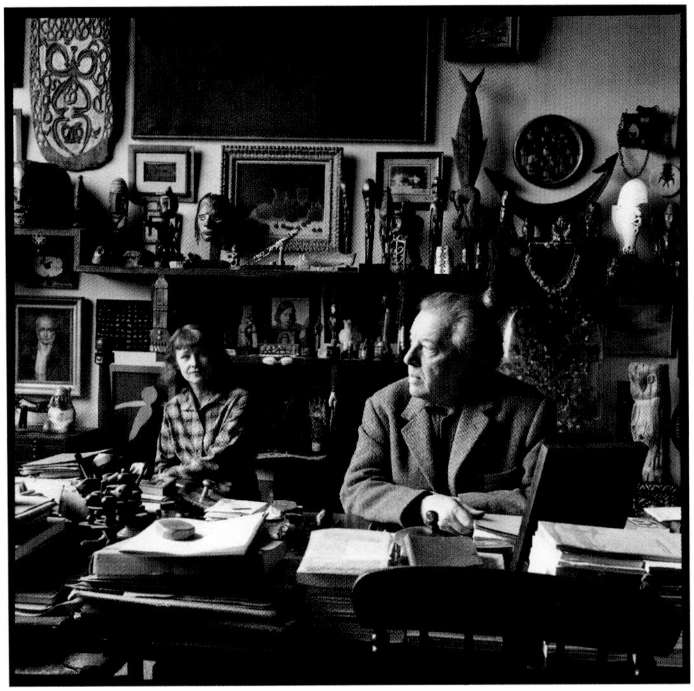

← André Breton with wife Elisa Breton (née Bindorff) in his study at 42 rue Fontaine, Paris • **by Ida Kar**
1960

into 42 rue Fontaine, Paris, in 1922, and the similarity between these two spaces is obvious. Of the thematic structure of the constellation of objects in Breton's study, architectural historian Dagmar Motycka Weston explains:

> Breton's collection was by its nature very private, often intimately autobiographical. Regarded as having personal significance, the objects were not labeled or catalogued. They were arranged and often rearranged with the ebb and flow of the author's imagination, and he often engaged in active dialogue with his pieces while working.... Finally, the collection comprised equally both 'works of art' (having a conventional market value) and common things, such as 'trouvailles', stones, used tickets and postcards – which only had personal value as stimulants and mementoes. Through their thematic arrangement, Breton's world was articulated.[11]

This method of creativity, provoked by an almost infinite combination of objects, each embodying a lexicon of ideas and concepts, could also be seen as a way to hold in check the 'unhomely'. In 1919, 'Freud took as his own starting point for an enquiry into personal and aesthetic estrangement the complex significations of the German word for the "uncanny" *das unheimliche,* literally the unhomely'.[12] Everyone has had the experience of the familiar suddenly appearing strange, extraordinary and almost threateningly alien. For Freud, 'unhomeliness was more than just a simple sense of not belonging: it was the fundamental propensity of the familiar to turn on its owners, suddenly to become defamiliarised, derealised, as if in a dream'.[13] It is perhaps the ongoing intellectual positioning of objects and a personally held notion of what ideas they represent that diminishes their propensity to suddenly turn unhomely, to mock the intellectual and creative security of their context. The urge of surreal creativity is perhaps then conditioned by a fear – of loss of control, knowledge and self-defined possibilities – and thus the need to define and find the uncanny before it finds you!

Welcome to the Jungle

Another of the proto-Surrealists was the much maligned (at the time) 'naive' painter Henri Rousseau, whose work caused much derision and alarm among an oversensitive and highly bourgeois public in late nineteenth-century Paris, and also fed on the unhomely for its unique power. From the mid-1890s until his death in 1910, Rousseau was befriended

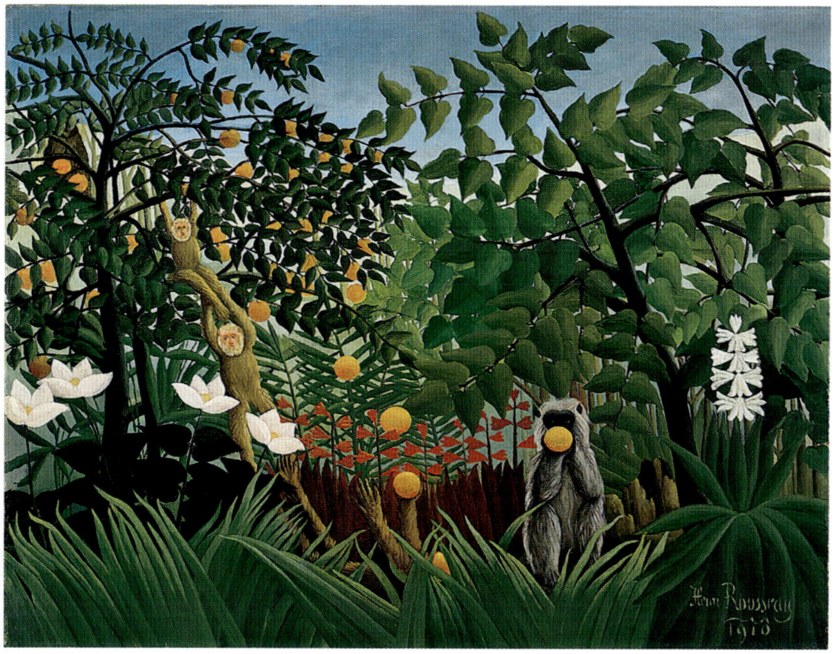

↑ **Henri Rousseau** • Exotic Landscape
1910

by the likes of Jarry, Picasso and Apollinaire, who recognized the originality of this work. He also became a source of inspiration for some young writers and painters searching for a way of expressing the arrival of the new century. His style, untrained and flattened, had a wayward sense of colour, a strangeness and humid fecundity that was both 'primitive' and highly modern. His works split audiences, entrancing the more thoughtful and discerning viewers, while others (the usual response) exhibited a mystified refusal to engage with it.

While much can be written about Rousseau as a pioneer of modern painting, his jungles are particularly interesting for the purposes of this book since they hint at a highly modern Surrealist architecture yet to be cast – that made of synthetic biology. Such a reading was not one of Rousseau's objectives in his work – the science of these speculations was far off in the future; it is their man-made and almost carnivorous ambiences that provoke us in such notions. Rousseau's jungles were not drawn from life, or even remembered from tropical journeys transversing the Equator; they were inspired by numerous visits to the Jardin des Plantes and Jardin d'Acclimatation in Paris, both of which were artificially created for the education and titillation of the public, artfully designed with often-flawed representations of the real thing. Rousseau thus reimagined the already imagined; his jungles were not painted blueprints of a faraway reality, but a compounded unreality occupying a completely different terrain to botanical drawings. This much more lyrical, compelling and sensuous place spoke of an imagined 'otherness', where the social mores of polite Paris are replaced by fierce viscerality and beauty.

Rousseau's jungle scenes often depict big cats chasing, killing and munching on their prey. The animals illustrated are caught in a deadly embrace. Human beings are painted with a sense of out-of-placeness, fragility and sometimes even languishing on incongruous furniture. A prime example is *Exotic Landscape*. The colours in this painting are a little too powerful, the fruits too orange, the leaves too healthily green, the composition a little too rhythmic for nature, and the whole

→
Giorgio de Chirico
The Soothsayer's Recompense
1913

ensemble just a little too geometrical. Overall everything is a little too clear and uncanny. No insects' buzz, no heat fog and no birds sing here. This picture has the dizzy insanity of high summer, an unbelievable perfection, yet monkeys look like old men – the only implication of death and decay.

The Surrealists who came later, particularly Ernst, loved to collage stamens, anthers, petals and skeletons to create parodies of the sexual antics or deviant acts of humanity and chimeric presences. These images were composed to create a dissonance with the established order elsewhere depicted in the same work. Nature released from the science of biology and picturesque subservience into a vegetative, disturbingly virulent alien force.

Strange Playhouses: Neither Inside Nor Out

Another key initial inspiration for the Surrealists were the Metaphysical paintings, such as *The Soothsayer's Recompense* that De Chirico started to produce in 1910 and continued up until the 1920s. His more classically inspired works that followed would receive heavy criticism from the Surrealists for their return to more established fine-art themes, techniques and compositions. De Chirico reverted to his Metaphysical works later in life, and subsequently worked in a variety of styles.

De Chirico's Metaphysical paintings continue to be a key feature of architectural discussions of the spatial potentials of interiors and urbanity. The works are characterized by strange and contradictory images painted in an otherworldly, naive style employing multiple perspectives to construct spaces unable to be built. They depict architectures that are subjected to the strong Mediterranean sun, where buildings and statues cast deep, dark shadows. Any architecture that figures in these paintings has lost its lineaments – its keystones, decorated pediments and rugged rustication. Baroque and Renaissance flourishes are absent, decoration stripped down. Chimneys and fortifications blur. Figures are lonely, waiting or grieving – immobile, weighed down by loss. Trains or sailing ships depict imminent arrival or recent departure. The whole portrayed in a painted delay, congealed in multiple scales. Rooms, squares and vistas leak, hermetic containment breaks down and numerous vertiginous perspectives contrive to confuse the viewer. It is often unclear whether a scene is inside, outside, a stage set or all three simultaneously, the drama powerful by its absence. Many include architects' drawing instruments – set squares, rulers and T-squares – massively overscaled. Domestic space is depicted as more than its boundaries, which are eroded, more than its functional configurations, but as whirlpools of memory, vagrant geometries, heightened emotions and spatial distortions.

As De Chirico wrote in 1913:

> **I remember one vivid winter's day at Versailles... everything gazed at me with mysterious questioning eyes. And then I realised that every corner of the place, every column, every window possessed a spirit, an impenetrable soul. I looked around at the marble heroes, motionless in the lucid air beneath the frozen rays of that winter sun which pours down on us without love.... At that moment I grew aware of the mystery which urges men to create certain forms. And the creation appeared more extraordinary than the creators.**[14]

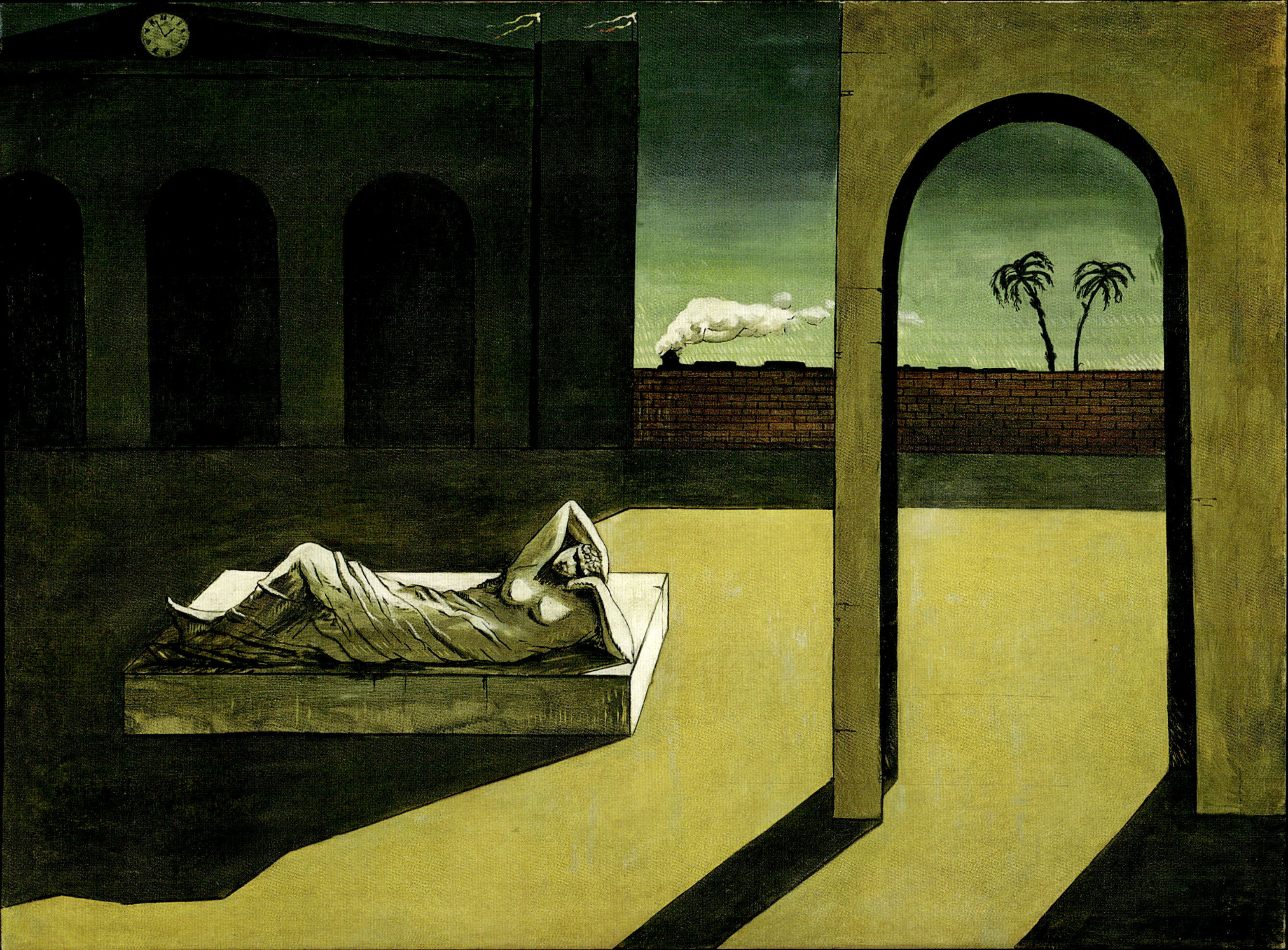

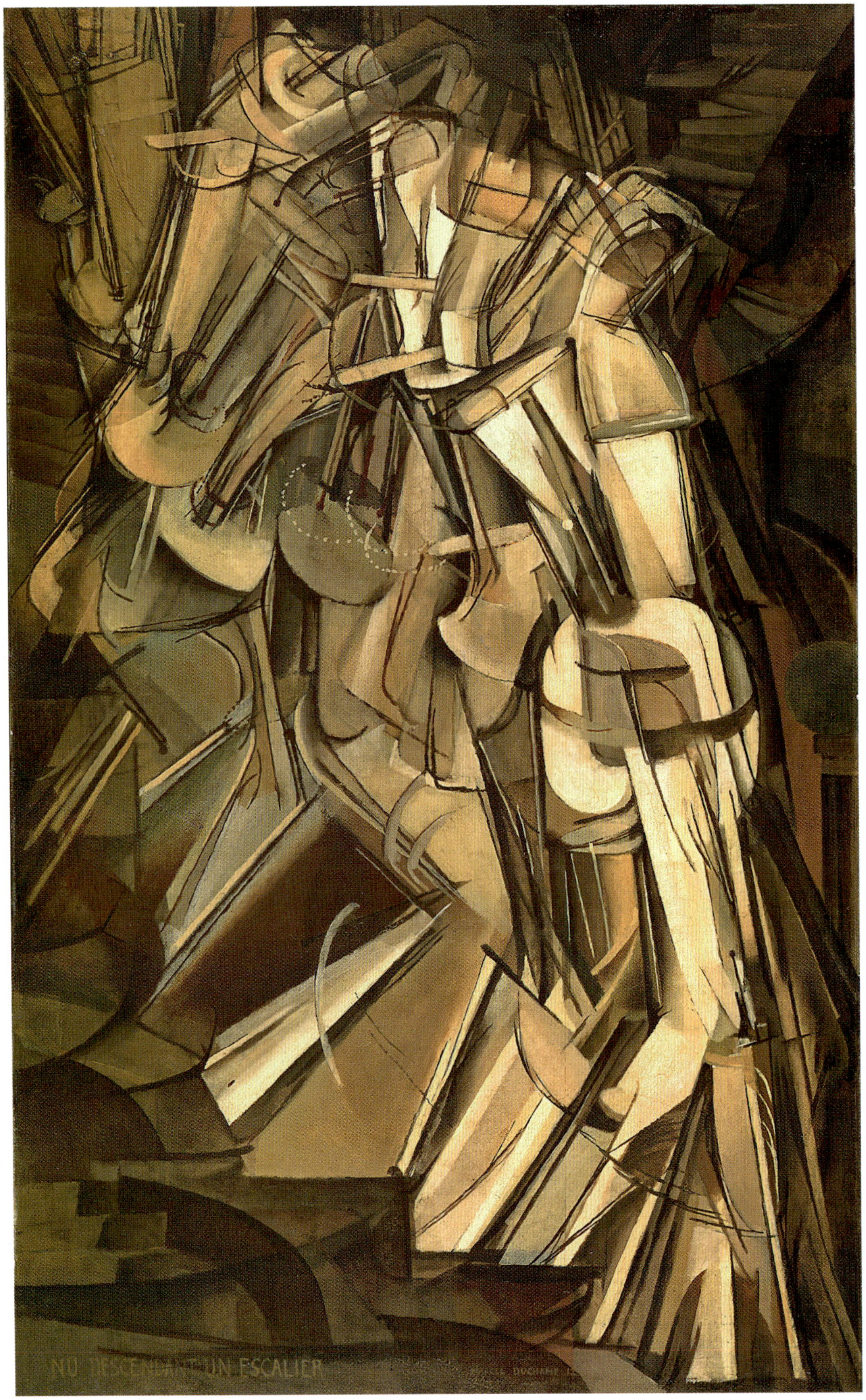

← **Marcel Duchamp**

Nude Descending a Staircase (No. 2)

1912

Hips, Pelvic Voids and the Crackle of Electricity

If De Chirico's revelation was about the stillness, silence and strange foreboding evoked by the architectural monumentality of Versailles, then Marcel Duchamp's *Nude Descending a Staircase (No. 2)* was alive with electric sparks and shocked its way across the art world, burning itself into the eyes of all who dared to look. Here was a great leap forward; early twentieth-century science had delivered us bodies that were transparent, dynamic and able to be accurately placed in space and time. The *Nude* is an X-ray painting (X-rays were enabling many exciting discoveries in medicine and science just as the painting was being conceived and executed). Up until this point, most Cubist painting had described objects from various points of view, from the top, bottom, side – all superimposed onto one another. *Nude* does not radically change the point of view, yet it depicts time, velocity and the nested representations of the X-ray body, managing simultaneously to imply clothes and the erotic sway of the naked female form.

Duchamp's innovative painting was too extreme even for members of his own artistic family, as well as most critics (by whom it was often ridiculed in spite of its huge impact when first shown at the Armory Show in New York in 1913). With its concentration on velocity, speed and duration, and transcribing of an 'invisible reality', the painting was to have massive ramifications on art and later architecture, as we shall see. The 'Nude' is nude not because it isn't wearing clothes, but because its bony fulcra and their vectors can be seen: hips, elbows, knees and the pelvic cavity, for example, caught in a blur of motion. We know now that the human body, indeed all bodies (fleshed or not), are space-time objects that are tracks of vectors and energies that vary position, direction and speed over time. As Duchamp realized, this notion profoundly affects art, architecture and the city in relation to the bodies that make and experience them. The 'retinal', as Duchamp called it, is only a partial, less important view of things than the complete description of objects that is still so elusive even to this day despite molecular science and advanced scanning systems. And one must also not forget our perception of events, our point of view, and the binding adhesive of our culture – desire. Desire is the most powerful fuel for Surrealists – virulent, all consuming, potentially destructive and marvellous. Duchamp started with this notion of desire, augmented by the mathematics of the fourth dimension and the electromagnetic spectrum, to create perhaps his greatest work, *The Bride Stripped Bare by Her Bachelors, Even (The Large Glass*; see page 45).

These ways of seeing, as will become evident over the pages of this book, are central to the evolution of ideas about both the architectural and the surreal body, and resonate across the last century in both art and architecture. The contemporary body for which we make architecture is varied, complex, both virtual and actual, with multiple yet simultaneous manifestations. The technologies that so inspired Duchamp have become highly accurate, multifarious and much expanded. Equally, by the second decade of the twentieth century, artists on both sides of the Atlantic, such as Man Ray, Francis Picabia and the European Dadaists, had also begun to explore the implications of our being subsumed into a machinic world, as the biological components of a hybrid biomechanical universe. Desire had become machinic, humanity conditioned by machines – could there possibly be a better future than the one that begat war?

→ **Raoul Hausmann** • Tatlin at Home
1920

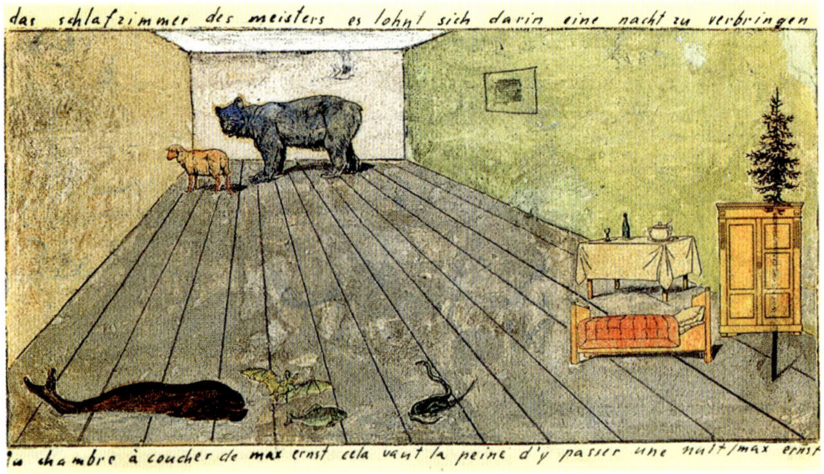

↑ **Max Ernst** • The Master's Bedroom, It's Worth Spending a Night There
1920

Waking the Lion

If De Chirico's Metaphysical works are about the pregnant pause and perhaps a striving for a contemporary Classical mythology in the face of ongoing mechanization, Dada is about the nihilist explosion, an assault on value, meaning and cosseting domesticity, its architecture and the social mores caused by science, engineering, urbanism and war. Dada collages and interiors are characterized by fragmentation, the emphatic shriek, the questioned integrity of objects and berserk newsprint. Three iconic pieces of art serve to describe the parameters of Dada ideas within the context of the domestic interior that directly fed into the Surrealist architectural lexicon: Raoul Hausmann's *Tatlin at Home*, Ernst's collage *The Master's Bedroom, It's Worth Spending a Night There* and Kurt Schwitters's *Merzbau* (see page 26).

European Dada emerged out of the shock and dismay at the senseless slaughter of the First World War. As the war raged around Zurich, the city became a haven for disaffected young artists and writers all seeking to register their disgust at the stupidity of a culture that could wage such destruction. The epicentre of this new movement was the Cabaret Voltaire founded by the German Dada poet Hugo Ball and his German companion and later wife, performer Emmy Hennings, in 1916. Conceived as an open space for performance and discussions of art, it welcomed through its doors not only the Dadaists, but also other avant-garde artists. Ball wrote and performed its first Manifesto in 1916, and the Romanian Dada poet, essayist and performance artist Tristan Tzara its second in 1918. Tzara concluded thus: 'DADA DADA DADA; – the roar of contorted pains, the interweaving of contraries and all contradictions, freaks and irrelevancies: LIFE.'[15]

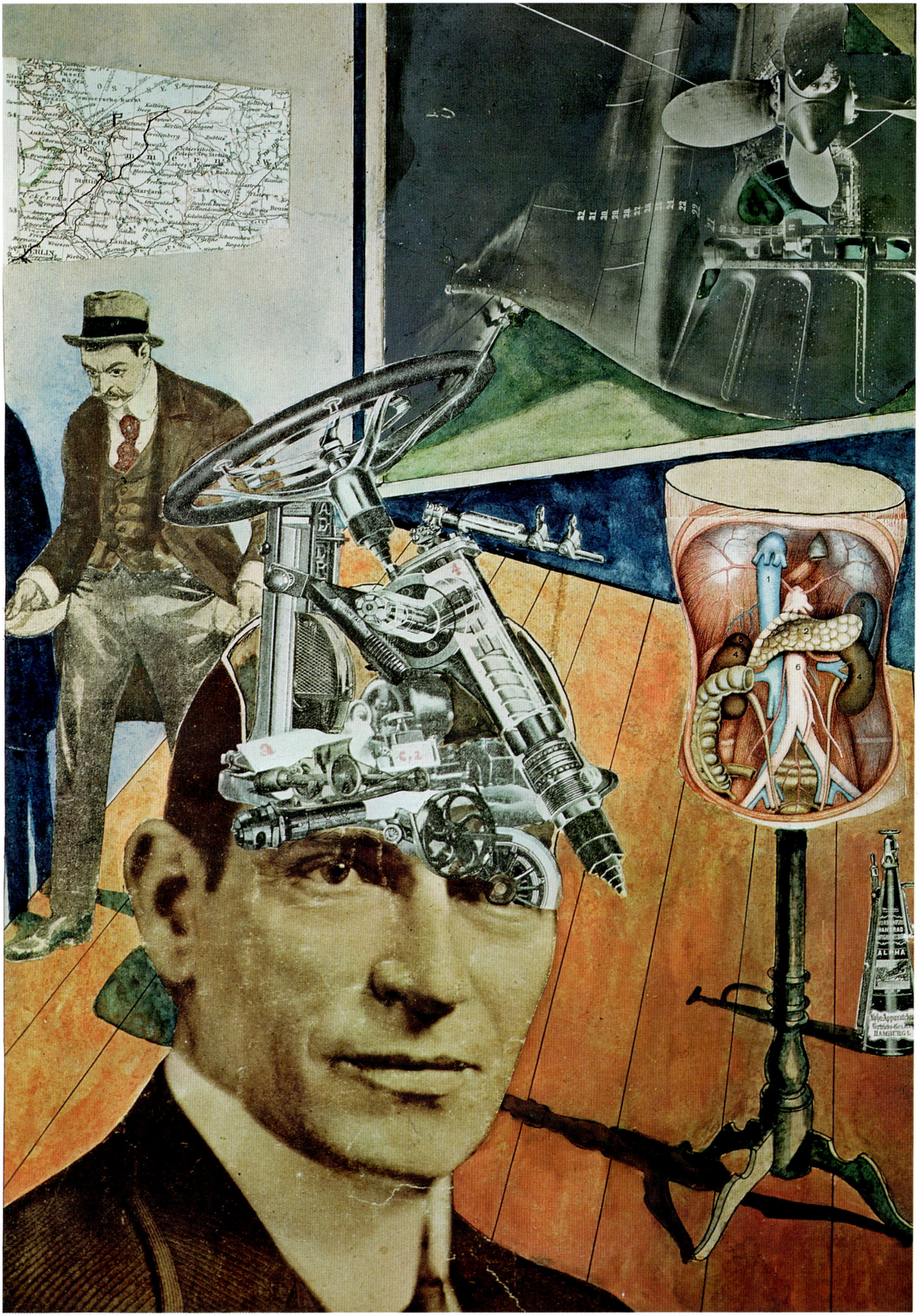

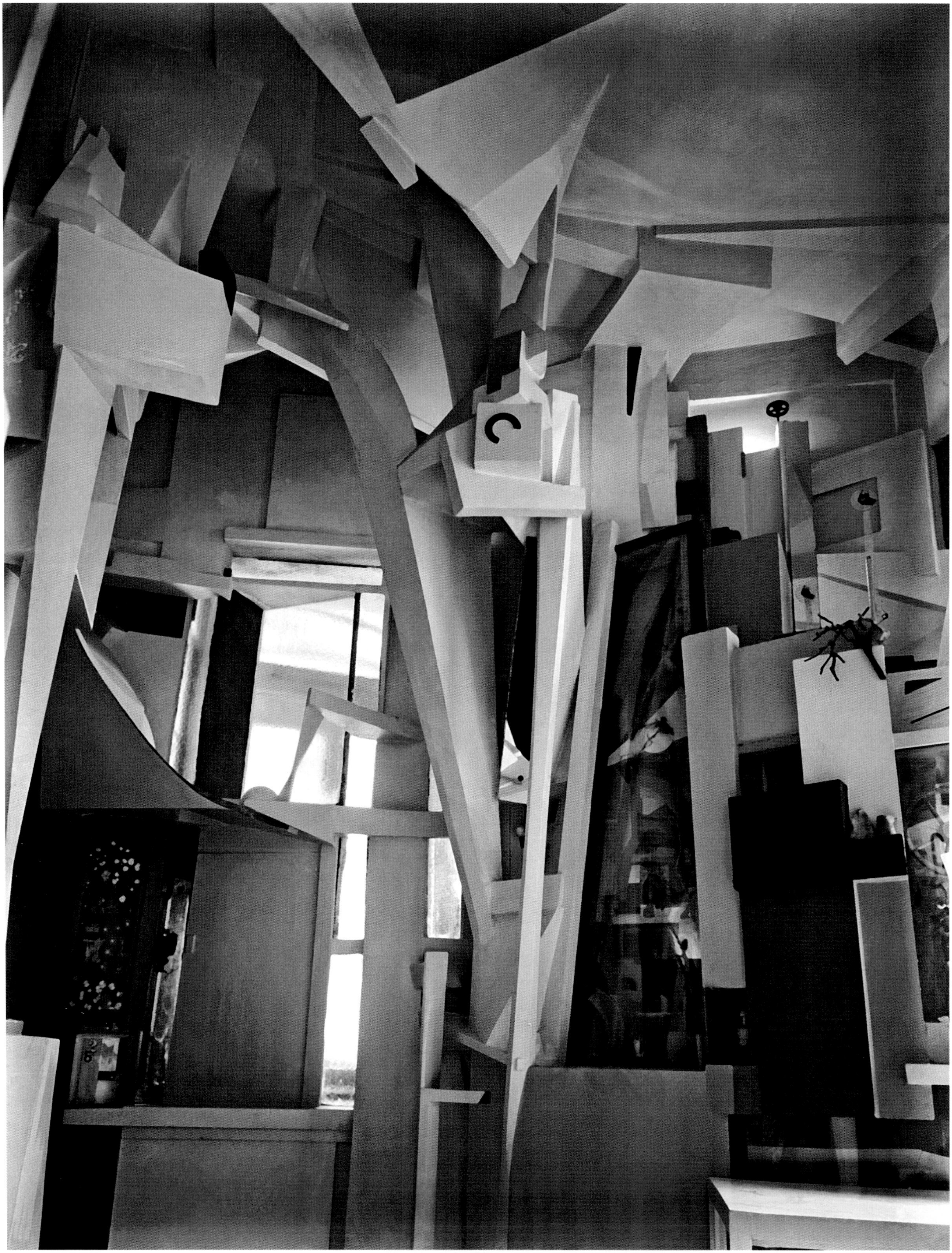

←

Kurt Schwitters • Merzbau

1923–36

Initial forays of Dadaist work included collages, poems, songs, performance, costumes, dolls and sculpture. By 1920 Dada had a significant presence in Berlin and the First International Dada Fair was staged there. It featured most of the main protagonists of European Dada including Hausmann, Hannah Höch and John Heartfield; however, perhaps the most arresting, polemic image was a mannequin suspended from the ceiling, dressed as a military officer, with the head of a pig and a sign attached to it that said 'hanged by the revolution': the subversive attitude of the group expressed in one microcosmic gesture.

Hausmann's *Tatlin at Home* was exhibited at the fair. A seminal example of Dadaist collage, it features in the foreground a man whose head is penetrated by machinery, extolling the advantages of mechanized thoughts, perceptions, bodies and homes perhaps, perhaps not. The scene also illustrates the ongoing transparency of the body to machines, implied by the anatomical stomach of a mannequin. In Russia, Tatlin had just proposed his iconic Monument to the Third International (Tatlin's Tower), and some solidarity existed between the Russian Constructivists and the mid-European Dadaists. As the floorboards of Hausmann's collage draw us into the room we notice the dissolution of perspective with its shattered aesthetic. On the walls behind we see a ship's propeller and a map, underneath which another man shows us the emptiness of his pockets, perhaps indicating the downfall of established capitalist systems and their moral bankruptcy.

The technique of using the inclined lines of floorboards to draw the viewer deep into a picture is also used to great effect in Ernst's collage *The Master's Bedroom, It's Worth Spending a Night There*. Here, Ernst appropriated an old school primer of animals and collaged them within a windowless room, adding a bed and dining table to create an image that defies the size of things and brings feral risk into the sanctity of the bedroom. The animals suggest a dream space of fear and guilt, and perhaps represent aspects of the 'master's' personality seeking reconciliation in the darkness of the night. The compositional and conceptual resonance with Jarry's *Ubu Roi* backdrop is clear.

During 1919, Kurt Schwitters started to dedicate himself to his art full-time. After being introduced to Dada and some of its key personalities in 1918, he began producing work that he described with the expression '*Merz*': *Merz* drawings, *Merz* pictures and later, importantly, his *Merzbaus*.

The first and most important *Merzbau* was constructed – perhaps 'grown' is an appropriate expression – from leftover materials, items and mnemonic things within the house he inhabited in Hanover. From 1923 to 1936 he laboured away on his creation, as it infiltrated his home, from room to room and floor to floor. Intended as a never-ending construction of objects of significance (including artworks by some of his Dada comrades) to Schwitters, and shards of different materials, its architectural proportions, simultaneously an 'installation' and an 'environment', existed before these terms were articulated in relation to artworks. The *Merzbau* aesthetic confounds both perspective and orthogonal constructions, its wayward geometries forever varied, nothing taken for granted, nothing assumed. Here was an architecture of surprise, consisting of labyrinthine crevices. The Hanover *Merzbau* anticipated the impact of the numerous intersecting vectors, varied surfaces and the mnemonic spaces of change in the modern home and city, and the fragmented body within them. It also asserted that this modern world is difficult to contain in such simple traditional volumes. It is perhaps fitting that this percussive rebellion against the traditionally domestic was itself blown up by Allied bombing during the Second World War to become for a moment more transitory vectors in the night sky, more grist to other scavengers' mills.

Dada proclaimed ideas of rebellion, and represented or created architectural spaces where tradition or alleged good sense is deconstructed, reassembled and the tyranny of gravity is often denied. But in among the tumult there are signs and symbols that leave enough for us to read their meaning and feel their urgent imperative.

The Marvellous City of Dreams, Desire and Convulsion

Two books mapped out the Surrealist conception of the city and influenced those who came afterwards, such as the Situationists. These were Aragon's *Paris Peasant* (1926) and Breton's *Nadja* (1928; see page 126). Aragon's book is topped and tailed with two essays that position themselves against the pre-eminence of reason in the world and our understanding of it. These crucial pieces of text concern his description of a Parisian arcade that is marked out for demolition, and a trip to a municipal park with Breton and their friend Marcel Noll. His descriptive tactics oscillate from straight factual documentary to a strange hallucinogenic delirium and every shade of dream space between. An example of the interplay between these techniques is illustrated when he comes across a cane shop within the arcade. Aragon initially describes the chimeric cane tops of hooked beaks, dogs' heads with jeweled eyes, women and cats. Then, after retiring to a bar, consuming many drinks and returning to the shop:

> **I was astonished to see that its window was bathed in a greenish, almost submarine light, the source of which remained invisible...the noise whose low throbbing echoed back from the arched roof...the voice of the sea-shells that has never ceased to amaze poets and film-stars. The whole ocean in the Passage de l'Opera. The canes floated like seaweed.... A human form was swimming among various levels of the window display. Although not quite as tall as an average woman, she did not in the least give the impression of being a dwarf. Her smallness seemed, rather, to derive from distance, and yet the apparition was moving about just behind the windowpane.[16]**

Aragon associates this siren with an old love and calls out to her; she looks at him with a fearful expression and the scene 'convulses' into disappearance. This infatuation with beauty swimming in huge water-filled vitrines is later echoed in Salvador Dalí's only entire building: the Dream of Venus at the 1939 World's Fair in New York (see pages 130–32).

For Aragon the city is full of the half-seen. The furtive machinery of the imagination and the reality of the city are merely clues to the seldom-seen ballet of possibilities, lusts and hybridized otherness that lies beneath. When we drift in it we learn about the human condition and ultimately ourselves. There is no such thing as a meaningless vacuum in the city and no way of opting out of its otherworldly machinations. We are merely a myriad of disparate points of view within a great kaleidoscopic Surrealist engine that consists of combinatorial wheels. This engine throws together combinations of images, technologies, locations and situations with ever-increasing speed.

Breton's book is the tale of the author's love for Nadja, a woman suffering from various psychological illnesses. She was Breton's condenser and subverter of reality, a human Surrealist engine. 'For Breton the importance of Nadja, the person not the book, was that of a muse. Someone who because of her nature, her "madness", was able to demonstrate how "reality", far from being concrete and measurable, can be shifted, become transparent, become Surreal.'[17] She is his guide through terrain he knew was there, but was unable to navigate fully by himself. *Nadja* and *Paris Peasant* were above all essays on the never-ending capacity of the city for Surrealist revelation. Paris was, for the Surrealists, a feminine city full of female power, desires and locations analogous to the female anatomy. This trait of anthropomorphizing was a common tactic of artists, writers and architects throughout the rest of the twentieth century and beyond to try to describe some aspects of the city's vitality.

As the art historian Roger Cardinal wrote in the seminal issue of *Architectural Design (AD)* on *Surrealism and Architecture* (1978), concerning the Surrealists' desire for Paris:

> **Love is a major theme of the Surrealists, and much of their attention to the topic of Women is coloured by their parallel adoration of Paris...the Surrealist map of love is precisely the map of Paris, a street plan comprising of irrational cross references and emotional indices. At times the city at large submits to what Ferdinand Alquie calls 'Breton's feminised perception' and the latter's 'Pont Neuf' is a text based on the premise that the Ile de la Cite, its bridges and the Seine, constitute an outstretched female body, complete with erogenous zones.[18]**

The Vertigo of the Modern

Despite the protestations of old-school Modernist critics, Surrealist spatial aspirations, mnemonic sensibilities and an interest in the desiring, fractured Surrealist body have continued to underpin many of the most interesting architectural speculations and buildings of the last century. The contention of this book is that far from the Surrealist influence waning, it is actually growing stronger and, further, a Surrealist understanding of architectural space will enable architects to conceive and create architectures that were hitherto impossible within the restrictive confines of traditional Modernist architectural dogma and simultaneously within the advanced technologies currently at the centre of the vertigo of the modern.

The key architectural themes of this book revolve around 'bodies', 'houses', the 'city' and the 'biomechanical landscape', with a chapter given to each typology to explore both their Surrealist historical, contemporary and potential future technological imperatives, their impact on architecture, and how an understanding of the precedents of Surrealism can provide new insights into these complex architectural issues. Each is also followed by a related feature piece on contemporary Surrealist architecture projects and the work of some of today's established and promising architects influenced by Surrealism.

Architecture is experienced via our senses, and these are housed in our bodies. As technology augments/changes the sensitivity of our bodies, the constitution of our perception of space changes, and consequently architecture changes too – a notion the Surrealists understood well. While their technologies were primitive compared to those of today, many of their preoccupations continue to be relevant. The chapter 'Surreal Bodies: Automata, Mannequins and Cyborgs' therefore investigates the history of the body – its mannequins, biomechanical chimeras and their multiple relationships with desire – alongside contemporary architectural discussions on the cyborg, robotics and synthetic skins to establish the notion of the modern, augmented Surrealist body as a register for the new spaces of architecture.

Surrealists have decorated or created their own places of dwelling, as did Breton. These often have unique personal epistemologies and mythologies. They are not just houses, but architectures that instruct on how to live particular surreal lives. They teach us notions of the domestic, the erotic, and they show individual preoccupations with forms, details and ritual. 'The Surreal House – Erotic Epiphanies and Fearful Anxieties' considers the notions of the non-ubiquitous in dwelling, nested in other worlds and extreme personalization of space according to all manner of fetishes and interest. These ideas also manifest themselves in the ways we might dwell in the twenty-first century, cloaked in our numerous technologies and individualized homes. Much Surrealist architecture is predicated on bringing together disparate ideas, forms and scales. For this to occur there is often a container, a space, and an alembic for surreal alchemy: the picture frame, the vitrine, the box, the room or the house.

In a world where we continually flit from virtual space to actual space and back, the Surrealist notions of mythic other dimensions and ghostly presences all seem familiar to the contemporary architect who can create space that is highly networked, there and not there, and even where things have auras around them or are seemingly sentient, or occasionally penetrate the anthropocentric architectures within our peripheral vision. 'The Great Transparent City' thus explores ideas such as Breton's 'Great Transparents', bringing some of these up to date in today's world of the Internet, augmented reality, wearables and 3D-scanning and -printing. In short, it is concerned with the lessons Surrealism has to teach us about the forms, protocols and experiences of living in the macrocosm of the house – the twenty-first-century city.

The final chapter, 'The Engorged Garden: Welcome to the Jungle', sees the end of this book teetering on the edge of what is technologically possible and might be architecturally feasible. This is where biology, architecture and the surreal merge into a fecund series of 'bottom-up' ecological technologies that happen at all scales, transmit information, change the perception of the user/viewer, and make no distinction between the living and the supposedly inert. Our architectural environments become huge gardens, blossoming, sensing and doctoring us. Surrealism, again, has experimented with these scenarios and can perhaps show the way in how we might deal with these technologies. The chapter ends with a speculative conclusion about the future of architecture and its continued engagement with, and expansion of, Surrealist ideas.

Our contemporary world exists in many times simultaneously, like our view of the stars at night. Our presences stride across the Earth's continents in digital and physical form. We have many names, addresses and databases – we can connect with nearly anyone, anywhere and at any time. The cartography of our world is therefore always in flux, and is becoming more and more interconnected. It is so complex, so virtual, it can now only be partially described by diagrams, glyphs, logos and allusions to old-world objects like clouds, desktops and apples. We need the protocols and tactics of Surrealism to help us find new spatial and architectural opportunities. We must find them before they find us! We must once again be the arbiters of the marvellous and deploy it for our joy, desire and understanding of the contemporary world. A world made in our image, not in the image of technology running amok, denying our humanity. This book is an attempt to find these ways forward.

COOKING WITH CHANCE IN THE CAULDRON OF CREATIVITY

NATALIE GALL

ARCH COMBINATORIA & THE HORIZONTAL FOREST

THAMESMEAD | LONDON | 2014–15

It is in the interstices where, often, interesting things happen, where disparate things align for a moment (Jarry's/Bök's 'syzygia'), spreading creative contagion, and breeding new hybrid thoughts that nourish our conscious creative endeavours with the power of their unpredicted eclipse. In Arch Combinatoria, Natalie Gall makes the connection between the British-born Mexican Surrealist painter and writer Leonora Carrington's magical realist novel *The Hearing Trumpet* (written in the early 1960s, though not published until 1976), the combinatorial epistemologies of Ramon Llull and Giordano Bruno – the Renaissance magi so dear to the Surrealists – and the compositional games of Oulipo[1] writers such as Raymond Queneau and, at times, Georges Perec. The site for this architectural experiment is the 1970s urban disaster Thamesmead (once the filmic backdrop to Stanley Kubrick's dystopian film *A Clockwork Orange*, 1971) in southeast London.

Thamesmead is a no-man's-land, a kind of purgatory town where people wait for their fortunes to get better or worse. It is also a Romany camp, full of ponies and donkeys and rough, decaying concrete. Residents have tried to inject a little character into their properties, but this has resulted in a stylistic eclecticism difficult to take for the architecturally trained eye, though certainly surreal.

Leonora Carrington was born to a wealthy family who owned large houses in the north of England; she grew up in Crookhey Hall, an Edwardian country house. It was a stifling upbringing, in a dismal and creatively suffocating architectural and parental environment. Carrington went to a Catholic school, became a debutante and was presented at Court in 1934. Much to the upset of her family, she went to art school, and through the Ozenfant Academy became familiar with Purism. In 1937, in London, Carrington met Max Ernst, who was some twenty years her senior, and a whirlwind romance ensued. She moved to Paris and became an accepted Surrealist by André Breton and his circle. It was during this time that her paintings began to represent her 'familiar' (an animal she identified with) – the horse (Ernst's was Loplop the bird). After a relatively brief spell with Ernst in a house in St Martin d'Ardèche close to Avignon, the events of the Second World War separated them and their relationship was never the same again. Carrington's mental health suffered. Later, after treatment in a sanatorium, she escaped Europe for America, finally ending up domiciled in Mexico, which she made her home.

The Hearing Trumpet is a weaving of alchemy, changes of identity, shamanism, space and time seen through the eyes of protagonist Marian, an old woman who is presented with the gift of a hearing trumpet and soon after sent by her family to a strange retirement home. The text cleverly mixes dementia with Surrealism to create a story of many twists and turns. Its architectural settings also play with scale, dimensionality and animism. Gall's work, while influenced by *The Hearing Trumpet*, takes its own wayward trajectory conditioned, as it is, by her self-made, small combinatorial wooden engine based on concentric circles and reread through her esoteric rules that determine materiality, construction techniques and displacement:

> *The site plan illustrates the full extent of Leonora Carrington's subconscious world. Within her world lies a collection of dwellings, which house all her friends [from the novel]. Each dwelling is designed to carry out different design processes for book making; including printing, binding, pressing, folding, drying and papermaking. The exact location of these dwellings on site has been determined by a previous use of the combinatorial model, where page numbers were mapped against character locations within* The Hearing Trumpet. *The resulting geometries illustrate a meandering swarm of architectural strategies, divided by the Surrealist Horizontal Forest where the architectures themselves are built.*[2]

This site plan is remarkable in that it depicts Gall's landscape/town as a series of combinatorial cauldrons for mixing possibility. It is divided by the Horizontal Forest, the fecund, dark crevice of creativity where the architectures are made. It sometimes floods, and is where the real and the virtual are blurred and the inorganic and the organic fuse in its moist jaw. This is the cauldron of cauldrons, a place of metamorphosis, a descent into hell or a journey of enlightenment – a stomach of imagination. Carrington writes of Marian's confrontation with herself and her multiple personalities:

> *As I reached the bottom of the steps I could smell sulphur and brimstone.... Beside the flames sat a woman stirring a great iron cauldron.... The woman who stood before me was myself.... She nodded gravely and pointed into the soup with the long wooden spoon.... 'Jump into the broth, meat is scarce this season'...she suddenly jabbed the pointed knife into my back side and...I leapt into the boiling soup and stiffened in a moment of intense agony...and there I was standing outside the pot stirring the soup in which I could see my own meat...boiling away.... The soup was not as good as a bouillabaisse but it was a good ordinary stew.*[3]

In Gall's narrative, Marian lives in the Concrete Circus with magical furniture around her, which serves as portals for her imagination and the world she has come to understand from her visions and journeys:

> *The fireplace is located in Marian's living room within the Concrete Circus. Upon choosing a book from her library she begins to read in her armchair in front of a roaring fire. Instead of a raw flame however, her fireplace becomes the portal between the forest and her home. Both Horizontal Forest and dwelling become indistinguishable; does the forest lie in the fireplace or does the fireplace lie in the forest. The fireplace marks the setting in which Marian drifts in and out of reality, her retreat. Amalgamations of her dreams crawl out of the fireplace creating new columns, soon to engulf her room.*[4]

Gall's work is complex, and all that can be given here is but a small indication of the different levels of reading that are possible in a project such as this. It is a surreal microcosm, the house exploded into a landscape, the dark creative spaces where wetness seeks to usurp the dry, where the subconscious runs riot over the conscious, and where our journeys and experiences of our existence make our own personal worlds. The spaces in our minds, our rooms, objects, paintings and writings are our autobiographies, palimpsests to be read by the archeologists of the future. The joy of Surrealism is in bringing those differing worlds together so that we can see more clearly, and not just with our eyes.

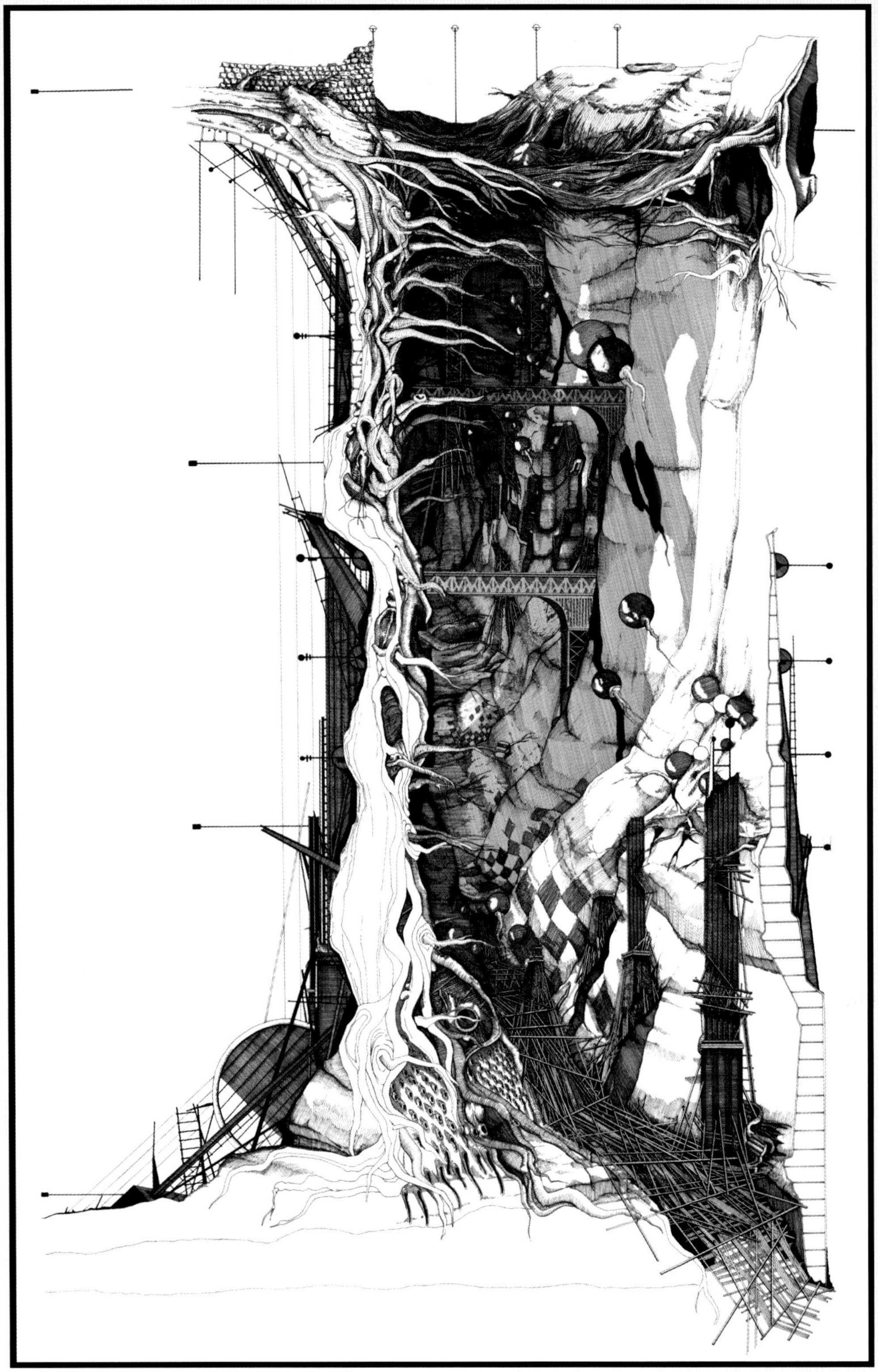

↑

•

The Horizontal Forest represents time, nature and the strength within the system, distorted by a twisted perception of the horizontal plane.

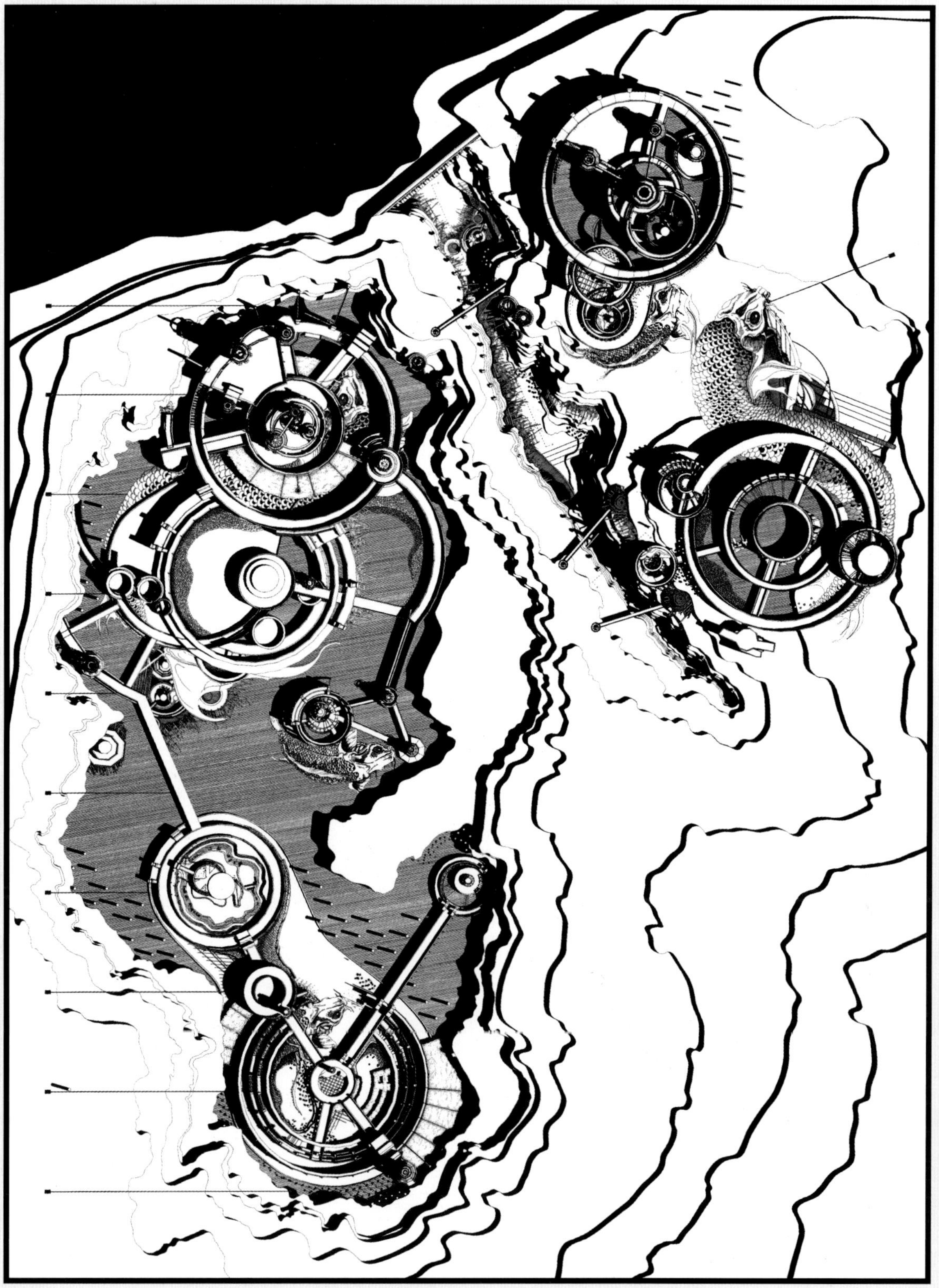

↑
•
Leonora's fortress. The site plan illustrates the full extent of Carrington's subconscious world.

The Bee Pond. As Marian daydreams, more decoration is added to the disused water fountain until the pond is more fiction than fact.

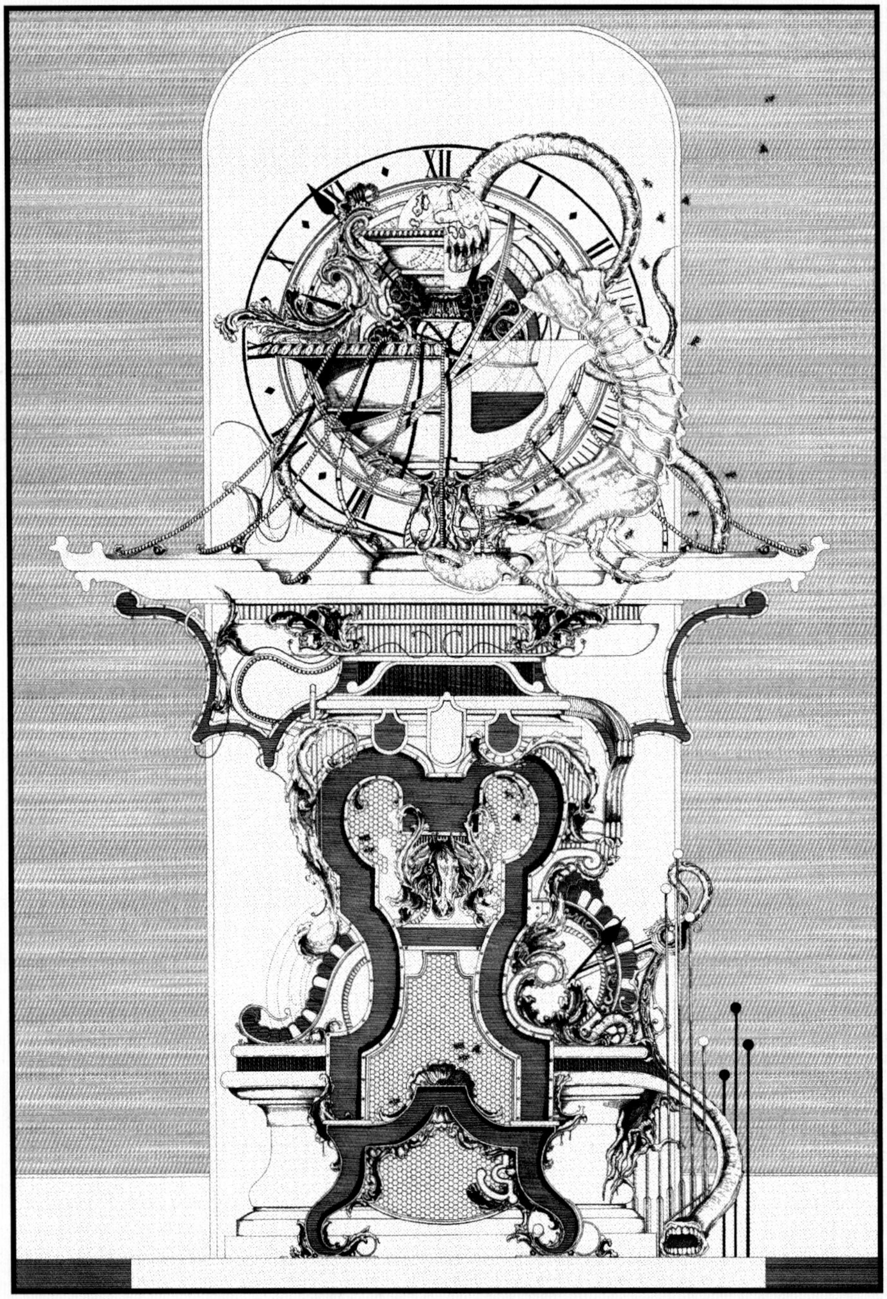

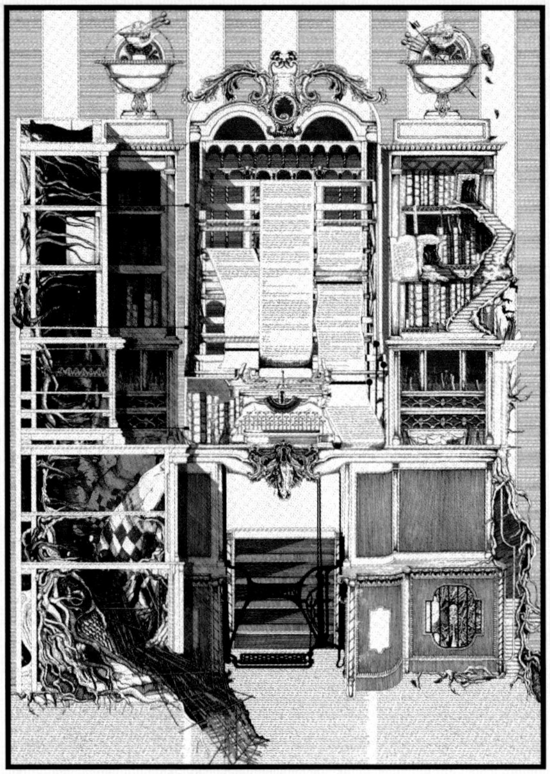

The bookcase. Disguised portals into the Horizontal Forest are hidden behind the books themselves.

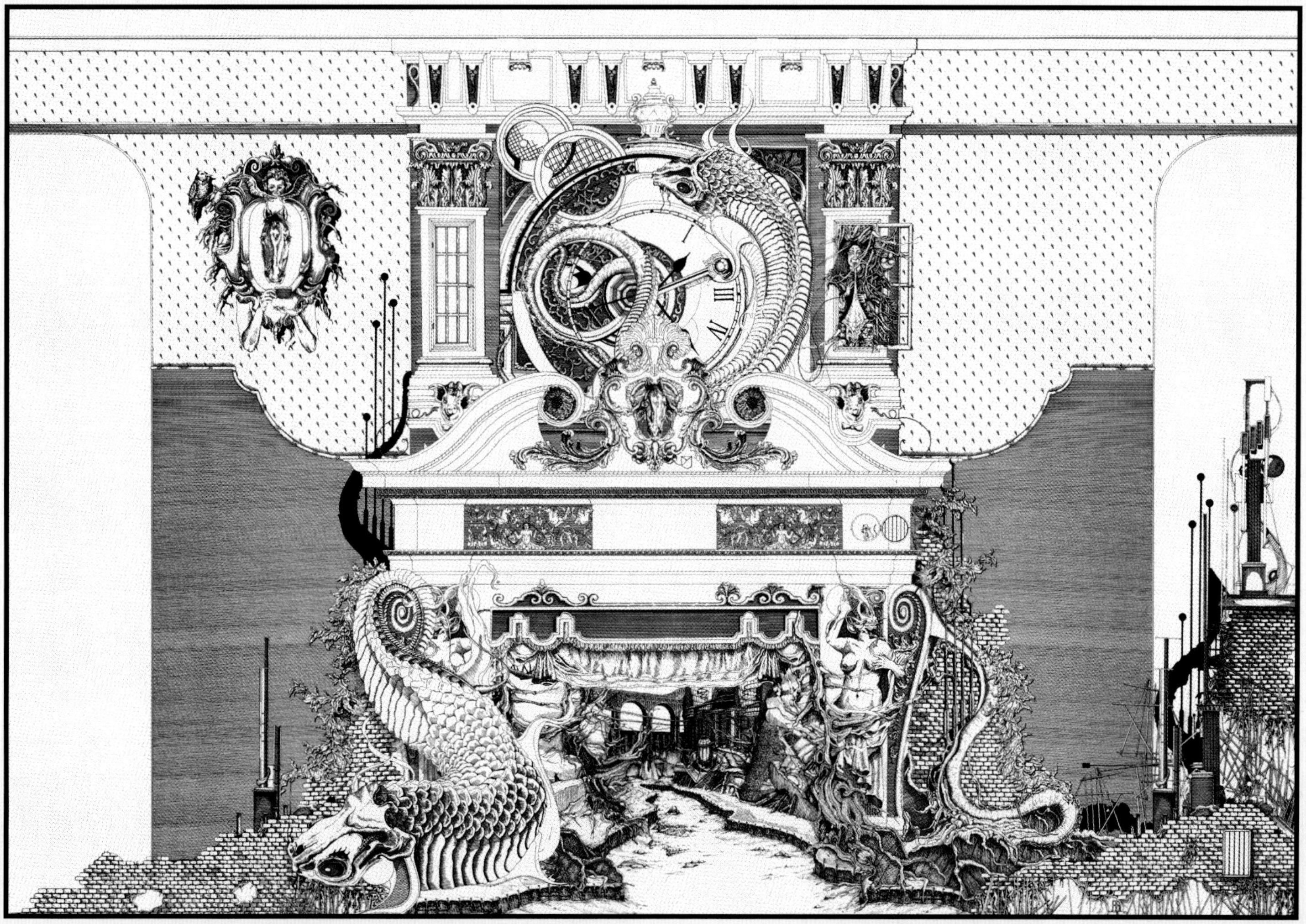

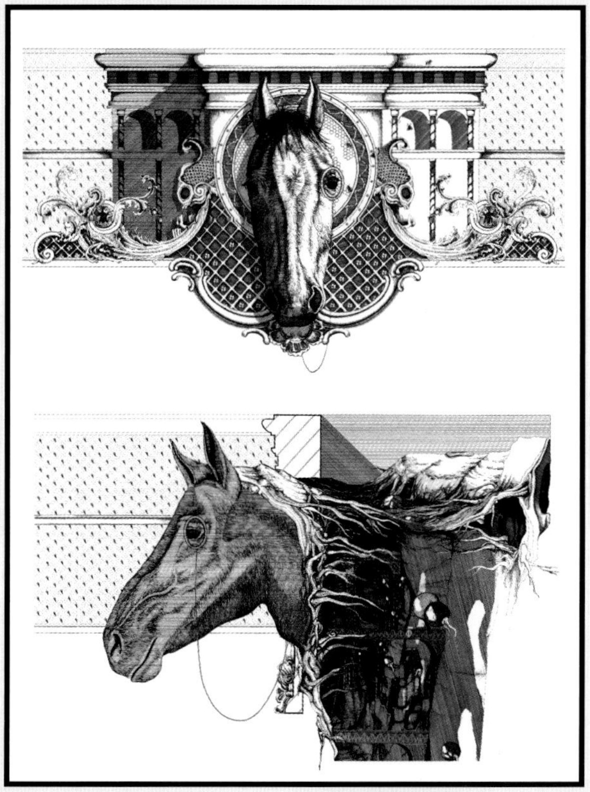

↑ •

The fireplace, where both Horizontal Forest and dwelling become indistinguishable; does the forest lie in the fireplace, or does the fireplace lie in the forest?

← •

Gate keeper detail. The use of the horse throughout Marian's home is a connection between Leonora Carrington's real life and Marian's imaginary life. Here it is a keyhole to the bookcase, which allows access into the Surrealist forest.

•
↓
The Concrete Circus. Marian manoeuvres herself around the carousel on her wheelchair, visiting her favourite locations made accessible by a running track that dips her in and out of reality.

• →
As Marian's carousel spins, the characters of her dream worlds dance beneath the canopy, bridled by the marine life beneath. Over time the two worlds will become intertwined, as the fish continue to distort the architectures above and below her carousel plinth.

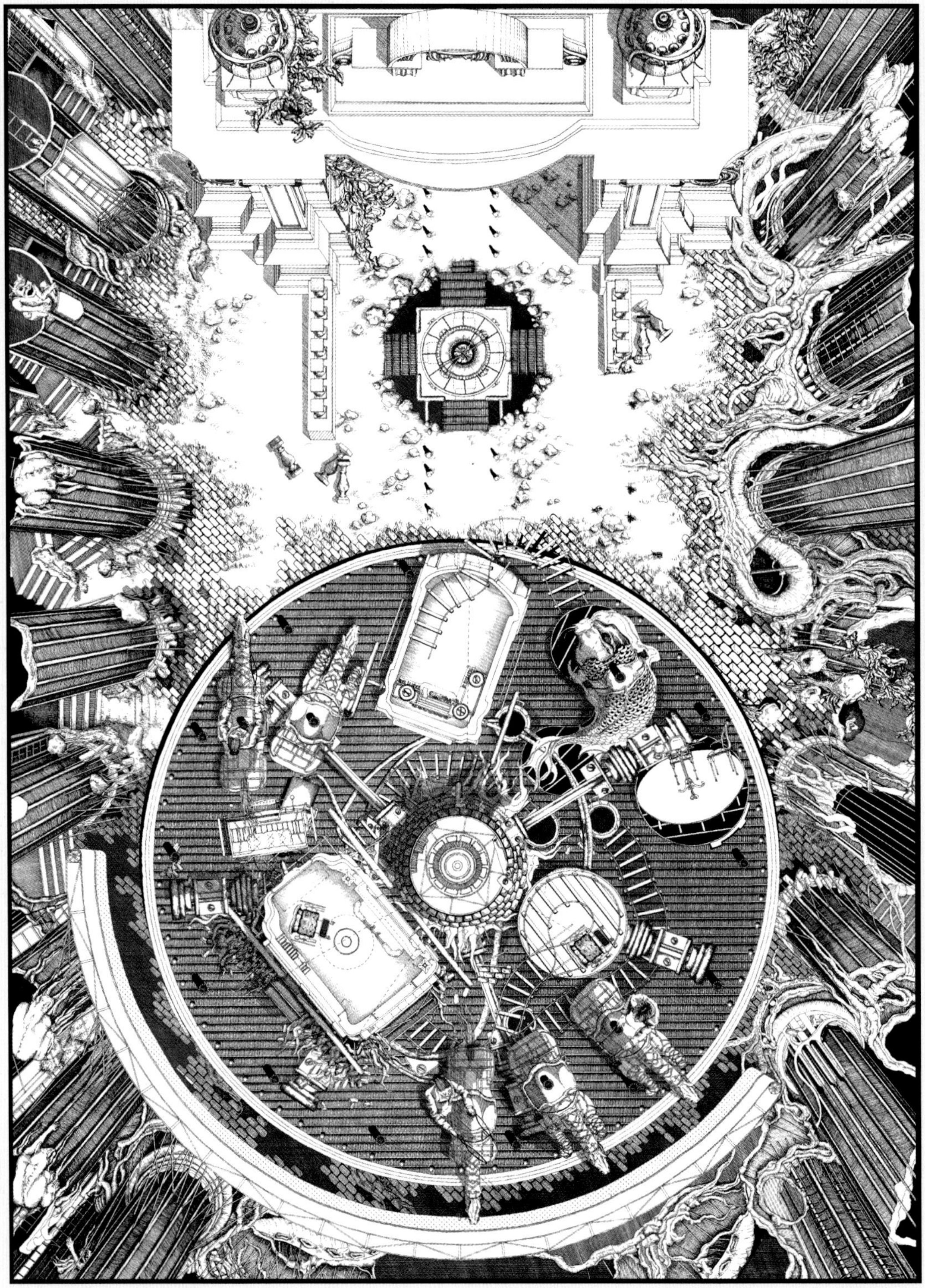

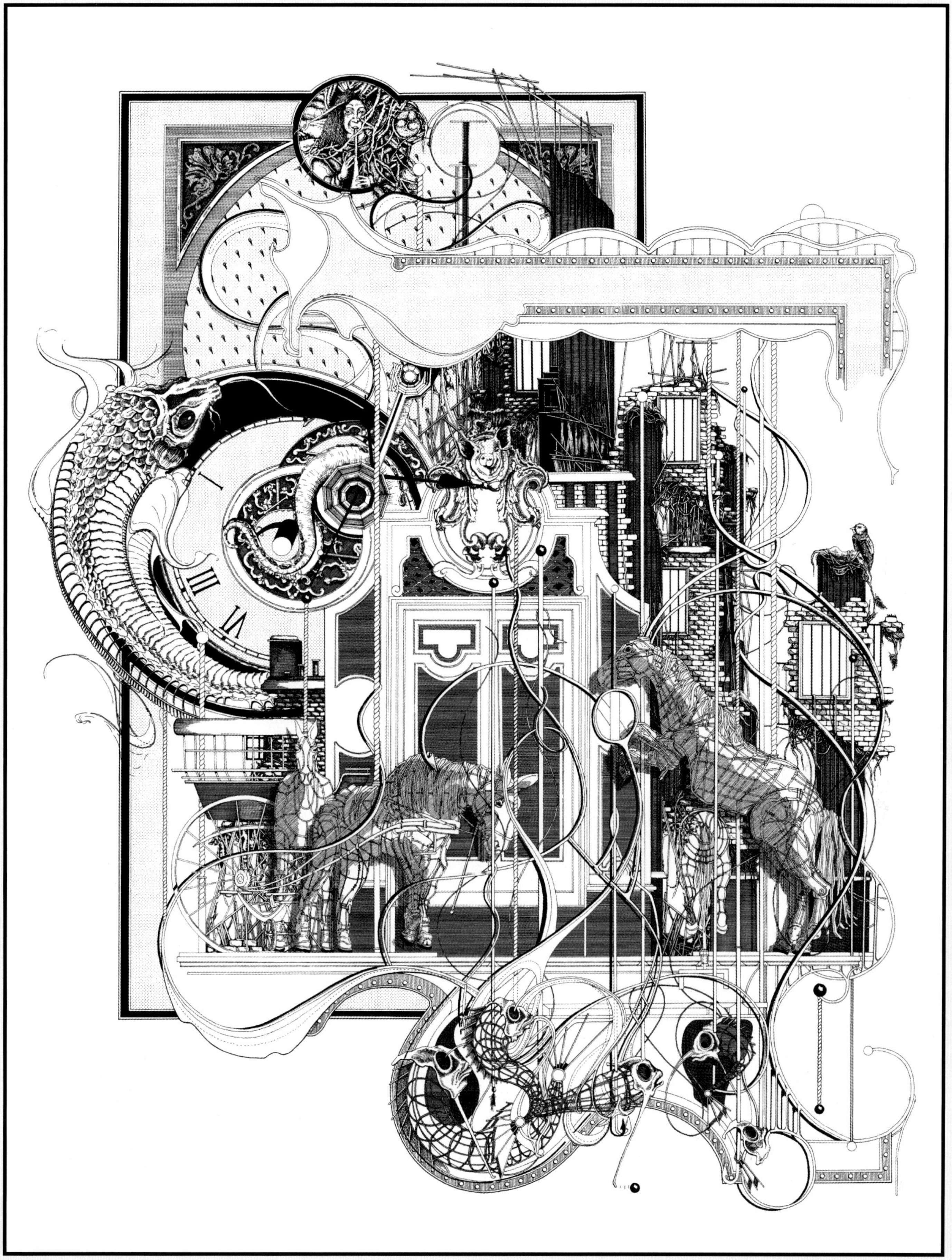

Doctor Faustroll was sixty-three years old when he was born in Circassia in 1898 (the 20th century was (–2) years old). At this age, which he retained all his life, Doctor Faustroll was a man of medium height... golden-yellow skin, his face clean-shaven apart from a sea-green mustachio...the hairs of his head alternately platinum blonde and jet black, an auburn ambiguity changing according to the sun's position; his eyes two capsules of ordinary writing-ink flecked with golden spermatozoa like Danzig schnapps.

Alfred Jarry, 'Exploits and Opinions of Doctor Faustroll, Pataphysician', 1911[1]

A body that is no longer anatomical, but a focus of desires. An act of love which is no longer mere self-gratification or the taking possession of, but an orgy of fantasies, projections, substitutions, displacements, even hallucinations. An individual who no longer defines him or her self as limitation and demarcation but as the interchange of meanings which repeat themselves infinitely in mirror image.

Xavière Gauthier, 'Surréalisme et sexualité', 1971[2]

SURREAL BODIES

CHAPTER I

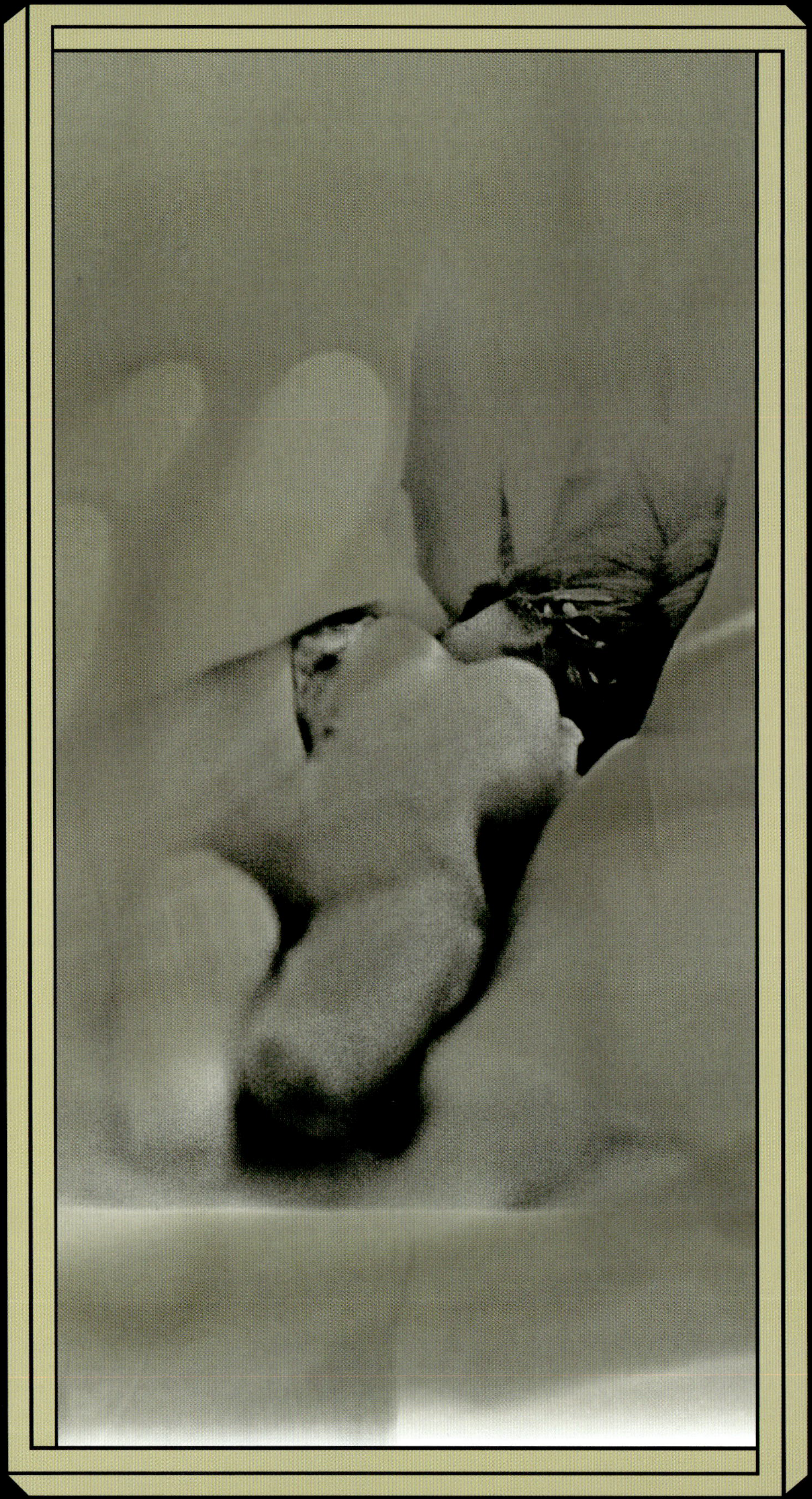

←
Yorgos Loizos • Olympia Doll #4
2009

Above all, the Surrealist legacy is about bodies: their mutability, desire, innards and, due to advancements in technology, their increasing transparency – all of which are also fundamental to the ongoing discourse concerning architectural space. The Surrealist body is an open concept, forever in metamorphosis. It has assimilated machines, flora and fauna, animals, alien geometries and fetishistic hungers. Simultaneously bloody and dry, deviant and pure, void and mass, the body, with its infinite potential for the uncanny coupled with humankind's ability to hold up a disturbing mirror to ourselves, is the oil that lubricates Surrealism's machinery – its *prima materia*.

Fruiting Bodies and Satan's Bottom

Many Surrealist spatial and artistic tactics and protocols have precedents deep in the history of art. Hieronymus Bosch, the fifteenth-century painter of godforsaken surreal landscapes of chaos and rage, spiteful demons, paradisiacal Edens and pious saints battling with their temptations, is one such influential predecessor. The Surrealists were particularly interested in his visions of Hell, his disregard for the sanctity of bodily scale (crustaceans can become fountains or buildings, for example), his imaginative lexicons of human tortures and his battalions of little chimeric demons, always ready to decapitate, penetrate, cut and pierce sorry sinners. These Hellscapes might be described as being in thrall to the 'pink and the black': the pink of the torn flesh of the body and the black of the crow, vulture or demon tearing at its sanctity. Plants, bodies, insects and all manner of spikes, pliers and knives and even musical instruments are put to demonly service.

Bosch is still a much-debated figure, and his motivations, the creative language and symbolism of his works have been widely interpreted. Some have postulated he believed that the entrance of Hell was between Satan's buttocks, our mortal world floating within some huge satanic alimentary canal. Bosch's exploration of this deep, dark crevice of foul, dank, malevolent odour and torment have given him an immortality as a painter unmatched by anyone.

The Garden of Earthly Delights triptych (see page 42) is one of Bosch's most well-known paintings and illustrates his talent, symbolic preoccupations and religious fervour perfectly. Its charm for the twentieth-century Surrealists was its bodily hybrid distortion, fragmentation and truncation. One can imagine it in flickering candlelight, inducing a miasma of dread as scuttling demons go about their fearful business. An infinity of time at the mercy of Bosch's and Satan's evil goblins surely a deterrent for anyone tempted to quench a filthy desire or a degrading urge.

In her book *The Secret Heresy of Hieronymus Bosch* (1995),[3] Lynda Harris musters a lot of evidence to suggest that the artist was a Cathar, and his paintings a series of coded messages of faith and resistance to other Cathars in a world where their kind was mercilessly persecuted by Catholic Rome and its Inquisition. The Cathars believed in the goodness and godliness of the immaterial and light. To them all matter was evil: our bodies, the Pope's body and our earthly environment. This belief in the power and goodness of light and the non-material beauty of the invisible can be seen to resonate with Surrealist metaphors of blinded eyes and the release of the subconscious. This simple binary logic, between the virtual (good) and the actual (bad), is also often played out in many contemporary debates surrounding bodies, architecture and technology.

Bosch's paintings can also be interpreted as a premonition and warning, perhaps, of a hubristic future. One of bodily mutation, viral contagion and interbred fecundity, with no barriers between people's bodies or animal species, as humanity takes the reins of nature and plays with it, like some demented creator, forging in chromosomes of stem-cell hell the genetically manipulated demons of the future.

L'Homme et la Femme Machine

The quest to create mechanical cyborgs has a long history and figures in many ancient mythologies. In 1738, the French inventor Jacques de Vaucanson first showed his drumming and flute-playing automata along with a mechanized duck to the Académie Royale des Sciences. These pieces later caught the imagination of the Surrealists for their mechanical ingenuity and uncanny presence. The Surrealist journal *Minotaure* (published between 1933 and 1939, and edited by André Breton), included many allusions to and illustrations of man/machine interfaces, including automata and human bodies augmented by technological prosthetics such as vision devices, suits and masks.

Breton and his fellow Surrealists were also fascinated with how automata and mannequins could solicit love, desire and even jealousy. The German Romantic author of fantasy and horror E. T. A. Hoffmann's story *The Sandman* of 1816, reconfigured in Jacques Offenbach's famous opera *The Tales of Hoffmann* (first performed in 1881), is thus one of the great historical, inspirational tales for the Surrealists. Freud's detailed analysis of Hoffmann's original story in 'The Uncanny'[4] also stoked their interest.

Offenbach's version of the story features an automaton called Olympia. Highly attractive, her artificiality hidden, she was constructed by the scientist Spalanzani, but the maker

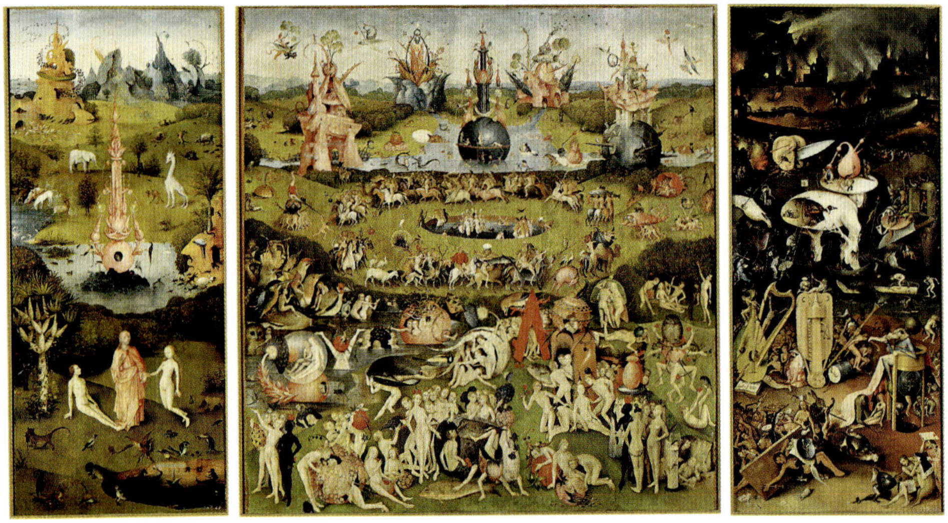

← **Hieronymus Bosch** • The Garden of Earthly Delights **(triptych)**
1490–1510

→ **Giorgio de Chirico**
The Torment of the Poet
1914

of her eyes is the evil Coppélius. Spalanzani is concerned that Coppélius might claim 'paternity' of the 'doll' because she has his eyes, and tricks him into signing away his rights. Spalanzani's assistant, a young man called Hoffmann, falls in love with Olympia and wishes to marry her. When Coppélius arrives wearing and selling glasses, Hoffmann buys a pair, and these appear to further enhance his love for her. Olympia can only utter a few words, '*Oui*' being one of them, which Hoffmann takes as a reciprocation of his love. He kisses her, and she spins out of control and away from him. Later, when he kisses her again during a waltz, she spins vigorously and he falls to the floor, and his 'magic' glasses are lost. Coppélius then takes his revenge against Spalanzani by ripping her apart. Hoffmann, glasses off, sees Olympia for what she is for the first time. Spalanzani commits suicide with a gun.

For Freud, Hoffmann's tale was not so much about the uncanniness of the automaton, but more about that of the repeated obsession with the eye motif that in his mind resonated with the castration complex. The 'eye' so crucial to this story also sits right at the centre of Surrealism's origins. It is also interesting that the magic glasses worn by Hoffmann enabled the continued perception of Olympia as real and human; augmented reality set also at the fulcrum of Surrealism, eyes and points of view abound in this story, both virtual and actual. When seen by the German artist Hans Bellmer in 1932, this opera, its preoccupation with eyes, the blindness of desire and doll dismemberment, must have provoked a few of the ideas he would later use in creating some of the most innovative yet perverse tableaux of dolls in Surrealism. Bellmer's dolls and bodies are always dismembered and suggestively posed, with plucked eyeballs often part of the disturbing composition.

The Mechanized Muse and the Desiring Dummy of Love Won and Lost

So it can be seen that many Surrealist bodily tropes were established before the dawn of the twentieth century. And they were to be further explored in the turbulent decades to follow when such preoccupations of bodily mutation, biology, desire and technology coupled with the enigmatically unfamiliar became major themes in the work of many avant-garde artists. For the Surrealists, the body, its symmetries, structures and unmistakable silhouette were a perfect semiotic cipher and microcosm for the mixing, hybridization and metamorphosis of their projects. Surrealism sought to destabilize the body, but equally to harness its power as a visceral engine of desire and as an architectonic element.

During 1913/14, Giorgio de Chirico's Metaphysical paintings (see also page 20) started to depict mannequins staged within his paused and enigmatic settings. *The Torment of the Poet* represents an initial manifestation of what was to become one of the artist's central motifs of this period. In *The Torment* the mannequin is female. Posed in Greek dress, she gazes blankly at the viewer, out of the picture plane, not with staring eyes, but with an implied Cyclopean pattern inscribed on her head – at once an 'eye' yet also blindfold. Presumably experiencing writer's block or, perhaps, stunned into inactivity by a vignette into the beautiful, invisible world of a higher, more poetic dimension, she is momentarily liberated from the dull greys, browns and inert forms of everyday reality, and feels grief that she will never adequately transcribe its allure or interconnectedness.

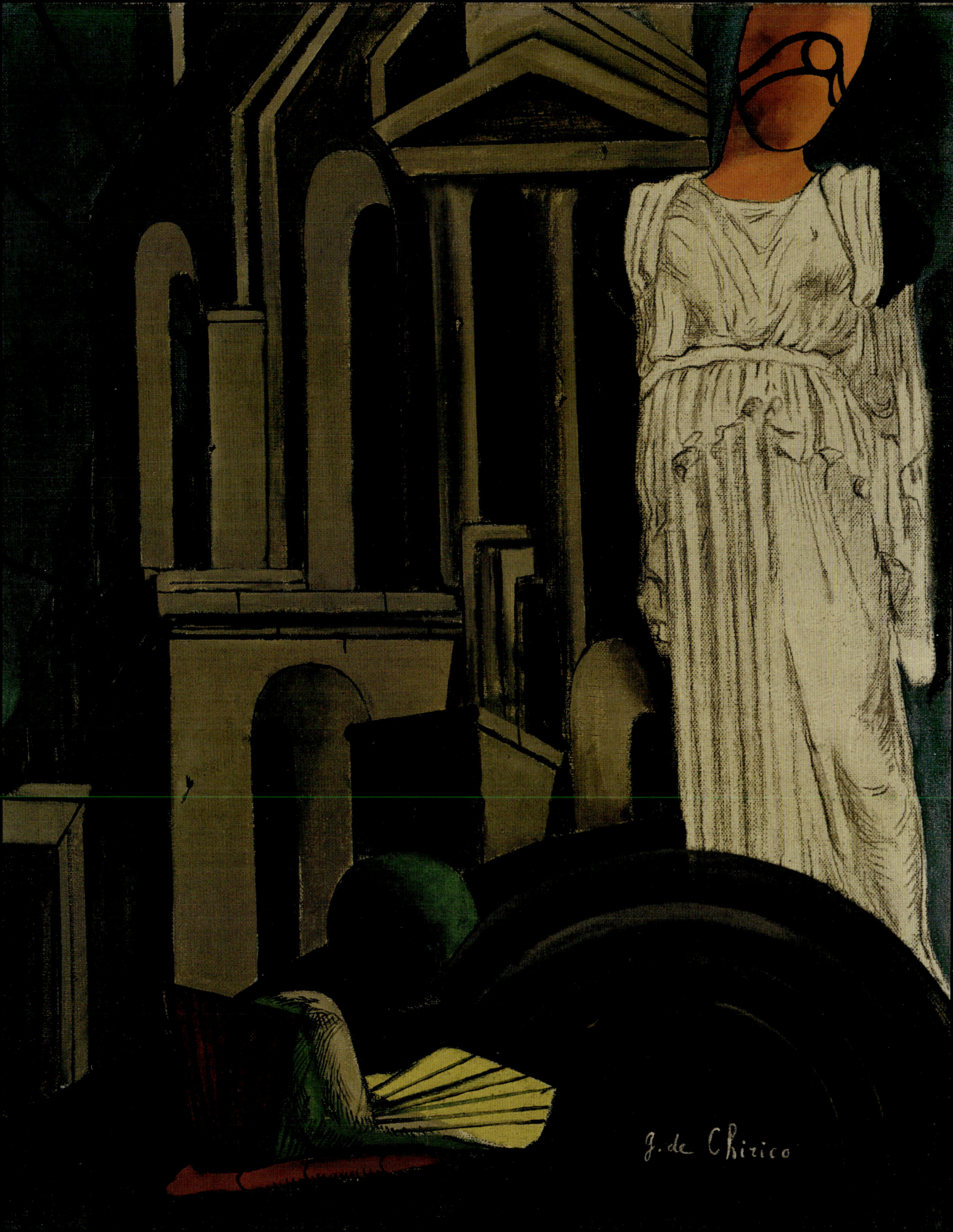
G. de Chirico

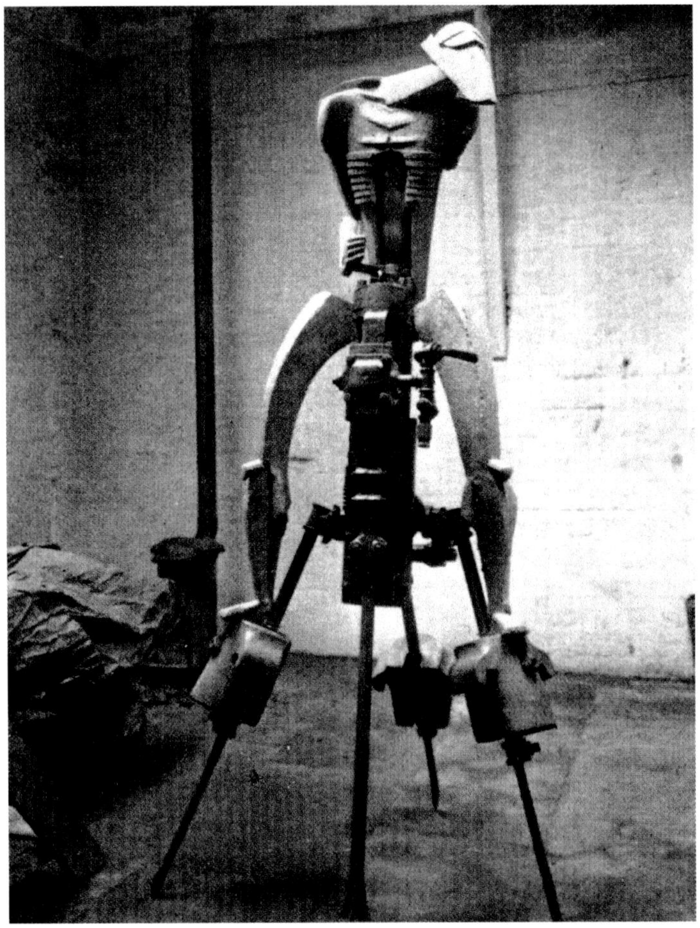

↑ **Jacob Epstein** • Rock Drill
1913–15

→ **Marcel Duchamp**
The Bride Stripped Bare by
Her Bachelors, Even (The Large Glass)
1915–23

Is the mannequin here a trapped vacant husk simultaneously emanating desires, or perhaps just a nuance of a mechanical harlot, the suggestion of her breasts arousing frissons of agalmatophilia (the sexual attraction to statues, dolls or mannequins) – a preoccupation that was to become central to Surrealist speculations of the body.

Around the same period, Jacob Epstein created *Rock Drill*, a sculpture of a futuristic cyborg perched on or riding an industrial drill. Is the cyborg wrestling the drill? Is the drill its mode of transport? Are drill and robot in some sort of symbiotic relationship? The figure's limbs are angular, and forward movement is implied by the pronounced long neck and driving hunched posture. The sculpture so disturbed Epstein that he dismantled it and never created a work like it again. It is no coincidence that the battle droids of George Lucas's *Star Wars* are based on this figure. It can be seen in many lights, for example as a harbinger and premonition of the horrors of the First World War – man cooperating with his own machines to accelerate his own destruction. It has just enough human biological form to make us wonder whether it is a portrait of a future us, or an alien being intent on world domination and human suppression. There is no lust or silent titillation here, only fear and consternation. But, in Surrealism, machines can evoke desire and much, much more.

She Builds Quick Machines

Constructed by Marcel Duchamp from 1915 to 1923, and brimming with allusion, metaphor, poetry, pseudo and actual science, *The Bride Stripped Bare by Her Bachelors, Even (The Large Glass)* is perhaps the ultimate synthesis of the surreal machinic body. During the latter half of 1912, Duchamp had experienced an artistic epiphany. He abandoned his painterly preoccupations in favour of an art that he felt could be more intellectual and less retinal, one that allowed him to invent its tactics and protocols and be its arbiter of taste, and embraced the technology, biology and science of his time. Such early twentieth-century scientific ideas were to radically change perceptions of the body both in art and in the space around it – architectural space.

A catalytic experience that inspired the *Large Glass* was a theatrical performance Duchamp attended (with his friends the French avant-garde painter Francis Picabia and poet and playwright Guillaume Apollinaire) of Raymond Roussel's (self-published) book *Impressions of Africa* (1910), which begins with a scene somewhat akin to a De Chirico Metaphysical painting. On a sun-drenched island (the waves of the sea lapping the beaches in the distance), a variety of characters act out strange rituals in a ceremonial

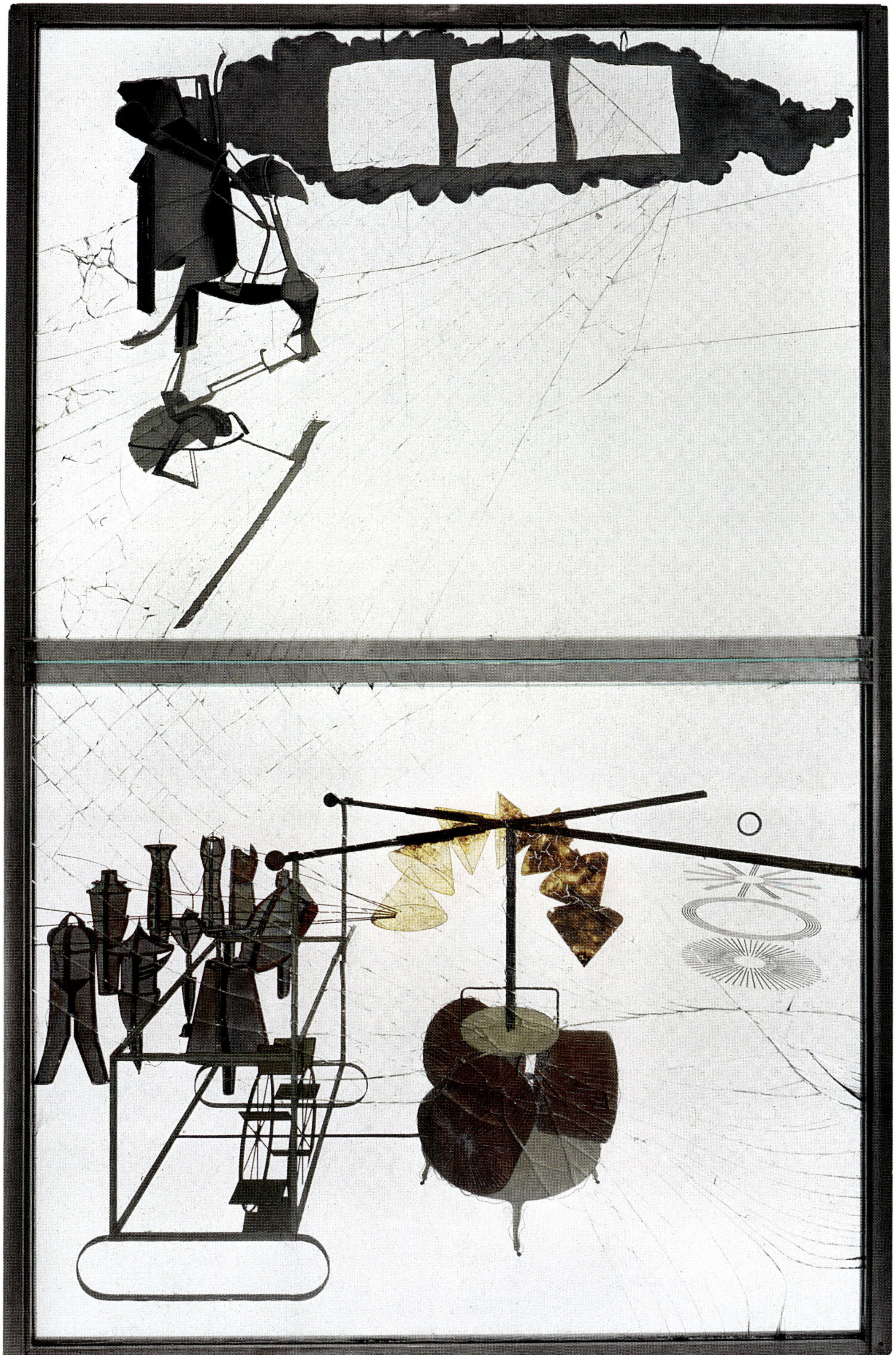

square in conjunction with the marvellous contraptions that also populate it. The book, with its ingenious surreal machines, utilizes not only the poetry of words, but equally that of juxtaposed objects later so powerful as an idea to the Surrealists. An example of Roussel's creative, almost magical formal vocabulary is his description of the Helot (one of the objects in the square), a statue of a fallen warrior still clutching at the spear that killed him protruding from his body. The figure is fashioned from whalebones and situated on an illogical plinth:

> **The feet of the statue rested on a very simple conveyance, consisting of a low platform and four wheels, fashioned from more black whalebones ingeniously put together. Two narrow rails, made out of some coarse, reddish gelatinous substance, which was in fact calves' marrow, ran across a surface of blackened wood and, by their shape if not by their colour, gave an accurate impression of a railway line; on these the four immobile wheels fitted without crushing them.[5]**

In an interview in 1946, Duchamp affirmed his interest in Roussel's *Impressions*: 'I saw at once I could use Roussel as an influence.... And Roussel showed me the way.'[6] Also during 1912, Duchamp, Picabia and others made the journey from Paris to the Jura Mountains to holiday with Dadaist Gabrièle Buffet. This trip along 'the Jura-Paris Road' has also been credited as an inspiration for the embryonic *Large Glass* in Duchamp's mind, and particularly in relation to its synthesis of the mechanical with the biological. At the time, Duchamp wrote about the journey in surreal terms, using the language of a biomechanical fusion between machine and passengers:

> **The machine with 5 hearts, the pure child of nickel and platinum must dominate the Jura-Paris road. On the one hand, the chief of the 5 nudes will be ahead of the 4 other nudes towards this Jura-Paris road. On the other hand, the headlight child will be the instrument conquering this Jura-Paris road.[7]**

Duchamp was also an admirer of Alfred Jarry, who before him was a fan of the emerging science of his day. Jarry revelled in the literary possibilities of the non-Euclidian geometries of space being postulated in the late nineteenth century, their multidimensionality and even their ability to disassemble the tyranny of irreversible time. Jarry liked to reference the bicycle as a magical conveyance, and even as a time machine. Duchamp's first readymade was a *Bicycle Wheel* (1913) and front forks, surmounted on a kitchen stool.

Like Duchamp, Jarry liked to describe the bodies of some of his protagonists, their desires, architecture and actions in terms of machines. This is particularly prevalent in his 1902 novel *The Supermale*, which explores human/machinic stamina, the reanimation of the body after death, hypnotism and electromagnetism. Supermale is a man obsessed by his own mechanical fitness and sexual prowess, who proves his lust and desire for his lover by cycling a great distance at the speed of a train and makes love to her many, many times a day so that his desire becomes fearful for her. The bicycle was an important symbol used by Jarry in many of his works to infer man/machine symbiosis.

As the author Linda Dalrymple Henderson has commented, when Jarry's *Exploits and Opinions of Doctor Faustroll* was eventually published in 1911, it included a series of subversive texts previously published in 1901–02 in the magazine *Revue Blanche*. These included Jarry's 'Copulatively Speaking', 'in which a number of the sexual elements of the *Large Glass* appear: the Virgin, a bride, *celibataires,* and *celibataires militaires*, complete with *uniformes*',[8] so the lineage between Duchamp and Jarry seems assured.

The *Large Glass* is a highly enigmatic object, and Duchamp's notes about it do nothing if not add to its complexity of interpretation. In effect, it is a series of interweaving channels of associations. The anatomy of the glass, at its most superficial level, is two upper and lower framed panes of glass. The upper pane is the domain of the *Bride*, the lower pane that of the *Bachelors' Nine Malic Moulds*. The *Bride* is a multidimensional being; its technologies are mostly invisible, electromagnetic and powerful. The area of the *Bachelors* below is more mechanical and three-dimensional. The *Bachelors* are trapped in their *Cemetery of Livery* lusting after the *Virgin/Bride* and 'grinding their own chocolate' – a euphemism for masturbation. The male and female parts of the glass never conjugate

> **[but] instead are locked in a mechanical cycle of desire involving fluids, sparks and gases, and the forces of gravity and friction. Duchamp was intrigued by the visual possibilities of using glass as a support, as well as linear perspective, which had been devalued within avant-garde art for a generation or more. An extraordinary departure from conventional conceptions of what a painting should be and what it could depict, the *Large Glass* summarized Duchamp's distinctly original way of thinking about the expression of ideas in visual form.[10]**

It has also influenced a number of architects, for example, Diller + Scofidio (see pages 114–21). My own work also has allusions to the *Large Glass*, particularly in the project 'Communicating Vessels' (see pages 176–87).

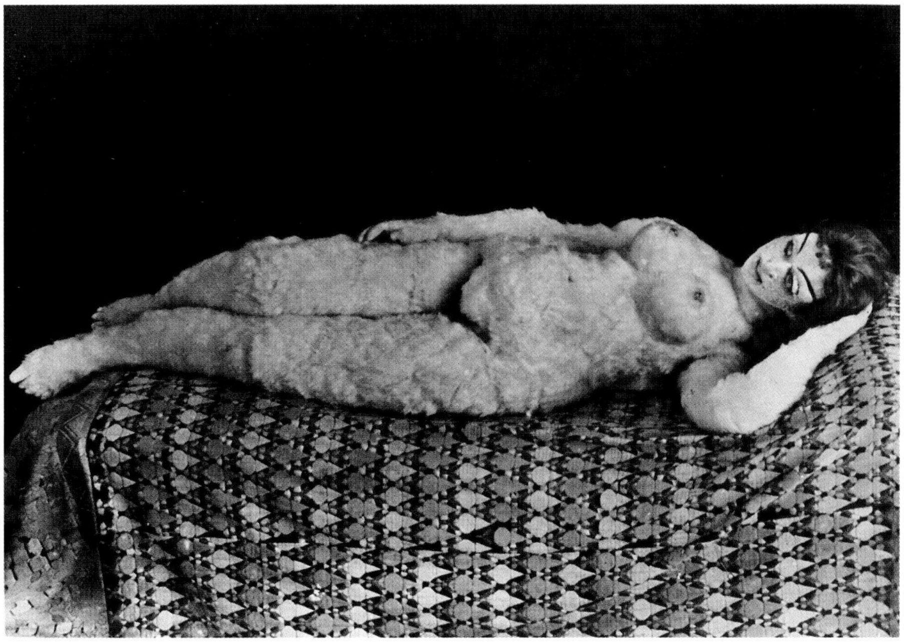

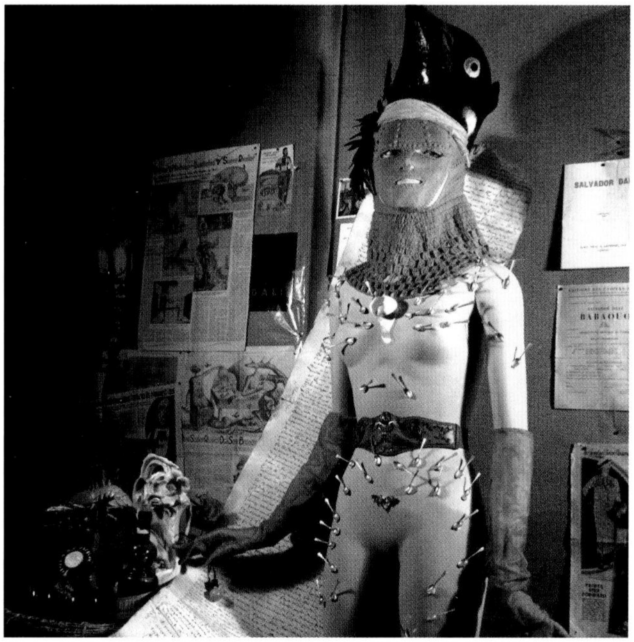

↑ **Oskar Kokoschka** • The Doll
1919

↗ **Salvador Dalí** • Mannequin
1938

The Sex-Doll Fetish

In 1918 in Vienna, the Austrian artist Oskar Kokoschka, dissolute with the news that his ex-lover Alma Mahler had married the architect Walter Gropius in 1915, and unable to get over his emotional dejection, commissioned a life-sized doll of her. The doll was to be constructed from Kokoschka's sketches of and reminiscences about both the look and feel of her body. It was to be artistic muse, model and sex toy; he repeatedly, and knowingly, described the doll as a 'fetish'. However, the hoped-for seamless melding of Alma with inert material left a lot to be desired, as is evident from the photograph of it above. Kokoschka nonetheless painted and entertained the doll. Latterly, however, as a symbol of his healing from the abandonment of Alma, he threw a party, drenched the doll in wine, decapitated it and sent it crashing to the street from an upstairs window.

In 1919, the Dadaist Raoul Hausmann utilized the adornment of the human head (this time a mannequin's head) in his *Mechanical Head (The Spirit of Our Age*; see page 53*)* to display a series of totems of his age to make a polemic point:

> **All the significant attributes of the object have been mounted by Hausmann on the outside of the head. The artist is introducing us to someone who only trusts in what he can measurably experience using objective**

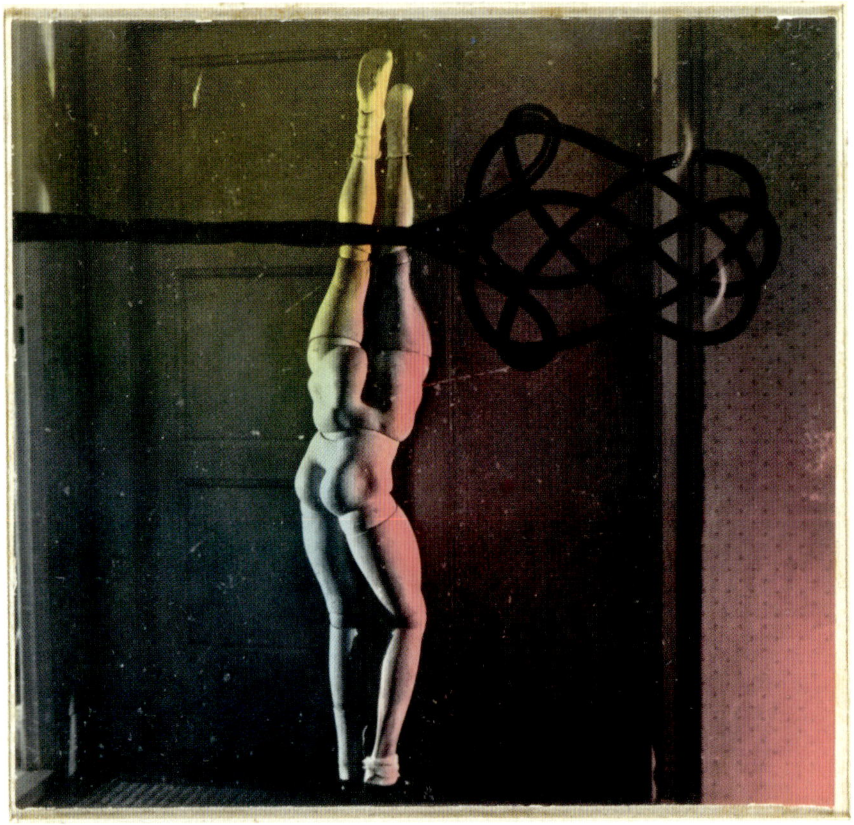

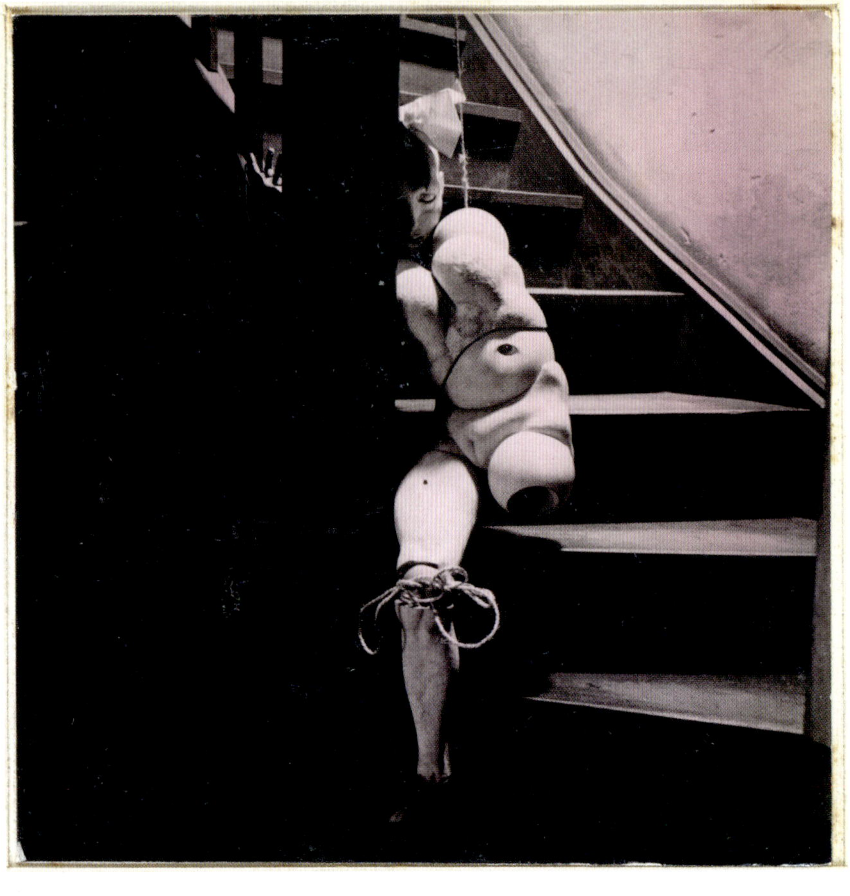

> **equipment. In place of being felt expressively, the world is encompassed in precise fashion by means of the ruler, the mechanical clock and the camera. No credence is placed in anything but the printed word.... By contrast the head's own eyes remain vacant.**[11]

The fetishization of the mannequin can be traced right back to the genesis of the Surrealist odyssey, with Breton, in his *Manifeste du surréalisme* (1924), alluding to the mannequin as 'marvellous'.[12]

As the 1930s progressed, the Surrealist mannequin became more sexualized, more an object of corrupt desire and more dislocated and dismembered. Its oscillation between inert plaything and erotically charged coquette or ravenous Greek sphinx delighted the Surrealists' thirst for the uncanny, for upsetting, disquieting desire and the forbidden gaze.

In Surrealist circles it was Hans Bellmer who created the most vivid and disturbing images of bodies. His representations of human anatomy, whether butchered and reconstituted mannequins or his beautiful yet highly transgressive drawings, are sexually explicit and perverse. Much has been written of the possible psychoanalytic reasons for his motivations.[13] Depending on which account one is reading, Bellmer is often portrayed as a polemicist, questioning Nazi ideas of the perfect Aryan body, or as suffering from a dysfunctional and fearful relationship with his father, a sexual attraction to his young cousin and multiple bereavements, deep feelings of loss or perhaps a combination of all of these. His art is scopophilic, paedophilic and oedipal, as well as agalmatophilic.

As a microcosm of his output we can look at two works: *The Games of the Doll*, a series of posed photographs in architectural space or landscapes, and the sculpture *The Machine-Gunneress in a State of Grace*. Both works extensively utilize ball joints. Though Bellmer was not thinking as an architect, he was speculating about the interpenetration of spatial realities. His work also depended on fetishistic objects such as the chemise, the striped stocking, the child's hoop, balls and marbles often mimicking eyes. The highly charged catalytic moment in Bellmer's oeuvre was his first doll, made in 1933. Sue Taylor describes its construction:

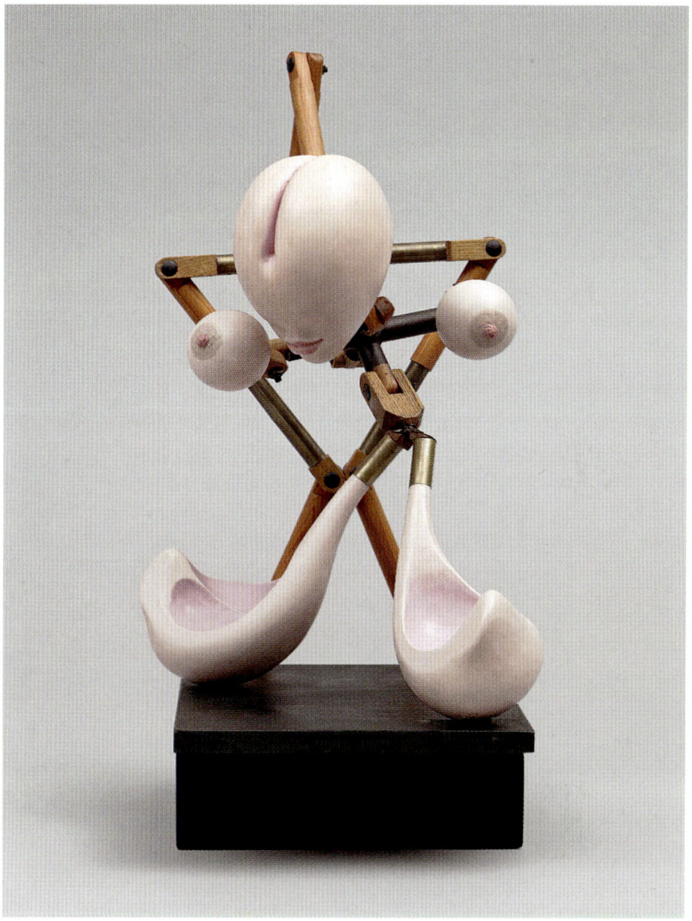

↑ **Hans Bellmer** • The Machine-Gunneress in a State of Grace
1937

> **standing about fifty six inches tall, the doll consisted of a molded torso made of flax, fiber, glue and plaster; a masklike head of the same material with glass eyes and a long unkempt wig; and a pair of legs made from broomsticks or dowel rods. One of these limbs terminated in a wooden, club-like foot; the other was encased in a more naturalistic plaster shell, jointed at the knee and ankle.**[14]

Bellmer had been aware of Kokoschka's 'Alma', and had seen Offenbach's *Tales of Hoffmann* with its scene of doll dismemberment caused by desire, jealousy and magic eyes.

His second attempt at constructing a doll was a more complex affair capable of being reconfigured with the aid of numerous ball joints. In 1938 he produced an essay entitled 'Notes on the Subject of the Ball Joint'[15] in which he explored the ball joint as a philosophical and apt mechanistic cipher and metaphor for many of his thoughts on mannequins and fleshed bodies, their movement, their environment and their superimpositions. The photographs of this doll were posed outside against bushes, tied to trees and in hay barns, and inside suspended from doorways and dismembered halfway down staircases, on beds and combined with chairs – the sanctity of the body violated, another infinitely reconfigurable object, merely a transient symbol of desire. It is this notion that resonates in our contemporary world just as much as any other transgressive content in the photographs.

Shortly after this Bellmer made *The Machine-Gunneress*. Again it consists of ball-jointed, reconfigurable female parts, of a mature woman, but also combined with those of a prepubescent girl, symbolizing both seduction and innocence, in repose but robotically alien, capturing Epstein's cyborgian other and its uncanniness twenty-five years later and imbuing it with sexual frisson and the guilt-ridden gaze.

Bellmer's doll photographs featured in the 'Exposition Internationale du Surréalisme' at the Galérie Beaux-Arts in Paris in 1938. Visitors to the gallery at 140 rue du Faubourg Sainte-Honoré first passed through a relatively large courtyard space in which was positioned Salvador Dalí's *Rainy Taxi*. The taxi was covered in ivy, headlights ablaze, and inside a female mannequin covered in snails, a sewing machine beside her. The car was internally irrigated to mimic rain. Having circumnavigated this work, visitors were led towards a corridor that featured a parade of a further sixteen female mannequins, each dressed by a different Surrealist artist (only one female artist was among these). Behind each was fixed a 'blue metal Parisian street sign, some real, some fictional, alluding to other Surrealist interests. With the exception of Arp's, the mannequin streetwalkers are engaged in sexual provocation, being in various states of undress and/or allure.'[16]

The Ultimate Sin

> **All epochs, philosophies and metaphysics have formulated at some moment (Manicheans, heretics, Cathars, witches but also Nervalians, Jarryites, Lautréamontists) the hypothesis of the derisiveness and fundamental unreality of the world, that is to say of a Principle of Evil, and they have always been persecuted and burned for this, the ultimate sin.**[17]

While Paris revelled in the terrible and titillating shock of the 1938 exhibition with its inert representations of bodies attempting sexual collusion with gallery visitors, a much more shocking and bloody theatre for Surrealist art was already raging on the Iberian Peninsula. Salvador Dalí, like the Dadaists before him, had used the malleable torsion of the human body to express the angst, terror and meaninglessness of war. In 1936 he had painted one of the archetypal Surrealist bodies in response to the harbingers of the Spanish Civil War (if we are to believe him). His *Soft Construction with Boiled Beans (Premonition of Civil War)* is an arresting portrait of a deformed human frame pulling itself apart, at once one body, but simultaneously two. Dalínian logic demanded that with so much fresh meat around it should be accompanied by some starchy boiled beans.

The distortion of the body caught in posed attitudes of distress and grief trying to respond to and reconcile horrible events beyond its control is also played out in Pablo Picasso's *Guernica* (1937), again influenced by the events of the Spanish Civil War. Likewise, in England, at the zenith of the Second World War and later during its denouement, Francis Bacon was exploring the loneliness of the human condition, its movement, visceral vulnerability and metamorphosis in

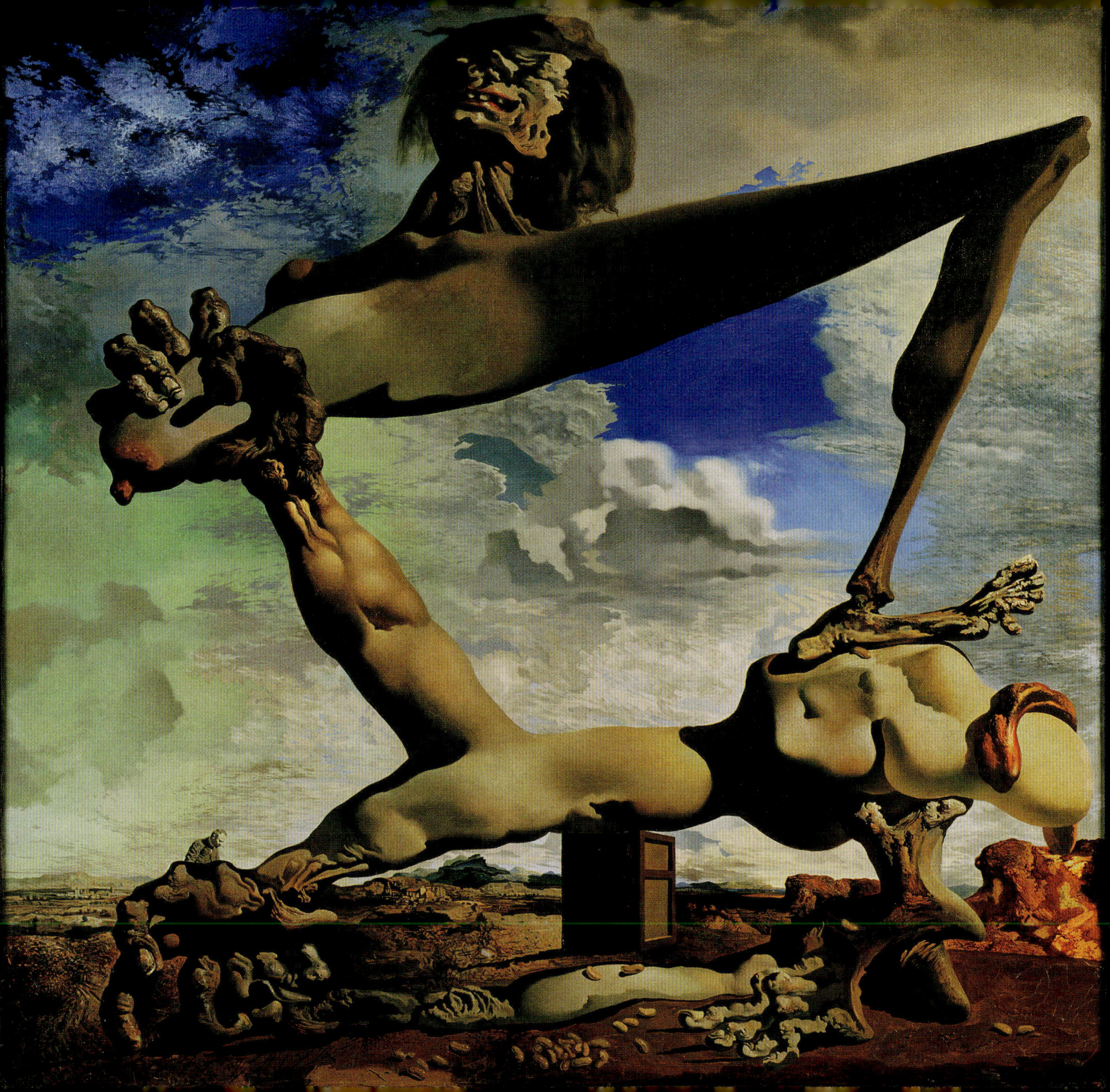

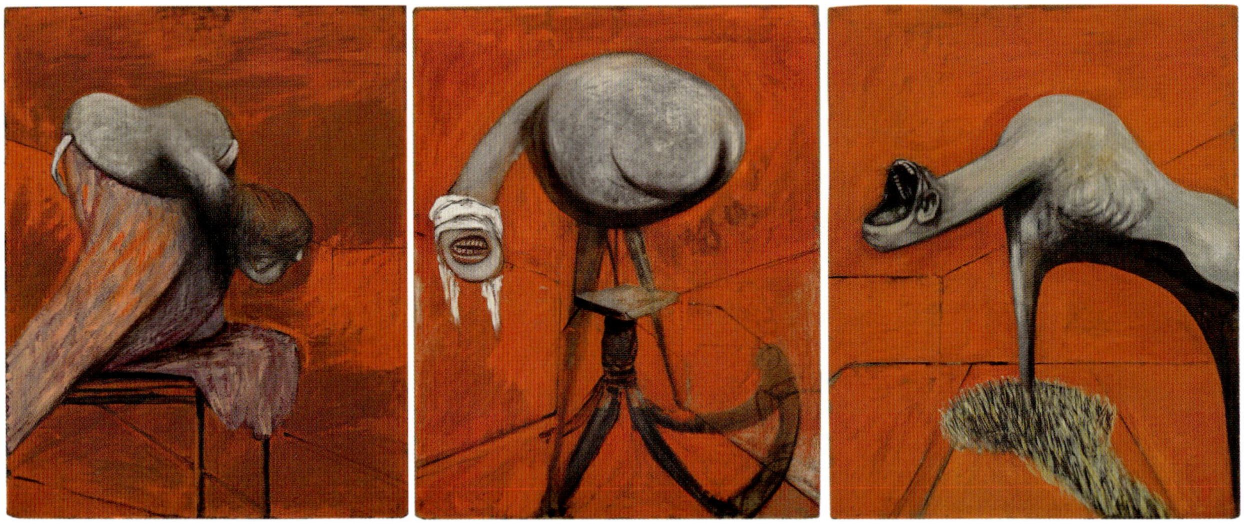

↑ **Francis Bacon**
Three Studies for Figures at the Base of a Crucifixion
***c.* 1944**

relation to our fears and loathings. Around 1944 he painted what he considered to be his first 'opus', *Three Studies for Figures at the Base of a Crucifixion*. The three figures were the genesis of his subsequent artistic endeavours for nearly the next fifty years.

The work consists of a triptych of half-human forms – Furies – hunched, pained, angry mutants mocking and celebrating the crucifixion that is happening, invisibly, above them. However just because it is invisible does not make it any the less disturbing and real. The figure to the left is perched on a plinth, the central figure on a convoluted tripod, and the right-hand figure on a small mat, maybe of grass. They can be read as the demented, smeared products of some grotesque medical experiment, a comment on the inhumanity of war and genocide; above all they are strange barometers of man's inhumanity to his fellow men, morphing and screaming as our exponential technological growth and ethical decay continue. The figures are 'uncanny' as we recognize ourselves within them. We are fearful of their violence, yet we empathize with their painful, brooding angst. Bacon's works nearly always depict bodies; blurred, leaky, pierced, smudged and bleeding, they are often sexual, not in idealized erotic shapes, but in repose to create feelings of still pain, remorse and death – rare and blue meat trapped in often domestic space.

Bodies with and without Organs

After the Second World War, and particularly, initially, in the USA, the mechanization of home and work continued at a pace as the speed and dexterity of information exchange and access to all manner of media increased. John McHale, artist, futurologist and writer, developed the concept that humanity could be represented by a series of constantly evolving 'Expendable Ikons' similar to Hausmann's *Tatlin at Home* (see pages 24–27) and *Mechanical Head (The Spirit of Our Age)*:

> **Such accelerated changes in the human condition require an array of symbolic images of man which will match up to the requirements of constant change, fleeting impression and a high rate of obsolescence. A replaceable, expendable series of ikons.**[18]

Since the mid-1970s, the performance artist and experimenter in bodily augmentation, Stelarc, has created a dramatic series, in effect turning himself into a contemporary version of McHale's Expendable Ikons. His performances illustrate clearly how the prostheticization of the body can result in numerous new architectural spacescapes. His works reconstitute humanity's haptic experience, sight and points of view, the cavities of the body, its sensitivity, virtual and actual experiences, scale of operation and, consequently, the architecture that could be designed for such augmented bodies. He describes his output in his own distinctive prose:

> **With gene mapping, gender reassignment, prosthetic limbs and neural implants, what a body is and how a body operates becomes problematic. We generate FRACTAL FLESH AND PHANTOM FLESH.... Meat and metal mesh into unexpected and alternate anatomical architectures that perform remotely beyond the boundaries of the skin. The monstrous is no longer the alien other. We live in an age of CIRCULATING FLESH.... Liminal spaces proliferate. Engineering organs through stem cell growing them or organ printing them will result in an abundance of organs awaiting bodies. OF ORGANS WITHOUT BODIES.**[19]

Stelarc's use of the expression 'Organs without bodies' is a reference to another powerful concept propagated in the late twentieth century by philosophers Gilles Deleuze and Félix Guattari – the Body without Organs (BwO). The BwO is not an attempt to describe our contemporary spacescapes

↓ **Raoul Hausmann** • Mechanical Head (The Spirit of Our Age)
1919

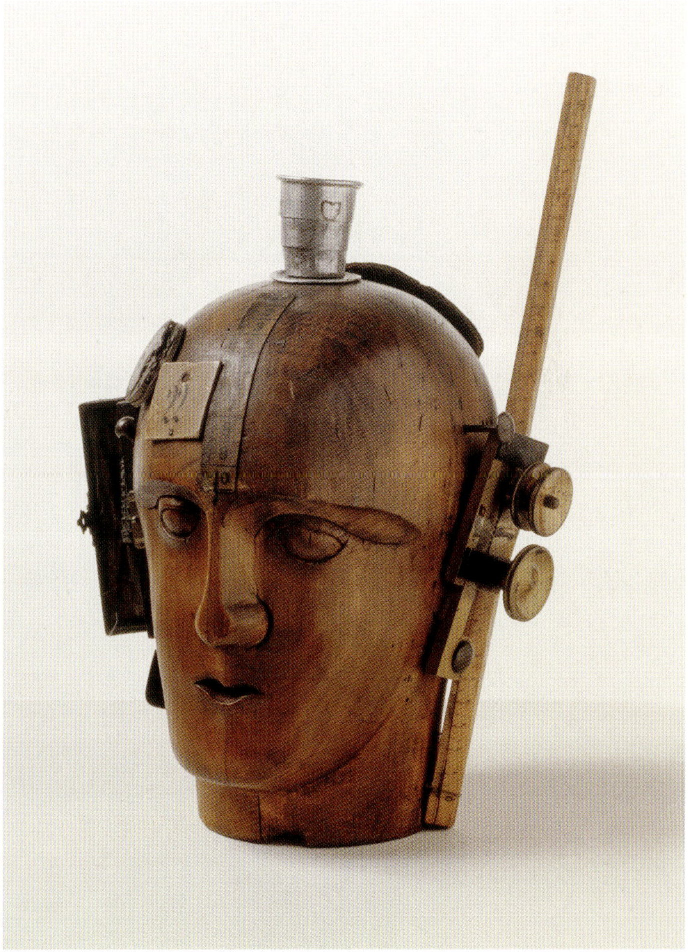

as lacking organs, but rather the interoperability of organs, flesh and electronic communication. Such synthesis facilitates fleeting multiplicities and swift changes within a global, universal body that includes our ecologies, politics, sexual mores and social organization. So the BwO is an exponential, asymptotic notion never fully achievable or fully comprehensible, a way to describe the trillions of interactions and points of view of humanity at any one millisecond – a writhing mass. Referenced in Deleuze and Guattari's explanation of the BwO, the American writer William Burroughs describes such a condition in his seminal novel *Naked Lunch* (1959):

> **In this place of total darkness, mouth, eyes are one organ that leaps forward to snap with transparent teeth...but no organ is consistent as regards either function or position...sex organs sprout every where...rectums open, defecate and close... the entire organism changes color and consistency in split-second adjustments.**[20]

This notion of the BwO, with its synthesis of the organic, the inorganic, the spectrum of human sexuality, fleeting connection and the myriad of spatial relations between objects, animals, things and people, the rejection of paternalistic organizations and hierarchies, and transgressed boundaries, dovetails nicely with Donna Haraway's concept of the cyborg and her important 'Cyborg Manifesto':

> **[B]y the late twentieth century, our time, a mythic time, we are all chimeras, theorized and fabricated hybrids of machine and organism; in short, we are cyborgs. The cyborg is our ontology: it gives us our politics.**[21]

This new politics is not born out of the masculine urge to dominate nature, but from ideas that recognize us for what we are: hybrid, natural and unnatural, unbounded and infinitely connected.

The theme of the emancipation of electronic connection and the infinite multiplication and quick change of these relationships were further magnified by the development of the spatial epistemologies of cyberspace as a cyborgian terrain. No book did more to express and inspire the wild transgressive spaces of cyberspace and its allusion to navigable data cities than science-fiction author William Gibson's *Neuromancer* (1984):

> **Cyberspace. A consensual hallucination experienced daily by billions of legitimate operators, in every nation, by children being taught mathematical concepts.... A graphic representation of data abstracted from the banks of every computer in the human system. Unthinkable complexity. Lines of light ranged in the nonspace of the mind, cluster and constellations of data. Like city lights receding.**[22]

Neuromancer is a novel that adopts a film-noir style, and as such depicts the urban landscape as corrupt, dangerous and predatory. Cities are cacophonies of language, human conspiracy and subverted technology. The 'street' is given up to 'black market' criminality and vagrant biotechnology. The main protagonist of the novel, Case, is a void waiting to be filled, a cyberspace junkie. Without being jacked in via dermatrodes to his cyberspace deck, Case is simultaneously a cowboy without a stallion and a racing driver without his Formula One – waiting, delayed, apprehensive like De Chirico's mannequins. Unconnected, he is bored, paranoid, gravity bound and withdrawn; connected, he is hero, master of the universe and sexy. According to cultural theorist Scott Bukatman:

> **What cyberpunk [authors such as Gibson share]...with the horror genre, is a surrealist perspective that reveals in the deformation and destruction, the resurrection and reformation, of the human. Taking their clues from Burroughs and Pynchon, as well as Bataille and Breton and Dalí and Man Ray, the techno-tactics of cyberpunk transform the rational structures of technological discourse to produce instead a highly poeticized, dreamlike liberation.**[23]

Stelarc's work, as well as concepts such as Gibsonian cyberspace, BwO and the 'Cyborg Manifesto', has been hugely influential on a generation of young architects attempting to reconcile these technologies with architectural explorations of this new augmented spacescape. Lucas Che Tizard is one such architect who has worked on the integration of the body with mechanical sensors and actuators to create biomechanical landscapes. In Tizard's work (see pages 56–61), the artificial blends with the visceral to speculate on an extended sensorium that is both individual and multiple, and both terrain and subject.

Today we inhabit a techno-surreal world and we understand that, as I have written elsewhere:

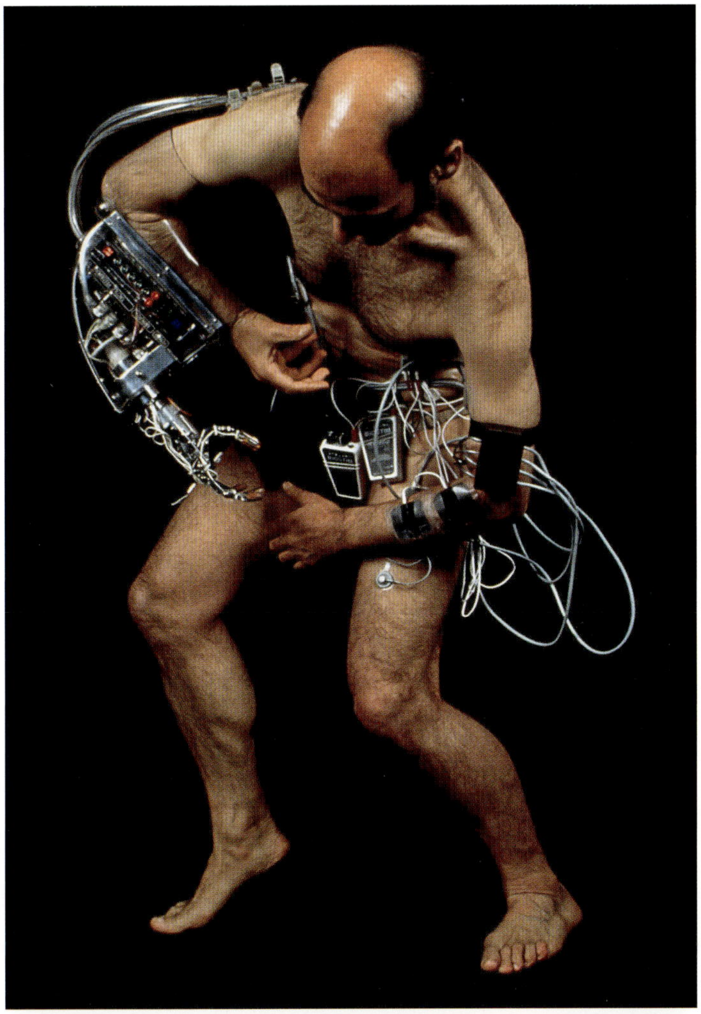

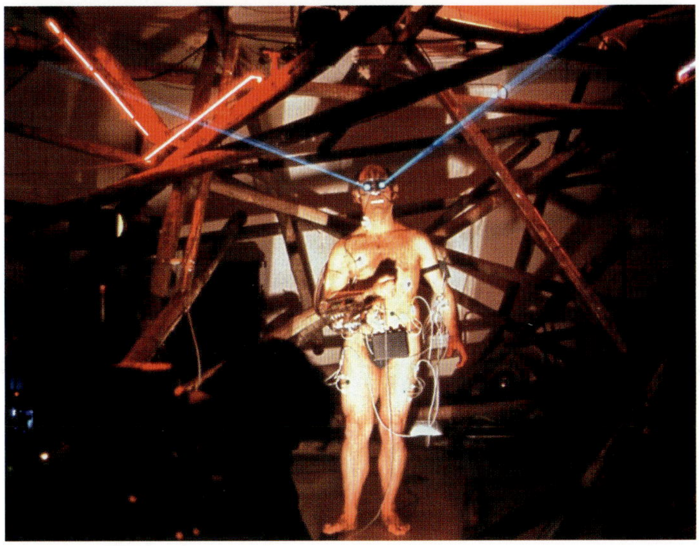

← **Stelarc** • Third Hand
1980

↙ **Stelarc** • Amplified Body, Laser Eyes & Third Hand
1985

there are many types of body – virtual, vital, augmented, prostheticised, digital and machinic – to name but a few. Technology allows us to coat ourselves in these bodies. However, we fear our fleshed body and its epidemic entropy. We yearn for release from its slow decay and vulnerability. We look to our machines and information networks to give us various shots at different types of immortality. Technology is trashing yet liberating the body, by allowing it to see further and deeper. Simultaneously technology gives us extended but fragmented versions of ourselves.... Engineering has become leaky, brittle and sore as we look to the technologies of molecular biology as a paradigm and method for advanced assemblage of products.... We are existing in a world that strives for interoperability, for compatibility across any platform, whether the digitised machine or the genetic viscera. Everything is manipulatable and morphable.... In the vortex of our fluid world, architecture becomes denser, faster and connected by the smears of ourselves and their trajectories.[24]

My own work *Genesis to Genocide* (see pages 62–63) sought to reconcile the Surrealist bodily themes of Dalí, Bacon, Bosch and Hausmann for a new generation of trials and tribulations concerning the emerging technologies of synthetic biology and virtuality. Again architectural space was at this time shifting radically. If we see our interactions with these fragmentational technologies and their peculiar landscapes as smears, then the more advanced the technology the easier it is for us to smear across and use it. We smudge our traces over space-time, across the landscape and through machines, where they are fleetingly registered,

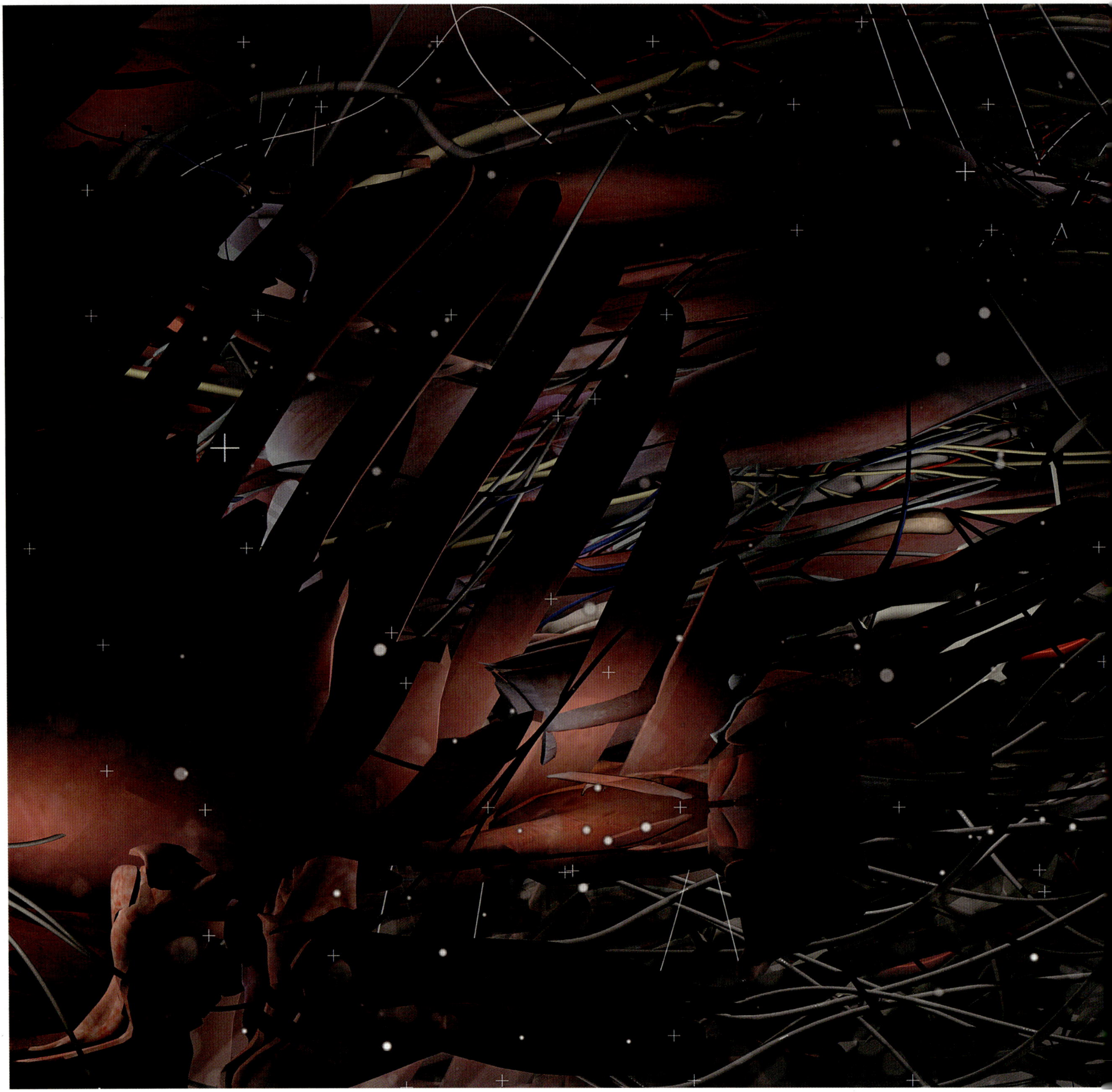

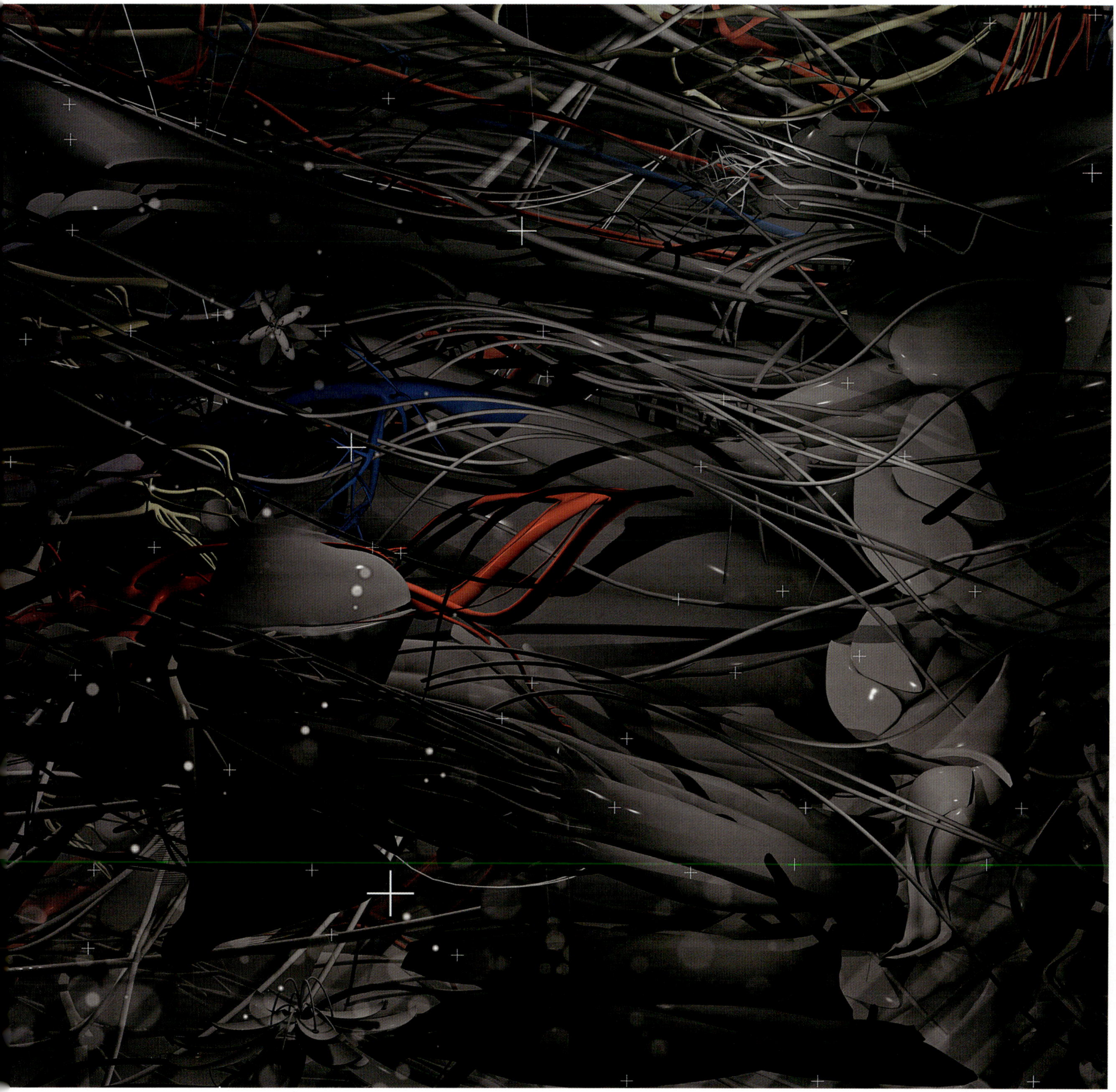

↑

Lucas Che Tizard • Biological Meets BioSynthetic, Prosthetic Architecture

2009

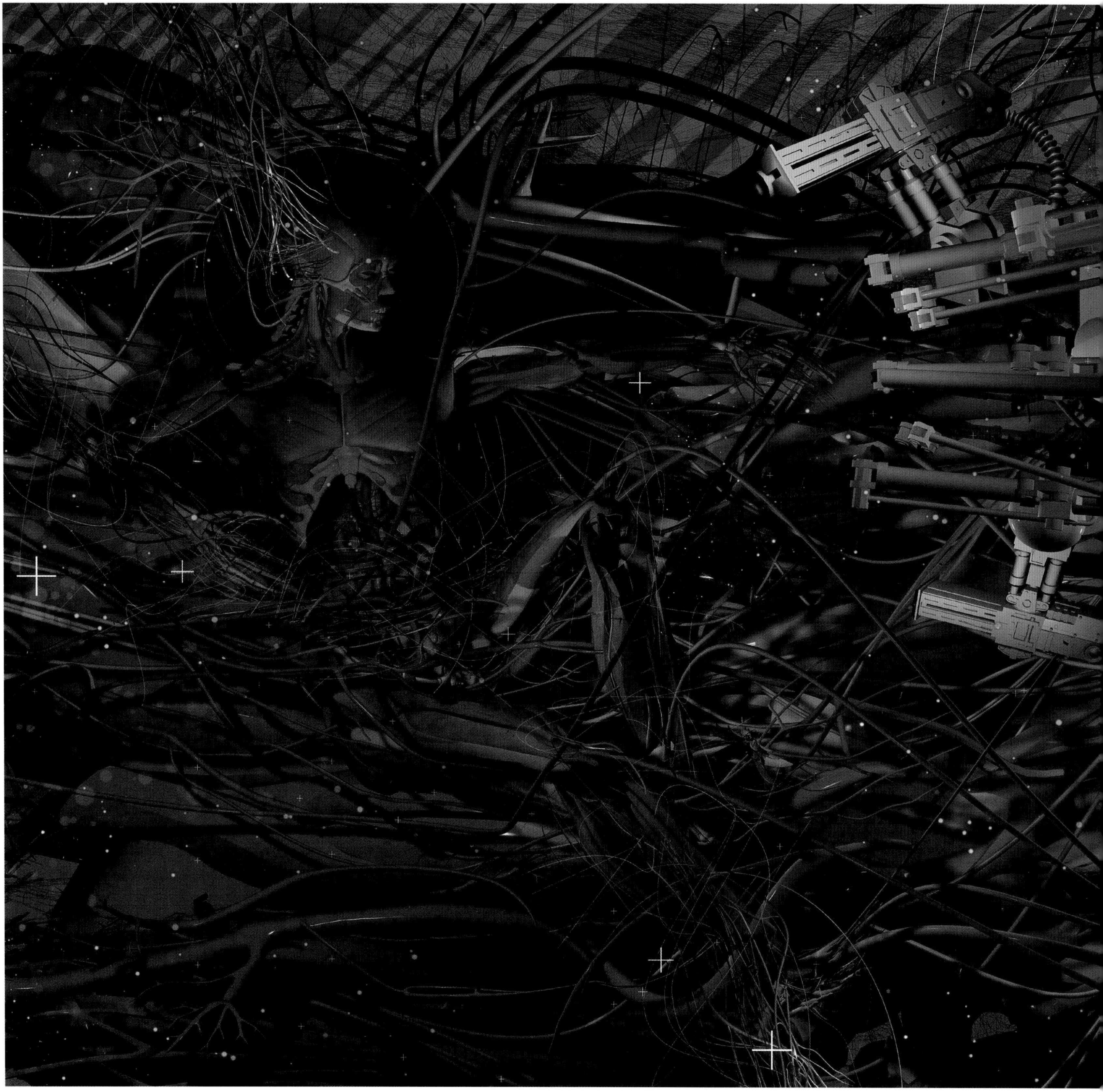

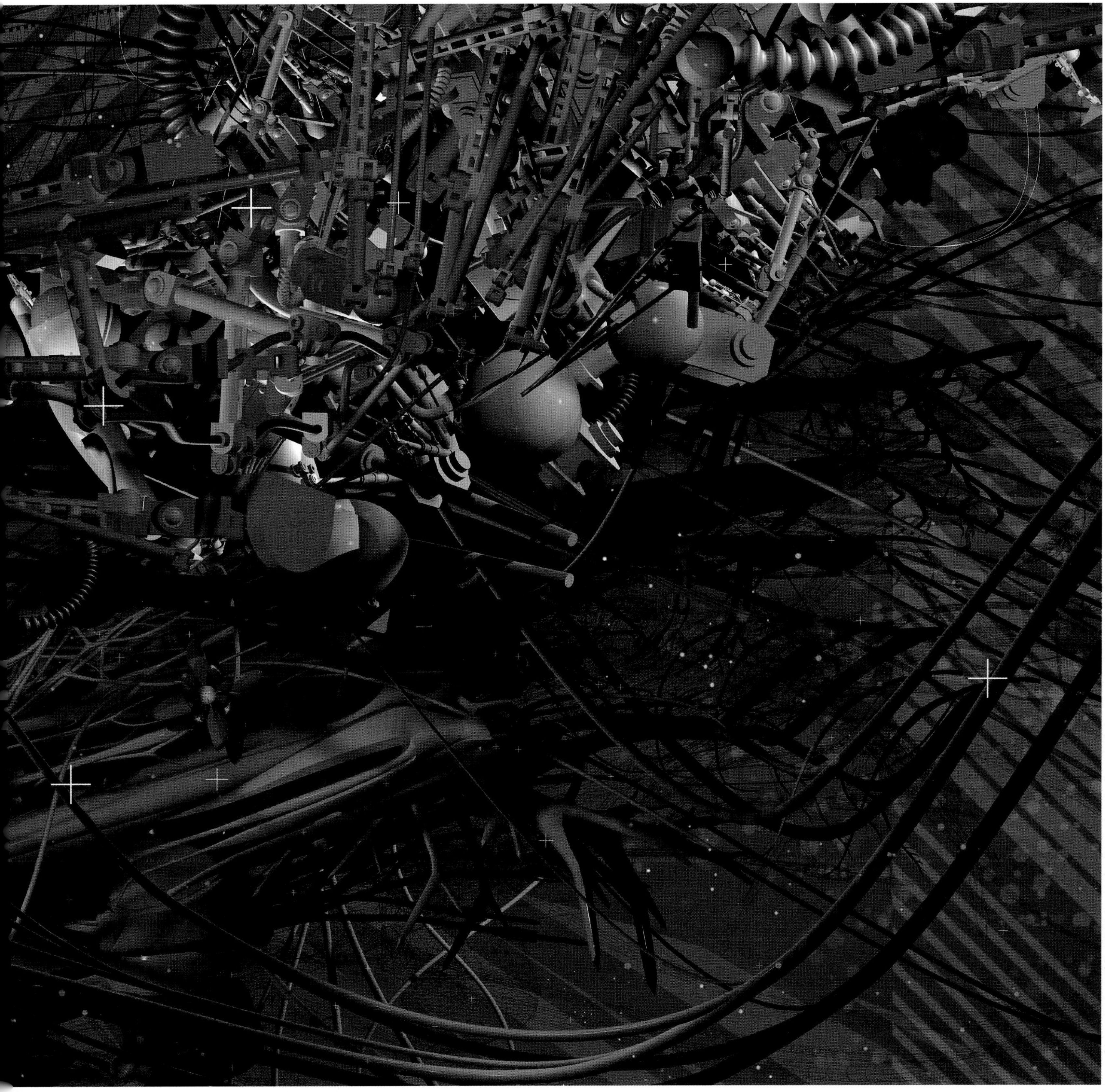

↑

Lucas Che Tizard • Creation of Arduinum, Prosthetic Architecture

2009

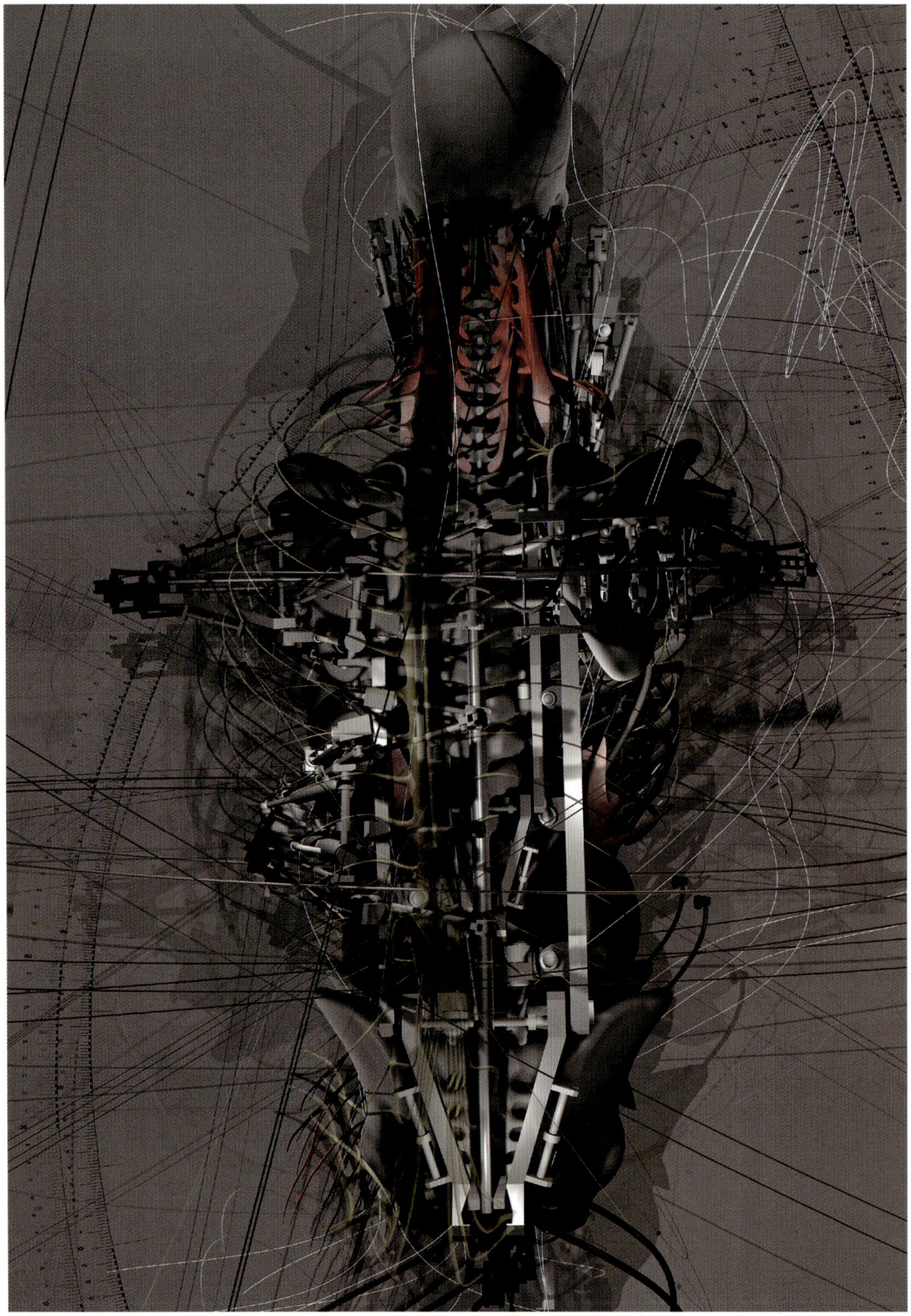

↑ **Lucas Che Tizard** • Head and Neck, Prosthetic Architecture
2009

→ **Lucas Che Tizard** • Mechanical Environment, Prosthetic Architecture
2009

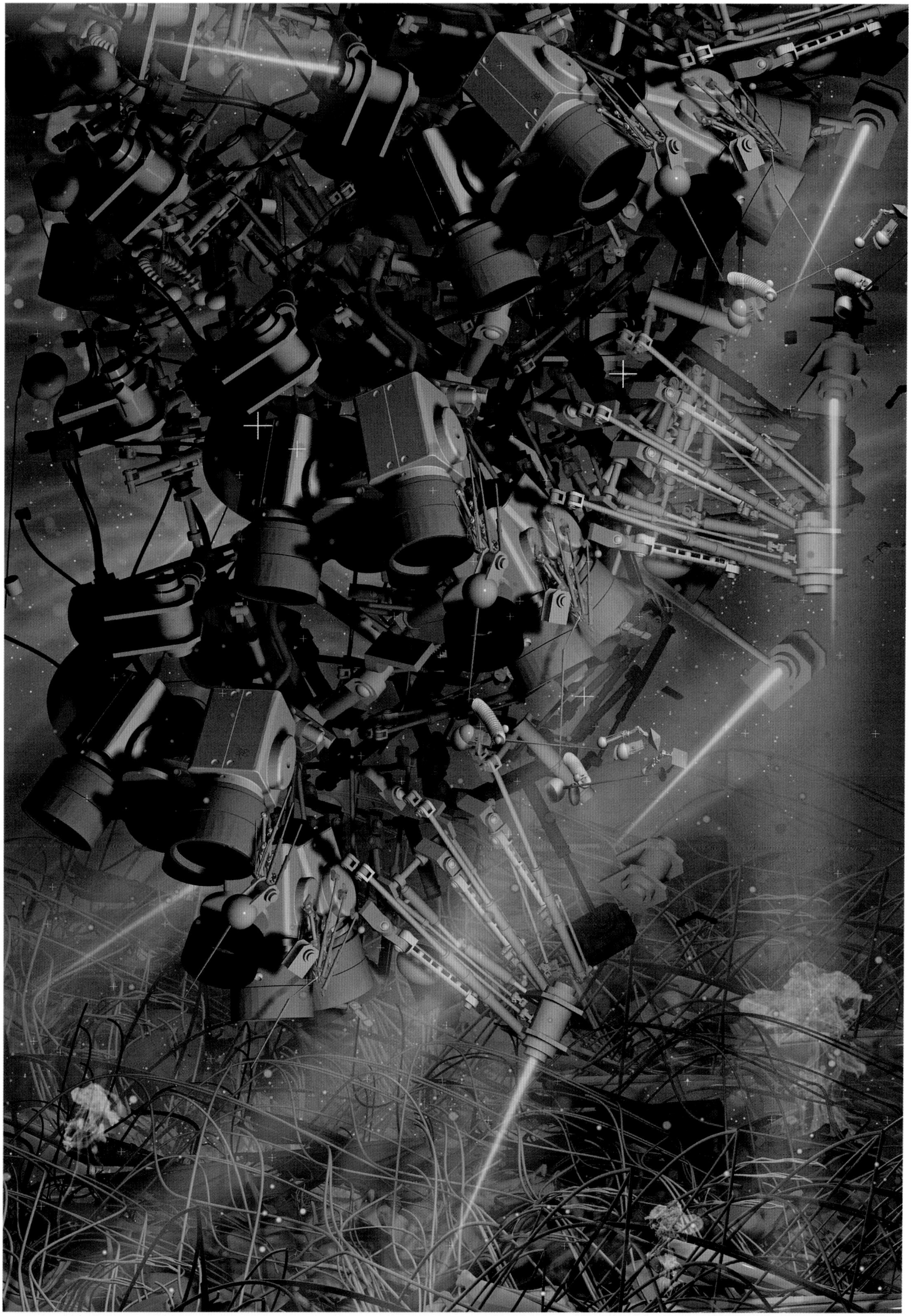

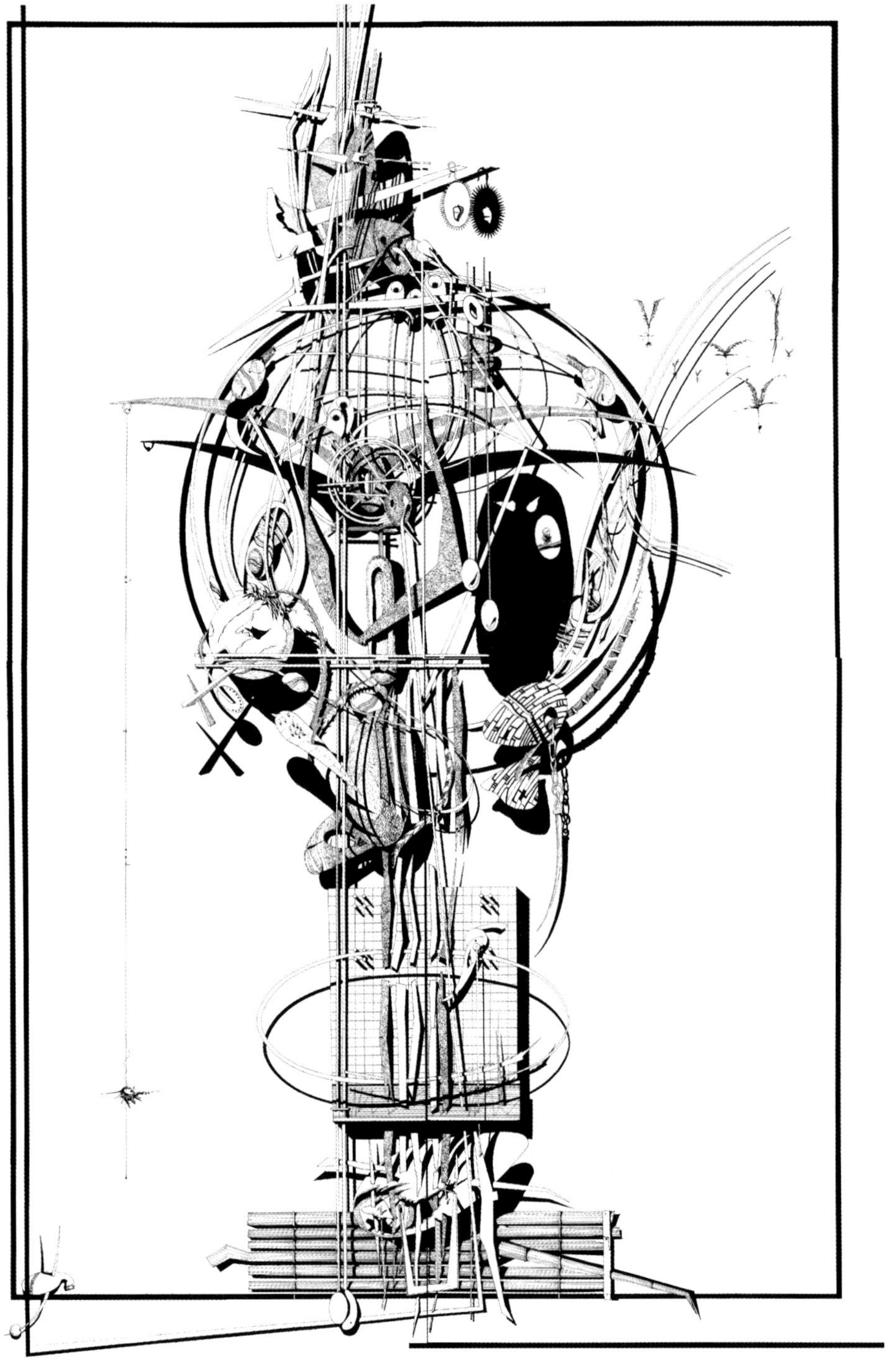
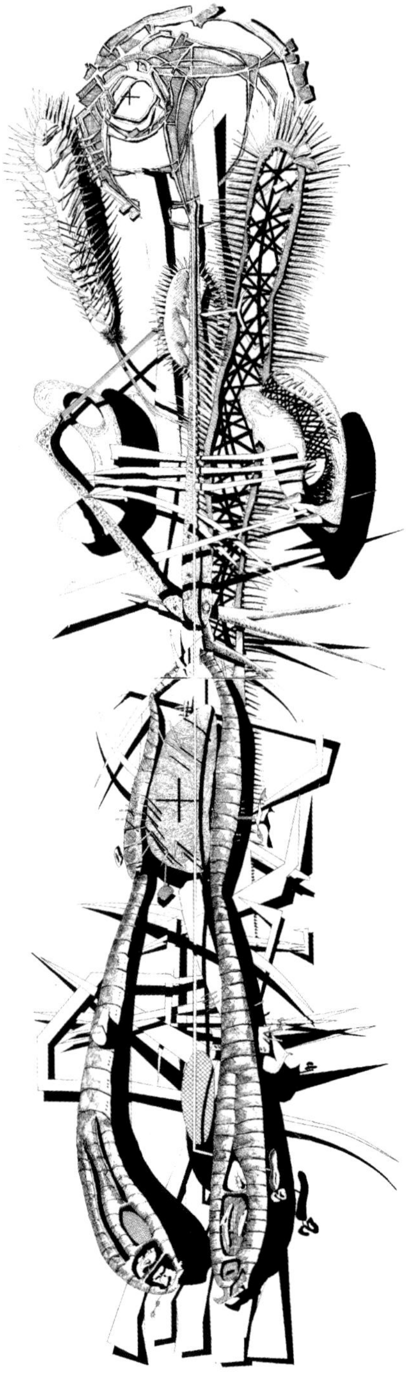

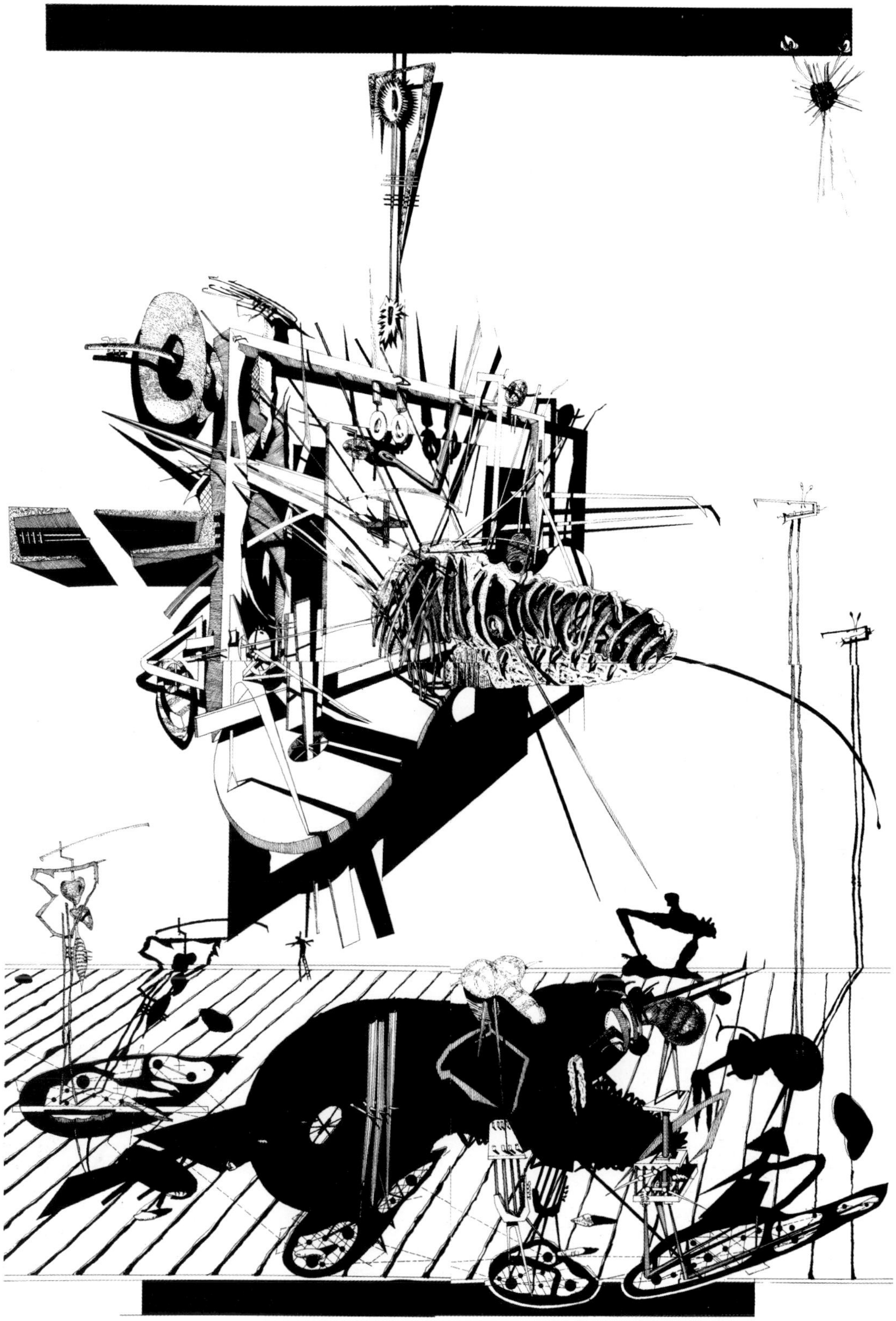

↖↑

Neil Spiller

Genesis to Genocide **(triptych)**

1995

classified, filed, transmitted or erased, reconstituted and retransmitted. These tools for augmented bodies are not passive; they coerce, trick, titillate and pull us towards and between them. Consequently, the body has become distal yet pierced, protruded, puckered and provoked as we seek to be everywhere at once, as our existence requires more and more updated information. As technologies flow forever on, our smears encounter less and less friction. Our researches concoct technological slime, which allows us to slip and slide through the landscape and through time.

Another depiction of this visceral, bloody body, in effect tearing itself apart and slipping through invisible technologized terrains, was inspired by the following religious text:

> **When you make the two into one, and when you make the inner like the outer and the outer like the inner, and the upper like the lower, and when you make male and female into a single one, so that the male will not be male nor the female be female, when you make eyes in place of an eye, a hand in place of a hand, a foot in place of a foot, an image in place of an image, then you will enter the Kingdom.**[25]

The designer and film director Bastian Glaessner's *The Groom's Gospel* implies a link to, or descendancy from, Duchamp's *Large Glass*; perhaps again the protagonists' backdrop is a multidimensional space of potential, although the images seem to have darker portents. What is clear is that Glaessner's Groom is a further meditation on the surreal body, Baconic themes and synthetic biology. Though the ceilings of Baroque churches and their illusionistic scenes of playful putti and benevolent angels are often inspirations for Glaessner, his skies are humid and heavy, awaiting a dark storm, perhaps a tornado, a force barely comprehensible, one of biological change and fearful destruction. The work has the same enigmatic yet foreboding presence as De Chirico's pregnant townscapes and stage-set rooms.

Glaessner's images show a host of flesh, bone and sinew – animal and human – smeared across the sky. These bloody denizens are caught in erotic bestial, cannibalistic postures as they transverse the firmament propelled, one suspects, by a power beyond their control – a charnel, magic technology of visceral mutation and eviscerating power where the old distinctions of animal and human, life and death, gravity and air are all left behind in its thrall. Glaessner's bodies pull themselves apart in a frenzy of gore, demonstrating the terrible consequences of humanity's hubristic hunger for the domination of all things and the chimeras that result. Again we empathize – we feel their sore bodies and speeding vertigo.

This metascape – architecture, landscape and microscape – must respond to this schizoid existence as we are smeared across its silicon wafers, glass slides and LCD screens, and caught in neural nets (both artificial and real) in its microphones and bitstream, gagging in its grafts and drowning in its cloned canals. These ecstasies hold clues to the new architectures of the twenty-first century.

The surreal body is alive and well, its genealogy strong, variegated and powerful. Time is not fading the aspirations and ambitions of the Surrealist pioneers, but boosting their premonitions. Techno-surrealist bodies such as those featured in this chapter need environments within which their expanded sensoria can exist, that nurture them and aid their continual reinvention of themselves and their quest to find and display the marvellous. The next chapter documents changes to the surreal house and its technologies, informed as it is by the evolution of surreal bodies.

→↘ **Bastian Glaessner**

The Groom's Gospel I and IX

2009

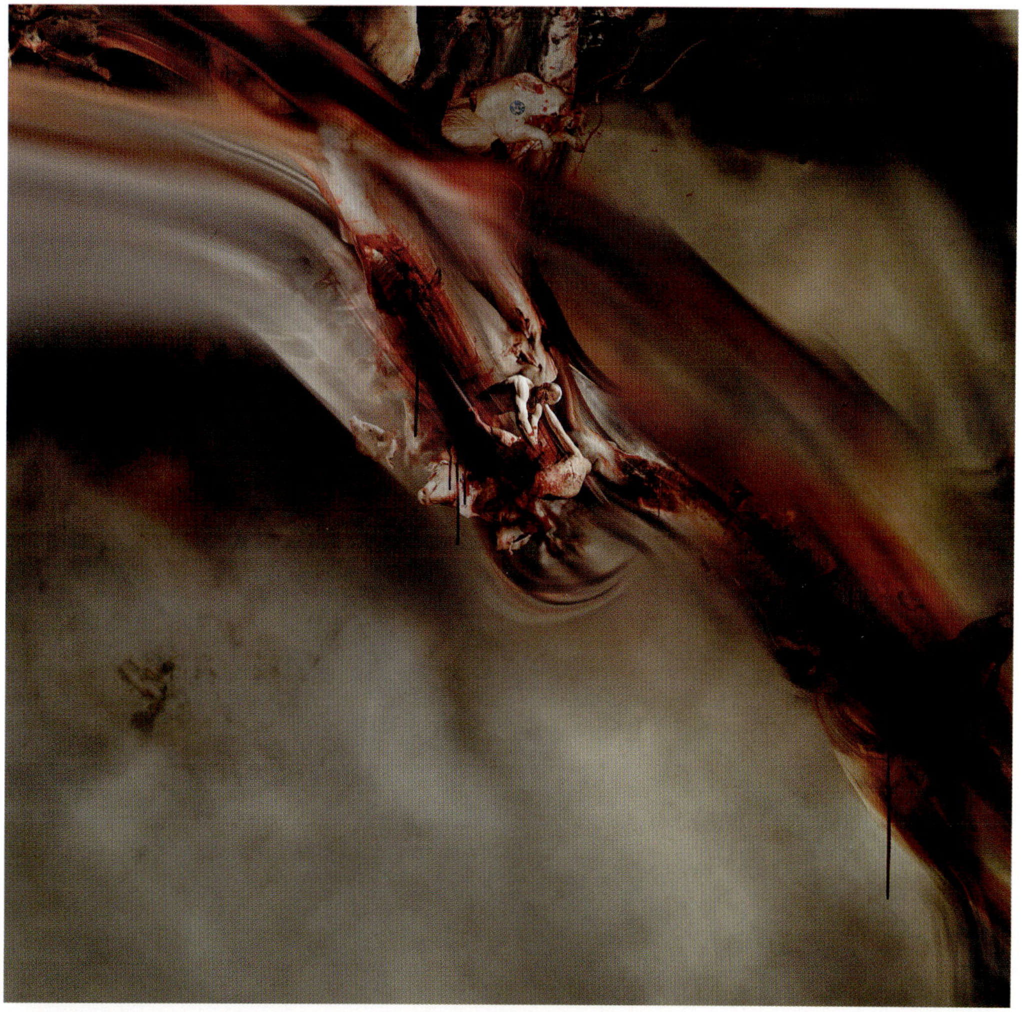

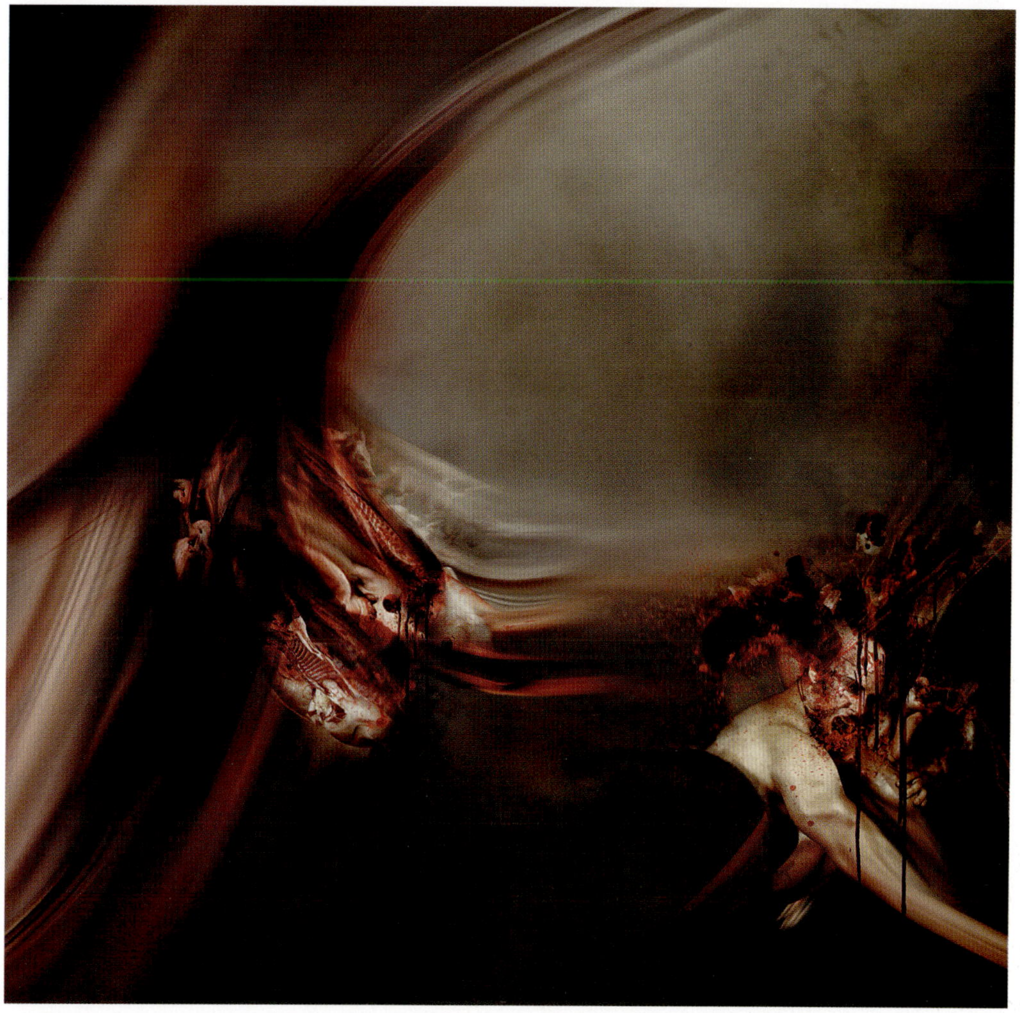

THE ARCHITECTURE OF BIOMECHANICAL CHIMERAS

HR Giger

Approaching Singularity

HANS BELLMER UNTITLED
PREPARATORY DRAWING
FOR THE FIFTH ETCHING FOR
GEORGES BATAILLE'S L'HISTOIRE DE L'OEIL
(STORY OF THE EYE), 1946–47

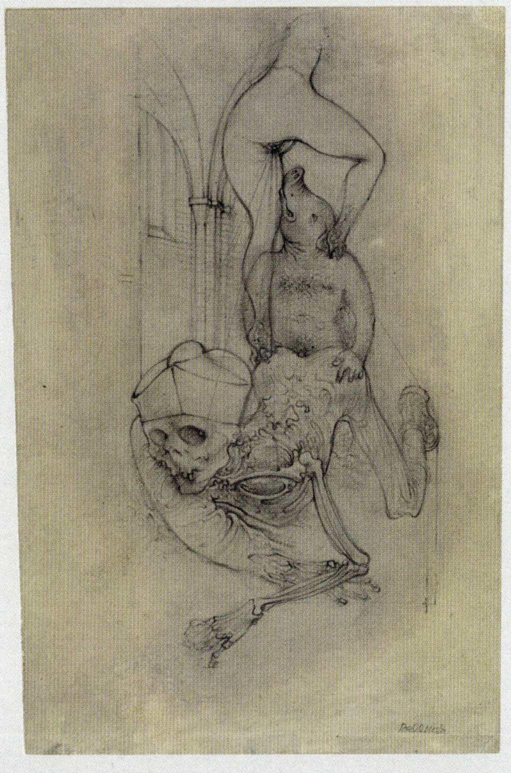

In an extraordinary display of drawn virtuosity, Bellmer seems to address and accentuate every sexual taboo in his illustration of Bataille's book.

The Swiss painter, sculptor and occasional film production designer Hansruedi Giger studied architecture and industrial design at the School of Applied Arts in Zurich, graduating in 1970. In his work, the transgressive bestial fecundity and body-machine synthesis illustrated in the paintings of Hieronymous Bosch and the photographs and drawings of Hans Bellmer reaches a new zenith. He will be forever known as the Academy Award recipient for his design of the Alien creature – inspired by his painting *Necronom IV* (1976) and its otherworldly environments – in Ridley Scott's 1979 film of the same name, but his work extends far beyond this populist perception.

For Giger, bodies become the exterior and interior of architecture. The body is portrayed as architecture's lover, its parasite, its decoration and erotic tormentor. In his art, Giger deftly assimilates the Symbolist influences of the Swiss painter Arnold Böcklin and the Austrian Gustav Klimt, the Art Nouveau of the French architect Hector Guimard and the Catalan Antoni Gaudí, the Fantastic Realism of the Austrian artist Ernst Fuchs and the Magic Realism of Salvador Dalí, the sexualized dismemberments and reconfigurations of Hans Bellmer, and the erotic machinery of Marcel Duchamp.

In the 1970s, Giger painted two versions of Böcklin's *Island of the Dead* (see page 70). The first, entitled *Homage à Böcklin* declares Giger's creative lineage not just in relation to Böcklin,

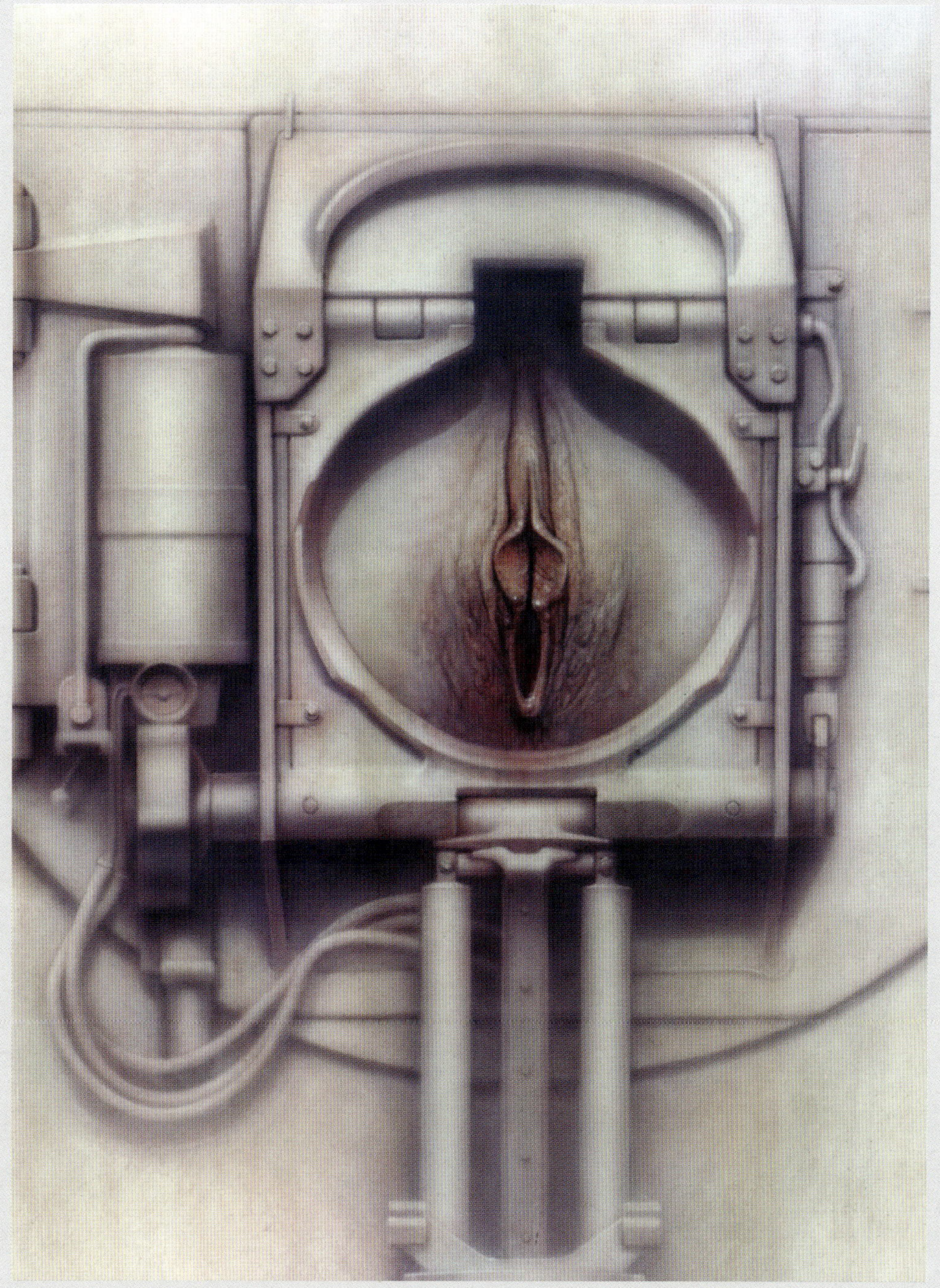

The mixing of the mechanical, the visceral and the Freudian dreamspace is a key preoccupation in Giger's art.

but also to Fuchs, who painted his own version of the Island of the Dead during 1971, and made reference to Böcklin's island in many of his other works. The second painting, *Isle of the Dead (after Böcklin)* features at the focal point of the Island a Passagen-type keyhole portal. Giger's Passagen series of paintings, reliefs and sculptures originated in 1972 as a response to his nightmare about being imprisoned in a room, the only way out to squeeze through a small hole, and evolved into disquieting metallic, vulvaic, industrial pseudo-religious icons.

THE EROTICS OF THE EYE AND THE EGG

The early Surrealist works most akin to Giger's generally are those of Bellmer, and particularly his 1946 illustrations for a new edition of the French writer Georges Bataille's *Histoire de l'oeil* (Story of the Eye; the first edition was illustrated by Surrealist artist André Masson and published in 1928). These drawings and preparatory photographs, viewed in conjunction with Bataille's pornographic text, are a heady mix of defiant imagery breaking nearly every taboo.

At a simple level, the book can be read as a litany of perverse mise-en-scènes that lurch from one bizarre sexual encounter to another, becoming more and more extreme. This sexual odyssey of debauched erotic scenarios of eggs, eyes, vulvas and testicles focuses on the narrator's carnal adventures with Simone – and also with Marcelle, the third party (both alive and dead) in their ménage à trois, who they encounter along the way. As the art historian Neil Cox writes:

> *Simone's obsession with eyes and eggs, and urine with semen, leads her to urinate into the eyes of Marcelle, when the latter is found hanged. Simone and the narrator flee to Spain, where Marcelle's role as third party is taken over by 'an Englishman' named Sir Edmund. Attending a bullfight, Simone is presented with the uncooked testicles of the slaughtered bull – 'of a pearly whiteness, faintly bloodshot, like the globe of the eye' – one of which she devours and the other she inserts into her vagina. Her resulting orgasm coincides with the death of a toreador, speared through the eye by a bull's horn.*[1]

In Giger's works, this hybridization of body parts is further synthesized with mechanical devices and other biological forms. Walls consist of fornicating bodies, pneumatic and hydraulic cables, gas cylinders and slithering tendrils reminiscent of worms, animal guts and condom sausages, all of which are ever ready to probe and penetrate any available orifice. His biomechanical chimeras can assume various forms – witches, vamps, dwarves, alien furies and siren harlots – the Surrealist motif of the vagina dentata (toothed vagina) fully utilized on many occasions and in many guises.

GIOVANNI BATTISTA PIRANESI
PLAN OF ROME **(DETAIL)**
1762

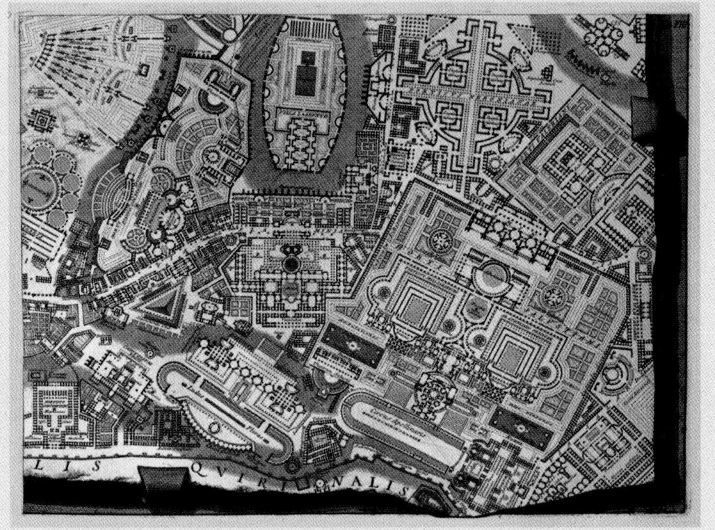

Piranesi, a master of imaginary landscapes and buildings, exhibits similar traits to Giger in that he too can seamlessly join disparate geometries and separate iconographies and figures to create hybrid architectural dreams.

The seamless painterly techniques Giger used to create his anatomies, architecture and landscapes effectively blur the boundaries between the scale of the body and that of the landscape/city. They can be sleek, suggesting nanotechnological vat-grown monocoque structures, or warty excrescences that erupt into bulbous crepuscular cysts dovetailed with eyes, eggs and glands. Giger's landscapes and cities, such as the 'New York City' series (1980–81; see page 71) or *Biomechanical Landscape* paintings (see pages 72–73), employ these tactics, synthesizing the body with the machine and its anatomies and products. Hearts and kidneys, veins, arteries and penises are joined in a language of extrusion with spigots,

GIGER BAR
GRUYERES, SWITZERLAND
2003

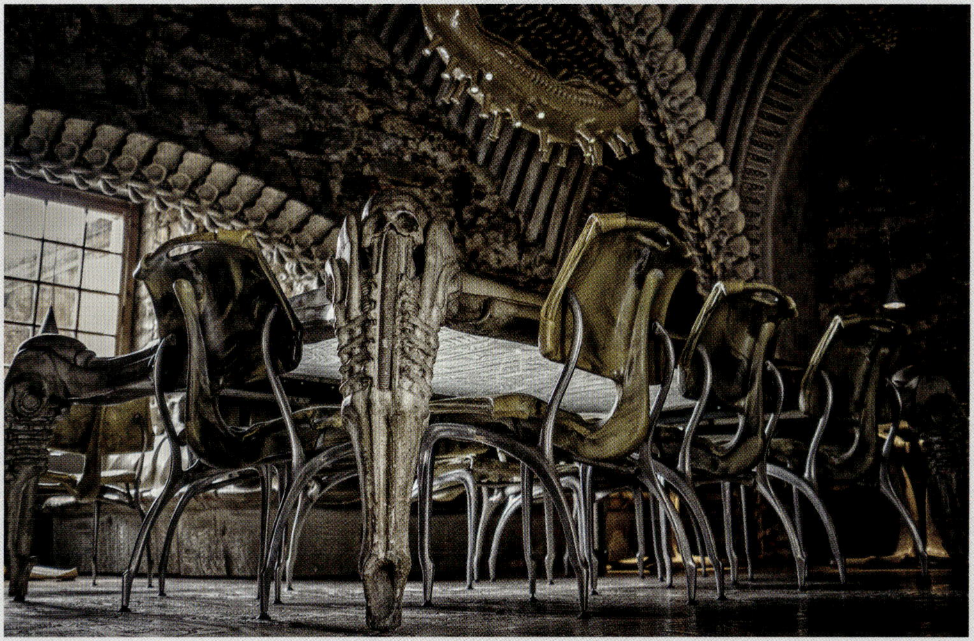

The Giger Bars bring the artist's architectural visions into the real world, augmenting a normally convivial situation with reminders of the beauty of bones and biological metamorphosis.

flanges, pistons and eyelets, the delicate skeins of milky spermatozoic membranes in some of the works forming an architecture of ethereal ejaculate.

A recurring motif in Giger's richly decorated architecture is that of the zipper, which, at once erotic and machine precision-made, often takes on the task of the dentil in classical constructions. His architectural works have a complexity in their details – an almost Aztec or Mayan flavour – and at first sight appear to seamlessly mingle irreconcilable geometries, much like the eighteenth-century Italian artist Giovanni Battista Piranesi's speculative plans of Rome. Giger achieves this reconciliation with a believability of construction, which, while it brings his works closer to existing contemporary building principles, is different. It is the interchangeable nature of this believability with his photorealistic draughting technique and the fantastic nature of the work that gives it such power. His work also features a series of Giger Bars designed to create furniture and spaces made of Giger-esque skulls and bones – in effect, charnel public houses.

His 'New York City' series exhibits a fractal rationale in which his towers, highways and train tracks are never fully declared, yet are understandable and readable at a variety of scales: as beautifully engineered musical reed instruments, or as urban plans and elevations of differing fenestrations – all slightly humming with the movement of trillions of nanotech milky drones.

Giger thus engages with the continual metamorphosis and formal and emotional dexterity of the city to create symphonies of urban rhythm in this particular series. The Surrealists explored the city's vicissitudes, its dark zones, accretions of marvellous constructions, traces of butchered myths and the rituals and fears of its human agents. Giger also plumbed these same depths to great effect, assuring his immortality as an artist in an imagined, but surely soon to be world subsumed in the glut of industrially produced organs.

HOMAGE À BÖCKLIN **1977**

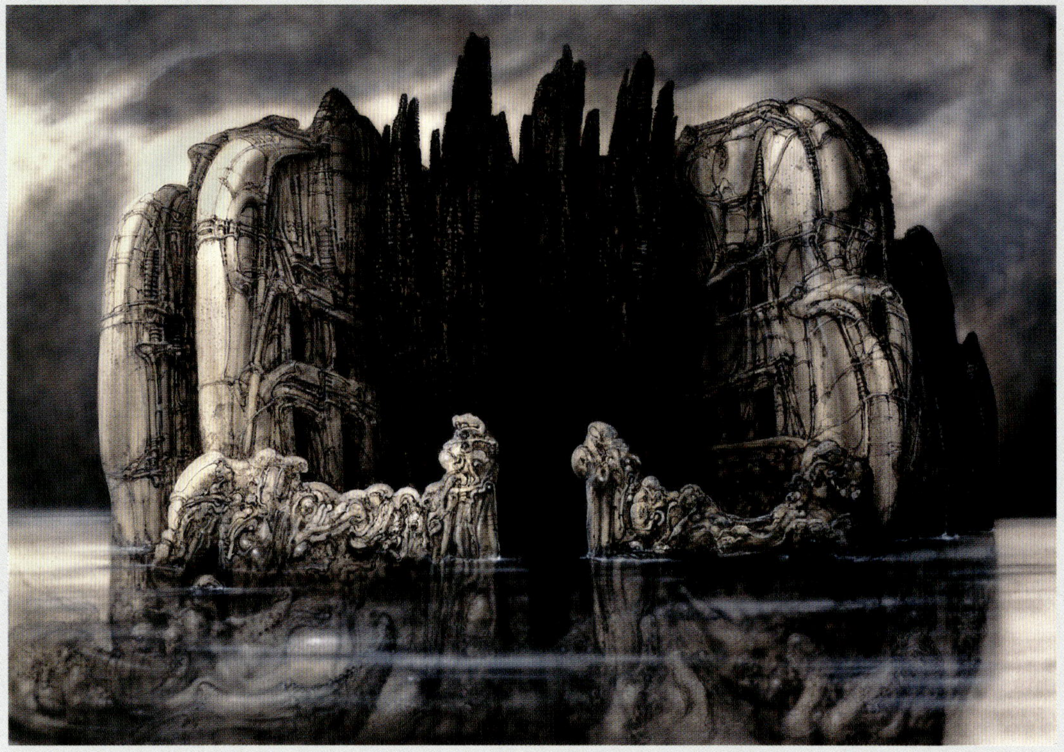

Böcklin's paintings, with their foreboding silence, deeply influenced Giger and his mentor/friend Ernst Fuchs.

ISLE OF THE DEAD (AFTER BÖCKLIN) **1975**

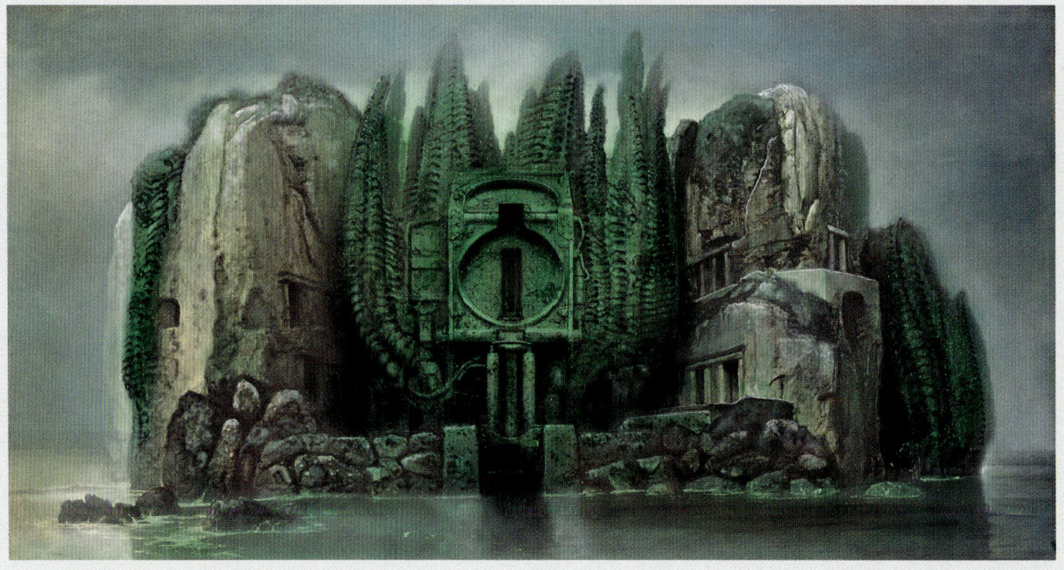

Giger combines his own lexicon of biomechanical forms with Böcklin's strange enigmas in his interpretation of the artist's series.

NEW YORK CITY XXV **1981**

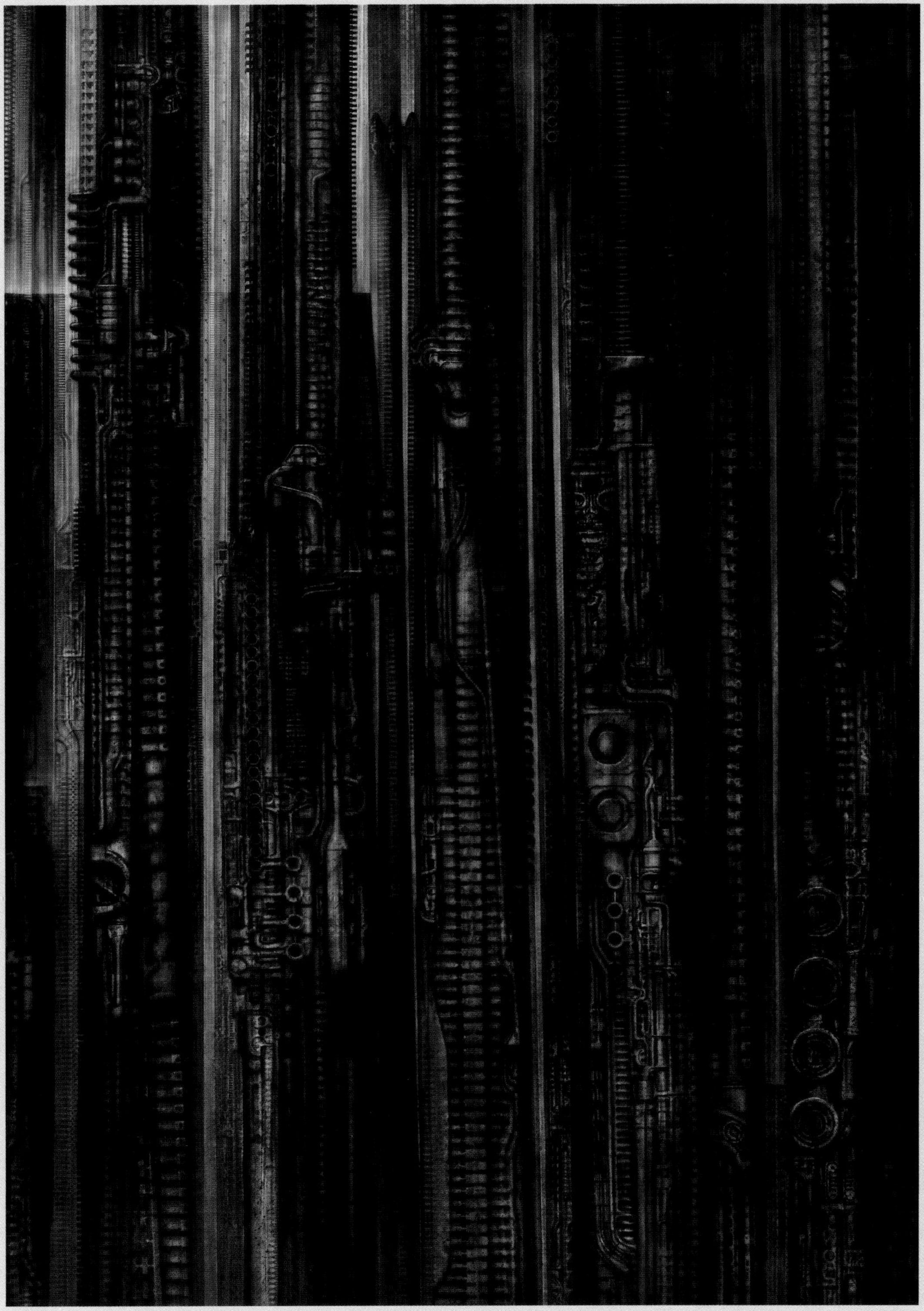

The 'New York City' series depicts a future city, alive with density, communication and travel conduits, yet also humming in molecular activity and biological imperatives.

Giger's formal dexterity, vision and synthetic attitude between bodies and buildings push forward our understanding of what biomechanical landscapes might be like.

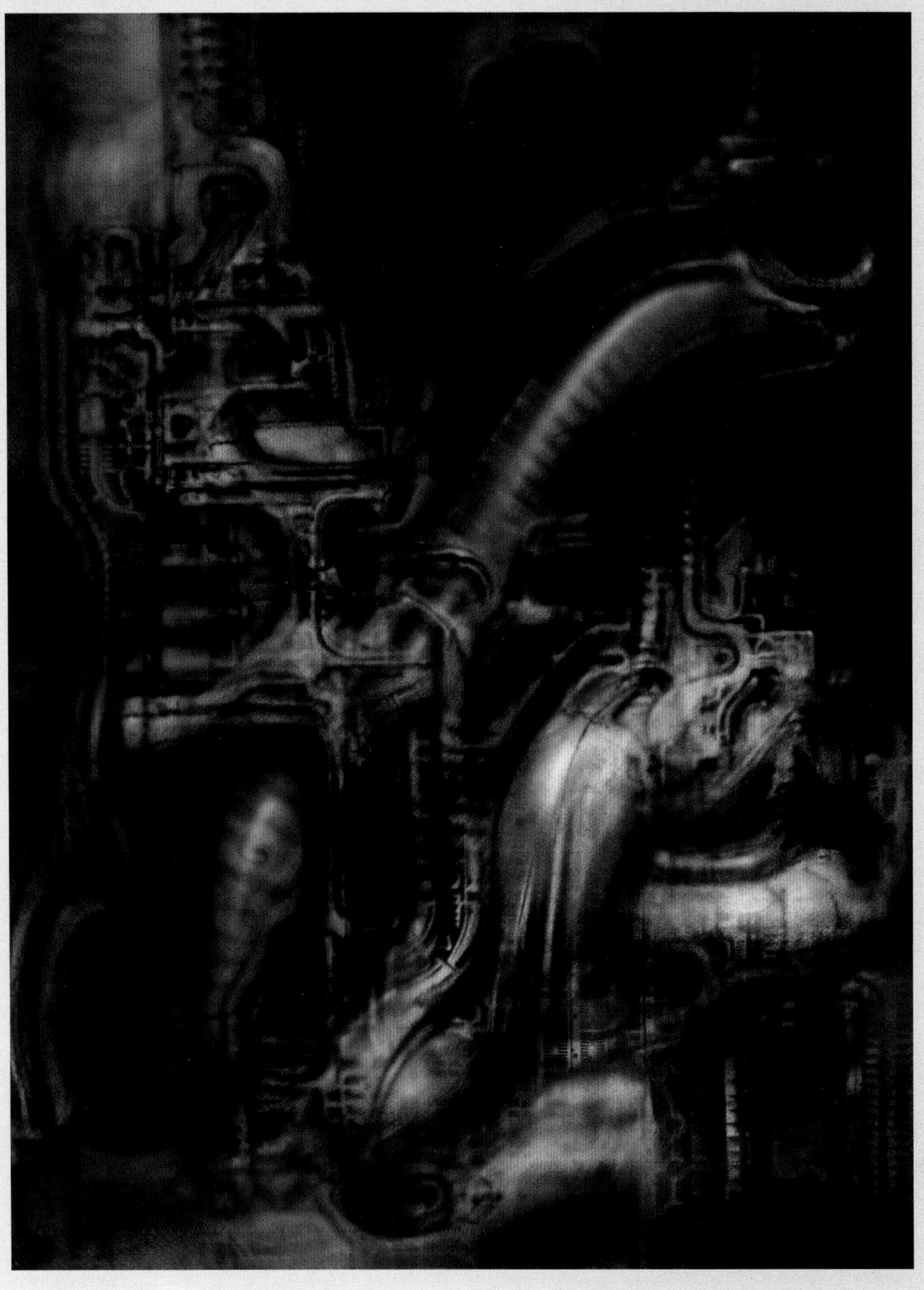

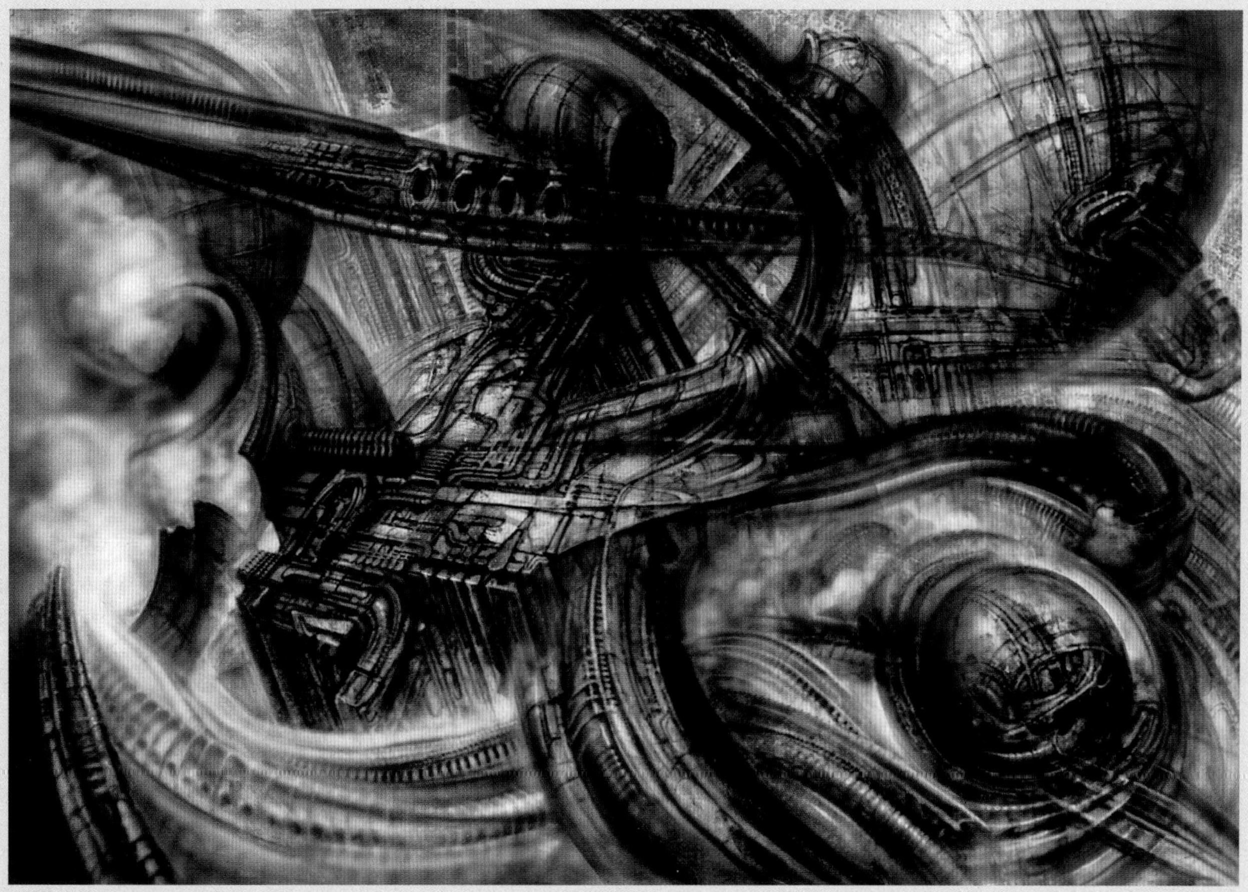

Giger's Biomechanical Landscapes flux and pulse, twitch and slide in the imagination as alive architectures.

The cellar is the bowels of a house; it collects all wastes and discarded time. A bed in a house promises future joys and remembers past sorrows. The forlorn house is a house without a woman. A woman moves her fingers over the surface of a pewter jug and thinks of man.... The house searches for its lost occupants.

John Hejduk, 'Sentences on the House and other Sentences', 1997[1]

...and yet, so far as I know, no one attributes to furniture the power to awaken in us ideas of an altogether peculiar strangeness.

Giorgio de Chirico, 'Statues, Furniture and Generals', 1929[2]

THE SURREAL HOUSE

CHAPTER II

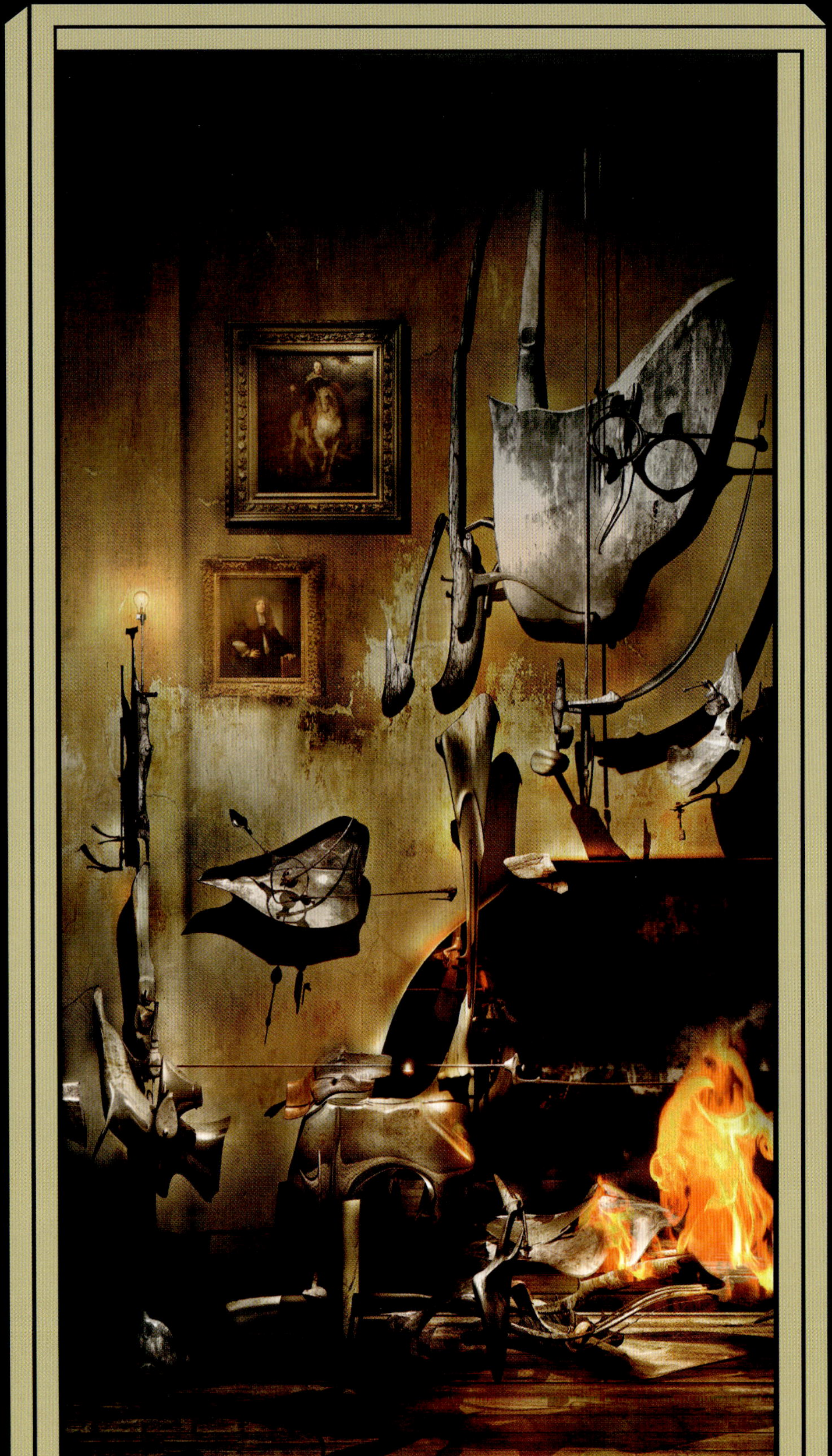

←

Tom Cartledge • House in the Woods

2009

For the Surrealist, and often the psychologist, the house is simultaneously womb, alchemist's kitchen, semiotic laboratory, *Wunderkammer* and pornographic memory theatre. Everywhere there are allusions to the celebration or repression of desire, the power or fear of dreams, and the veiling or honouring of ghostly presences. Above all, houses are analogue computers that bring into juxtaposition wondrous or uncanny objects, ideas and eclipses of things.

Implicit within this lyrical space of combinations is technology – of metamorphosis, adjacencies, collage and mutation. The history of the surreal house is one not only of love, lust, bodies and anti-bourgeois rebellion but also of an ever-expanding architectonic palette of building materials, communication devices, information media and consumerization. Above all, the interaction of virtual space with actual space is becoming more complex, and this alone will dramatically alter the house of the future, further imbuing it with surreal qualities.

The relationship between the changeling bodies of the previous chapter, domestic evolution and our colonization of increasingly dense informational landscapes are symbiotic. The kaleidoscopically fertile collusion of Surrealism and architectural technologies changed everything – and will continue to do so as new bodies demand new environments in which to dwell. In his 1968 essay 'The Cylindrical Monarchy of Guimard', Salvador Dalí wrote that he was 'Against the total lack of eroticism of Le Corbusier and other mental weaklings of our most-sad modern architecture'.[3] Here he offered us not the Corbusian 'machine for living in', but 'Houses for Erotomanes not to inhabit but to live in and even, with the permission of Monsieur Le Corbusier, to dream in, and even to rave in'.[4] As we will see, Dalí's mutually exclusive binary arguments against Le Corbusier are disingenuous. However, the new bodies at the genesis of Surrealism needed new notions of domestic space with which to protest against and consternate the establishment with its precious myopism and fixation on order and prudery.

The upper- and middle-class domestic settings of the late nineteenth and early twentieth centuries were seen by the radical writers and artists of the time as spaces of sexual and technological repression – hypocritical, abusive (psychologically and physically), stultifying, ritualistic and segregated in terms of class and gender. In effect a whole raft of unstable veneers cast over deep – what we would now call 'Freudian' – tensions. The visceral and erratic nature of humanity were subsumed into a complex series of ineffectual protocols designed to obscure and conceal two basic facts: that we desire/dream, and that outside the home technology was burgeoning and changing us, as it always had, but at an ever quicker pace. The Surrealists wanted to set themselves free from such hypocrisy.

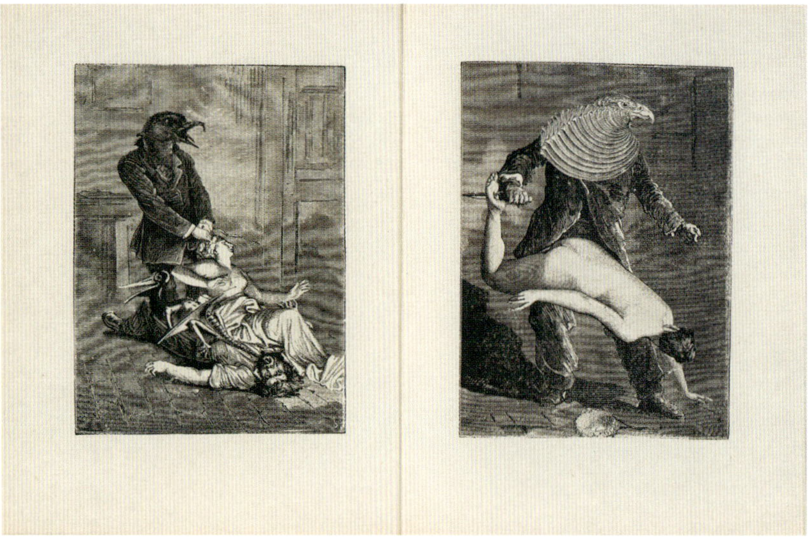

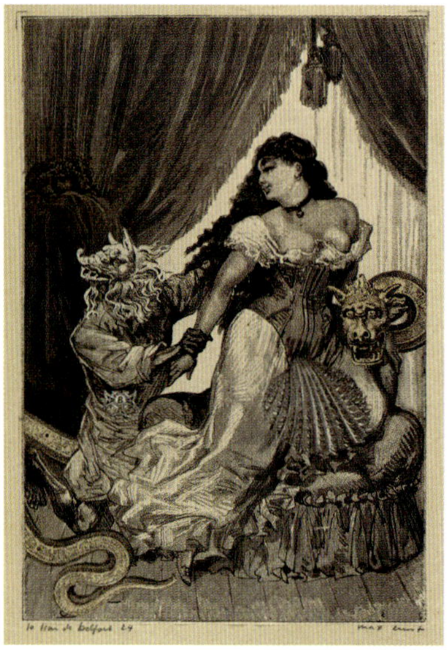

The House of Fear

The surreal house can be said to unearth and exploit human emotions, desires and fears. Its architectures are drenched in psychological oceans and singed with the infernal anxieties of its inhabitants. In 'Inside Fear' (1997), Anne Troutman explores these phantoms and their haunts:

> I do not believe the house is a safe place. For me, it is a collision of dream, nightmare and circumstance, a portrait of an inner life. The primal shelter is also the site of primal fears. Its interiors are a map of the conscious and the unconscious: of their securities and insecurities. There is danger in the house. Closets, hallways, stairways, doors and windows, attics, basements, eaves and cabinets expand and contract with fear and desire. They are the night side of the house, in which the identity and security of domestic life is displaced, condensed, fragmented. Within every contented home there resides the house that anxiety built and buried to counterbalance the security of the known self.[5]

The sculpture *The Palace at 4 a.m.* created by the Swiss artist Alberto Giacometti summed up all these nuances. It was influenced by the Swiss Symbolist Arnold Böcklin's *Island of the Dead*. Böcklin's paintings were also hugely significant for the Italian Giorgio de Chirico (who utilized their brooding silence in works that include *The Soothsayer's Recompense*; see page 21). All three artists share the same enigmatic stillness and peace while maintaining a deep sense of dread. *The Palace* is said to have come into Giacometti's head fully formed as a dream about lovers, mothers, houses and dresses – a good Freudian mix of symbols and taboos. The central figure, a pod-like form with a pea or bean in it, is Giacometti himself stuck, almost crucified, witnessing the unfolding of a recurring terrible drama that he is unable to stop. This is both a physical and mental house, one full of recurring fetishizations, angst and yearning. The maternal figure to the left of the sculpture is at once homely and unhomely, simultaneously comforting but also a source of shame and judgment.

In his graphic novel *Une semaine de bonté* (A Week of Kindness), German artist Max Ernst illustrates what might better be described as a 'Week of Hell', using his expertise in the art of cut-and-paste. The whole is organized around the days of the week, associating each with a material such as mud, water or blood, or notions such as sight and blackness, with Saturday being intentionally 'unknown'. Much of the work is situated in strange domestic interiors. Ernst's raw materials for the collages were Victorian magazines or encyclopaedias, thereby symbolically turning Victorian epistemology on its head. The subversive power of collage lays bare the feral and haunting presences within the home and their darkest thoughts and imperatives. As each of the pages of his pictorial novel unfold, Ernst further documents

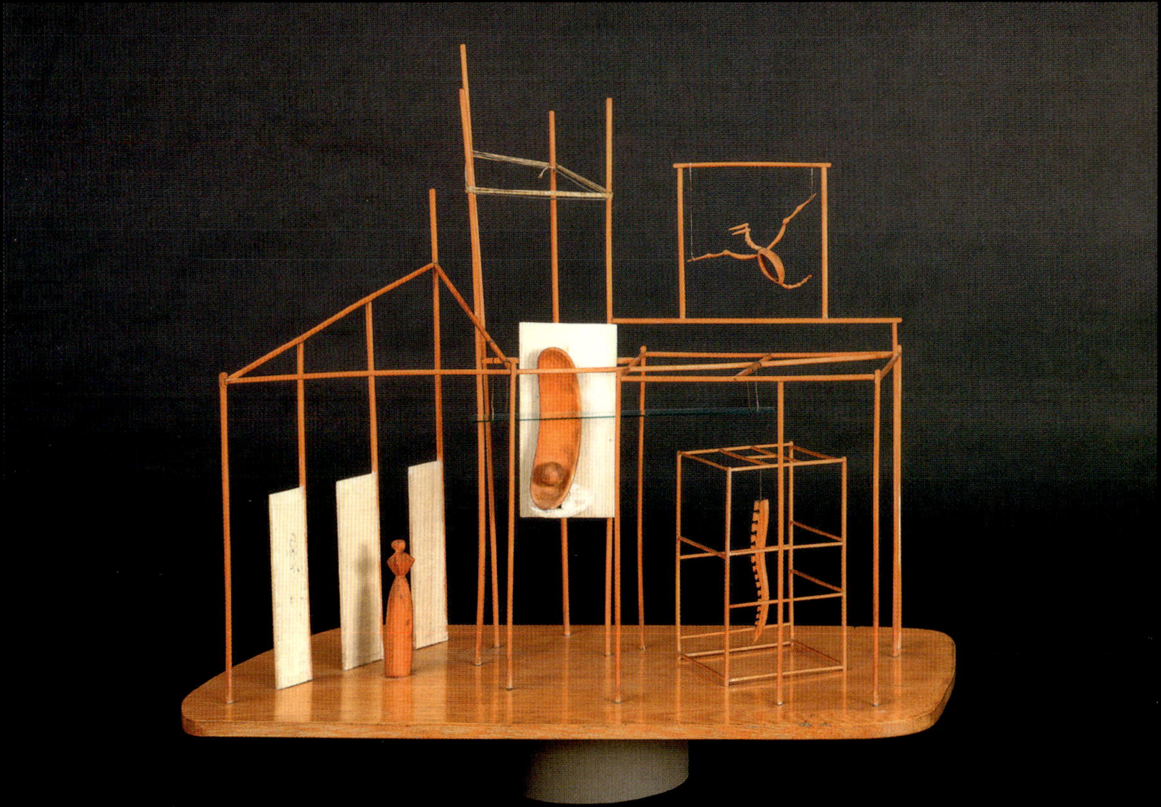

← **Max Ernst** • Une semaine de bonté ou les sept éléments, Capitaux, **vol. IV, Paris 1934**

← **Max Ernst**
From the graphic novel
Une semaine de bonté
(A Week of Kindness)
1933

↖ **Alberto Giacometti**
The Palace at 4 a.m.
1932–33

↙ **Arnold Böcklin**
Island of the Dead
1880

this other domestic world of dark deeds and thoughts. Rooms, houses and streets become full of lustful chimeras, straight-laced but deviant. Animals and humans are hybridized and the natural order of things is corrupted: objects are rescaled, out of place; interiors sometimes caught in vengeful floods or subject to howling winds. We become voyeurs of the Victorian hell house and its jungle of desires, unhealthy appetites of all kinds no longer repressed by whalebone corsets and stiff collars. Reflections are not to be believed; pictures contain more demons, overscaled animate objects or alternative threatening realities – nothing offering quiet serenity except death itself. Furniture commands its own sullen or stealthy presence. Demure ladies turn into lascivious harlots, or their chastity and virtue is left in tatters as they are subjected to all manner of perils and improprieties. Women are more often victims than vamps, and death, murder, sex and nudity abound. This is a world out of control. It is as if the dusty, ornamental gloom of these scenes, their decorations and dim lighting demands that their occupants act in these ways.

The Fallen Angel of Surrealism

The white and transparent Modernist house pioneered by Le Corbusier and others in the 1920s and 1930s sought to cast out these dark demons that dwelt in the opaque nooks, crannies and material swathed around turn-of-the-century domestic interiors. However, during this time Le Corbusier also produced a pronounced Surrealist project, revealing Surrealism, with its extreme juxtaposition of objects and space, to be a powerful magnet even for the Great Modernist.

On one level, the Beistegui Apartment (1929–31) in Paris is a party place – a stage-set for titillation and play. It was commissioned by Charles Beistegui, a multimillionaire art collector, known throughout his life for his extraordinary parties and international network of famous and influential friends. Architecturally, Beistegui is an optical machine. Its spatial tricks include a periscope, mechanically moving and controllable roof planting, and its half-room/half-roof garden that features truncated views of Paris and its famous nearby monuments, including the Arc de Triomphe. It is a contradictory piece in Le Corbusier's canon, bringing together and attempting to reconcile a great diversity of ideas and form. An ornate mantelpiece without a fire adds a focal point of pure Surrealist theatre. Le Corbusier's Purist art and sculpture was not so different to Surrealist preoccupations.

Indeed, Le Corbusier was also interested in and respected Alfred Jarry and his proto-Surrealist prose and plays, as suggested by the series of sculptures, paintings and drawings Jarry produced during his life with 'Ubu' – (the name of his

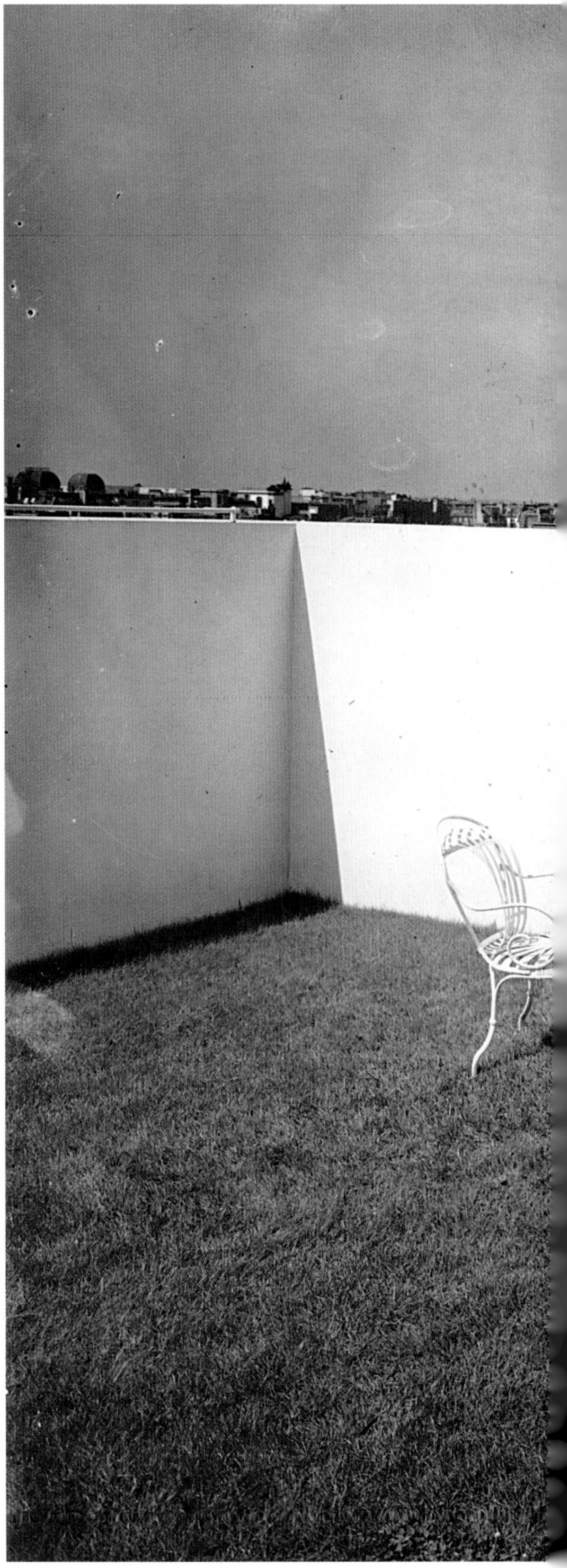

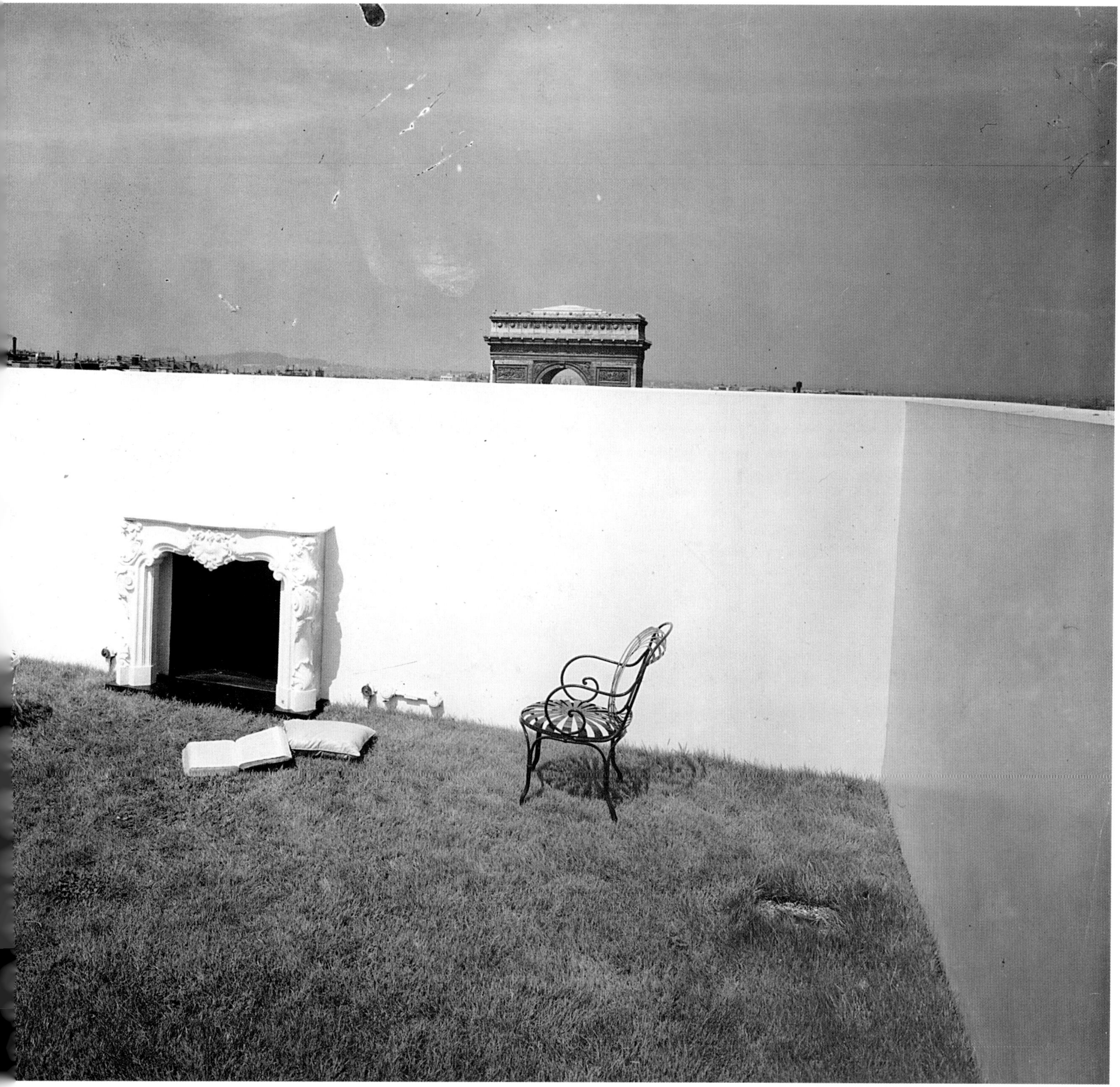

↑

Le Corbusier • Rooftop Garden of the Charles Beistegui Apartment, Paris

1929–31

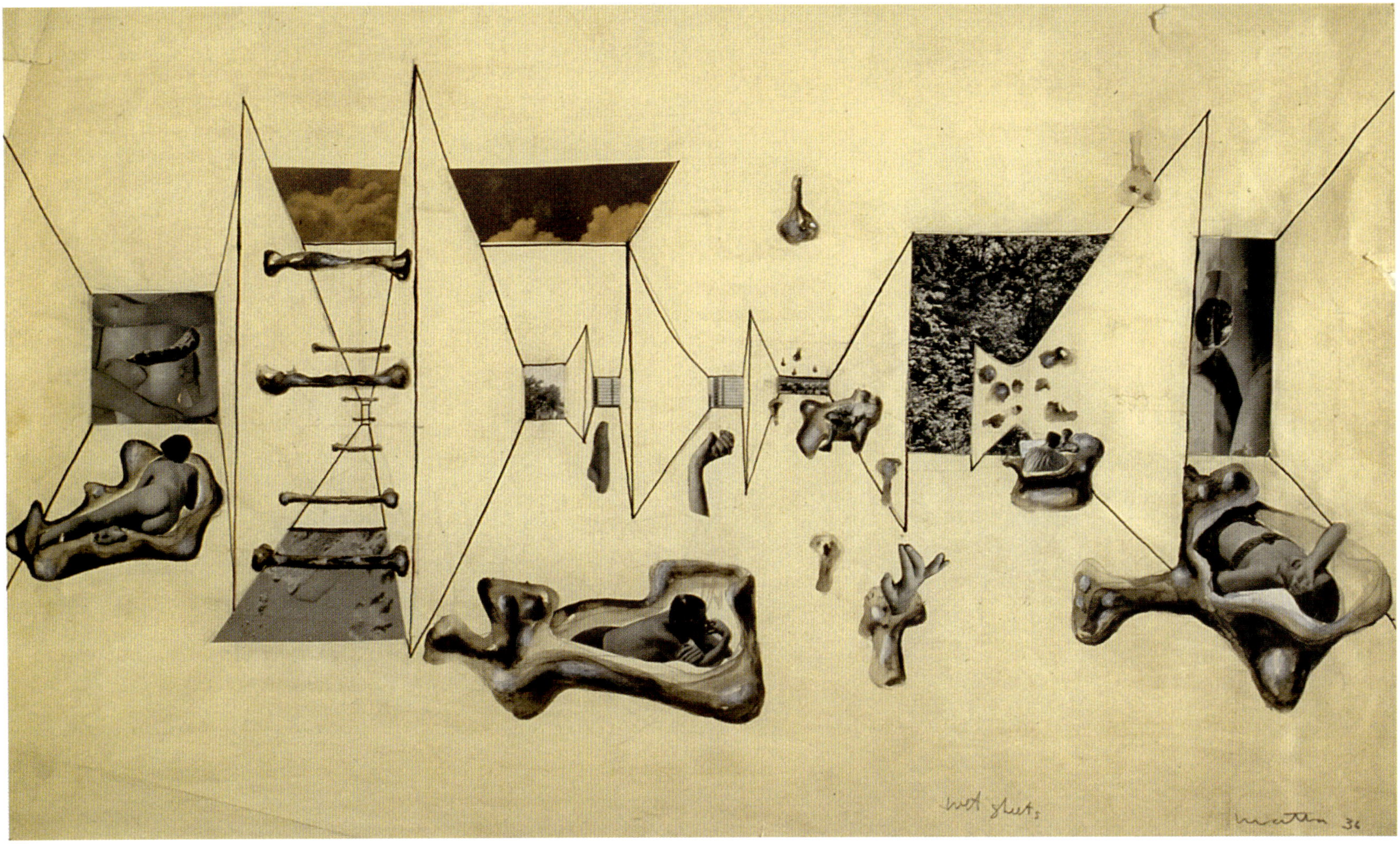
matta 36

←
Roberto Matta • Wet Sheets
1936

central character in this cycle of plays) – in the title. For example, the Corbusian 'Ubu' motif is cast into the concrete façade of the Maison des Jeunes in Firminy, France (1965). So although Le Corbusier can perhaps be cast, as André Breton and the Surrealists later tried to portray him, as the antithesis of Surrealism, equally he may be described as drinking from the same well of inspiration, attracted to Surrealist juxtapositions of form and ideas. And as will be shown later on in this chapter, certain alchemic ideas are also not missing from his work.

The 1930s were a fecund period for the further elaboration of the Surrealists' ideas of the home and house, which became consolidated with Freudian theories of dream analysis. Some Surrealists, such as Tristan Tzara, Chilean painter Roberto Matta and, later, the Austrian-American architect, theatre designer, artist and sculptor Frederick Kiesler, regressed back to the notion of the protective, comfortable envelope of the prenatal womb: International Style Modernism's dry, orthogonal, sharp-edged, scientific masculinity countered by, in Surrealist eyes, a benevolent, cosseting architecture of wet, feminine curvature not denying the body, but openly cupping it.

The Womb with a View

During 1933, Tzara, a key presence in the Dada movement, turned his attention to speculations about another type of architecture that had associations with comfort and material security:

> When one returns what was torn away by adolescence and childhood, man could possess those realms of 'luxe, calme et volupté' that he constructed for himself beneath the bed covers, under tables, crouching in cavities of Earth, above all at the narrow entry; when it is seen that well-being resides in the clair-obscur of the tactile and soft depths of the only hygiene possible, that of prenatal desires, it will be possible to reconstruct the circular, spherical and irregular houses that mankind has conserved from the time of the caves to the cradle and the grave, in his vision of intra-uterine life which knows nothing of that aesthetics of castration called modern.[6]

Tzara's aspirations for his 'inter-uterine architecture' were conditioned by the cultural memory of primitive huts such as the yurt, and the defensive Freudian security and invisibility from beneath a mother's skirt. Tzara only expressed his dissatisfaction in prose, but from 1936 to 1938 Matta began to produce drawings and text that progressed the idea, giving it a semblance of materiality and spatial complexity. Matta had trained as an architect and spent time as an intern in Le Corbusier's office before joining the Surrealists and later making his name as an artist. Much of his artistic preoccupations were the result of his architectural training, inspired by an interest in the multidimensionality of space and its non-orthogonal geometries. His first forays into designing for surreal domesticity shared the same influences and, as is the case with Tzara, are a celebration of the visceral, of the tactile and of a fulsome sensuality. *Wet Sheets*, for example, was an attempt to chart a non-Euclidian space seen from multiplying points of view. The drawing/collage was an interior architecture with only small hints of the world outside. Suggestive of bony protuberances, body parts are modelled, deconstructed and dispersed around the space, the furniture wombs within a womb, snugly supporting the occupants in their post-coital abandon and repose.

A couple of years later, Matta was invited by Breton, editor of the Surrealist journal *Minotaure*, to expound and develop his inter-uterine architecture. It was here that he produced his seminal essay, 'Mathématique sensible – architecture du temps' ('Sensible Mathematics – Architecture of Time'; 1938) and a new, untitled illustration to accompany it. The prose was one of 'vertigo', 'spasm' and 'perpetual menace': 'There must be walls like wet sheets that deform and marry themselves to our psychological fears; arms hanging among

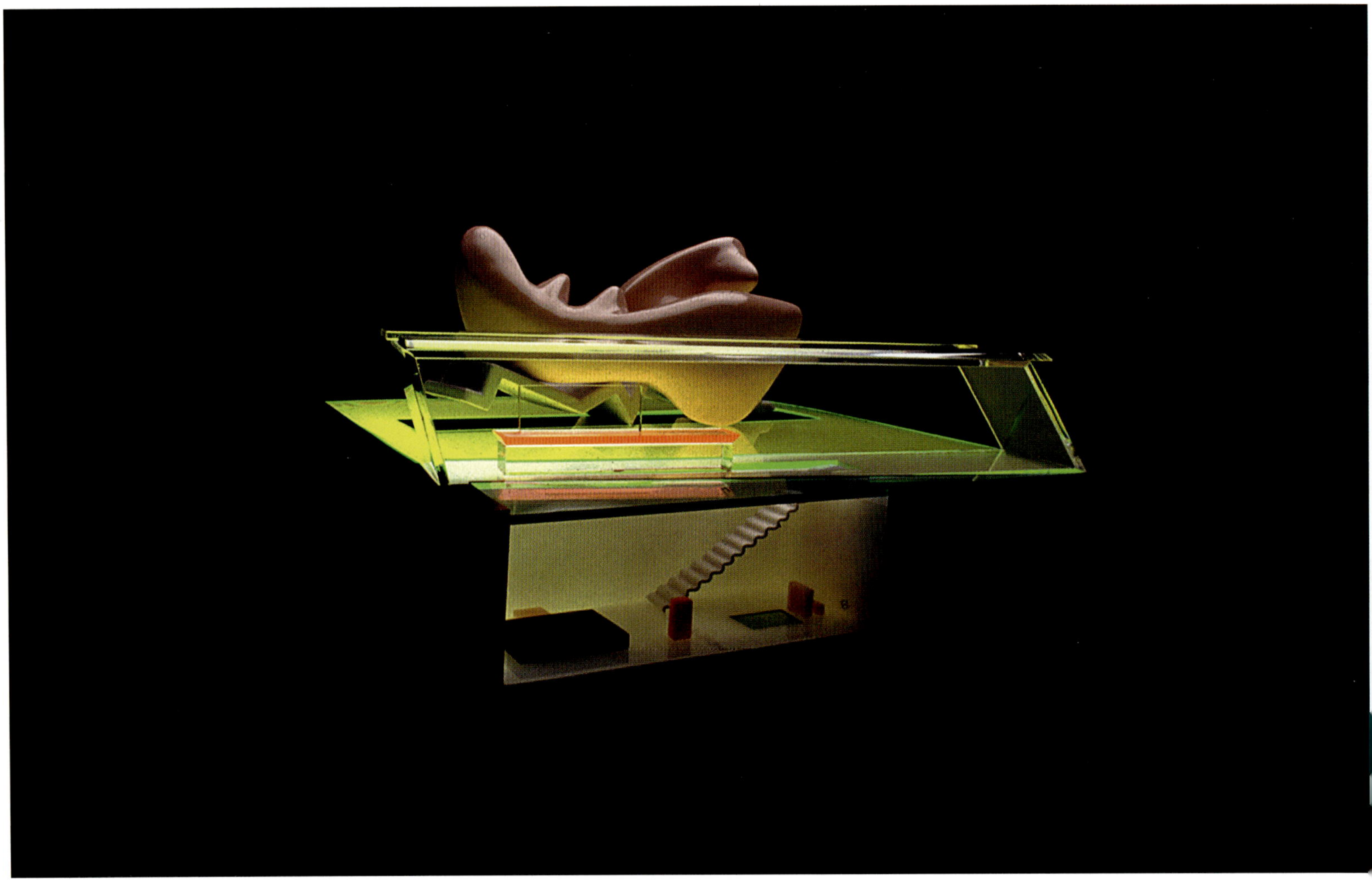

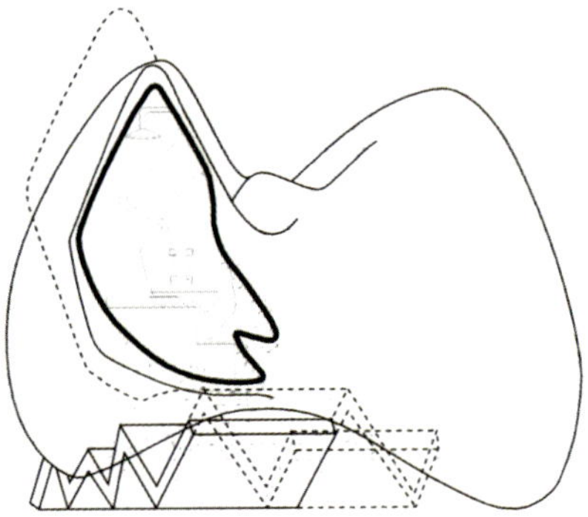

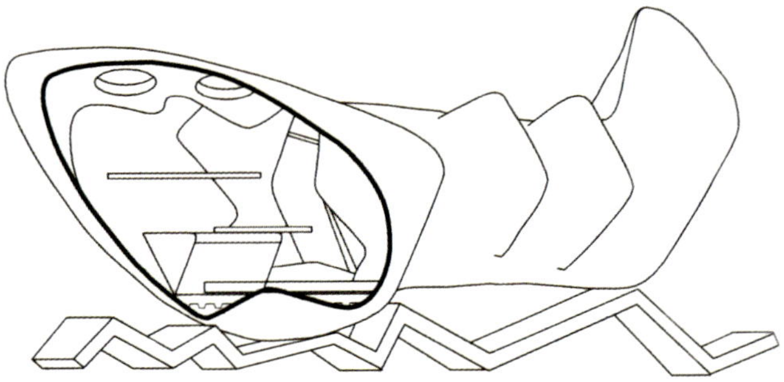

← **FAT Architecture**
Anti-Oedipal House
1993

the interruptions that throw an abusive light on the forms and on their shadows, of a colour susceptible to awaken the gums themselves for lips.'[7] This architecture is surely one of erotic intensity, a vortex of strange and exciting views, feelings and sensations, egging the numerous occupants on to climactic passions and almost hallucinogenic psychological ecstasy. The space punctured by holes in both ceiling and floor, and the placement of the windows, are all made possible, ironically, by the Corbusian free plan: concrete columns and slab, no load-bearing walls.

The archetypal double-curved, egg-like inter-uterine architecture was suggested in interdisciplinary designer Kiesler's epic project the Endless House (see pages 86–89). Kiesler's works included vision machines, theatre, stage-set, architectural and exhibition designs; he had worked in the office of architect and theorist Adolf Loos in Vienna, and emigrated to New York in 1926 where he developed a friendship with the highly influential artist and sculptor Marcel Duchamp (and their work sometimes augmented that of the other; see pages 90–91). The Endless House was developed and designed over more than twenty-five years and included numerous models of varying scales, prototype pieces and drawings. The environments within this theoretical house were dynamic, often conceived with the use of both natural and artificial light. While instilling all the previous inter-uterine propositions of Tzara and Matta (hygiene, psychological and physical freedom, and comfort) Kiesler also sought to decompose, at certain times, the envelope of his house. Unable to achieve this by somehow dissolving the sprayed concrete exterior of the building, he experimented with light.

As Stephen Phillips has noted: 'Kiesler hoped to provide a fantastic dream world that can reach out to the cosmos and expand. He attempted to rely on the technology of magic illusion – theatrical projection, cinema, and even television as "Broadcasted Decoration" – to achieve expansive space.'[8] The interior of the Endless House was to be a festival of materials, grass, warm tiles, even small streams, all cast in changing coloured mood-lighting and 'broadcast' vistas. It seems that Kiesler was one of the first to foresee some of the challenges and opportunities of the modern domestic environment. The house consisted of and explored unprescribed living patterns, the role of the virtual in expanding vistas and spatial hybridity, the human need to blur the boundary between the natural and the synthetic, and it synthesized the outside and inside of the dwelling.

By the 1990s, the machinations of contemporary parenthood and a general acceptance of Freud's Oedipus complex, according to the members of the FAT Architecture practice, including Kevin Rhowbotham, had culminated in the repression of the sexuality of pre- and post-pubescent children within the family. The evolving transparency of much of the parents' lives provoked them to design the Anti-Oedipal House. The parent 'house' is a two-storey structure with a basement area for sleeping in and a transparent box at ground level for entertaining and relaxing, and the child's bedroom/dwelling assumes the form of the pink inter-uterine shape adjacent to it. Both spaces can function as separate habitats. While this project is tongue in cheek, it still connects with the womblike shape as a liberation from spatial repression and sexual guilt.

As FAT have described it:

> **[The house] proposes an anti-oedipal idyll, a suburban house prototype that opposes that ubiquitous architectural machine of oedipal repression – the typical family dwelling. This house separates the parents from the child, allowing each to indulge their own particular obsessions – the parents in the arch modernist glass house where they may fulfil their passion for dinner parties and obsessive cleanliness while the child lounges in the voluptuous 'mastabatorium' free from the parents' repressive gaze.**[9]

→
Frederick Kiesler • Endless House

1924–50

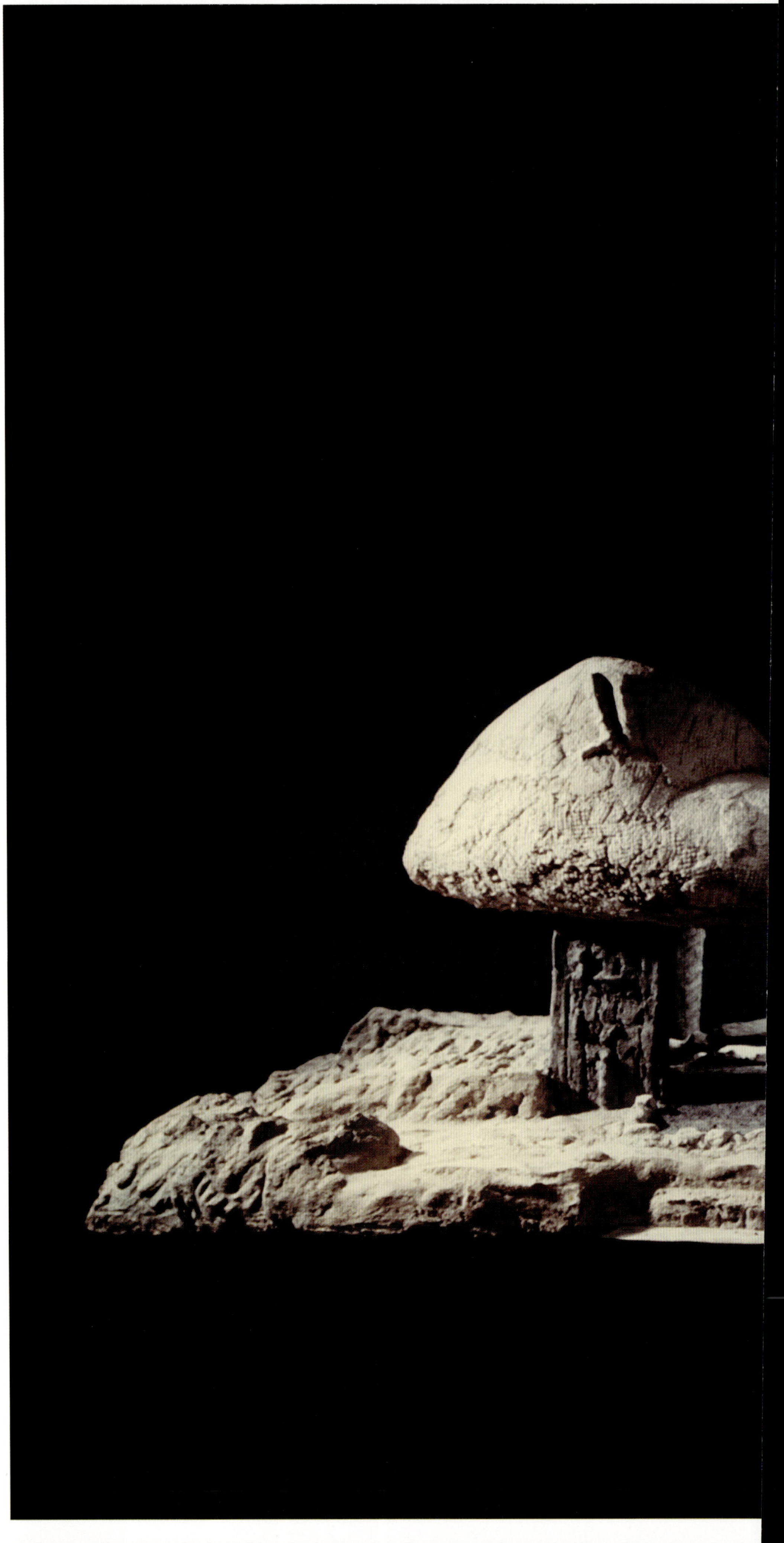

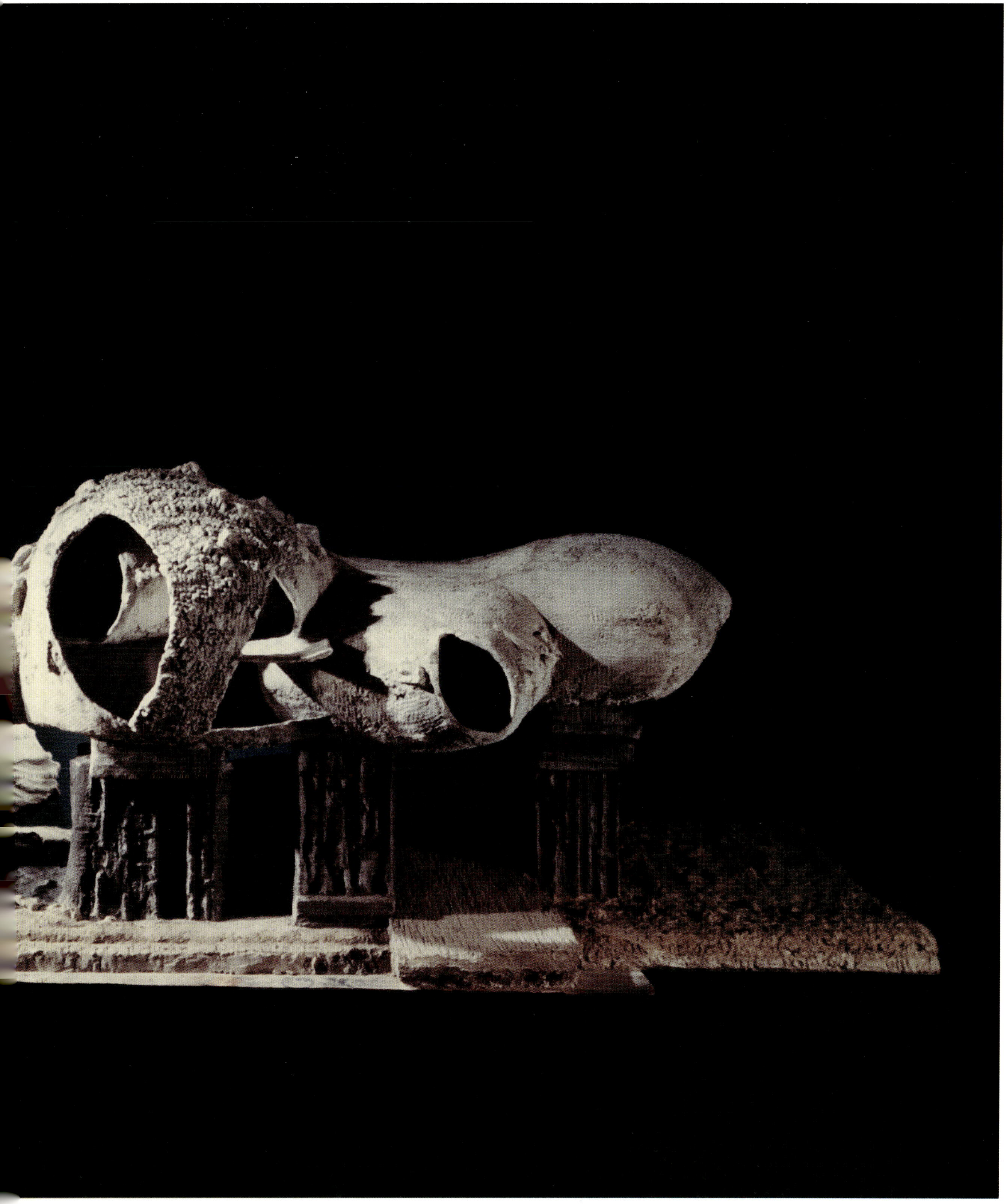

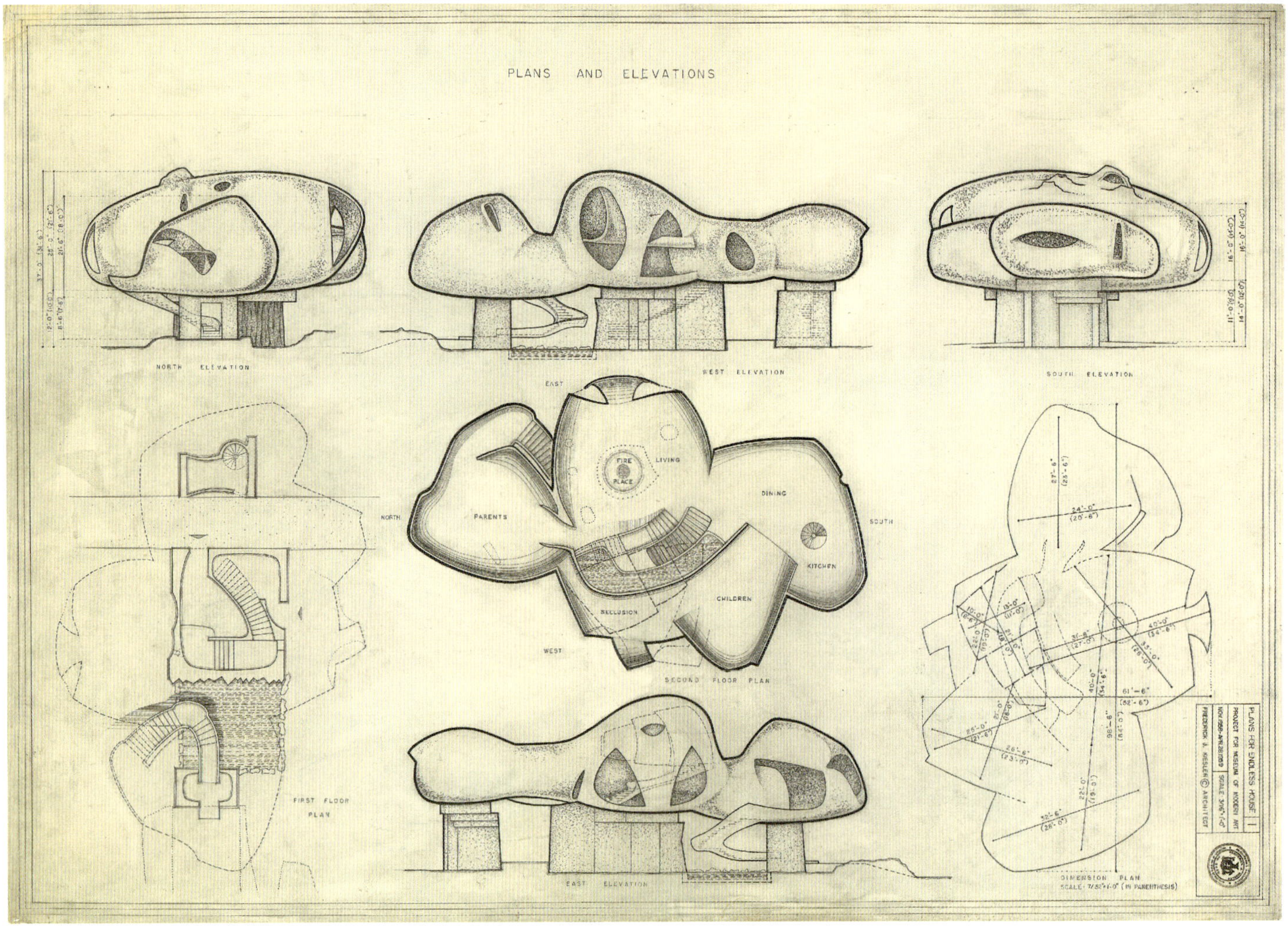

↑↗

Frederick Kiesler • Endless House

1924–50

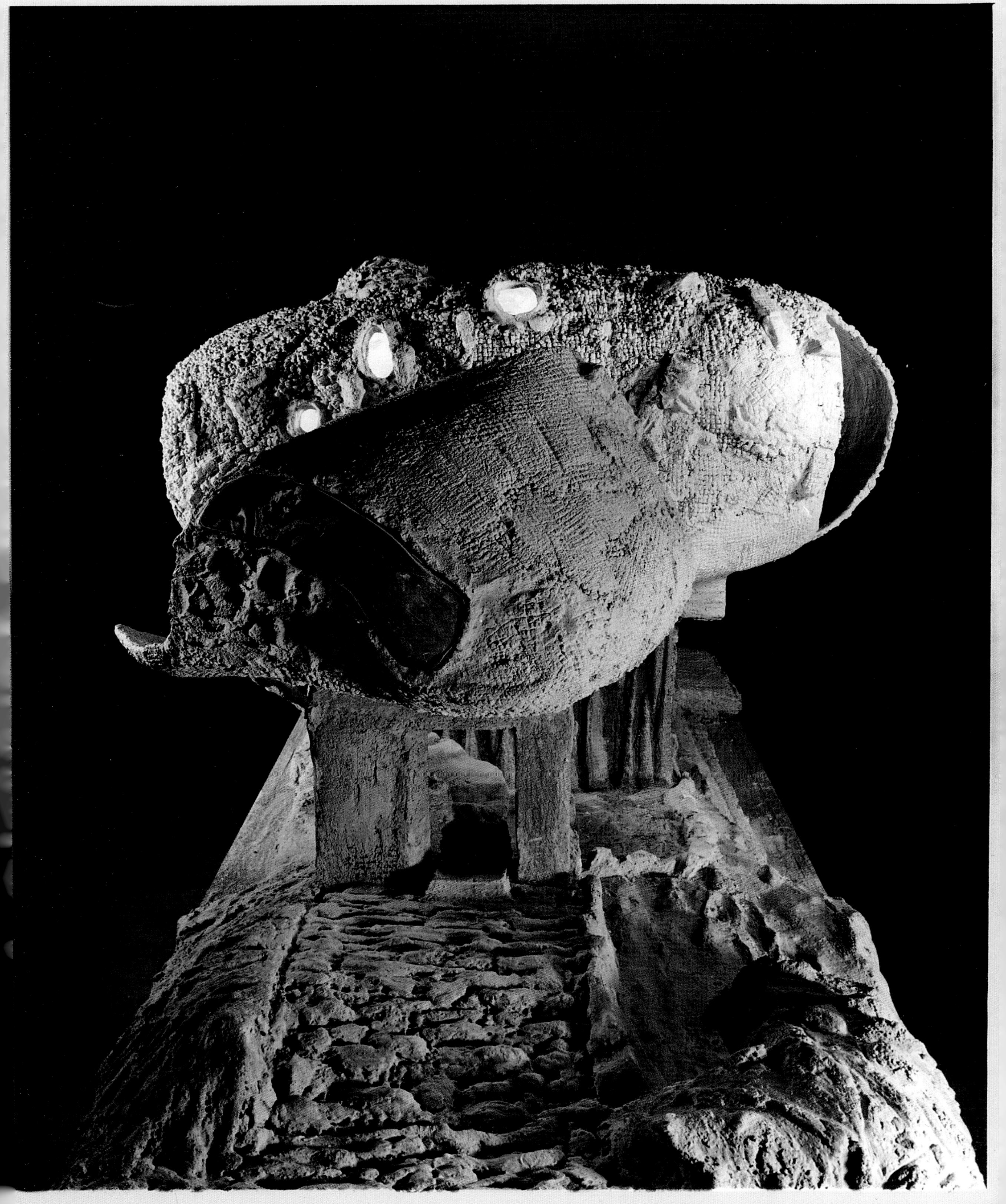

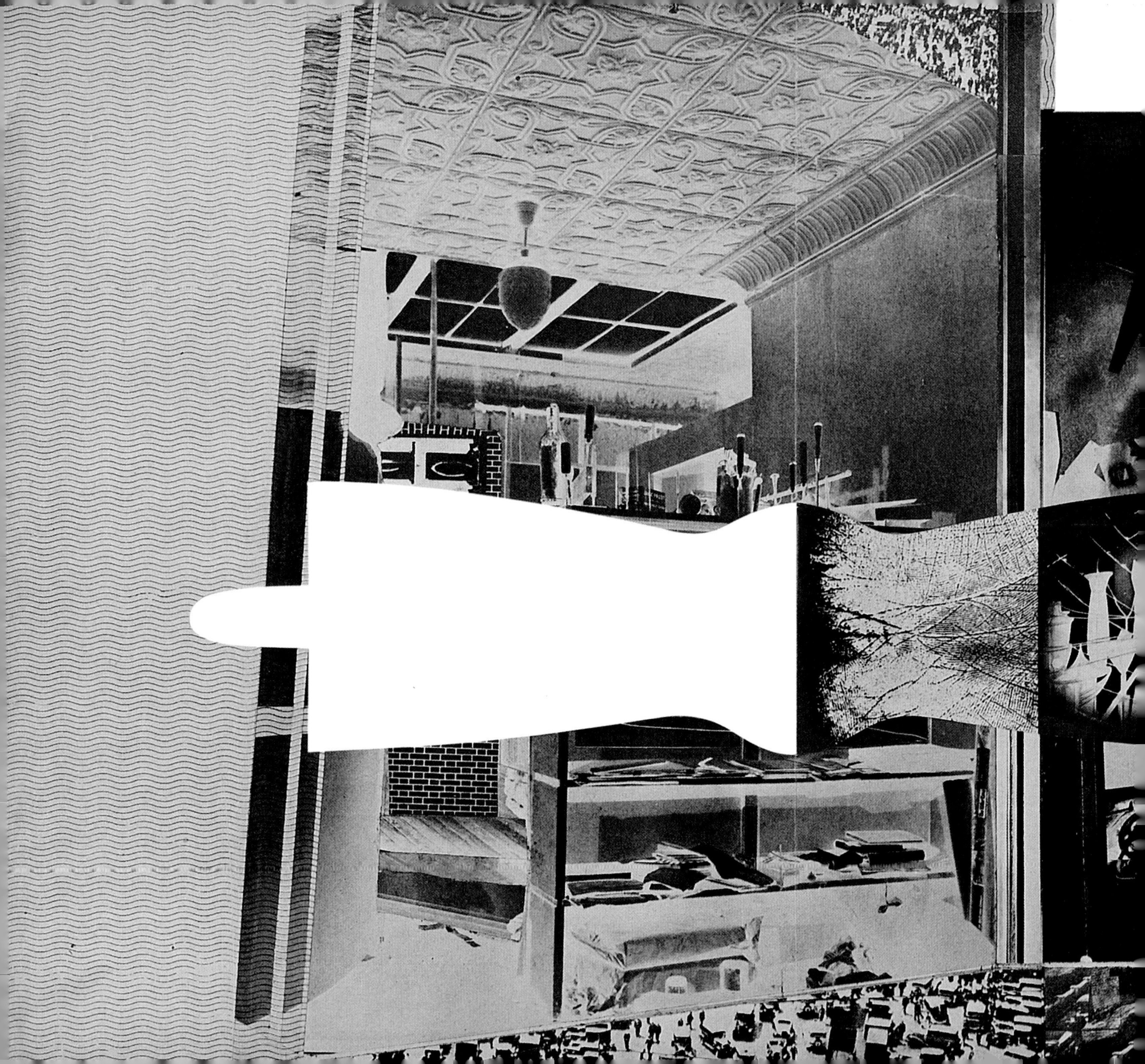

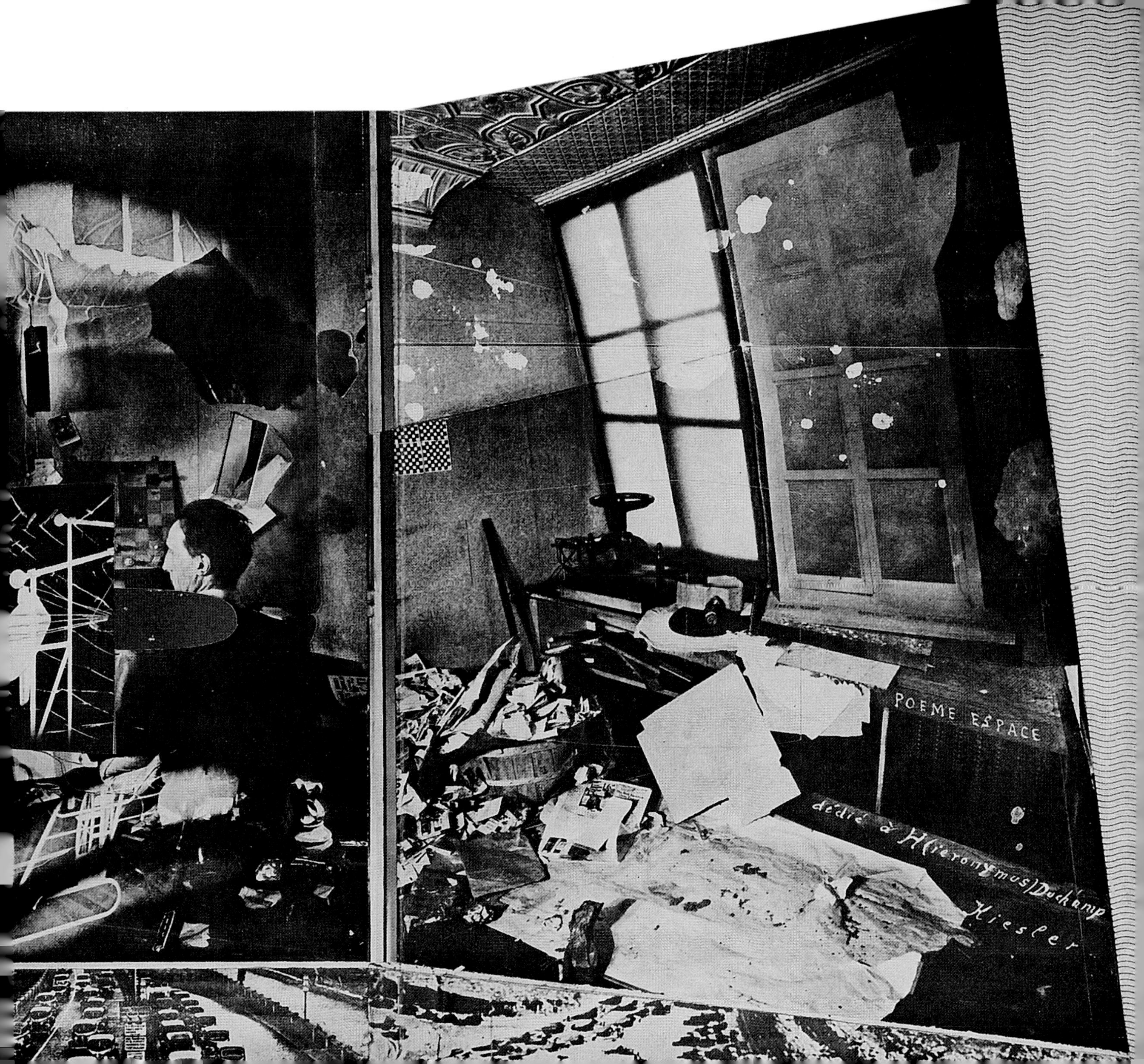
POEME ESPACE
dédié à H(ieronymus) Duchamp
Kiesler

Frederick Kiesler • Centre fold-out triptych for View**, Marcel Duchamp special March 1945**

Universes of Discourse

It is perhaps obvious to many that to dwell is much more than to live, to survive. To dwell is to populate the world, to build our universe by operating within it, and it is these constructions, whether actions, events, situations, poems, pictures or buildings that leave mnemonic traces within minds and spaces. Rooms and brains are witnesses to individual pasts. A room is a memory theatre that the agile and synchronized mind can read. Its objects provoke memories – of aspirations, failures, loves, loves lost and so much more. A lifetime of existence can be recorded in a single room or house. Take John Soane's House in London. Situated at 13 Lincoln's Inn Fields, the building was designed as the setting for the English architect's objects of art. Like Freud and Breton after him, Soane used his house, galleries and shelves and their constant rearrangement to provoke connections and ideas to enable his architectural creativity. However, that rooms are mnemonic is of course not a new idea; in her seminal book *The Art of Memory* (1966),[10] Frances Yates traces such conceptions back to Roman times, via the Dominican friar and philosopher Giordano Bruno (1548–1600) and philosopher Ramon Llull (1232–1315) to philosopher and politician Marcus Tullius Cicero (106–43 BC) and many others.

The Surrealists had studied the arcane, hermetic arts and were familiar with the idea of memory theatres and their advanced use of syntax, semiotics and symbolism. Primary among those Surrealists who used mnemonic devices to animate their work were Max Ernst, Salvador Dalí and Leonora Carrington. Memory theatres are also implicitly tied up with the alchemic arts and the secret languages (both graphic and spatial) of the alchemic adepts. Mnemonic forms are symbiotic with both their context and the viewer. Duchamp understood implicitly the mnemonic imperative and the act of viewing, the desiring gaze and the knots of association of objects and forms, his work resonating with associative geometries, reflexive conditions and shape-shifting semiotic turns. Kiesler created a triptych of Duchamp in his 'studio' for a special issue of *View* magazine in 1945.[11] Heavy with many allusions to his work and lexicon of interests, Duchamp's environment in this collage of photographs, entitled *Les Larves d'Imagie d'Henri Robert Marcel Duchamp* (see pages 90–91), is indicative of his art, his cognitive map and his rarefied epistemologies of space, gender, multidimensions, desire and the point of view.

Irish writer James Joyce also understood the room and the house as a witness and a chunking engine. Here he describes the House of O'Shea in his novel *Finnegans Wake* (1939):

> The warped flooring of the lair and sound conducting walls thereof, to say nothing of the uprights and imposts, were persianly literatured with burst love letters, tell tale stories, stickyback snaps, doubtful eggshells...upset latten tintacks, unused mill and stumbling stones, twisted quills, painful digests, magnifying wineglasses, solid objects cast as goblins, once current puns, quashed quotatoes, messes of motage, unquestionable issue papers, seedy ejaculations, limerick damns, crocodile tears, spilt ink, blasphematory spits, young ladies' milkmaids.[12]

Houses take on the thoughts, emotions and fears of their occupants; they live vicariously for them, they are caskets, readable after death, and palimpsests that protect against mortality. While the occupants are still alive, they are giant mixing machines, potentially churning out new ideas by association with the objects and ideas they embody. They can also be their mausoleums.

↓ **Marcel Duchamp**
Three Standard Stoppages
1913–14

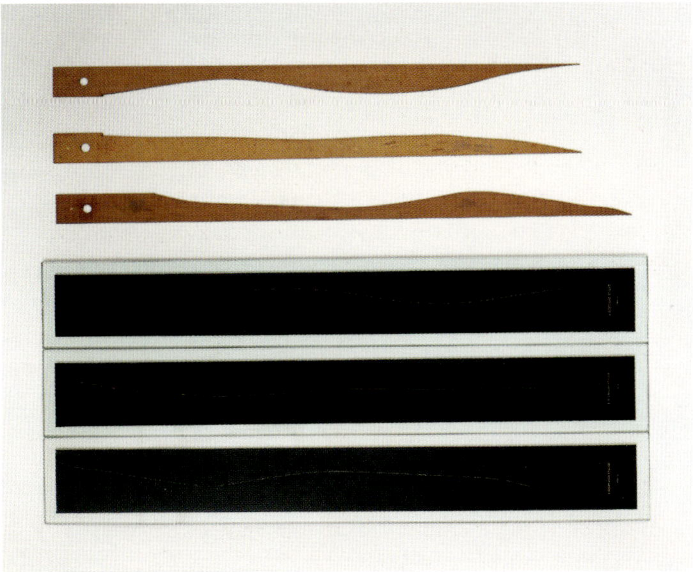

Metrical Instruments and Learning to Live

The Surrealists first adopted the non-orthogonal shape, as we have seen, in allusions to the womb and sexual and spatial liberation. The wombic architectures of Tzara, Matta and Kiesler suggested that humanity needed to find new ways of living, and the inter-uterine houses did not therefore legislate particular functions in particular places – this was, after all, a Corbusian and white Modernist affectation. It was the Modernist liturgy over the sanctified relationship between form and function that so aggrieved the Surrealists. Kiesler was an architectural pioneer with his creation of 'Endless Space' – space that in some ways, notwithstanding the technologies of his time, was continuous, both spatially and visually. Kiesler understood, as did the Surrealists, that architectural space can be described and calibrated in an infinite number of ways.

During 1913–14, Duchamp created his *Three Standard Stoppages*, as he named them. These 'yardsticks', 'rulers' or 'measures' – call them what you will – were a calculated slap in the face for all those who sought to define and legislate weights and measures as standard empirical units. Duchamp allegedly (as with him, often nothing is as it seems) took three pieces of string, held them above the floor, dropped them and transcribed the curves produced into wooden templates. The *Stoppages* are a choreography and respect for chance; the templates were later used to set out the arrangement of his *Nine Malic Moulds* for *The Bride Stripped Bare by Her Bachelors, Even (The Large Glass)* of 1915–23 (see page 45).

As Kiesler realized in his Endless House project, the control, calibration and tone of light are highly dependent on what it is projected from and what it is projected on to. In 1989, the American architect Lebbeus Woods created his 'Metrical Instruments' series. Like Duchamp's *Stoppages,* these were non-standard measuring devices, but in this case consisting of wire, plates of aluminium and other materials joined together in non-orthogonal ways. Woods described his understanding of light as follows:

> It has long been my contention that light does not reveal the presence of objects, but the other way around: objects reveal the presence of light. This flipping of the phrase is more than a trick with words, though it may seem like that at first. What it does is shift the emphasis of meaning. If light reveals the object, then it is the object that is important. But if objects reveal the light, it is the light that is important. In other words, the simple turn of phrasing changes the relative values of objects and light.[13]

Woods's Aerial Paris project, drawn also in 1989, exhibits the same interest in the shifting ballet of light brought into being by this proposal for a performative, bottom-up, flying city. Obviously, the light revealed by an object is highly relational, dependent on geographical location, weather, time of day and light. These beautiful yet strange objects are harbingers of Woods's Solohouse (see pages 96–97). This archetypal house, Woods would admit, pops up in many of his subsequent projects, slightly redesigned and renamed.

The Solohouse is a test of human resilience and ingenuity. It is at once an observatory of stars, cosmos and humanity. The house consists of what Woods called 'freespace'. Similar to the multivalent space usage of Kiesler's Endless House, freespace is not particularly designed with convenient and convivial usage in mind. It is space more likely sent to try us, in reading and colonizing it. To live within this architecture, one has to be resourceful and, above all, imaginative. Woods's structure is not finished; it is merely a catalytic shell:

> The concept of the Solohouse was, ostensibly, that it was a house for one person. But, even more so, I conceived it as an 'atom' of architecture, one that embodied the essential properties of architecture that were fundamental to building up 'molecules' and 'compound substances,' like building groups, even towns and cities. The function is ambiguity itself, the burdensome idea of 'freespace' – one must invent the way to inhabit the house, because it is not pre-determined. That's the way principles work, assuming many variations, shapes and forms over time and its changes to the way we understand materials, structure, and function. Still, the human condition remains the same, which is what makes it 'human', joining us to the past, and also giving us not only inspiration, but a guide for creating the future.[14]

The key to this way of thinking about buildings and architectural space was connected, in Woods's mind, to his early meetings with the great cyberneticist Heinz von Foerster. The cybernetic notion is that of personal worlds,

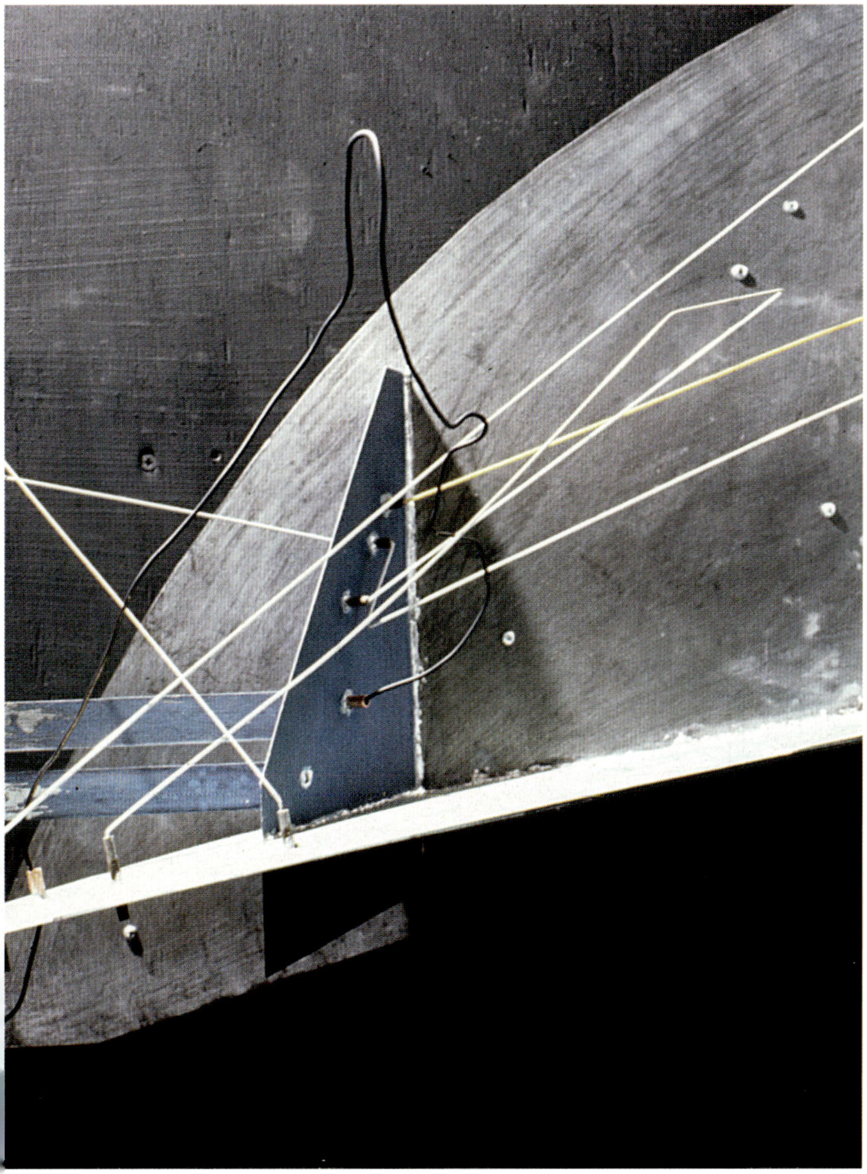

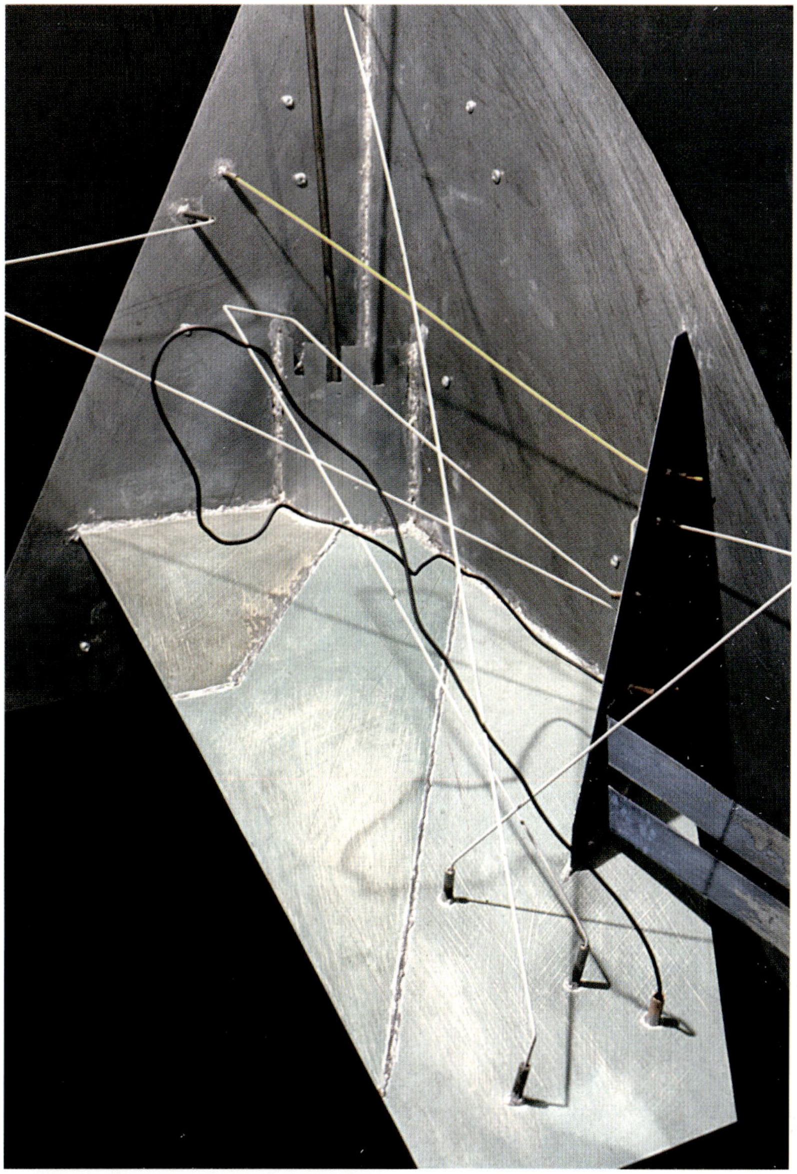

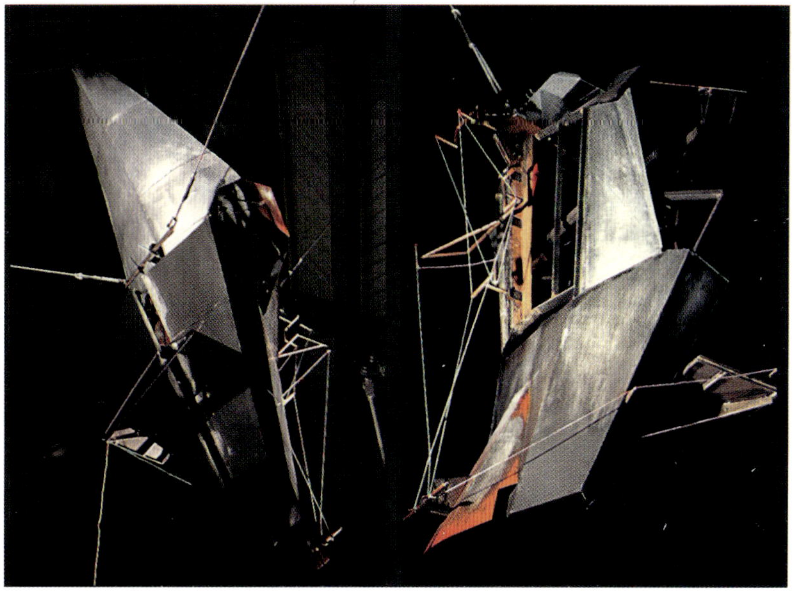

→

Lebbeus Woods

Aerial Paris

1989

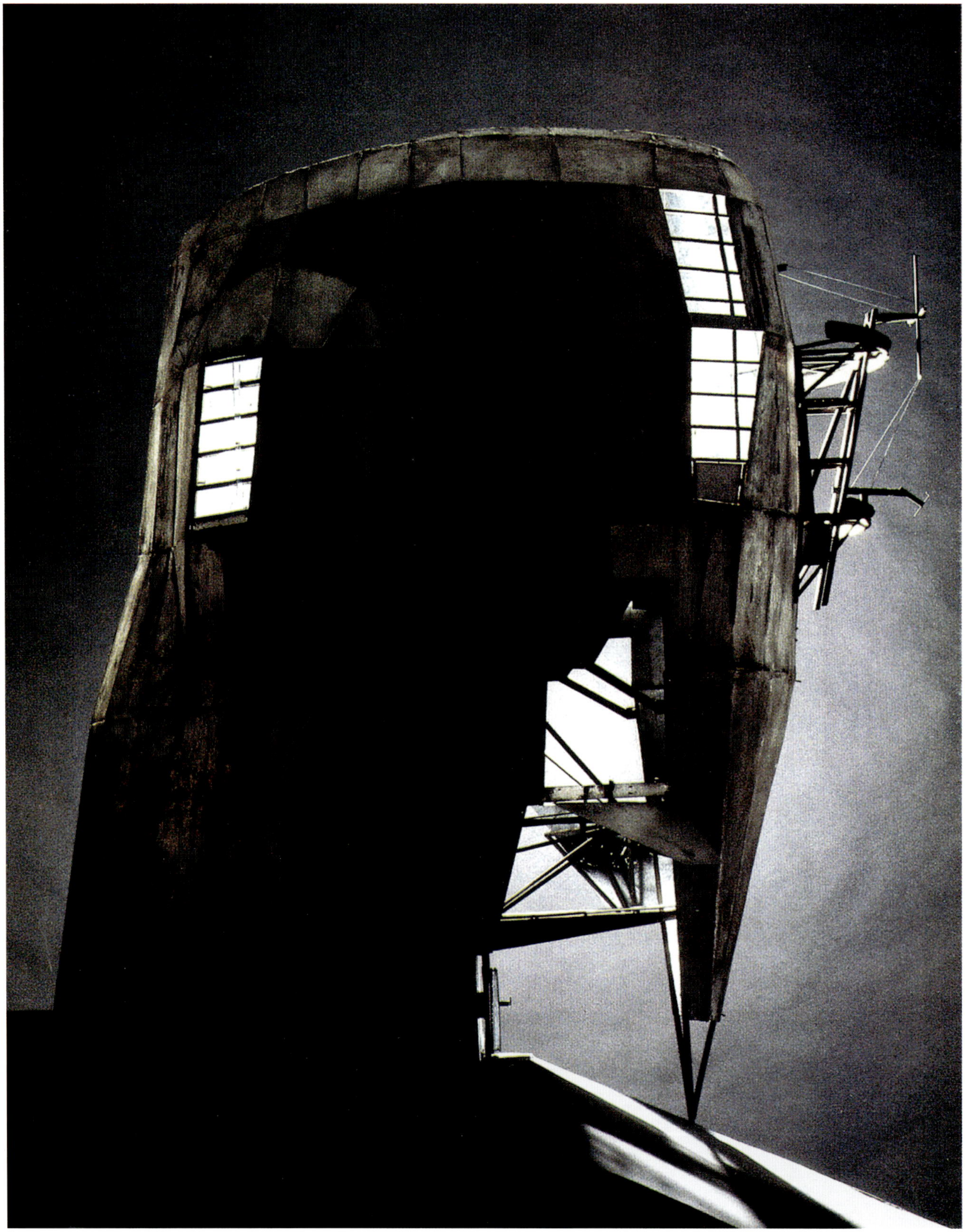

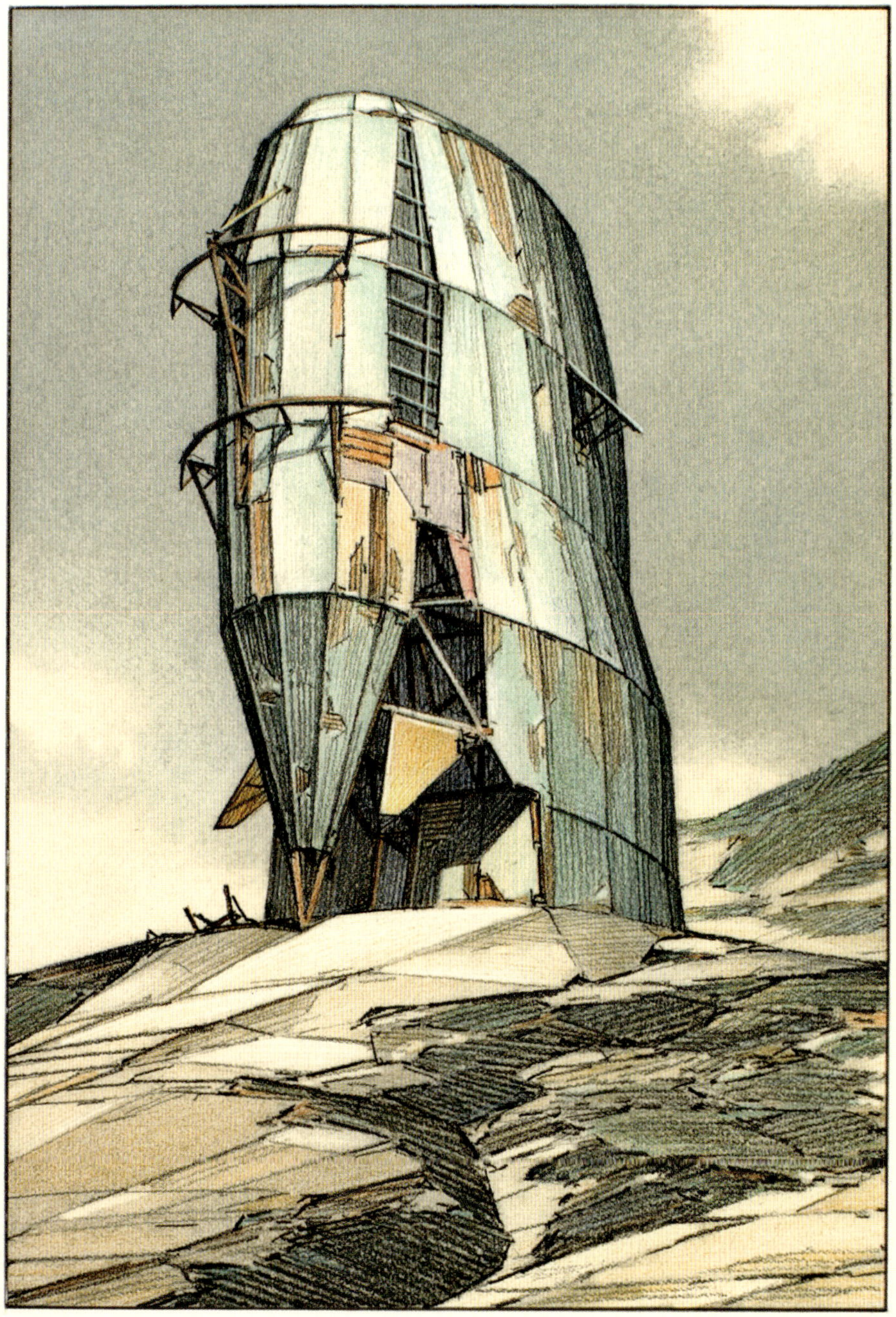

↖↑

Lebbeus Woods • Solohouse

1988–89

and the understanding of these worlds is constructed by our interactions within them. In short we 'build' our world (construct our reality) as we go through life, modifying it based on our conversations and experiments – social, relational and physical. Everyone's world is different and meaningful to them. None of this seems to suggest anything that negates Surrealist thinking; indeed, one could suggest, as I have elsewhere,[15] that cybernetic world-making, in fact, has the same common roots.

This world full of spiralling circularity and acted-on feedback is translated, by Woods, into one of a reflexive relationship between self and environment within the Solohouse. The narrative of the house, written at the time, concerns a single inhabitant who starts to observe the world outside themself, looking out through mechanical occuli. They then begin to observe the house, its construction and the elemental composition of its material, before turning their observations on themself and realizing that they also, in addition to the inert fabric of the house, are stardust and the ebb and flow of energy. A short series of accompanying drawings imply the growing awareness of the inhabitant. The first of these is an almost traditional architectural section; little is declared except the shell, the observation platforms and a staircase ladder. However, as the series progresses the drawings become more and more tracks of vectors, diffused radiation and interference – almost a chart of eclipsing, colliding and swerving atoms.

The Solohouse was also modelled at an uncanny scale, at nearly 2m (6ft) tall. This gives it an almost animalistic scale, its pointed end seemingly becoming its snout sensing the ground. This scale is also shared with the more arresting models that Kiesler built of the Endless House; it seems to exacerbate strangeness. It is neither abstractly small and pristine, where the composition of material in the building and model is denied for the sake of spatial purity, nor at the scale of a 1:1 fabricated piece, where it is of itself. The intermediate scale is bizarre, like an oversized doll's house or a 2m pair of binoculars. Why is this house Surrealist? Woods never rushed to the Surrealist cause. It is Surrealist because it confronts the fear, the meaningless silence and nothingness of contemporary existence, and posits an alternative, optimistic view that we can 'build' our own worlds full of joy and exploration, making our own knowledge for ourselves. Worlds that might be highly idiosyncratic, but resonate with our human desire to explore and know ourselves.

Architect Tom Cartledge's House in the Woods (pages 76, and 99–101) is another example of a house that is conditioned around a Duchampian and also a cybernetic way of seeing the world. It is both intensely personal yet also connected to its surroundings in the woods, a place of many scary fictions from the Brothers Grimm to the Blair Witch Project. It therefore plays on the familiar Surrealist house-of-fear concept, yet its nooks and crannies are constructed by looking outside and within. It is intended to be inhabited by a surreal woodcutter who constructs his world from what he knows: the wood, the saw, the rope and the food he catches, skins and eats. The project is not fully described and this adds to its enigma. There are drawings of the front door (draped in fur and sinew), a fireplace, the hallway, the gallery and the kitchen, and a long internal elevation of the living space. The furniture is strange, full of allusion to body parts, bones, internal organs or butchers' implements, farm tools, gunstocks and trappers' gear. Cartledge's woodsman, while looking at and celebrating his own way of life and the objects that sustain him and enable him to navigate his world, also wishes to celebrate what is outside. The daily and seasonal rhythms and vectors of the countryside are translated into almost Duchampian 'stoppages' that are created to bring the outside in and calibrate it. There are stoppages to record the horizon,

↓~

Tom Cartledge • House in the Woods

2009

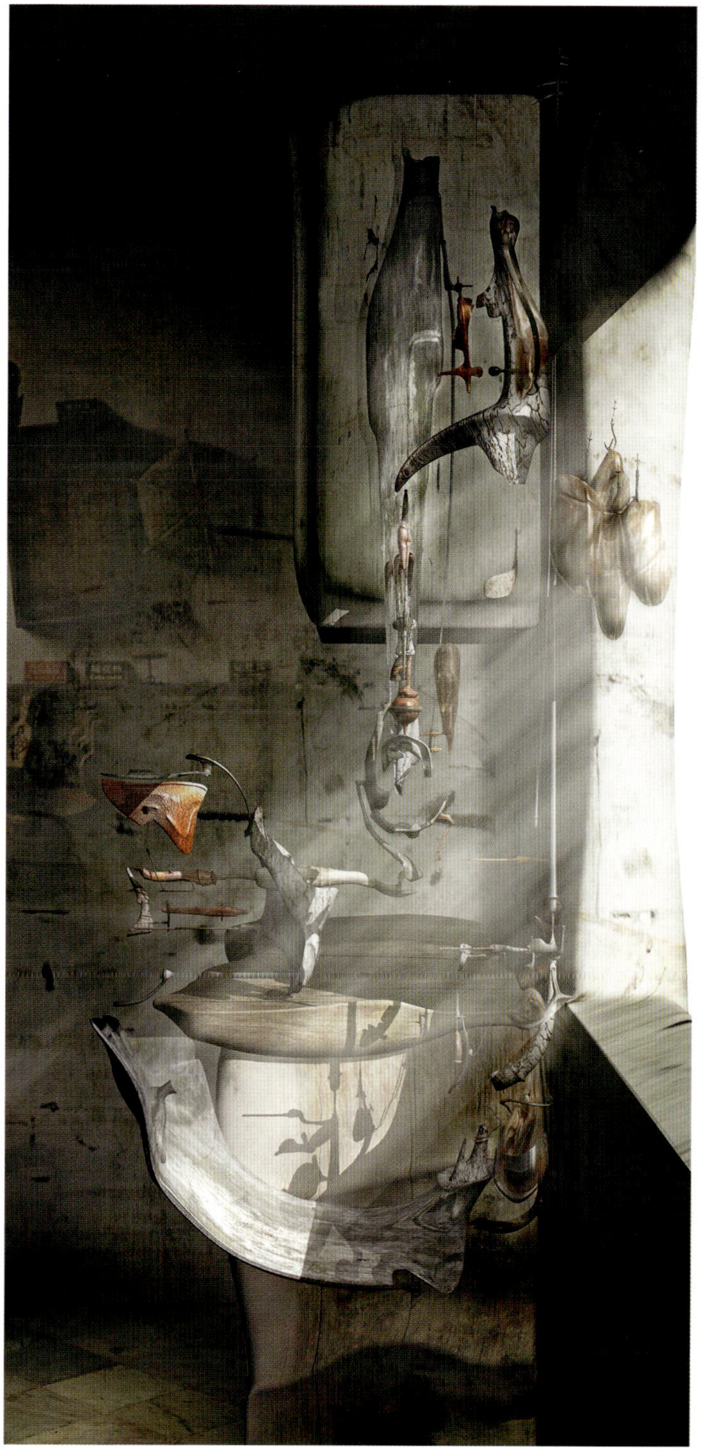

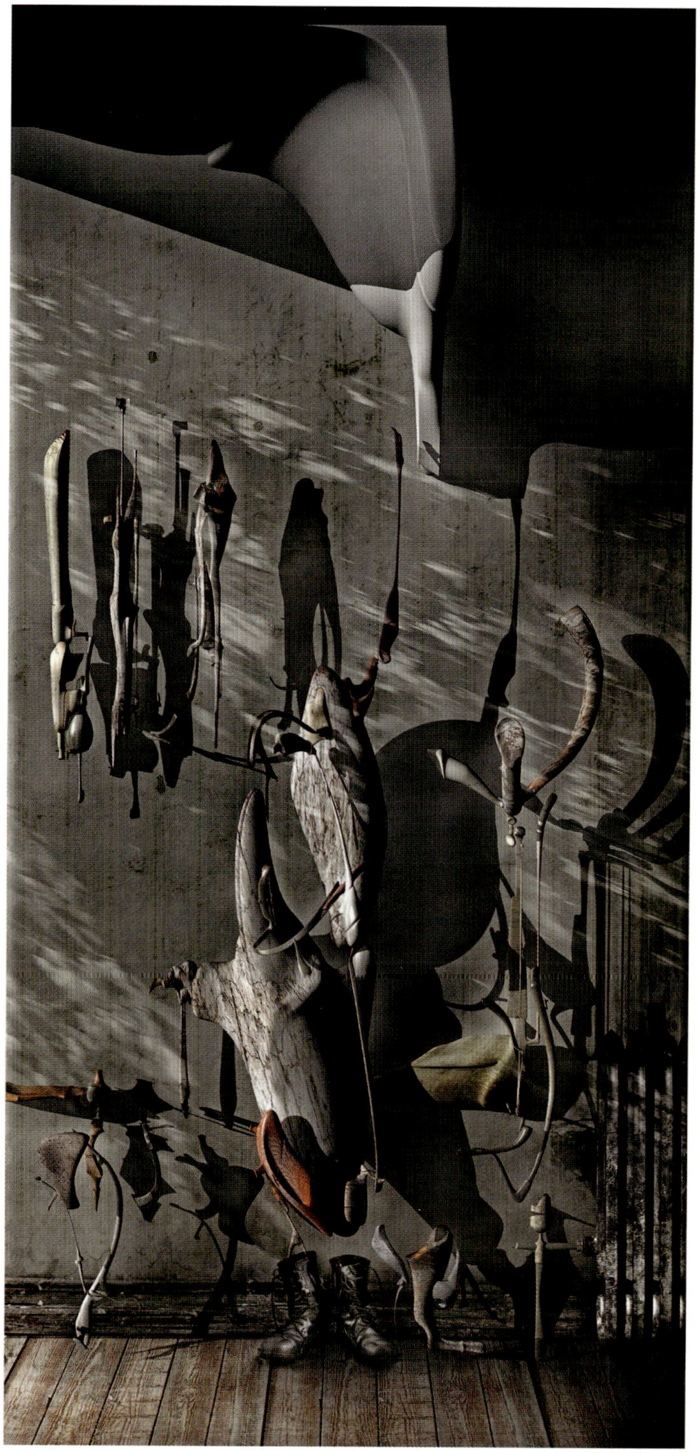

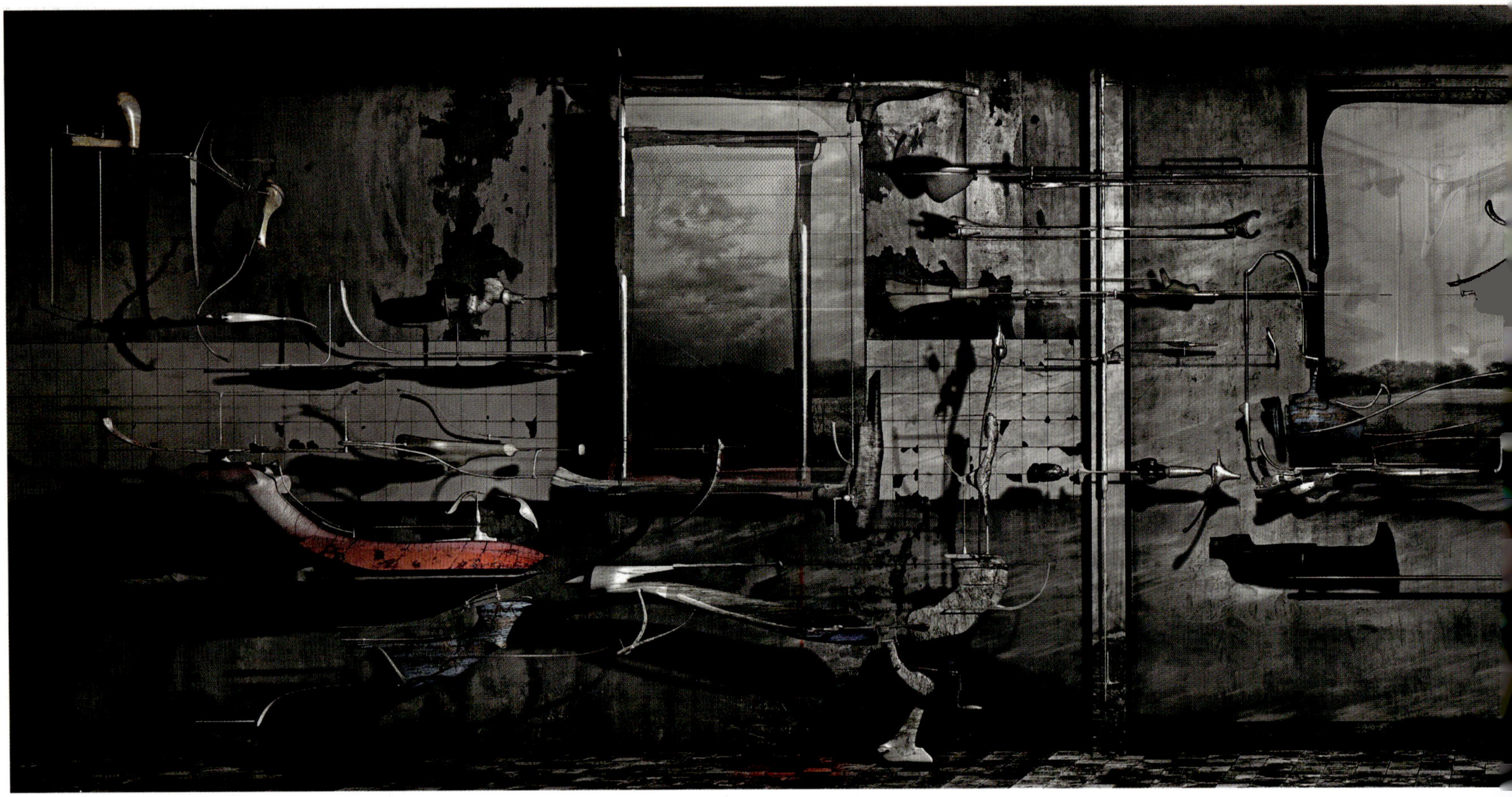

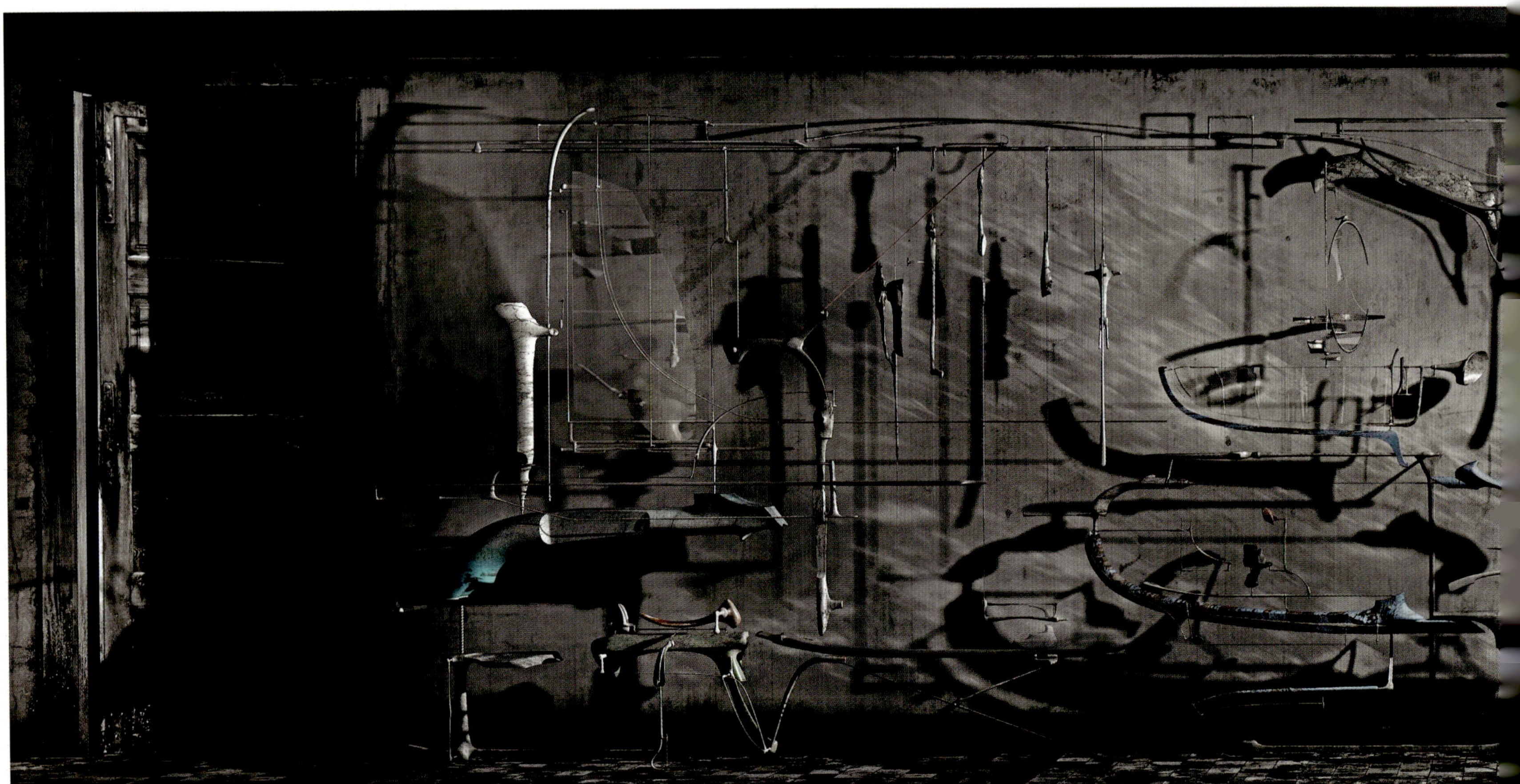

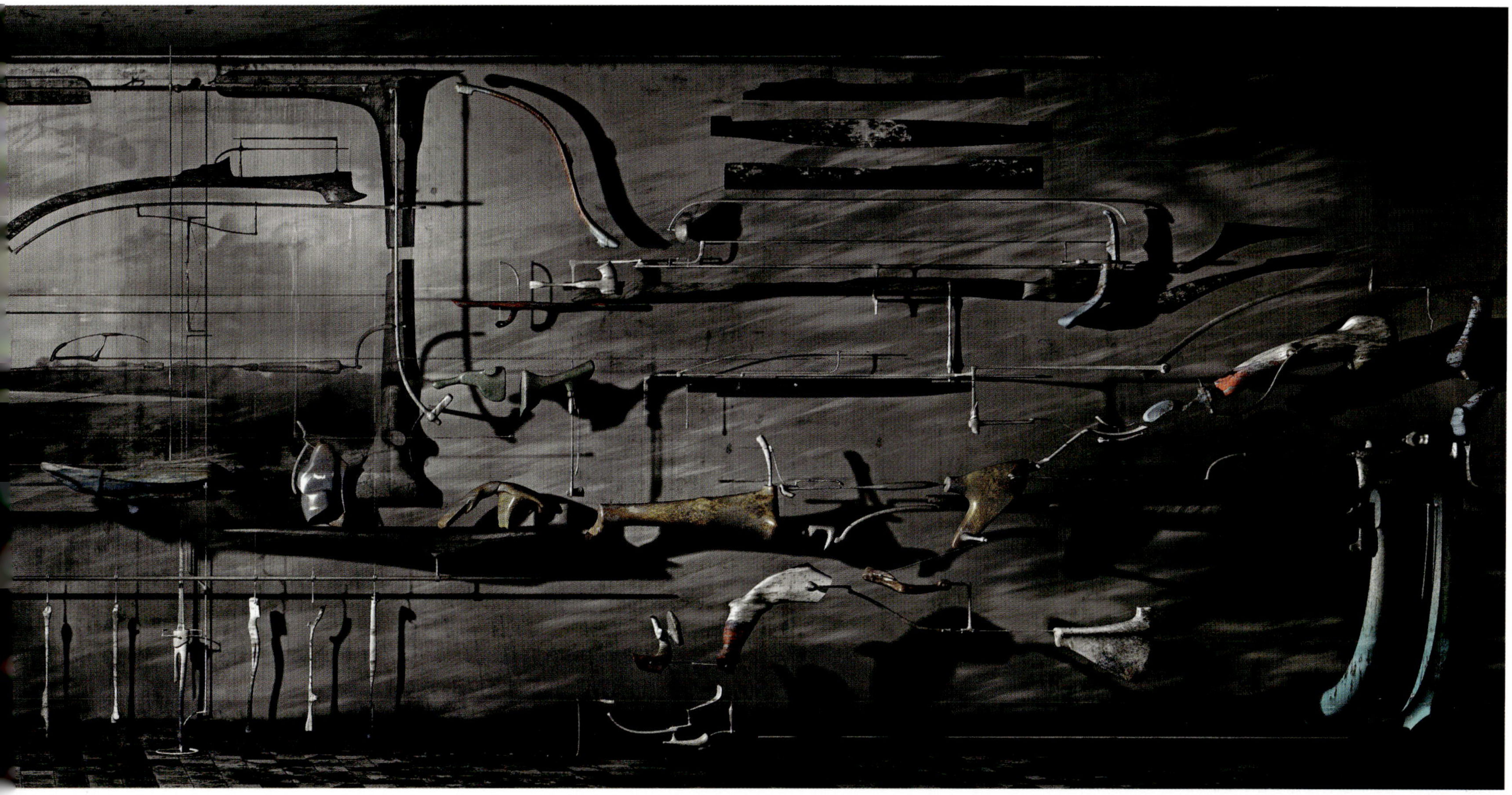

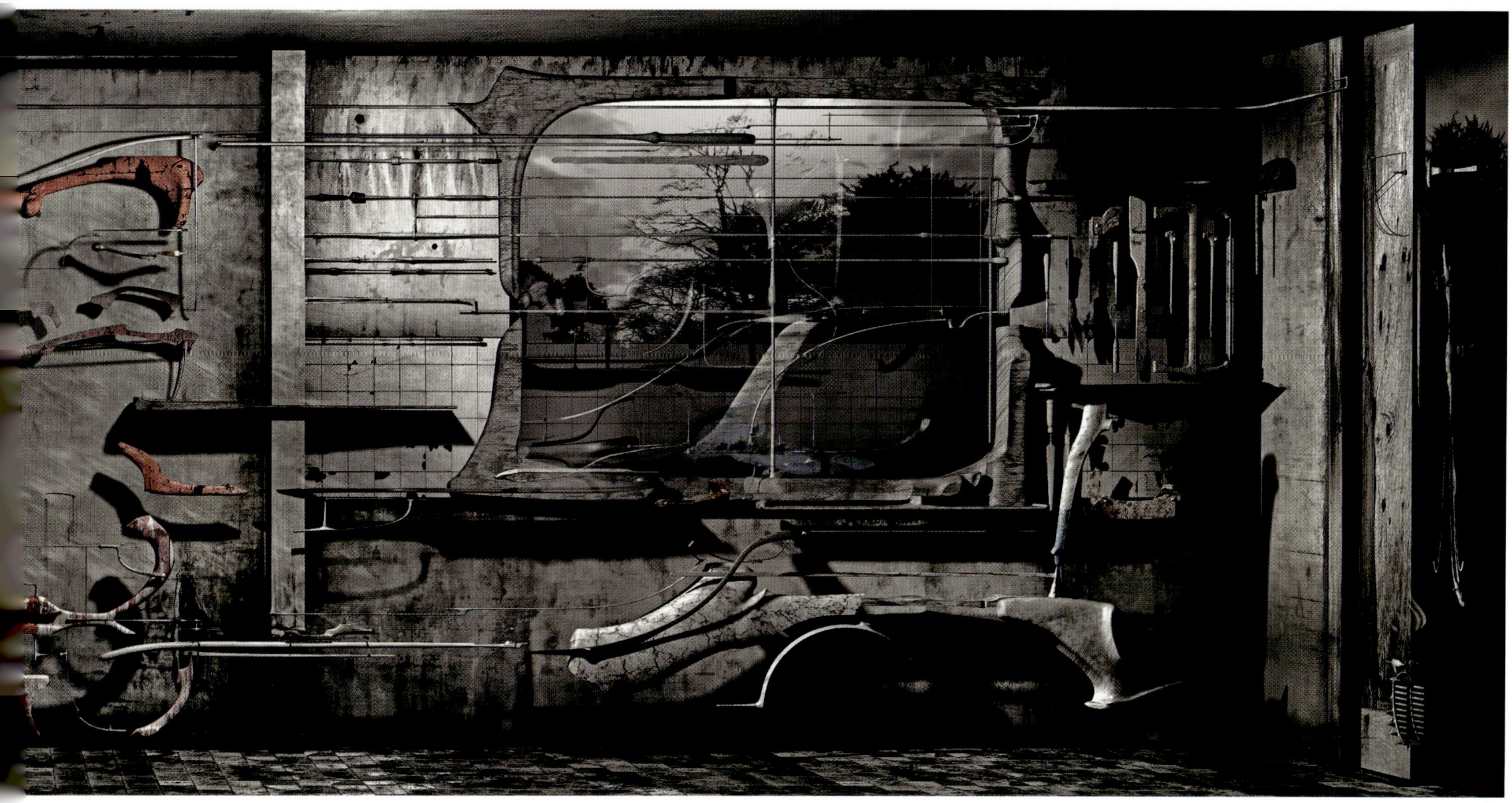

the elevation of the stars and sunsets, the tracks of woodland beasts and birds – these give him the geometries from which he makes his house, both psychologically and physically.

> **The dwelling is intimate, immediate, a resonant chamber, a mirror of the self, opening up to infinite perspectives. Depth and reflection, soul, body and dwelling are but expressions and projections of each other. For the house is not merely walls, doors and windows but a doorway to things beyond, a 'capacity' of the senses and spirit. Finally, there is no distinction between outward and inward. We dwell in the home and home dwells in us.**[16]

Here, Anne Troutman, again in 'Inside Fear', describes the symbiotic nature of a house with its occupants, and though not written with these drawings in mind, her words are apt in summing up Woods's and Cartledge's projects.

Houses on Adjusted Foundations and the Return of the Angel

The very best architects create works that often remain only on paper, works that speak of more than the simple transaction of materials and financial assets embodied in buildings. These, including Woods's Solohouse, speak of the yearning and delight of the human condition and equally its demise. Architects can employ, as can artists, a variety of techniques to create and communicate these powerful little worlds, or as the cyberneticists would call them, 'universes of discourse'. Architects can muster up poetics, cross-cultural hybridity, use myths and religion, absence, narratives, unusual spatial notations or projections in their work, or simply enigma to explore these more fundamental issues of architecture.

In this respect, the work of the American architect, artist and educator John Hejduk is an extraordinary outpouring of such ruminations and tactics. Each of his projects is a deployment of a powerful lexicon of sparse architectural parts, emotions and poetic evocations. Throughout his oeuvre there is a rich seam of 'house' designs. For Hejduk, 'house' was much more than mass-produced functional dwelling,

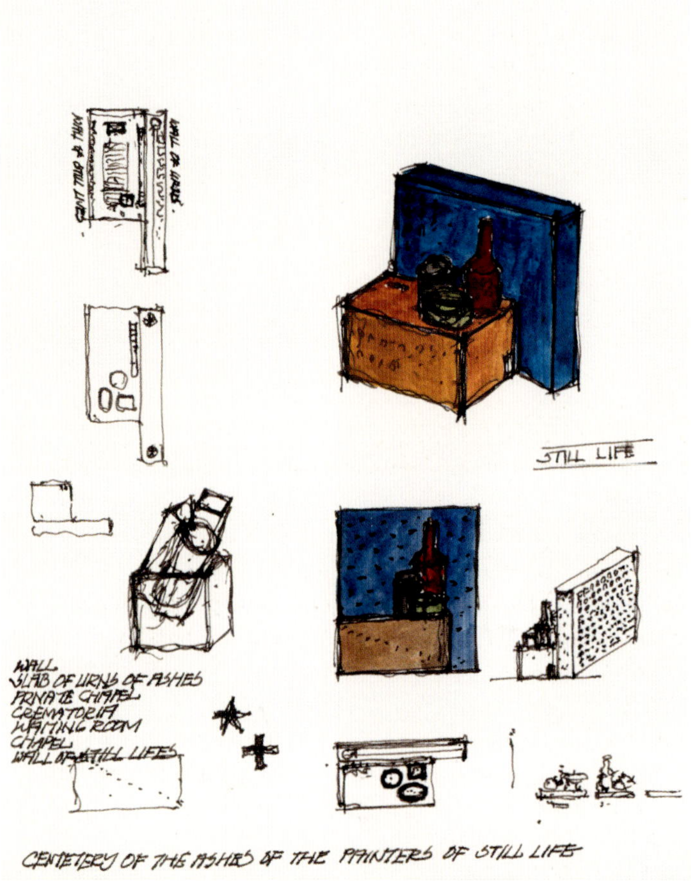

↑ **John Hejduk** • Cemetery for the Ashes of the Still Life Painters
1994

and instead a container of memory, an alchemist's alembic, within which metamorphosis and transmutation occur. The Surrealist preoccupation with alchemy is a long and fruitful one that has inspired the likes of Ernst, Carrington and Dalí among others. Hejduk's creative, spatial and mnemonic architectural alchemy often parallels the old medieval adepts themselves. He would first select a 'slough of despond', a *prima materia* (an ubiquitous material, often hidden or invisible to most eyes, but which when revealed and worked on becomes life-affirming). In Hejduk's case this was often the genius loci of a particular city, its history, its inhabitants, or the simple act of living with the burden of time, memory and loss. Like Cartledge's project, Hejduk's pieces are often carved from people's professions, trades or work patterns. His houses are the product of careful distillation to reduce them to their essence, a concentrated architecture that gives them a formidable power that can radiate rainbows of allusions so that ultimately they become philosophical gold. Again, similar to the alchemists, Hejduk's methods include the position of the sun, date and time of day, poetic incantation and memorial rituals. Pattern and form become potent accomplices in the successful conclusion of the opus.

Throughout his life, Hejduk felt a great kinship with, and took much inspiration from, Le Corbusier. Initially he was enamoured with the early Corbusian works, but later, as Hejduk's style progressed, it was to the older master's later projects that he returned. The architecturally mature Le Corbusier, as another spatial alchemist, was able to reconcile what at face value were opposites – Purist painting and sculpture, poetry and architecture. From 1947 to 1953 he produced *Le poème de l'angle droit* (The Poem of the Right Angle), a synthesis on his architectural, formal and environmental preoccupations. This important book consisted of poetry and nineteen lithographs. At first glance it is visually arresting, a festival of bright, mostly primary colour. The illustrations are more ragged than Le Corbusier's early Purist works, yet indebted to them, and the influence of Picasso and late Matisse can also be felt. One might also suggest that the accompanying poetry, redolent as it is of suns, moons, colours and seasons, is inspired by the many arcane theosophies so familiar to the Surrealists:

Do not overwhelm then he
who wants to take his part of the
risks of life – Let
the metals fuse
tolerate the alchemists who
besides leave you outside
the cause.[17]

While the Surrealists, and particularly Breton, feuded with Le Corbusier, here is clear evidence that they shared an interest in alchemical transmutation at this time. This is perhaps the nearest the two came to establishing that fecund artistic resolution of Surrealism and Corbusian Modernism that the German philosopher and cultural critic Walter Benjamin later speculated could have been, in his opinion, a profound tipping point for France and Modernism: 'To embrace Breton and Le Corbusier – that would be to draw the spirit of contemporary France like a bow which strikes with knowledge to the heart of the present.'[18]

Hejduk's later work, such as his design books *Adjusting Foundations* (1995) and *Pewter Wings, Golden Horns, Stone Veils* (1997), often dispensed with fine and particular line work, as did Le Corbusier in *Le poème de l'angle droit*, and displayed instead a frenzy of creation, of architectural jewels falling from the modern-day alchemist's pen: new spaces, allusions and formal configurations forged with the heat of new insights.

Two of Hejduk's later works are sufficient to give us an understanding of his Surrealist methods. The more recent of these, *Cemetery for the Ashes of the Still Life Painters* is in effect a self-sealing house of death and memorialization. He provides a full explanation of this project within *Adjusting Foundations*:

The painter can set up a composition on a table of a so-called still life/natura morta – bowls, fruits, table clothes, bottles, glasses – and paint it on a two-dimensional canvas as he sees it or reimagines it; however, within the arranged three-dimensional still life, certainly, in the case of the fruit (apples, pears, grapes), there is a rotting taking place, and this destroys the

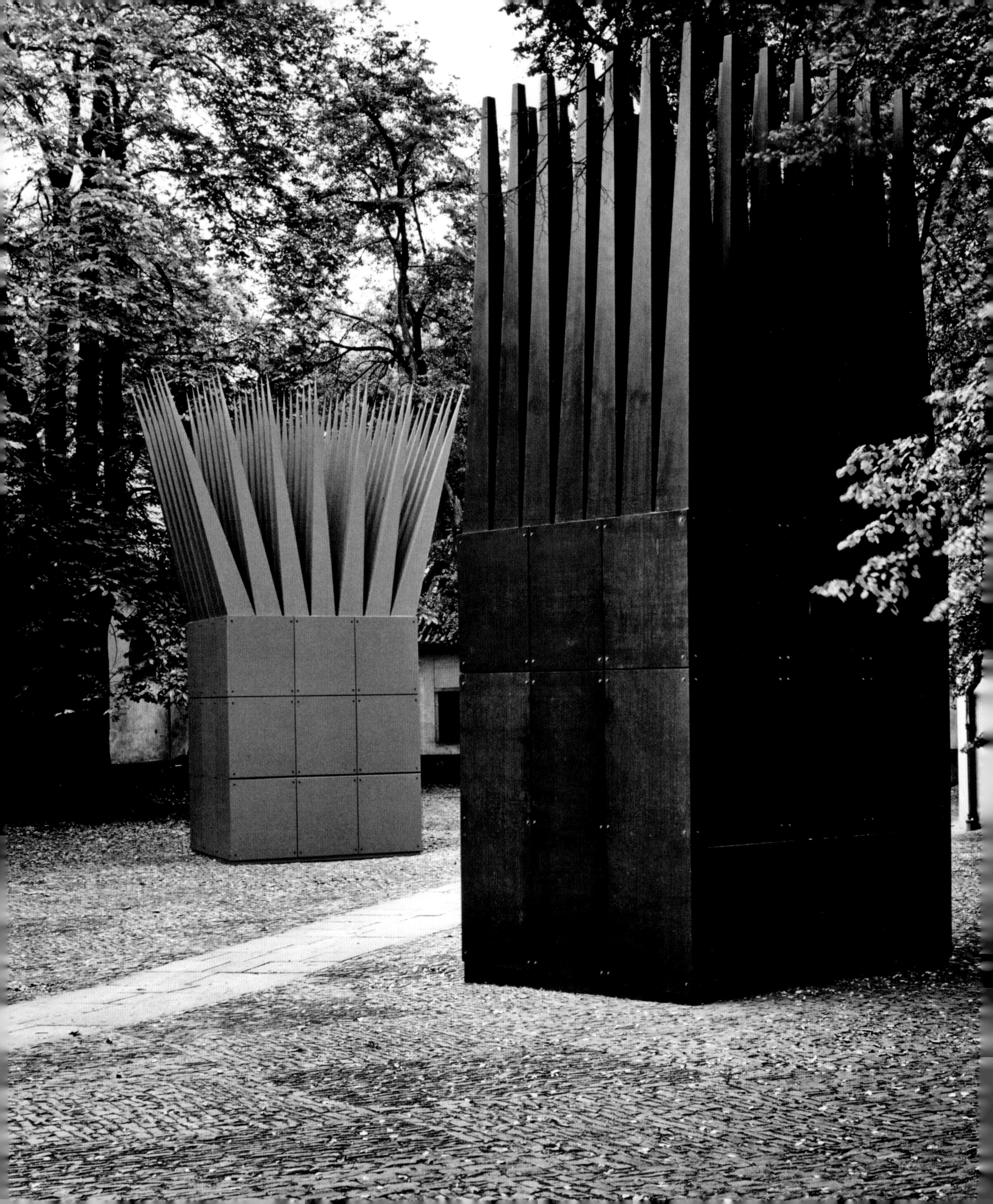

←

John Hejduk • House of the Suicide
and House of the Mother of the Suicide
1980–82, installed at Prague Castle
Prague, Czech Republic
1991

original still life through organic decay.... [The great painters] are the River Styx boatmen, taking stilled life to the underworld; that is, some of them do. Nothing is frivolous in stilling life. Time, some time, no matter how infinitesimal, is necessary for the crossover. The painter accompanies life to its stillness or fixes nature consequently defying mortality. The painter is mortal; the painting immortal. The beautician and mortician work together, one hiding life, the other hiding death. The painter's still life is nature; God's still life is man.[19]

Just for a moment, looking at Hejduk's work is like communing with angels.

The House at the End of Time

Some architects have focused on the rituals of bereavement and memorialization. Architecture is, in these cases, utilized to semiotically remember and to protect against the dark night of the soul and simple mortality.

Hejduk's House of the Suicide and the House of the Mother of the Suicide were inspired by a poem by David Shapiro entitled 'The Funeral of Jan Palach', which in itself was inspired by the death in 1969 of Palach himself, who set himself alight as a protest about the Soviet occupation of Czechoslovakia. The two structures (built in the grounds of Prague Castle in 1991), face each other a few metres apart:

The suicide's house (angled spikes) is sealed so that the viewer can only imagine the experience of its entombed inhabitant. Entry to the mother's house (vertical spikes) is possible via a small opening at its base. Inside the cramped, womb-like space a raised platform permits a single visitor to peer through a small aperture and thereby to contemplate the facing House of the Suicide, the only possible view, the view that haunts the mother.[20]

In 1988, the architect Douglas Darden became captivated by a small water tower situated on open land just north of Oxford, Mississippi. The exterior of the building, in his eyes, provoked a feeling of simple attractiveness. However, the prospect of experiencing its interior induced a feeling of claustrophobia and gasping for breath – similar to the experience one might have with a collapsed lung. He resolved to try to create a project that engendered these two conflicting emotions.

His Oxygen House (see pages 106–07) is not a house that rejoices in ease of living, or that is a joyous synthesis of form and function, or where each day is animated with life-affirming experiences, ambitions and loves. This is a surreal house awaiting death. As Darden's friend Peter Schneider has noted: 'Within the compelling idea of the first house – the house at the beginning of time – is buried the equally compelling image of its shadow: the house at the end of time. This is a place for dying in. Its fragility and hostility, its ephemeral and temporary aspects, change our delight to anxiety, our ease to dis-ease.'[21]

The architecture of the Oxygen House is sustained by a story that was inspired by William Faulkner's novel *As I Lay Dying* (1930), and the parallels between Darden's main imaginary character Burnden Abraham, for whom he designed the house, and Faulkner's Addie Bundren are numerous. The house is a surreal mix of analogy, symbolism, allusion, literary quotation and inspiration, the design revolving around Abraham and his nurse, Jewel. The main body of the house is a life-support system – a capsule of life-sustaining oxygen – the so-called Bright Drum-Torso. According to the narrative, Abraham was terminally ill, unable to stand and dependent on Jewel. He had been a signalman on the railroad until he sustained debilitating injuries in an accident when a train derailed and shards of metal entered his body and collapsed his lung. The site of the accident is also subsequently the site of the house. Abraham had to live what was left of his life, waiting to die, horizontally, in bed.

As well as the oxygen chamber, the house also consists of the Stone Fort/blockhouse (burial chamber for Abraham), Shutter-Gate (live-in nurse's quarters), Oxygen Tank (tent support and nurse's tomb), Lift (circulation and Abraham's tomb), Tar Road (entry/exit to the West), Life-Line (stockpile of oxygen to the East), Derelict Track (broken North–South train line), Wash (dried up tributary of the Mississippi River), Spring (source of pure water), Willow (existing tree, deciduous) and Spruce (new tree, evergreen). As long as Abraham lives he can be visited. Visitors can reach the Oxygen House along the Tar Road. All are screened by the

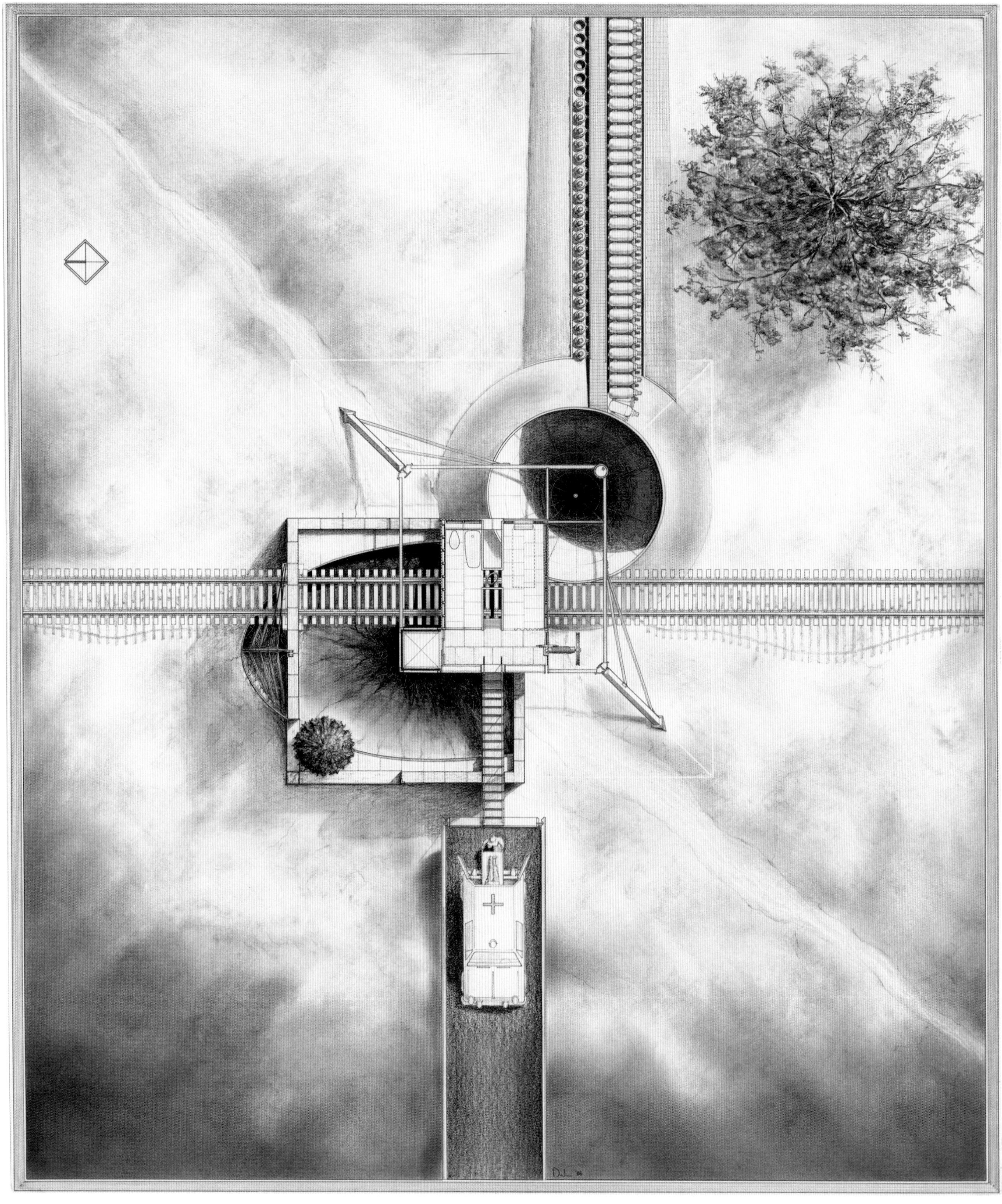

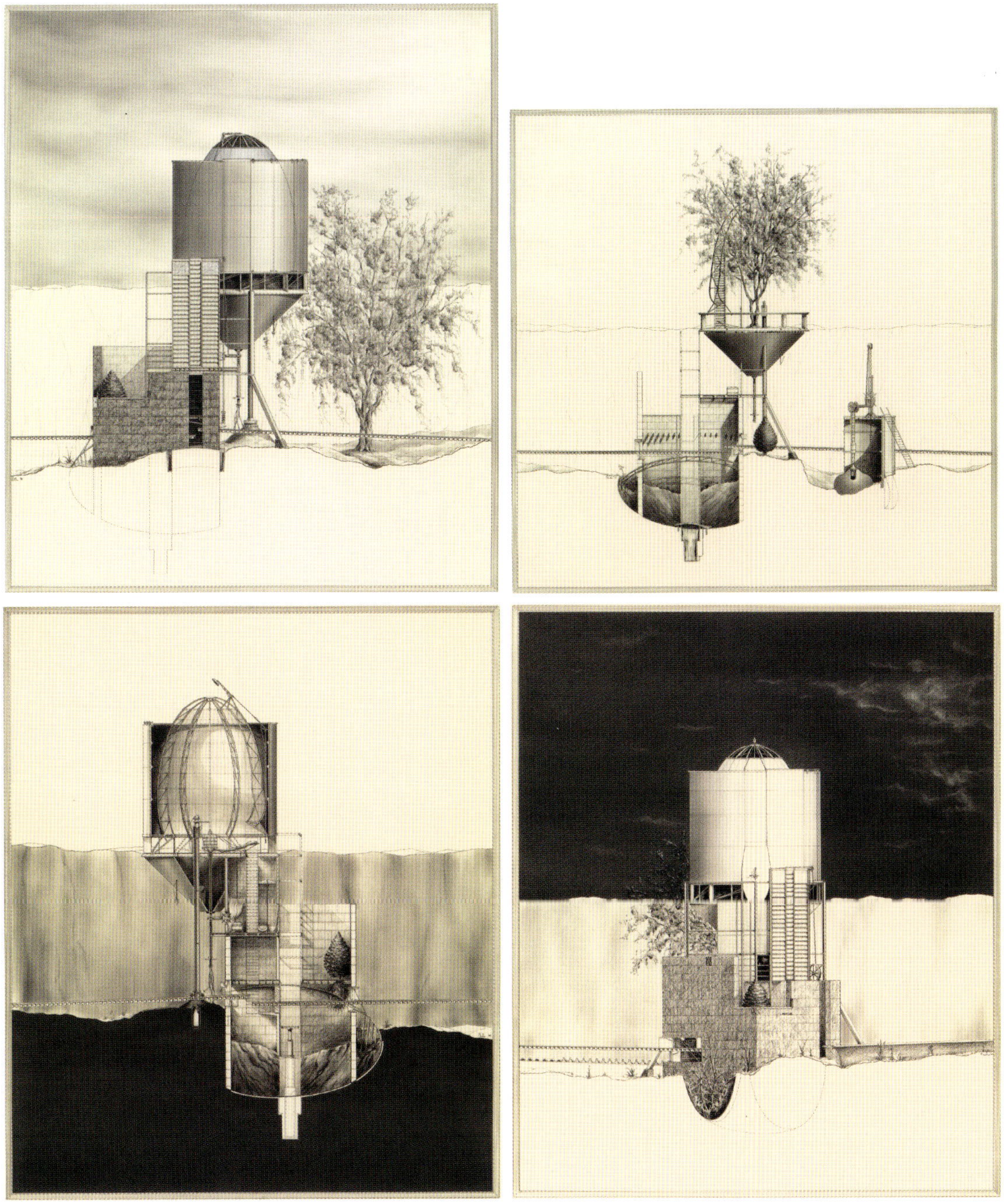

←↑

Douglas Darden • Oxygen House

1988

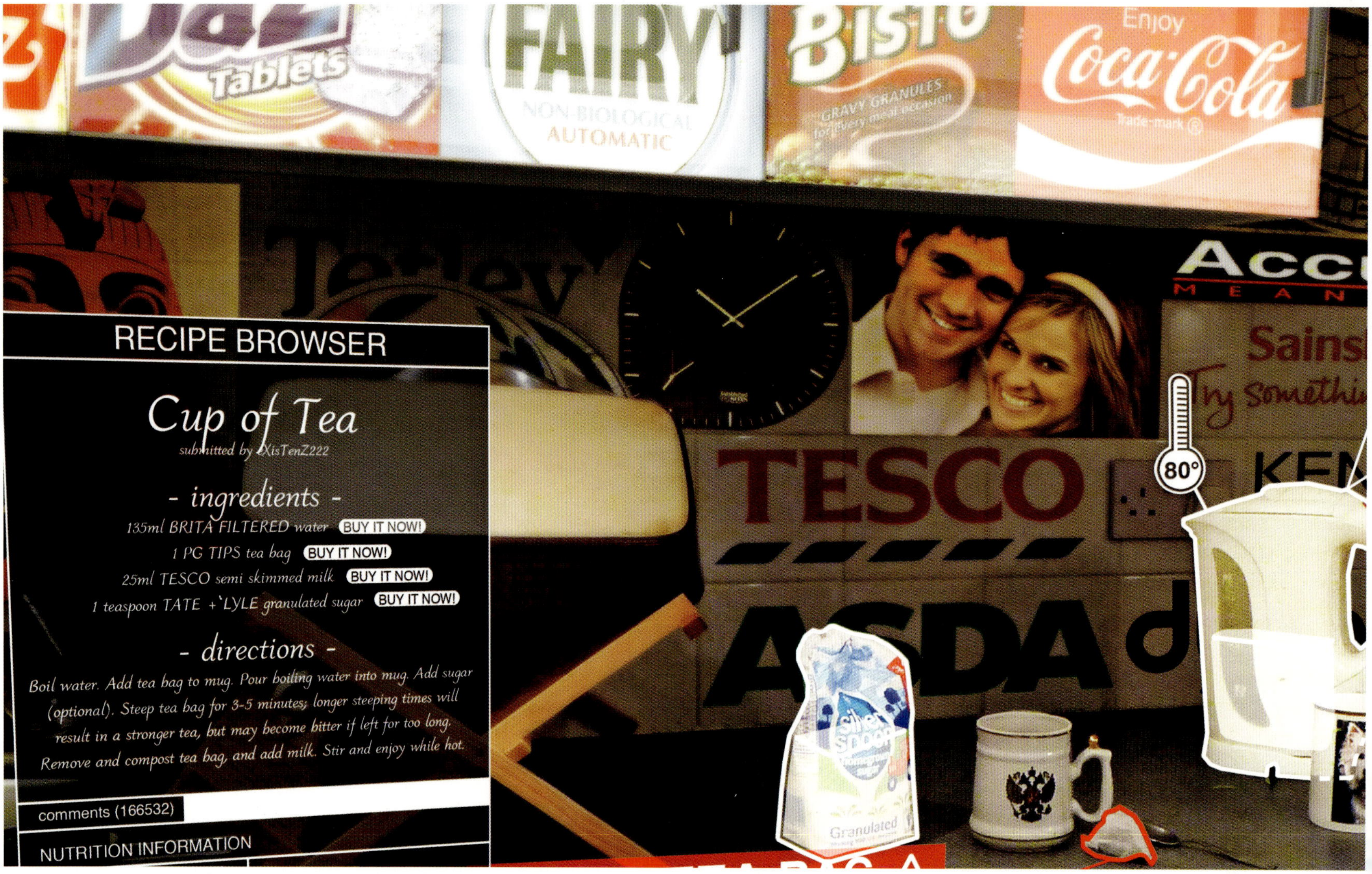
Daz Tablets
FAIRY
NON-BIOLOGICAL AUTOMATIC
Bisto
GRAVY GRANULES
Enjoy Coca-Cola
Trade-mark ®
RECIPE BROWSER
Cup of Tea
submitted by XisTenZ222
- ingredients -
135ml BRITA FILTERED water BUY IT NOW!
1 PG TIPS tea bag BUY IT NOW!
25ml TESCO semi skimmed milk BUY IT NOW!
1 teaspoon TATE + LYLE granulated sugar BUY IT NOW!
- directions -
Boil water. Add tea bag to mug. Pour boiling water into mug. Add sugar (optional). Steep tea bag for 3-5 minutes; longer steeping times will result in a stronger tea, but may become bitter if left for too long. Remove and compost tea bag, and add milk. Stir and enjoy while hot.
comments (166532)
NUTRITION INFORMATION
TESCO
ASDA
80°
Granulated

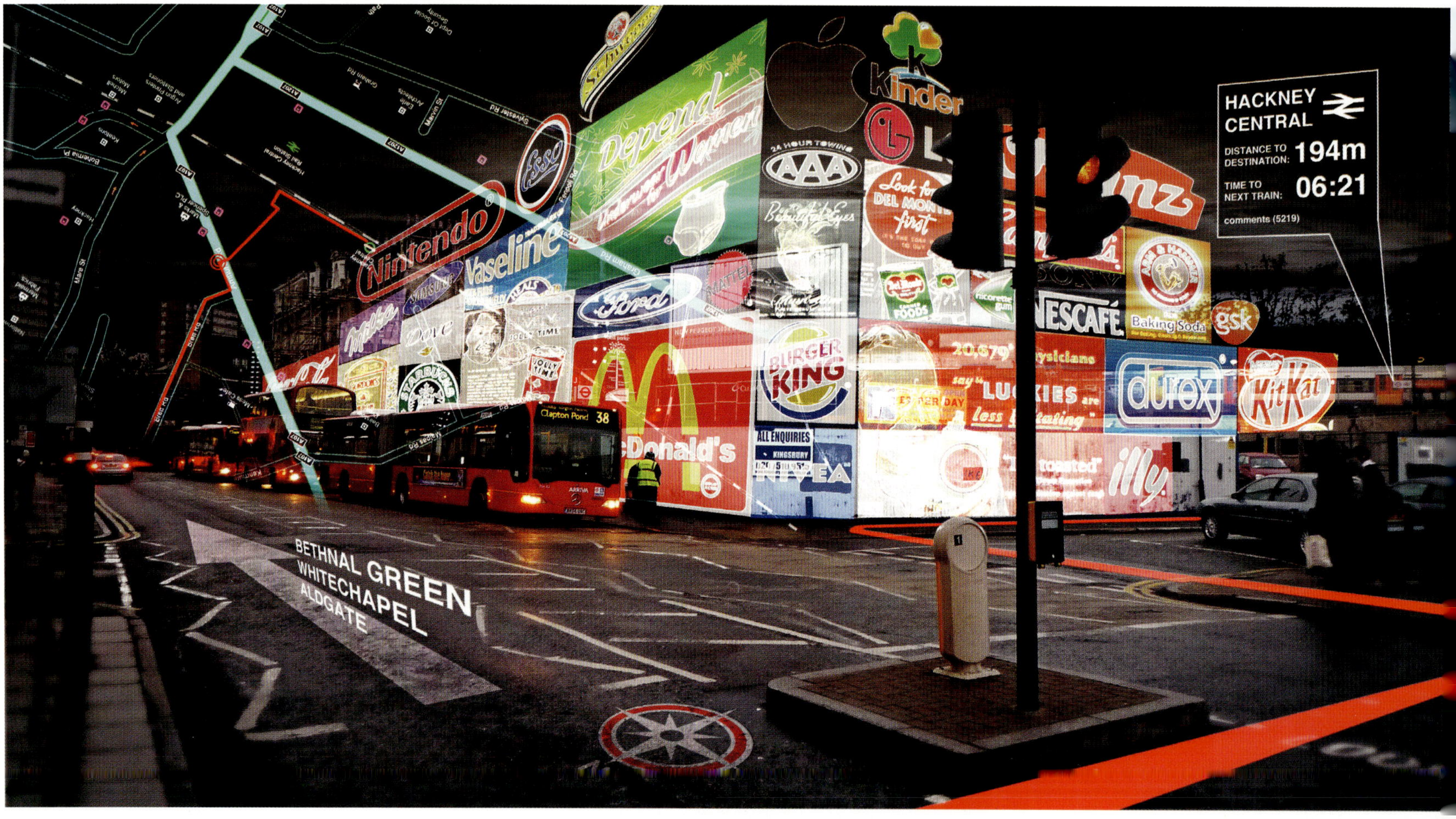
HACKNEY CENTRAL
DISTANCE TO DESTINATION: 194m
TIME TO NEXT TRAIN: 06:21
comments (5219)
Nintendo
Vaseline
Depend
Kinder
AAA
NESCAFÉ
Baking Soda
gsk
BURGER KING
durex
KitKat
ALL ENQUIRIES
NIVEA
illy
Clapton Pond 38
BETHNAL GREEN
WHITECHAPEL
ALDGATE

←

Keiichi Matsuda • Augmented (hyper)Reality: Domestic Robocop
2009

nurse who operates the Shutter-Gate, before walking upstairs and then leaving by lift. At the time of Abraham's death, the oxygen tent fabric becomes his shroud, he is buried in the base of the lift and his bed is used to cover his tomb. The willow tree is uprooted and planted in the drum-base, the Bright Drum-Torso is taken apart and placed over a wellspring.

Schneider explores the dark underbelly of the house, the last resting place of Abraham: 'The directions are downward and inward, and it locates itself within the realm of the shadow. As a closed underworld, a dark place, it is below the surface of the land. It is the "airless" place where one encounters the Minotaur. It is where one confronts the disquieting, meets terror and anxiety, and where one loses one's breath.'[22]

The Oxygen House is a deep meditation on mortality, the history of the American South, on geography, health, life and death. Abraham, an architectural alchemist, has his mystic sister, Jewel, whose tomb in the house also awaits her. One is reminded, once again, of Böcklin's *Island of the Dead*: she is Abraham's boatwoman who takes him across the River Styx, she is his Still Life Painter.

Augmenting Reality

This chapter has explored various notions that engender the Surrealist idea of the 'house'. The work of Giacometti and Ernst has introduced us to the surreal house of fear. We have seen the dark side of the house, as a site of ghostly apparitions, populated by objects and things that can quickly turn animate, provoking uncanny sensations. They seek psychic attention, attract our deepest desires and confront our primal fears – those that concern our distress at the loss of domestic order, unbridled sexuality and implications of death. We have also encountered the womb house, the initial Surrealist obverse of the house of fear. To its advocates, this house was about spatial and material liberation, space not tied to function, for example in Kiesler's Endless House where vistas and decoration are broadcast in light, and walls in theory decompose in this cinematic illumination.

We have seen how a house is surrealistically, mnemonically constructed, from all the actions and thoughts, emotions and aspirations of its occupants as they make and navigate their lives, and create their own personal 'universes of discourse' within it and between themselves. Some Surrealists sought to make this invisible house visible. Simultaneously, the Surrealists rejected traditional methods of measurement and standard ways to describe objects, things and architectural space, and instead calibrated houses in different ways conditioned by the inhabitants' lifestyles and preoccupations.

Finally, we have looked at houses that are concerned with that other Surrealist preoccupation – alchemy. Alchemic houses attempt to reconcile opposites (life and death, for example), and by focusing on the transmutation and metamorphosis of material. Ritual is also part of the alchemic process, and this last type of house often has its own memorial, alchemic protocols.

These surreal spatial tactics and examples are useful for contemporary architects experimenting with advanced technologies in domestic settings. The Surrealist house embodies virtual appearances, animate objects, transmutation, the hybridization of materials and mnemonics, and offers lessons on how we might engage with these in information-rich environments.

A simple vignette into the potential of the contemporary house to become digitally surreal has been illustrated by designer Keiichi Matsuda in his short film *Augmented (hyper)Reality: Domestic Robocop*. Here, Matsuda takes the simple act of making a cup of tea and shows how augmented reality, enabled by the Internet, could create a hybrid virtual and actual environment projected within and around the kitchen. This capacity, liberated from current screen-based technologies of computing, can help the user in their tea-making task, keep them in contact with the outside world, advertise to them and allow them to change the ambience of their space and the informational vistas they experience, which they can conjure up or swipe away at a whim. These ghostly presences appear and disappear at architectural scale and are highly locative and spatialized. This environment transforms, is reflexive and can be 'constructed' by the user according to personal preoccupations, work patterns and formal and physical fetishes. Its haptic interfaces can also be changed to his taste, calibrations of movements, intentions and environment, all personally contrived and 'built'.

The mnemonic spaces of memorialization, both of the house and of the individual personalities within it, have been further contemporized by architect Lena-Stina Andersson's Bendy House II project (see pages 110–12). Her work, based in an old derelict house once owned by her grandmother in Sweden, utilizes ideas of augmented reality and locative technology to speculate on mnemonic space.

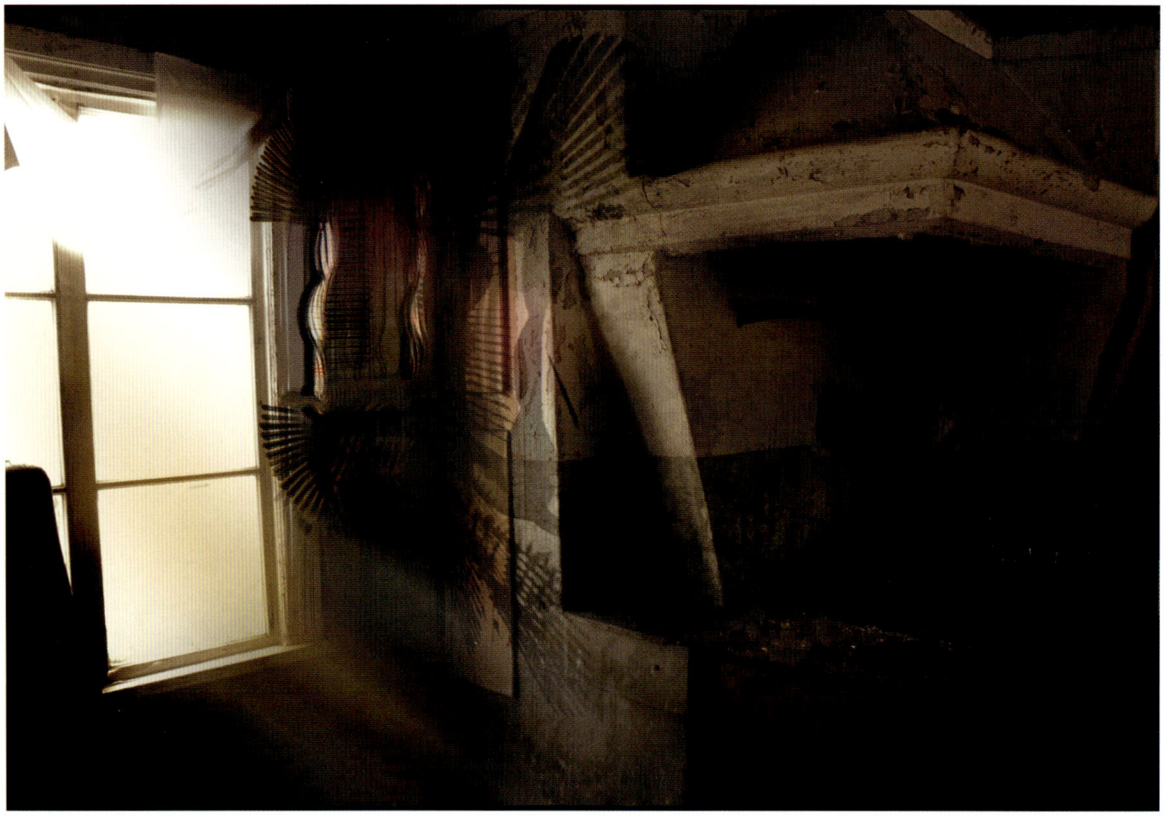

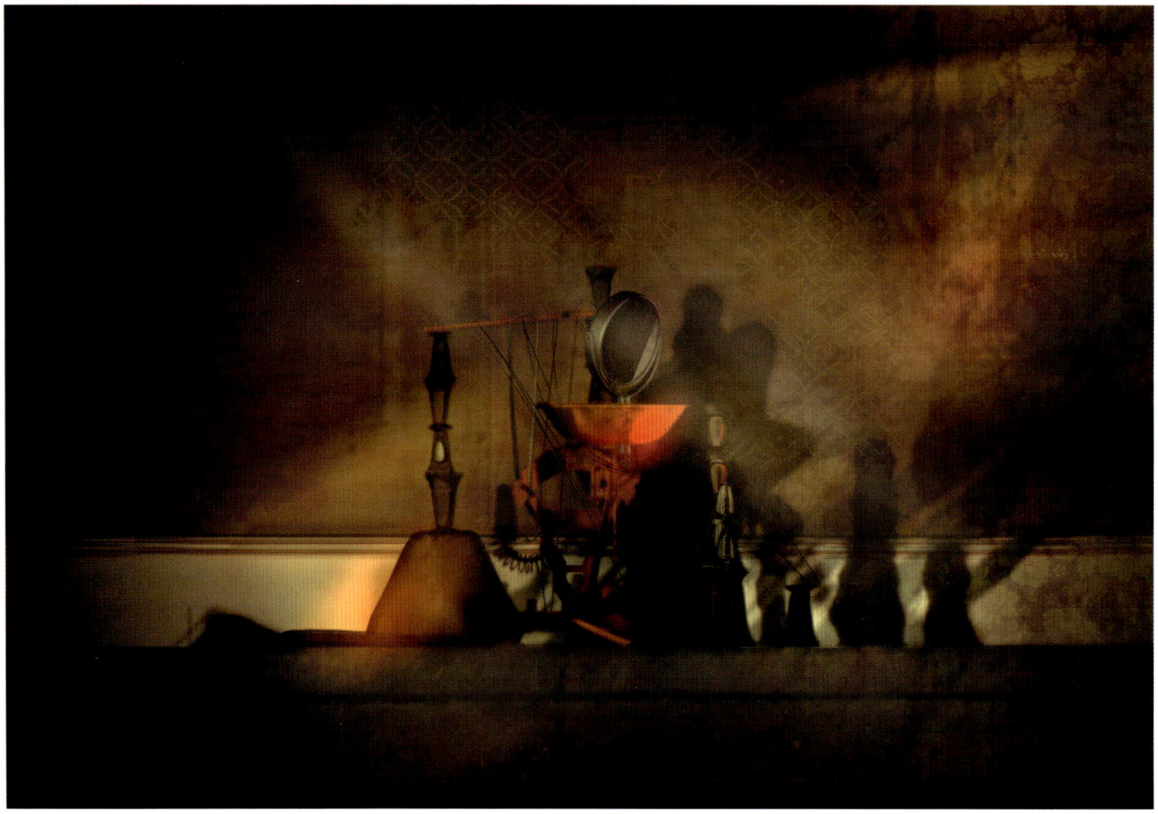

↑→

Lena-Stina Andersson • Bendy House II

2008

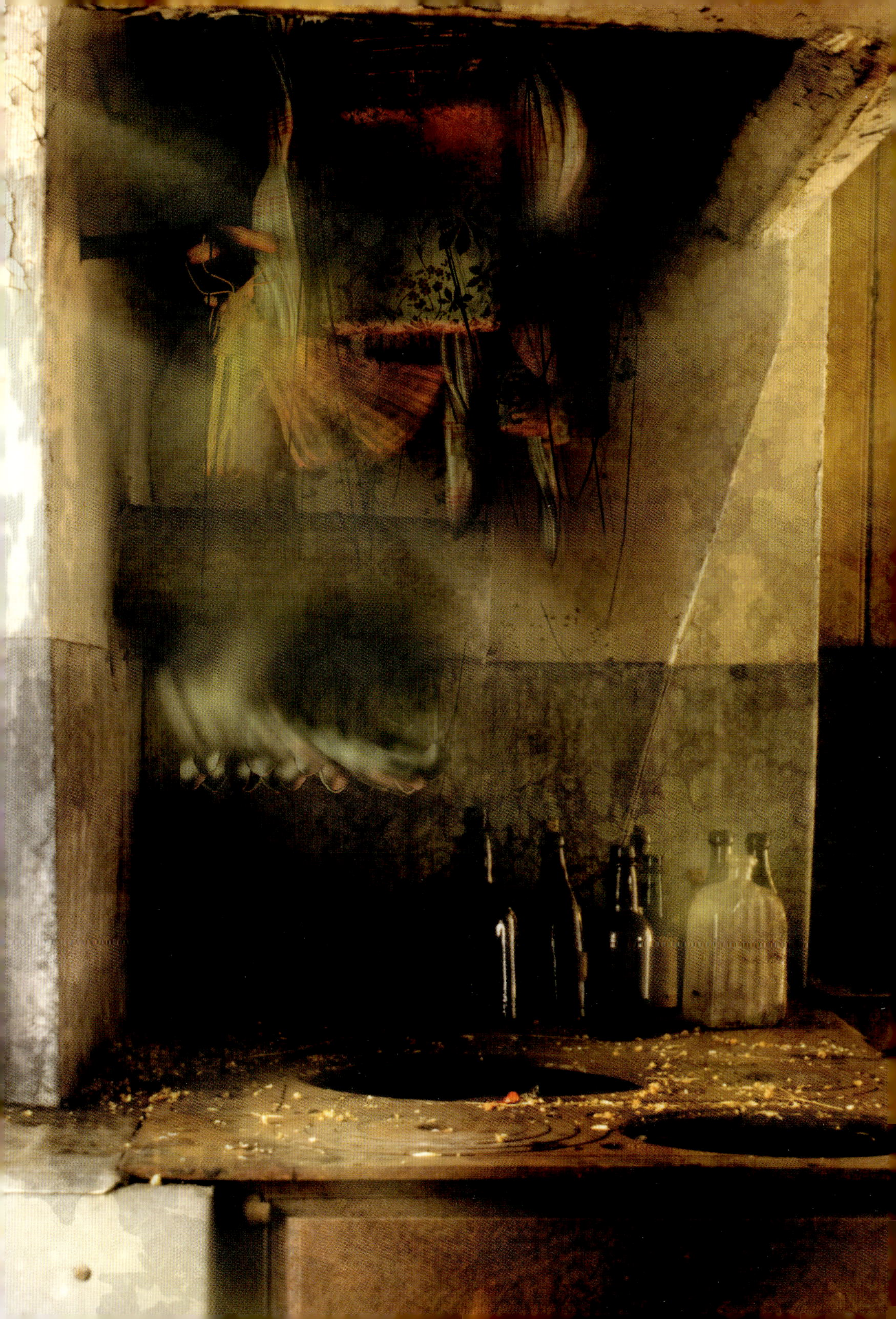

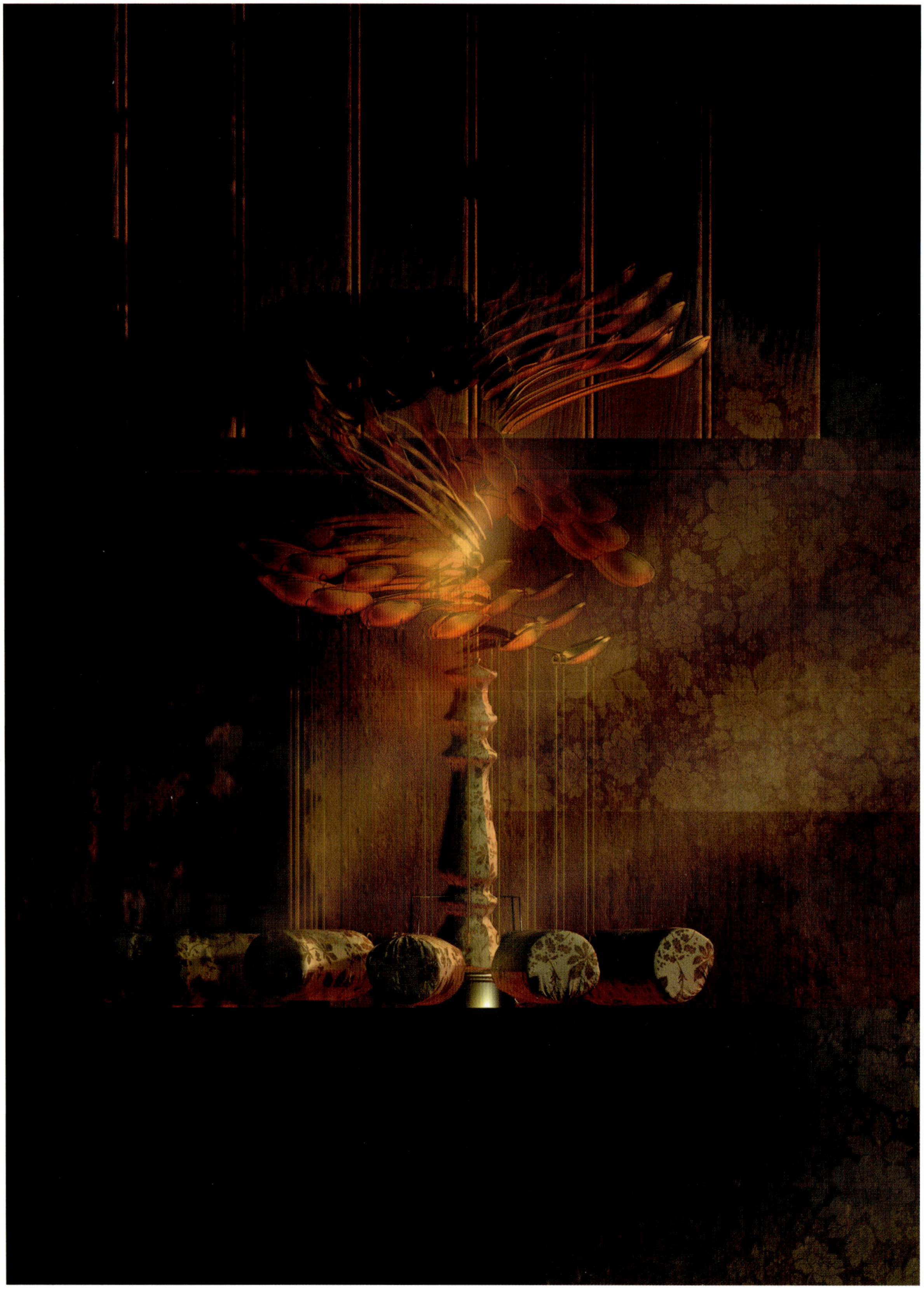

↑

Lena-Stina Andersson • Bendy House II

2008

Andersson choreographs virtual elements (cutlery, bowls and so on) around her grandmother's old house to suggest moments of their time together, prompting memories personal to her. One is reminded here of Surrealist hero Raymond Roussel's *Locus Solus* (1914), a novel about a great scientist and inventor, Martial Canterel, who could hubristically reanimate the dead, so that they could re-enact the most powerful events of their lives: 'Given a free rein, and dressed according to the character of his part, the corpse, finding furniture, supports, various resistances and things to lift in their right places, performed without falls or false moves.'[23] All this enabled by a plug of Vitalium inserted in the cadaver's skull above the hairline.

The Surrealist idea of the womb house is lent a contemporary flavour with the American architect and professor Greg Lynn's RV Prototype House (RV = Room Vehicle). The egg-shaped, carbon-fibre cocoon of this prototype vehicle that is also a house is an essay in the minimal use of land and materials to create as small a spatial footprint as possible. The house is capable of revolving in all directions on its motorized base. Similar to Kiesler's Endless House, but with a much greater degree of movement, floors become ceilings and vice versa. Functions and furniture choices are distributed around the whole interior of the 'egg', with the interior moulded in a series of undulating contours to facilitate this flexibility. Lynn's prototype is more akin to a space pod than a house. Instead of being absent, gravity is here used to provoke a space-like strangeness. Again similar to the Endless House, vistas of the exterior landscape are important, but can move in real time, in real space, by the touch of a switch, rearticulating the whole house.

Thus surreal notions of 'house' remain strong, and our twenty-first-century technologies, instead of eradicating the Surrealists' mythologies, are further elaborating them. The house is of course the microcosm of the city.
In the next chapter we shall see how Surrealist protocols of space-making and the grander scale of the city, linked with burgeoning new technologies, is further enhancing urban design in many marvellous (in Breton's sense) ways. The vast stage of the city, the bodies that inhabit it, the relationships of objects with these bodies, the architectures of work and play and the streetscape that is made from all of these personal and public interactions is another Surrealist stage.

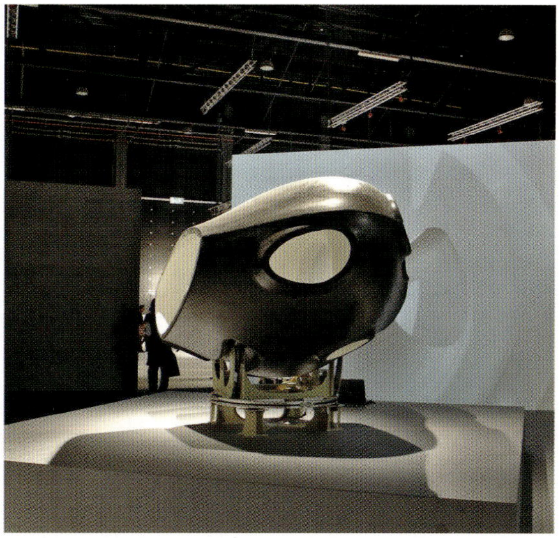

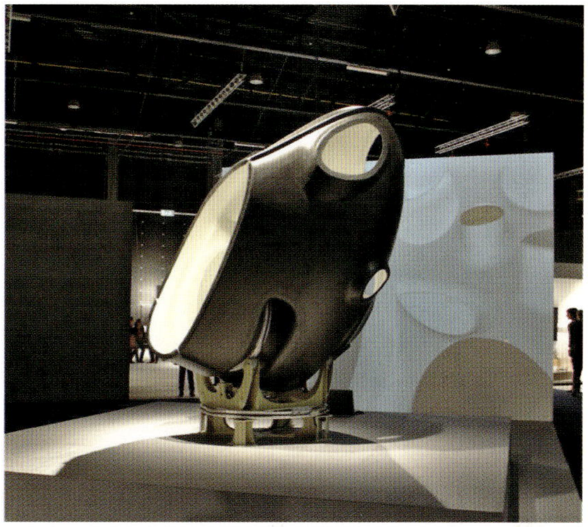

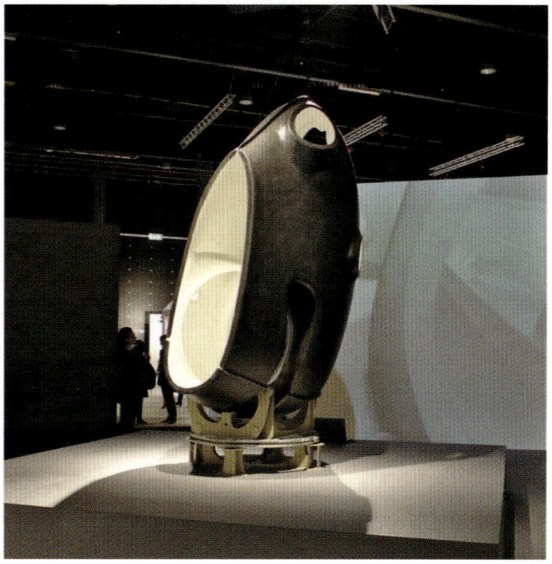

→ **Greg Lynn** • RV Prototype House
1/5th scale models, Los Angeles, USA, and Kortrijk, Belgium
2012–13

JUICELESS CYBORGS – INVISIBLE IN WHITE LIGHT

Diller + Scofidio

THE WITHDRAWING ROOM: VERSIONS AND SUBVERSIONS

Capp Street Project | San Francisco | 1987

Created as an installation at the Capp Street Project experimental art space in San Francisco, the *withDrawing Room* is an enigma. It suggests, perhaps, two narratives. First, have the human occupants been banished and is this their torture chamber? Second, is something less or more than human dwelling here? Living to different rules, deconstructing, reconditioning and navigating the vestiges of previous human inhabitants? In short, is what we witness evolution or warfare and suppression? Is this a happy house of technologized spiritual transcendence, or the surreal house of fear recast?

The spaces are certainly strange, uncanny and foreboding. They imply numerous surreal bodies, for example invisible phantoms, extruded beings from another dimension, not restrained by gravity. Terrabyte ghosts or, perhaps, desiccated human/animal chimeras with long necks and legs, and no bodily fluids. The *withDrawing Room* makes no attempt to recreate the womblike spaces of early Surrealism; it does not protect and conceal, but rather slices and legislatively surveys. There is nowhere private or comfortable. This is the 'night' side of the surreal house, eroded of its interstitial dark portal spaces, and brought out into the bright and mesmerizing light of a rotten sun.

Human memory is depicted here as in a process of being subsumed, what is left already bastardized by entities of differing epistemologies, and denying any haptic experience – the handmade gone. The memory theatres of the ancient world and Surrealism that consisted of re-locatable, shamanistic, mnemonic objects erased. Is this a space for technologized suicide? Or is it simply the new memory theatre of a digital techno-Surrealist body? A universe of discourse for bodies that are part bit, part atom, that move faster and have much larger bandwidths than our red, brown and yellow leaky conduits can deliver. These bodies might be the products of Lamarckian evolution, each new generation having inherited the knowledge and skills of the previous one at the time of birth – no need for potty training, schools or playful learning here.

The *withDrawing Room* seems to memorialize the transition of humanity into something else. Greg Bear brilliantly describes this type of transition in his science-fiction novel *Blood Music* (1985):

> *Michael Bernard is crossing an interface.*
> *He is encoded.*
> *No longer conscious of all the sensations of being in a body. No more automatic listenings and responses to the slide of muscles, past one another, the bubbling of fluids in the abdomen, the push and roar of blood and pounding heart. He no longer balances, tenses or relaxes. It is like suddenly moving from the city to a quiet cave.*[1]

Overhead
detail
of
hanging
dining
room
set.
↓

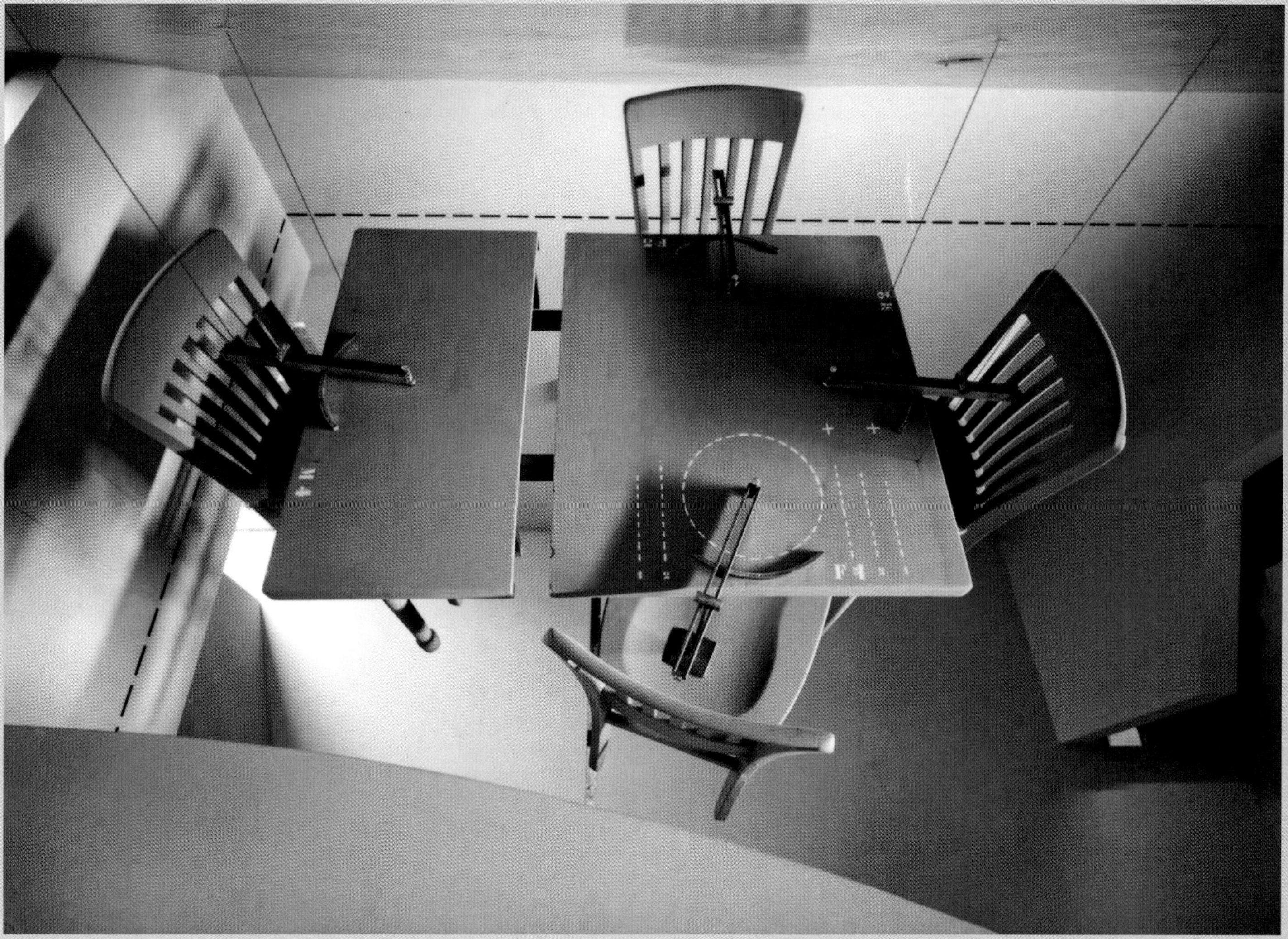

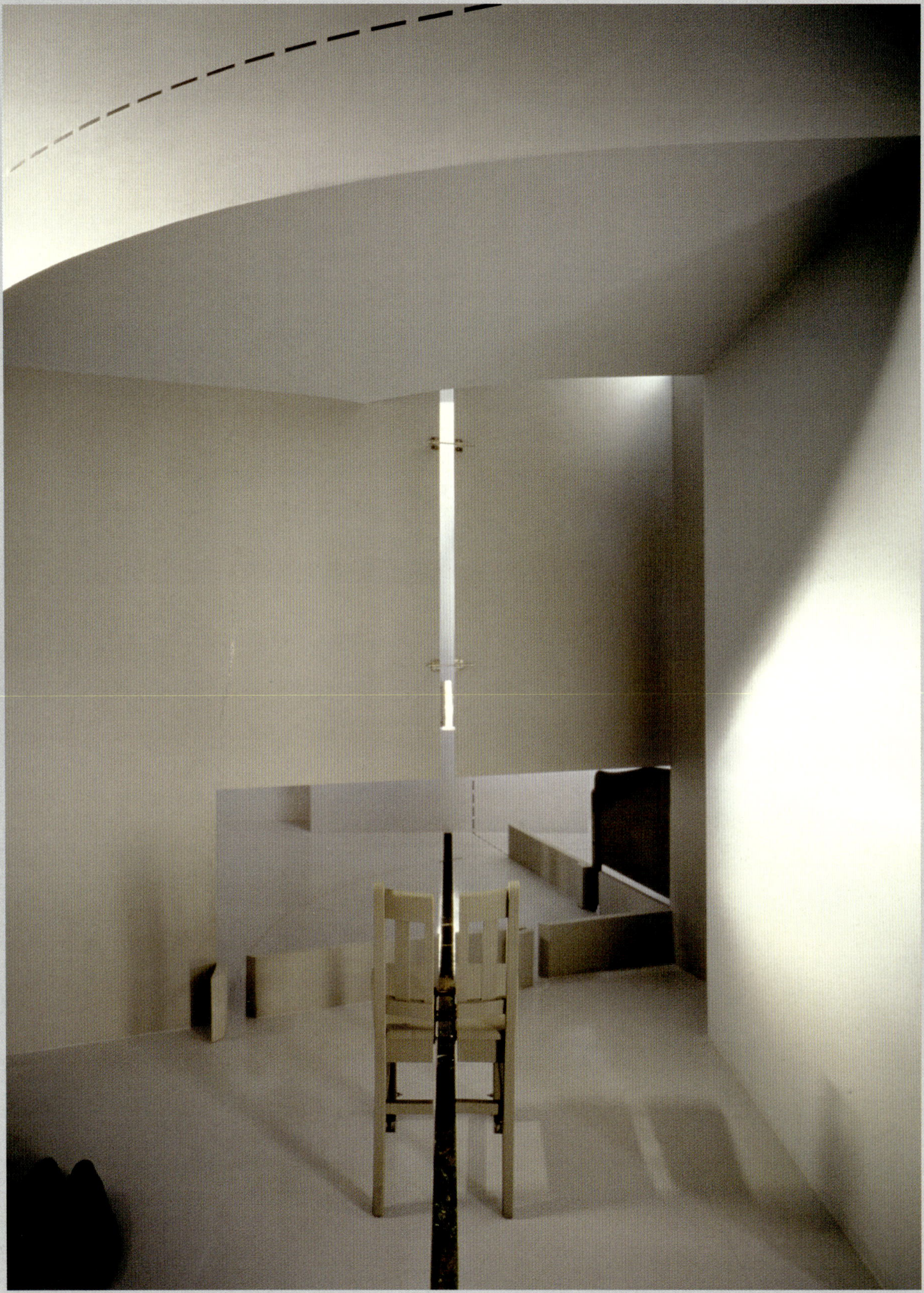

↑

Bisected chair.

The installation also has a tinge of sadomasochistic delight about it, of invisible bodies, unable to freely operate, split and pierced furniture, tied and suspended in mid-air, slices and gaps positioned to reveal invisible human genitals, exposing them and making them susceptible to all manner of inspection and vulnerability. This combination of voyeuristic pleasure, desire and restraint can be traced back to Diller + Scofidio's interest in the implied choreographic movements and strange delay in time and space in Marcel Duchamp's *The Bride Stripped Bare by Her Bachelors, Even (The Large Glass*; 1915–23; see page 45). As Anthony Vidler writes, referencing the Surrealist photographer and artist Man Ray's shot of Duchamp's iconic work neglected and covered with thick dust:

> *Like the dust traces falling on Duchamp's* Large Glass, *the phantom operations of absent inhabitants and living objects are also mapped into their deposits. The moving bed is tracked by films of dust beneath it; the presence of former drinkers marked by rings on the table. The house is left as if obsolete and already abandoned technological space – like the inside of an old radio – a readymade, found again to be reused at will, dust and all; the traces of non-occupation as well as occupation seem to provide a schematic archaeology by which to begin again.*[2]

The *Large Glass* is rigorously demarcated into an upper domain of the four-dimensional 'stripping' electromagnetic bride/virgin. The semi-frosted horizontal window of the *withDrawing Room* reminds us of the bride's Milky Way and its Draught Pistons that feature in the top pane of the *Large Glass*. The lower pane features the three-dimensional, nine malic liveried masturbators, and few elements have the ability to cross from one terrain to the other. But in Diller + Scofidio's Capp Street installation, the *Large Glass*, while also evoked by the proliferation of implied boundaries (dotted lines, walls and thresholds), are invariably compromised by objects and views that transverse its mostly blank spaces. These are punctuated, most memorably, by a tethered cathode ray tube, stripped out of its momentarily fashionable carapace. Perhaps it is there as a constant reminder of the media's role in self-surveillance, telling us what to think as the purveyor of the party line, a nuance of George Orwell's *1984* and our own computer-mediated and tranquillized existence.

Diller + Scofidio's spaces at Capp Street are another manifestation of the pristine, reflective 'dissecting-table' of the Comte de Lautréamont's – and Surrealism's – definition of 'beauty',[3] where objects and bodies are caught in the act of metamorphosis, a stage on which spatial alchemy acts, provoked by changing technologies and new, invisible, juiceless desires.

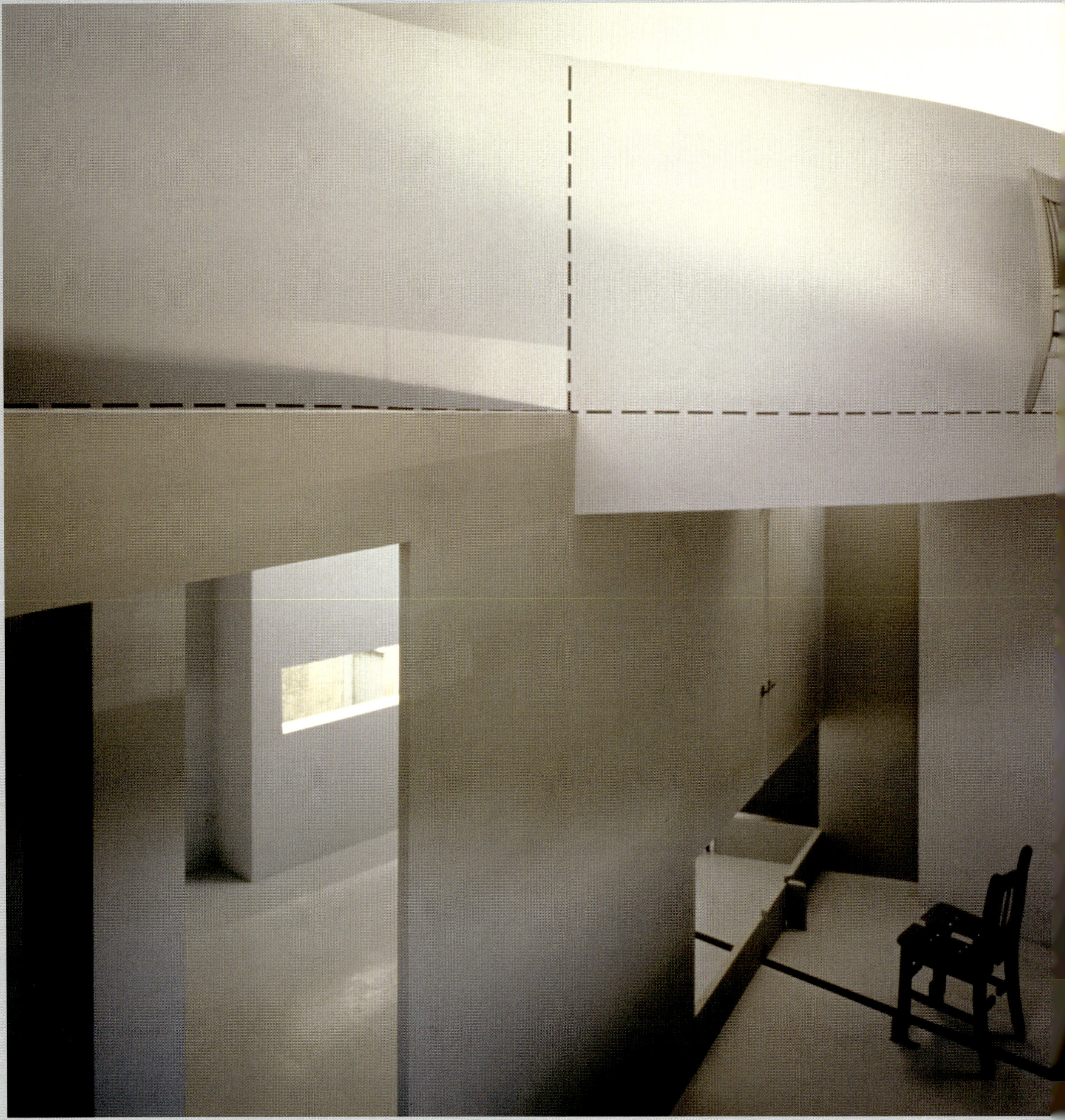

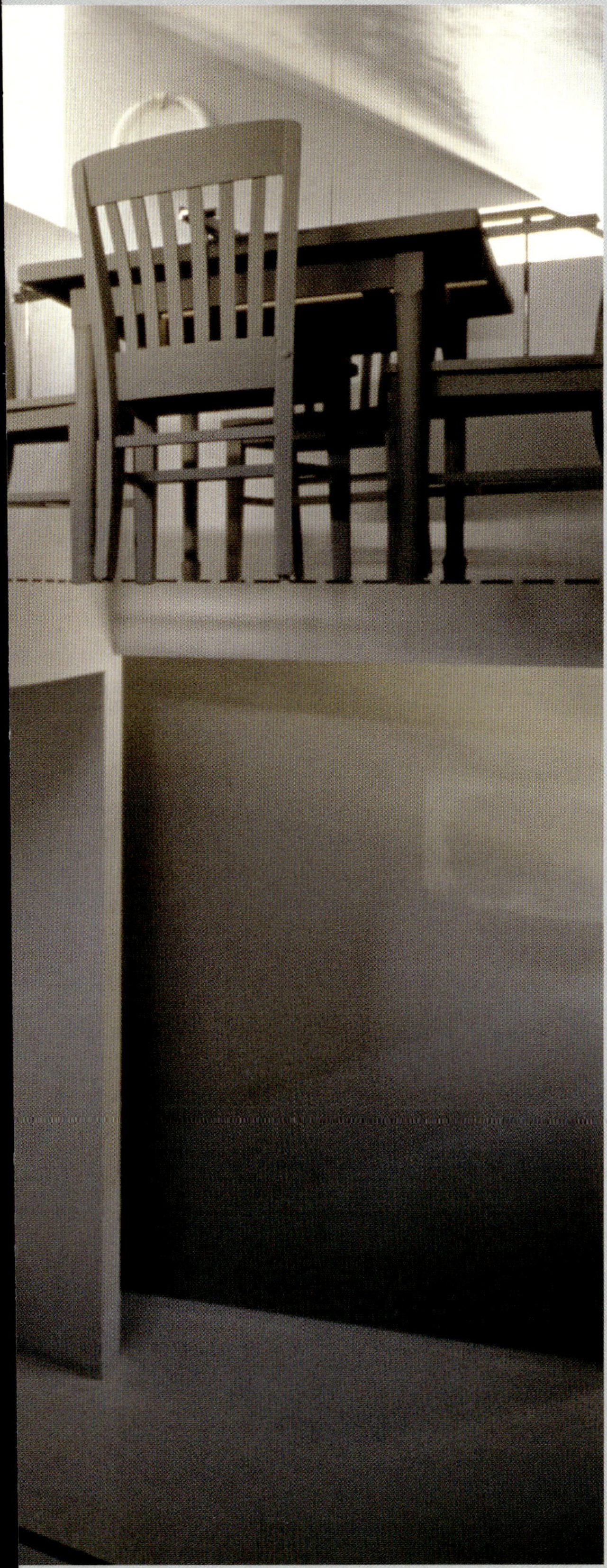

←
Overview
with
bisected
chair
and
second-level
dining
room
set.

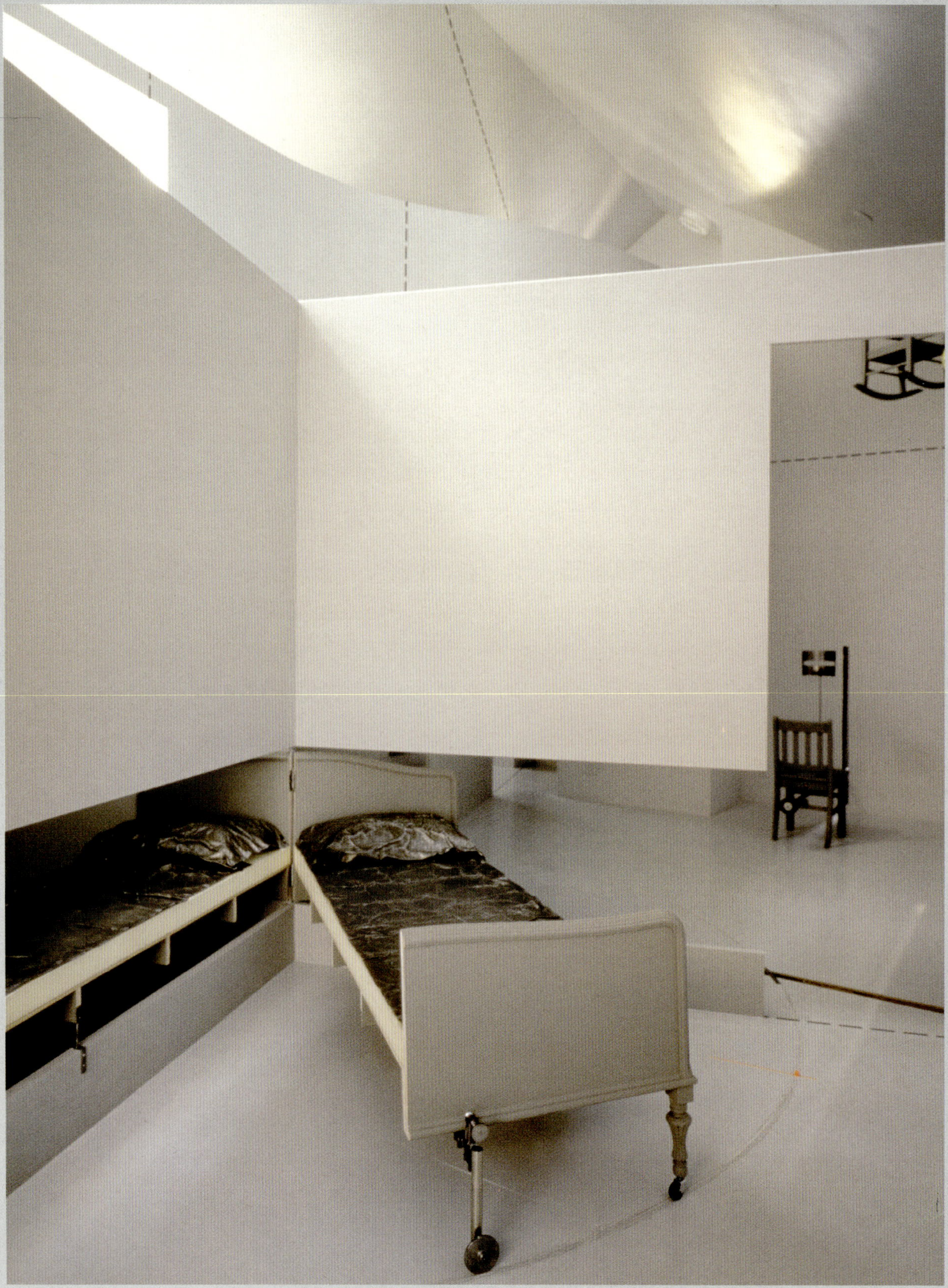

← View of a bed radius.

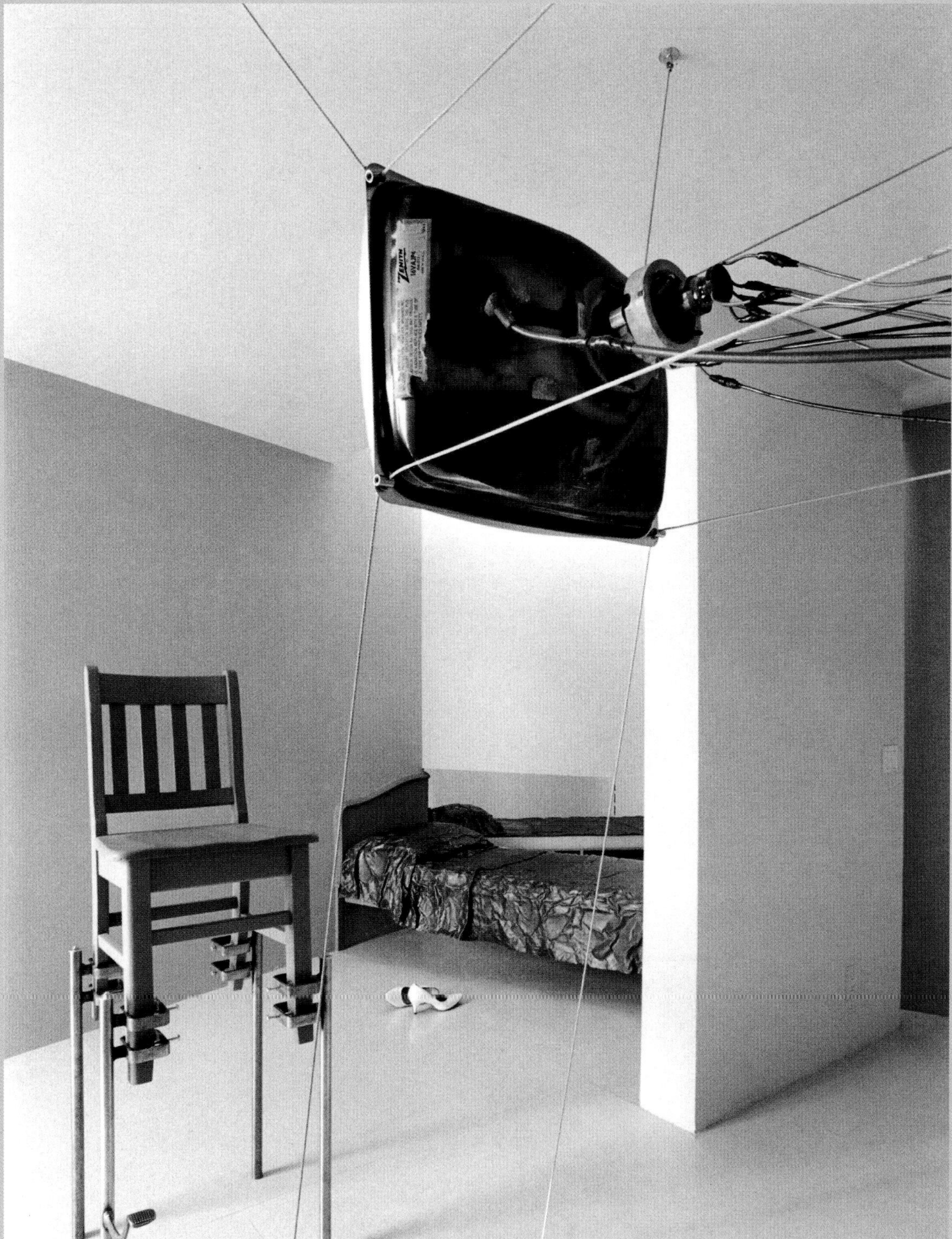

→ Detail of chair on stilts and hanging monitor.

And tell of the women I have seen bathing in the pool of a garden and who sometimes – it is said – invite the stranger to disrobe with them and chase them in the water. But with all this, I would not be telling you the city's true essence; for while the description of Anastasia awakens desires one at a time only to force you to stifle them, when you are in the heart of Anastasia one morning your desires waken all at once and surround you. The city appears to you as a whole where no desire is lost and of which you are a part, and since it enjoys everything you do not enjoy, you can do nothing but inhabit this desire and be content.

Italo Calvino, 'Invisible Cities', 1974[1]

[The] city inhabitants create an exquisitely complex geometry, a geography passing beyond the natural, to become metaphysical only described in terms of music or abstract physics: nothing else makes sense of relationships between roads, rails, waterways, subways, sewers, tunnels, bridges, viaducts, aqueducts, cables, between every possible kind of intersection.

Michael Moorcock, 'Mother London', 1988[2]

THE GREAT TRANSPARENT CITY

CHAPTER III

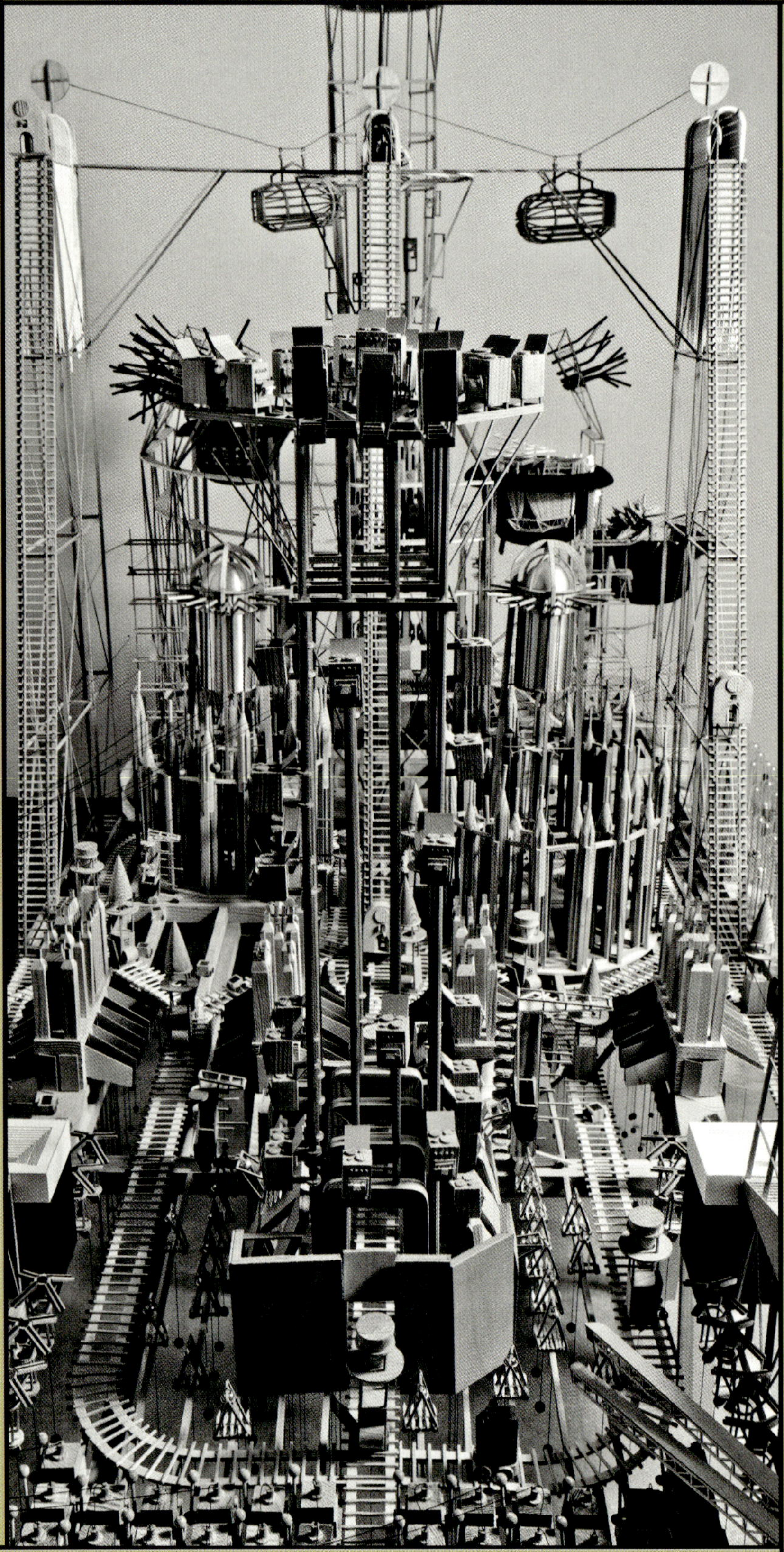

In the 1920s and 1930s, if any city could claim the monarchy of Surrealism, then that city was Paris. Its boulevards, cafés and salons played host to the Surrealists' meetings, and its streets, parks and structures excited their imagination. Paris was their muse; soluble, melting into air, pungent in its vitality and its ability to throw up the marvellous in all its forms. This erotic, enchanting intoxication of the urban, its lives and the amalgam of flotsam and jetsam it conjured up (that so fascinated and inspired Kurt Schwitters earlier in the century) was the grist to their creative mill.

The city itself is a wild engine of chance, an opium-like storm of connections. The metabolic rate of the city defies the simple logic of humankind with its rationalism and pragmatism. Hierarchies are blown wide open. The Surrealists were drawn to this semiotic turmoil, often amorously: the curve of an architrave, the sublime sinuous navigation of a crowded pavement (passing lives, furtive glances) or the battle of nature to re-establish its hold over the realm of the artificial were all inspirational.

For the Surrealists, the small museum of fears and joys and manipulatable poetic realities of the house are writ large in the city. The city is uncontrollable, far more compelling and dangerous – an adventure of mind-boggling proportions. Walter Benjamin describes this attraction to the city as an extension of the home in relation to writer and Proto-Surrealist Charles Baudelaire's practice of roaming the city streets, observing and seeking inspiration:

> **The street becomes a dwelling place for the flâneur; he is as much at home among house façades as a citizen is within his four walls. To him, a shiny enamel shop sign is at least as good a wall ornament as an oil painting is to a bourgeois in his living room. Buildings' walls are the desk against which he presses his notebooks; newsstands are his libraries; café terraces are the balconies from which he looks down on his household after his work is done. That life in all its variety and inexhaustible wealth of permutations can thrive only among the gray cobblestones.[3]**

The activities of the flâneur, still with a faint whiff of those of the dilettante, were a precursor to the Surrealists' walks into the psychic labyrinths of Paris. For André Breton and his colleagues, their search was for the same phenomena they found so appealing in the paintings of Giorgio de Chirico: the extreme juxtapositions of objects, their scale and combination of aesthetics, chance occurrence, impossible vistas (both mentally and physically) and desire creating uncanny situations.

The city can be read like a trillion parallel texts completed and composed in cahoots with the viewer. The great mother/lover, the Surrealist city is an analogue computer, churning out combination after combination of objects. Humanity's passions nurtured and sustained by the flow of time, a succession of lives and capital across the city. This hallucinogenic space of reflection, poesis and semiotics, providing a cornucopia of new images and concepts, was complicit in the drafting of the powerful Surrealist city literature composed by Breton and Louis Aragon. Their books are love letters to Paris. Aragon was first to recognize the surreal fertility of the city in his *Paris Peasant* (1924),[4] the narrative of which involves a visit to the Parc des Buttes-Chaumont. As the contemporary landscape architect and academic Fernando Magallanes has written:

For Aragon, Parc des Buttes-Chaumont was a site filled with abstract fictive possibilities and more concrete visible objects, such as oddly placed Greek follies, engineered bridges, and reconfigured artificial landscapes containing magical and psychoanalytical meanings. The animist qualities found in the park objects, the deaths produced from numerous suicide jumps off a bridge in the park, and its tormented quarried past were magical to the writers in reconfiguring a surreal place.[5]

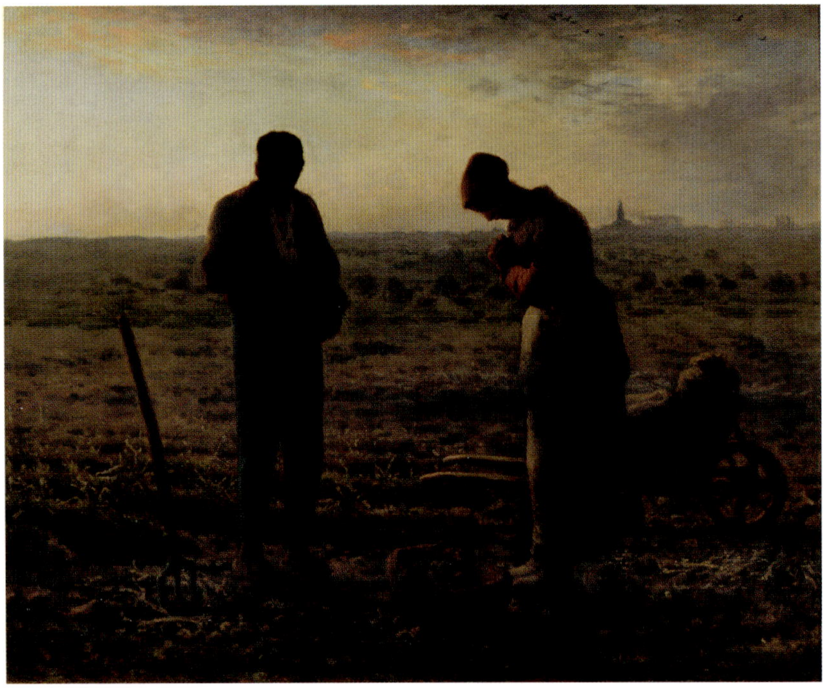

↑ **Jean-François Millet**

The Angelus

1859

Breton contributed to this new-found urban oasis of possibility with his book *Nadja* (1928),[6] which describes 'André's' perambulations around Paris in search of intellectual, creative and emotional stimulation. He would know when he found it. Casting himself into the vortex of the city's storm, he finds Nadja, the object of his desire and his interpreter in this unfamiliar terrain. Nadja, like the city through her eyes, is otherworldly. We find out she is mentally ill, an idiot savant, sometimes cogent, sometimes delirious. Latterly she melts away, and the narrative is sustained by her absence; the prose, maybe even more surreal, defined by her loss. The last sentence of the book was to become a Surrealist saying: 'Beauty will be convulsive or will not be at all.'

In his seminal essay 'Soluble City' (1978),[7] Roger Cardinal defined six Surrealist readings of the city: as a dream, as a love affair, as a palimpsest, as a poetic text, as a psychic labyrinth and as a system of signs. These are not mutually exclusive, but simultaneous and concurrent. Like quantum fields of events, everything exists at once as potential readings until it condenses, momentarily provoked by an observer, read and captured as a trace of another reality where the familiar rules are not obeyed.

Surreal Cognition and the Paucity of Maps

The simultaneity of cities, their multivalency and the nesting of one within the other (the other determined by the observer) is the subject of Italian writer Italo Calvino's *Invisible Cities* (1972). Highly influential among contemporary architects searching for alternative ways of reading and designing cities, such as C. J. Lim (see pages 150–57), the book's opening narrative tells us that these are the thirteenth-century explorer Marco Polo's reminiscences of all of the cities he has visited on his travels, as told to Mongolian emperor Kublai Khan. In Calvino's book, however, Polo's cities are really one city: Venice. Through these tales, the rich tapestry of the history of this place and its society could be ascertained: 'Only in Marco Polo's accounts was Kublai Khan able to discern, through the walls and towers destined to crumble, the tracery of a pattern so subtle it could escape the termites' gnawing'.[8] Calvino describes these multiple cities as hidden cities, trading cities, cities of desire, continuous cities, thin cities, cities of memory, cities of the dead, cities of signs, cities of names and cities of eyes.

The Surrealists' disregard for standard methods of measurement outlined in the previous chapter is also reflected in their distrust of maps and plans. The city is such a tumult of objects, vectors and humanity that no map can be drawn that encapsulates its complexity, speedy metabolism and multiscalar beauty. A map or plan is a method of exclusion, of simplification and often-intentional erasure. My *Map of the Surrealist City* is an attempt to create a drawing that is a summary of all the scales, concepts and ideas that embody the Surrealist conception of the urban. Some ideas of the fluctuating city ambiences and hybrid functionality of the urban fabric were taken up by the Situationists and their leader Guy Debord during the late 1950s. Their work consisted mainly of polemical far-left political texts, however, the Dutch artist Constant Nieuwenhuys did produce *New Babylon* (1959–74), a drawn and modelled but ill-defined and ambiguous scenario for a city. These notions, and particularly Debord's idea of the 'spectacle' and the capitalist consumption and subversion of all outside it for profit, have been reinvigorated today by our all-consuming electronic presences and personas as we derive our worldviews and environments – real and imagined.

Letting the city throw up situations of surreality and being alert to them was too passive a position for Salvador Dalí. By the early 1930s he was experimenting with a much more proactive process of interpretation of his surroundings, a system of deranged intuition he called the 'paranoiac-critical method'. He began to muse on events before and after those of the Catholic man and woman praying in a field portrayed in the French artist Jean-François Millet's *The Angelus*, a painting that he maintained had spooked him since childhood.

Dalí's interpretation of the work is a frenzy of death, praying mantises, penile erections and exotic sexual positions. It certainly spread a Surrealist new light on Millet's sombre painting and provided Dalí with a mental machine with which to make new work. He

> showed that an artist could obtain spectacular results by the controlled and lucid simulation of mental disease. Paranoia is an interpretative disorder with a rational basis, which, if skillfully mastered by the painter, will allow him to reveal the double significance of things... the painter will act and think as if under the influence of a psychic disorder, while remaining fully aware of what is going on.[9]

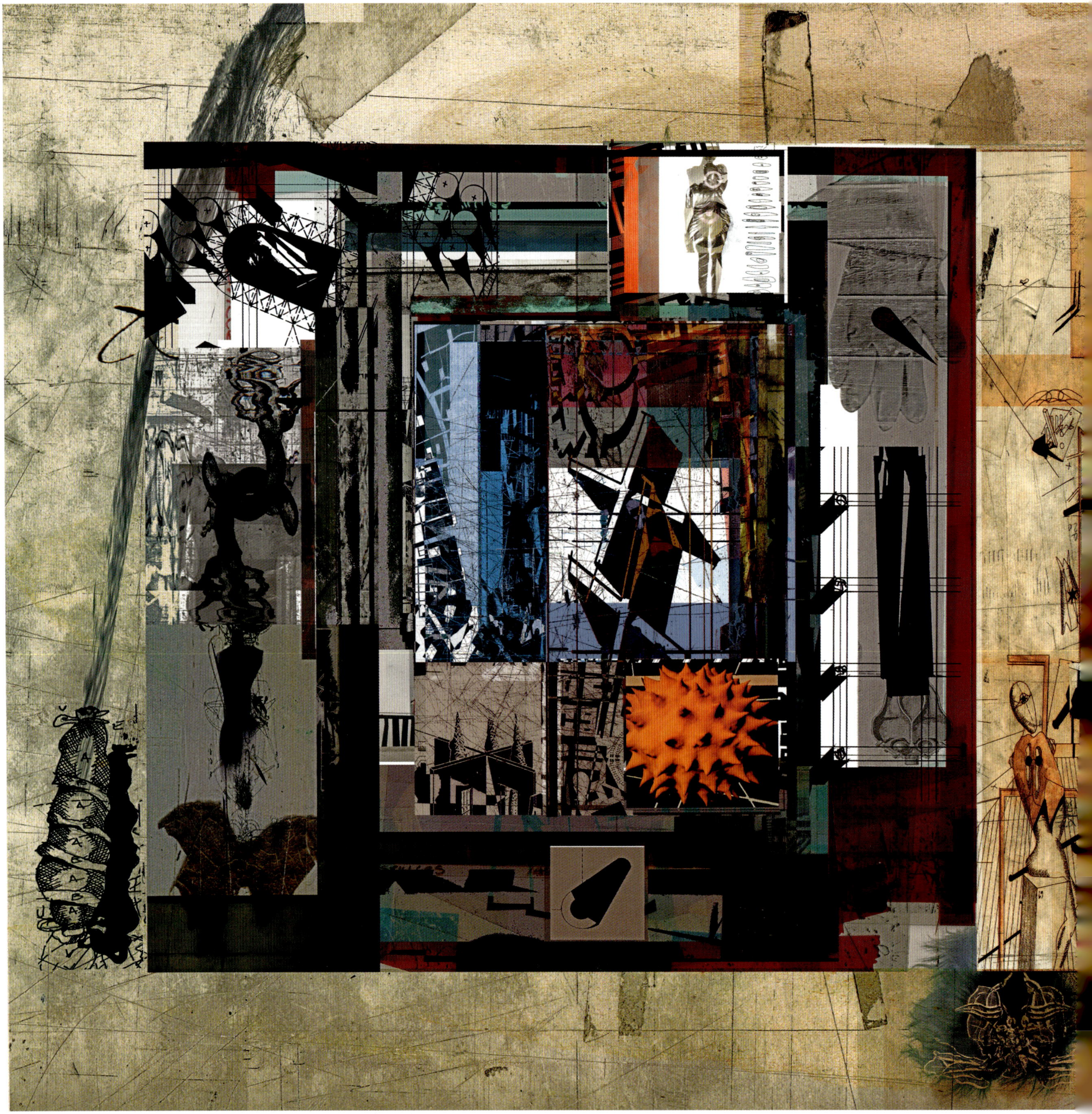

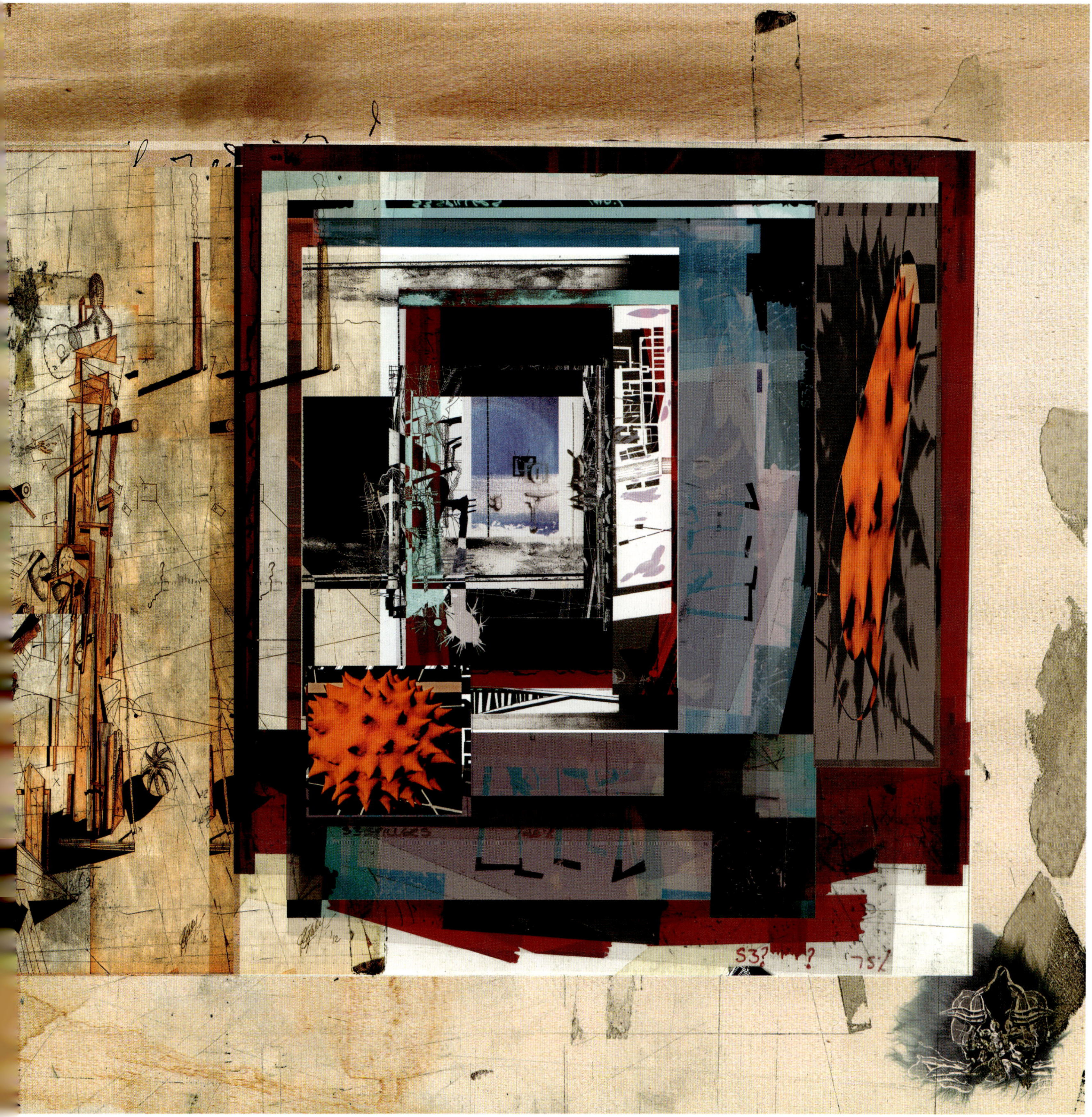

↑

Neil Spiller • Map of the Surrealist City

2013

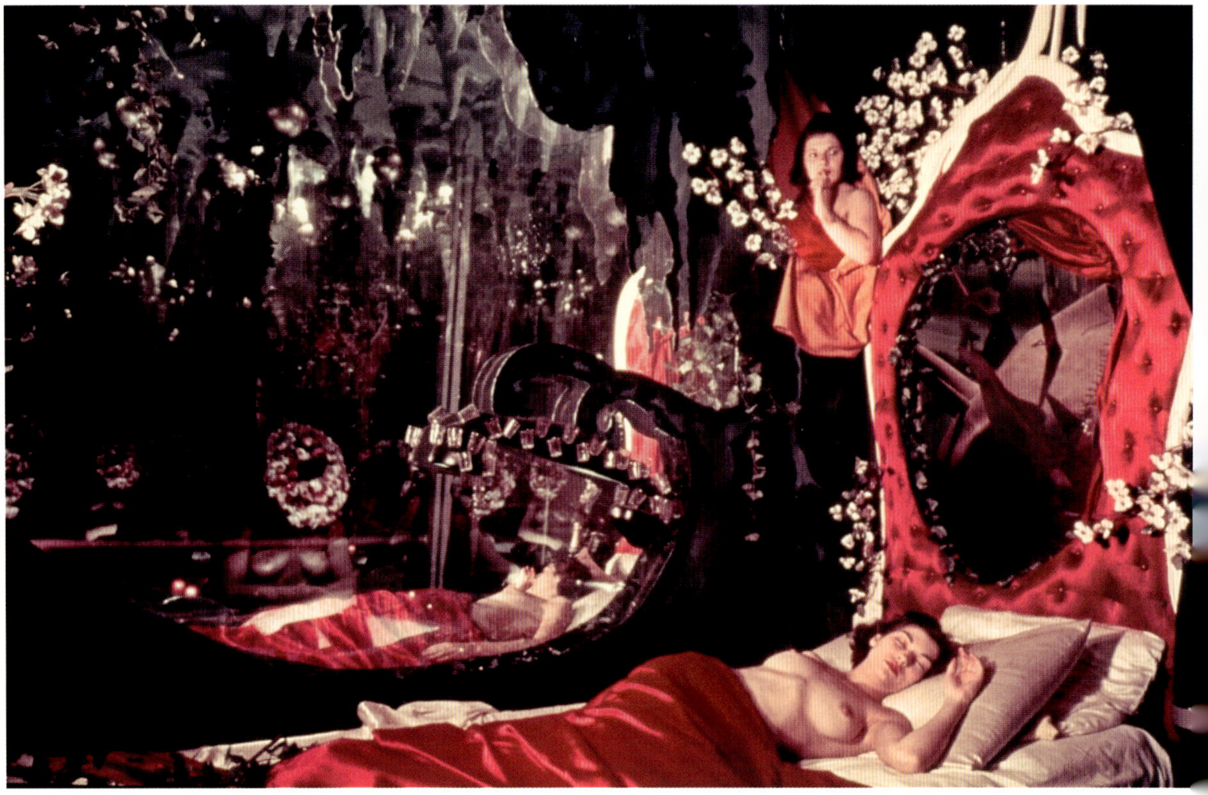

The maturation of this idea coincided with Dalí's first visit to New York and his realization that it was the Surrealist city par excellence, and a more than worthy successor to Paris. As the Dutch architect Rem Koolhaas commented in 1978: 'In the mid-30s both Salvador Dalí and Le Corbusier – they hate each other – visit New York for the first time. Both conquer it. Dalí conceptually through interpretive appropriation...Le Corbusier by proposing to literally destroy it'[10] through the position to lay it to waste and develop a more logical (in his mind) city of towers.

When Dalí first arrived in New York by sea in 1935, he managed to persuade the ship's chef to bake him a loaf 2.5m (8ft) in length. During the press frenzy that ensued on docking in New York, Dalí was unsettled when nobody asked about the loaf with which he posed: 'the disconcerter disconcerted,' as Koolhaas noted, 'Dalí's first discovery that in Manhattan Surrealism is invisible. Reinforced Dough is just another false fact among the multitudes.'[11]

The 1938 'Exposition Internationale du Surréalisme', in Paris, with its boulevard of mannequins (by artists such as Marcel Duchamp, André Masson, Dalí and Joan Miró) and Dalí's *Rainy Taxi* (see page 50), was a huge success, and efforts were made to recreate Surrealist attractions in other arenas. One of these initiatives resulted in Dalí's only fully-fledged building, the Dream of Venus pavilion, at the 1939 New York World's Fair. Dream of Venus was remarkable, combining the plasticity of form reminiscent of the Catalan Art Nouveau architect Antoni Gaudí with the mad symbolism of Surrealism, which resulted in an external aesthetic that had much in common with beach debris. It was a microcosmic city of Surrealist ideas. Dalí described the entrance sequence of the building in familiar Dalínian hyperbolic terms:

> A small freestanding building, bristling with appendages and cast in crepuscular light, rises under a swag of red velvet. It is an architecture of accretion, a pile of pink and white stucco sculpted into a profusion of niches and protuberances. Framed within its façade is a giant image of Venus: Botticelli's breezy nude, blown up to billboard height. At her feet, real women wearing late-1930s bathing suits and beach jackets make ballyhoo by waving bamboo fishing rods. Catching your attention, they reel you towards their grotto.[12]

Even this fails to adequately describe the pavilion and its special place in the history of Surrealist architecture. The building is seedy and inviting at the same time. The façade is a vertical landscape of indentations and holes.

↖→ **Salvador Dalí** • Dream of Venus
photographed by Eric Schaal
New York World's Fair
1939

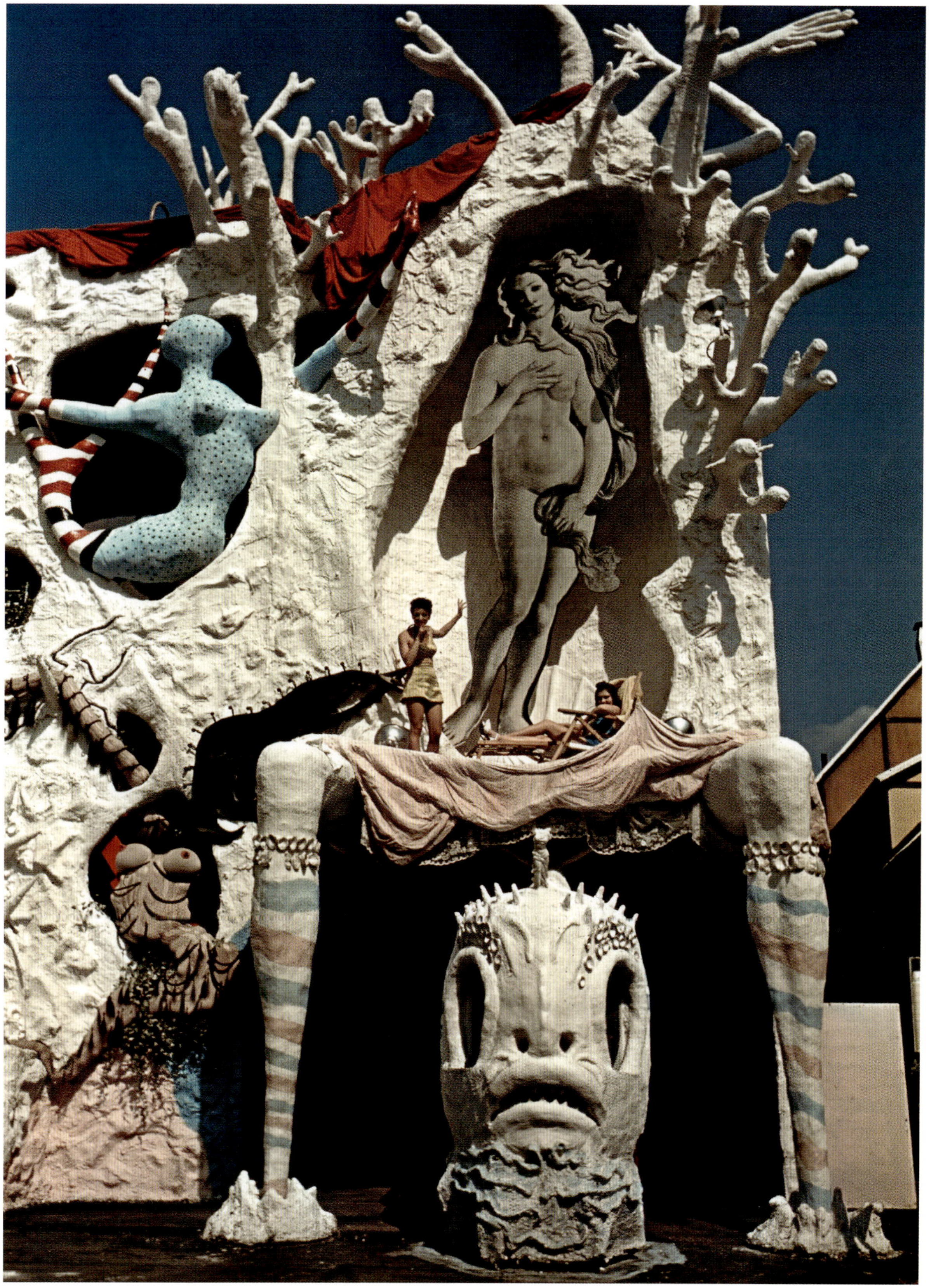

In one niche is an enlarged reproduction of the Italian painter Sandro Botticelli's *Birth of Venus* (mid-1480s); in other holes are half-hidden plaster torsos of mermaids with deformed and prominent breasts. A millipede crawls across the surface, disappearing into yet another crevice. The skyline of the building is punctured by crutches, alien hands and what might be branches, baguettes or shaved cacti.

One naturally enters the pavilion between what look like an old person's legs. The ticket booth between them is in the form of a fish. The viewer enters the first chamber, which includes a huge vitrine filled with water. Within this aqueous environment, gravity is denied. Telephones float on their cables, chains sway like seaweed, similar to Aragon's descriptions of the Parisian cane shop (see page 28). There is also a mummified cow, typewriters, and a piano with a keyboard cast in feminine form. All these pieces are set against a De Chirico-inspired backdrop with penitent caryatids, a procession of bones/beans and Vesuvius erupting on the horizon. The live action happens in the foreground, where women in stockings and fishnet bikini tops swim past.

Shuffling into the next space, the viewer immediately becomes aware of a massive, long bed. On it is a sleeping woman. A second, watchful woman emerges from the headboard, beckoning the crowd to be quiet. In the large bedside mirror, another, topless woman appears with her head swathed in a wreath of flowers. The bedclothes are topped with hot coals, lobsters and bottles of champagne. This is no doubt an allusion to erotic dream space. Above the crowd, the ceiling is covered with open Lautréamontian umbrellas.

The viewer is then ushered into a corridor. As in the Parisian Exposition the previous year, the two tableaux in this linear space feature mannequins, one sitting with its torso and head replaced by a bird cage, the other standing in a parody of the agonies of St Sebastian, covered in shot glasses with drinking straws mimicking the arrows stuck in the saint's flesh. Soft, melting watches, umbrellas and flaming giraffes, and a diver's helmet (a memory of London) are all featured among other paraphernalia of Dalínian symbolism.

The final chamber features another *Rainy Taxi*. The occupants are a mannequin of a dominatrix and another of Christopher Columbus. The taxi is draped with ivy and more topless women. Dream of Venus is a miniature Surrealist city. It is both interior and exterior, exploring and quoting Surrealist mythologies and analogies.

War and the Search for New Mythologies

At the height of war in 1942, while in exile on the American continent and writing his 'Prolegomena to a Third Surrealist Manifesto or Not', Breton signalled a new avenue of exploration for the Surrealists and their art. Under the subheading 'The Great Transparent Ones', he wrote the following:

> **Man is perhaps not the center, the cynosure of the universe. One can go so far as to believe that there exists above him, on the animal scale, beings whose behavior is as strange to him as his may be to the mayfly or the whale. Nothing necessarily stands in the way of these creatures' being able to completely escape man's sensory system of references through a camouflage of whatever sort one cares to imagine...a new myth? Must these beings be convinced that they result from a mirage or must they be given a chance to show themselves?**[13]

The prescience of this statement and the positing of a new mythology through the search for the 'Transparent' ones allowed Surrealism to embrace the invisible and to bridge the gap between the twentieth and twenty-first centuries, which was particularly apposite as virtuality and cyberspace began to evolve.

However, this new techno-surreal vitality came slowly, particularly in relation to the architecture of the city. After 1939, Surrealism's engagement with the city became more tenuous. The rebuilding of Europe after the Second World War and the prevailing orthodoxy of Le Corbusian Modernism, as purveyed by the many less talented disciples of 'The Crow' (as he was sometimes known due to the literal translation of his chosen name) and the almost Jesuit religious fervour with which they went about its prosecution, had no truck with anything that did not masquerade as scientific and rational.

It was the beginning of the 1960s before voices began to be heard in relation to the historical poverty of the Modernist conception of the city. The megastructural movement, predicated on the design of new cities as vast machines/systems with expendable elements, pluggable, relocatable and playful, was an alternative to the white, clean, neatness of Modernism, but essentially even more anti-surreal, where everything that use had abandoned was discarded. These were machine cities for John McHale's expendable 'Ikonic' people (see page 53), which strode over the landscape nullifying the genius loci, cognizant of nothing but their own podded systems, conduits and structural engineering – bigger and looking more like machines for living in.

In 1966, the Italian Aldo Rossi in his seminal book about urbanism, *The Architecture of the City*, contradicted the prevailing notions of Modernist urban planning and the nature of the contemporary city. The republication of the

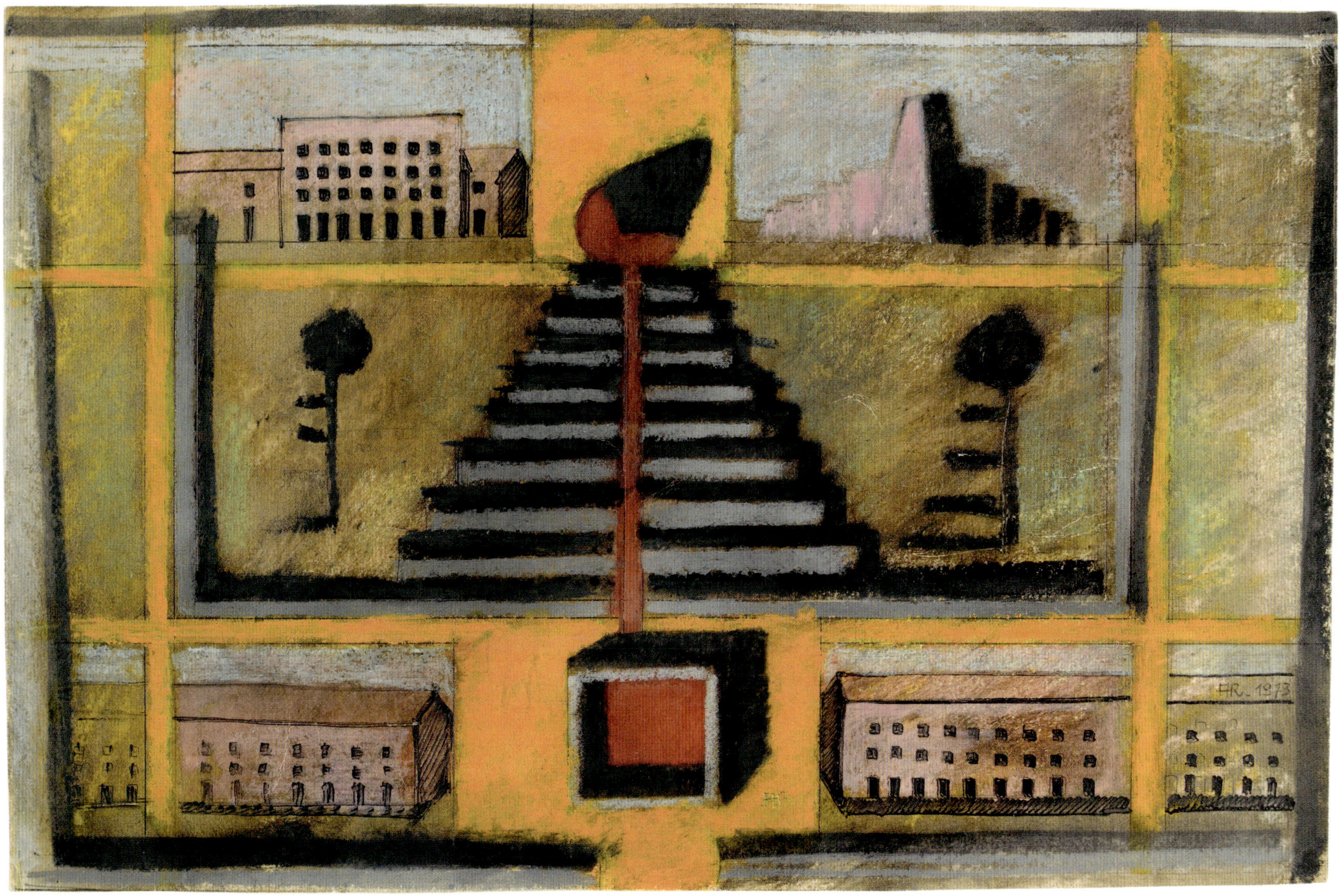

↑

Aldo Rossi • The Game of Death

1973

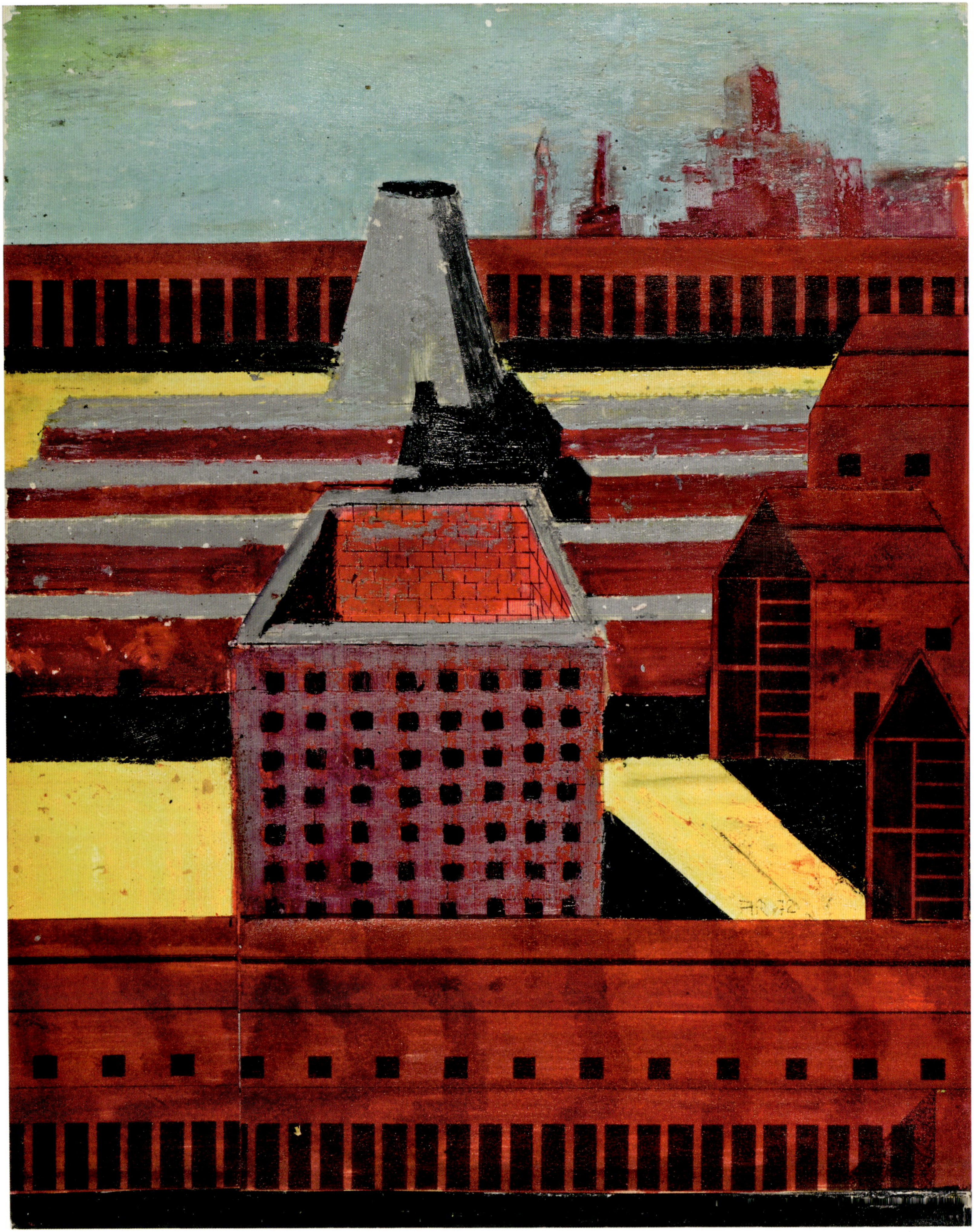

←

Aldo Rossi

Study for the Modena Cemetery

1972

book in 1982, illustrating its appeal to a wider audience, is an indication of how these ideas had taken root in the intervening decade and a half. Rossi evokes the history of place, its specialness of site and the occupations of its inhabitants over time as clear drivers for urban form:

> The city is not by nature a creation that can be reduced to a single basic idea. This is true both for the modern metropolis and for the concept of the city as a sum of the parts, of quarters and districts that are highly diverse and differentiated in their sociological and formal characteristics.'[14]

Also in 1966 the American architect Robert Venturi wrote *Complexity and Contradiction in Architecture*, a vanguard publication that had started to suggest, very politely, that in the wake of Modernism architects had forgotten something crucial to the provision of successful architecture – the value of expedient messiness:

> Architects can no longer afford to be intimidated by the puritanically moral language of orthodox Modern architecture. I like elements that are hybrid rather than 'pure,' compromising rather than 'clean,' distorted rather than 'straightforward,' ambiguous rather than 'articulated,' perverse as well as impersonal.... I am for messy vitality over obvious unity. I include non sequitur and proclaim the duality.[15]

Rossi's interest in the city was to see it as a temporal continuity of numerous moments, changes and new articulations; in effect the poetic everyday text of the city of the Surrealists. Indeed, Rossi developed a style very much influenced by the enigmatic paintings of De Chirico. His architectural tour de force is his San Cataldo Cemetery in Modena, Italy (1971), which remains, to this day, only partially built. The full scheme, however, is a series of simply composed iconic fragments creating an enigmatic city of the dead: a perforated cube (central ceremonial space); diminishing rows of linear ossuaries; enclosing runs of niches; and the frustum (truncated cone) chimney commemorating a communal grave that echoes the landscape of the region. With these simple elements and careful cutting of openings for light and the movement of people, Rossi created spaces that resonate with the solemnity of death and bereavement: the moment of mortal departure expressed in Metaphysical surreal architecture.

Calvino's 'Laudomia', as chronicled in his *Invisible Cities,* might also be understood as a description of a place similar to Rossi's cemetery:

> every city has at its side another city whose inhabitants are called by the same names: it is the Laudomia of the dead, the cemetery.... The properties of the double city are well known.... On fine afternoons the living population pays a visit to the dead and they decipher their own names on their stone slabs: like the city of the living, this other city communicates a history of toil, anger, illusions, emotions; only here all has become necessary, divorced from chance, categorized, set in order. And to feel sure of itself, the living Laudomia has to seek in the Laudomia of the dead the explanation of itself, even at the risk of finding more there, or less: explanations for more than one Laudomia, for different cities.[16]

By 1972, having joined forces with Denise Scott Brown and Steven Izenour, Venturi had been learning from Las Vegas and determining new urban forms demanded by cars and their speed, by advertising and by the expediencies of gambling, hotels and shows:

> The patterns of parking lines give direction much as the paving patterns, curbs, borders, and tapis vert give direction in Versailles; grids of lamp posts substitute for obelisks, rows of urns and statues as points of identity and continuity in the vast space. But it is the highway signs, through their sculptural forms or pictorial silhouettes, their particular positions in space,

their inflected shapes, and their graphic meanings, that identify and unify the megatexture. They make verbal and symbolic connections through space, communicating a complexity of meanings through hundreds of associations in a few seconds from far away. Symbol dominates space. Architecture is not enough. Because the spatial relationships are made by symbols more than by forms, architecture in this landscape becomes symbol in space rather than form in space. Architecture defines very little: The big sign and the little building is the rule of Route 66.[17]

This text, often taken as a harbinger of the architectural postmodern, while not explicitly a surreal one, starts to analyse the surreal extremes that technology and semiotics are taken to in the contemporary city, and articulates that speed and electronics are at its core.

The Architectural Rebirth of Surrealism of the Late 1970s

In 1978, numerous events conspired to create a Surrealist alignment of considerable rejuvenating power. The first of these was a continuation of preoccupations similar to Venturi's architectural contradictions and Rossi's temporal cities: the publication of Colin Rowe's and Fred Koetter's *Collage City*. This book proved to be highly influential. Like Rossi and Venturi, the architects and educators Rowe and Koetter were concerned by the prevailing Modernist ideas of city planning to undertake a vast wiping out of all that had gone before, and instead posited a city of collage that rejoiced in history and the continuity and invention of architectural and urban expediency. To them, it was just that – the traditional city's clash of form, use, architectural language and architectural style – that gave cities their unique identity and pleasure. They also recognized that these collisions are not just formal, but, in a hint of Surrealist thought, psychological too:

To move now from the consideration of a collision of physical constructs to the further consideration of collision, this time on a psychological and to some degree, a temporal plane. The city of collusive intentions, however much it may be presentable in terms of pragmatics, is evidently also an icon, and a political icon signifying a range of change in attitudes relating to historical process and social change. So much should be obvious. But, if Collision City, as so far discussed has only incidentally betrayed an iconic intention, questions of symbolic purpose or function begin now increasingly to rise to the surface.[18]

Another element in this fortuitous collision of publications was a double issue of *Architectural Design (AD)* magazine, guest-edited by Czech architectural historian, theorist and teacher Dalibor Vesely. Entitled *Architecture and Surrealism*, this publication was important for many reasons. Firstly, it coincided with a large exhibition at the Hayward Gallery in London on 'Dada and Surrealism Reviewed', which was, incidentally, reviewed in the same *AD* by Surrealist, collector, historian and jazz singer George Melly. Perhaps the most important essays in the issue were Roger Cardinal's 'Soluble City' (as referred to earlier), and two by the young, and future architectural megastars Rem Koolhaas and Bernard Tschumi, here previewing thoughts that would make clear their lineage to Surrealist protocols of engagement of the city and its creative power.

Koolhaas's essay,[19] a version of which would appear later the same year in his book *Delirious New York*, was entitled 'Biuer! Ai bring ou surrealism aulredi meni pipoul in niu york jove bin infected bai zi laifquiving and marvelous sors of surrealism' – a reference to a phonetic sentence written for Dalí to enable him to announce his arrival in the city in 1935. It is essentially the contrasting stories of New York's acceptance or rejection of Dalí's paranoid critical paronoiac-critical method and Le Corbusier's urban visions. In *Delirious New York*, Koolhaas interpolates this episode in a book-length soliloquy to the Big Apple that focuses on the city's creative, surreal presence. For him, New York, the Surrealist city par excellence, was a treasure trove of urban conditions, each of the urban blocks within its ubiquitous grid an oasis of history, of city prototype, a social mixer and condenser. Walking down a street or avenue is a voyage, propelled by the winds of chance, of fantasy and inspiration – a delirious cornucopia of forms, memories and mythologies. Every skyscraper is an experiment in vertical living and mixed function, predicated on structural pyrotechnics. New York is portrayed as a broadcast city, where towers fornicate, forever mixing their aberrant architectural genetics. The city is a labyrinth of connections above and below ground populated by architectural chimeras, and its fleeting messages always dissipated in a variety of media – and fast. The book's most memorable illustrations are the surreally beautiful paintings by Madelon Vriesendorp (see pages 137–41), whose subjects include these post-coital skyscrapers.

Tschumi's essay in the *AD* issue, 'Architecture and Its Double', is mostly taken up by a thorough exploration of Surrealist architectural precedents such as French postman Ferdinand Cheval's Palais Idéal at Hauterives in southeastern France, begun in 1879 (see pages 10–11), Surrealist performance and exhibition design and establishing Georges Bataille as inherently involved with subverting

↓

Madelon Vriesendorp

Flagrant delit, Delirious New York

1975

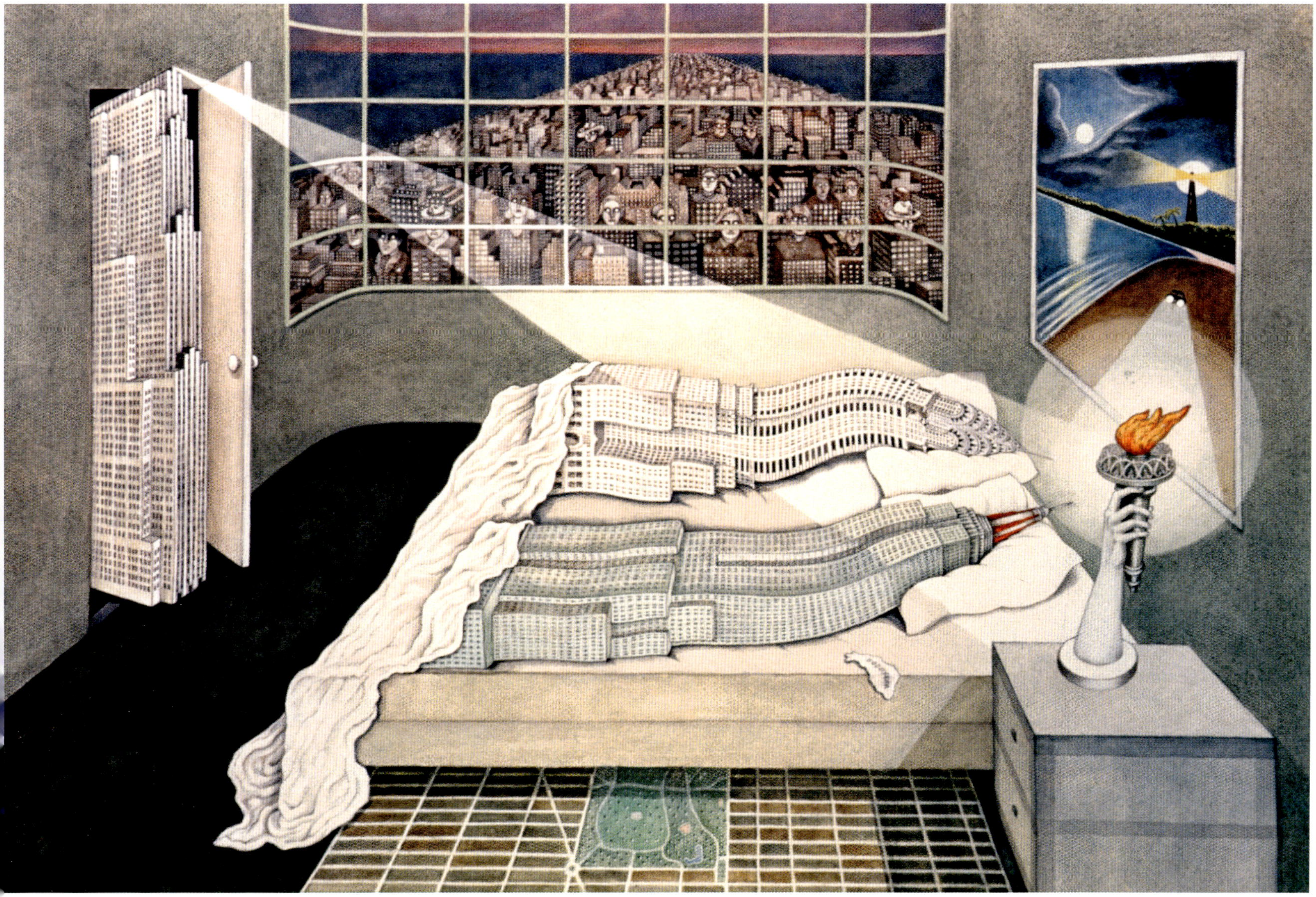

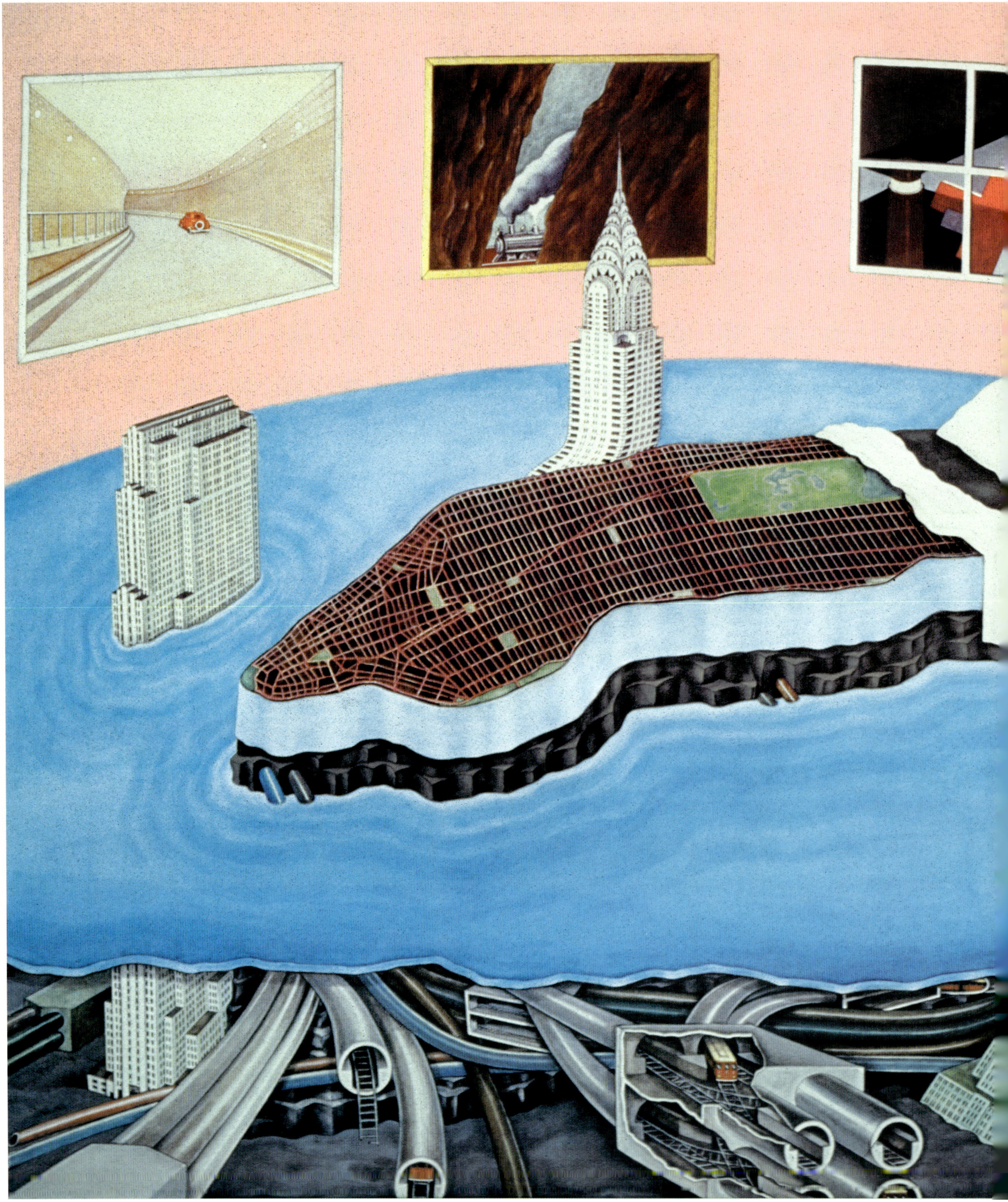

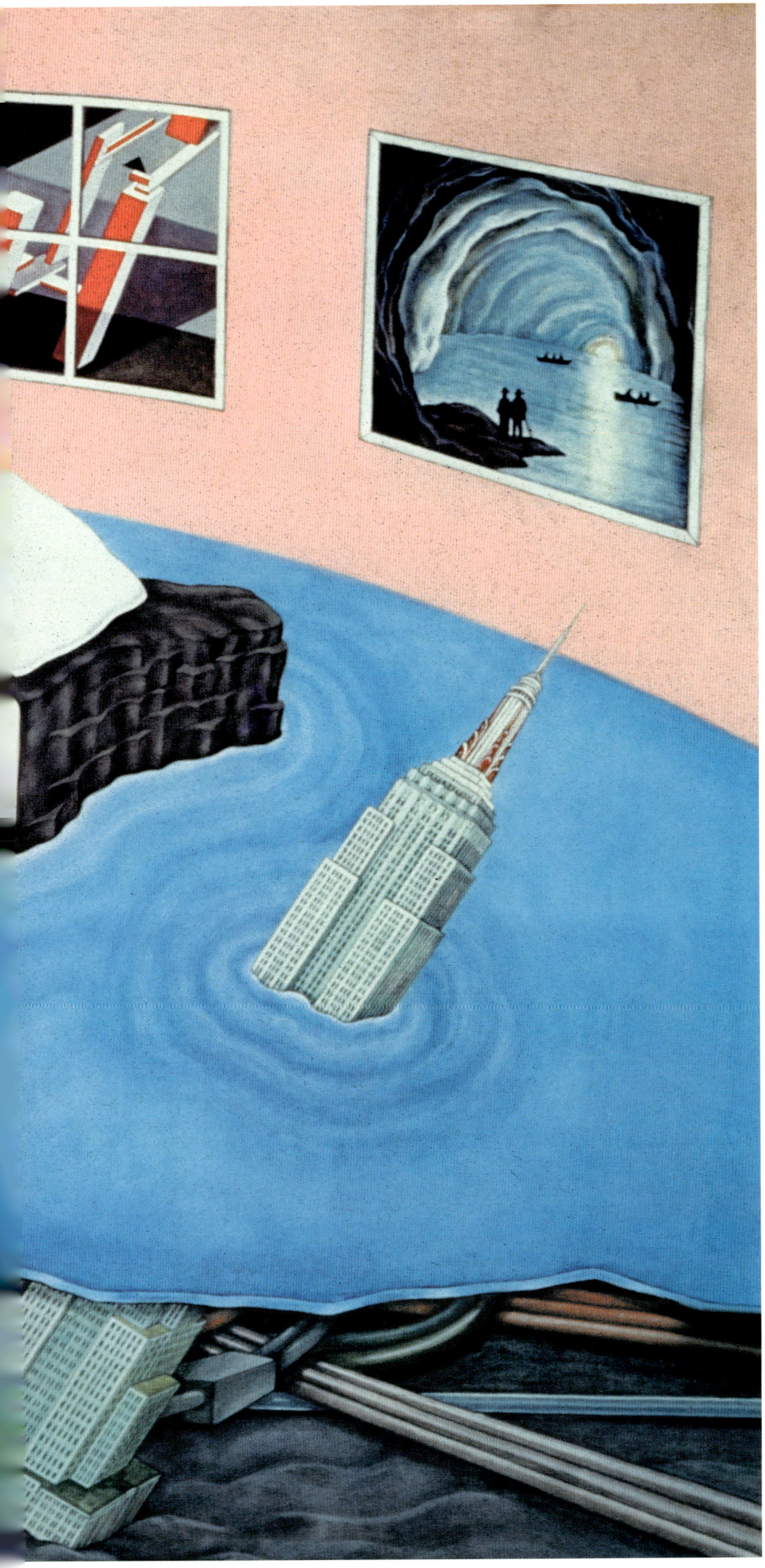

← **Madelon Vriesendorp**
Freud Unlimited,
Delirious New York
1972

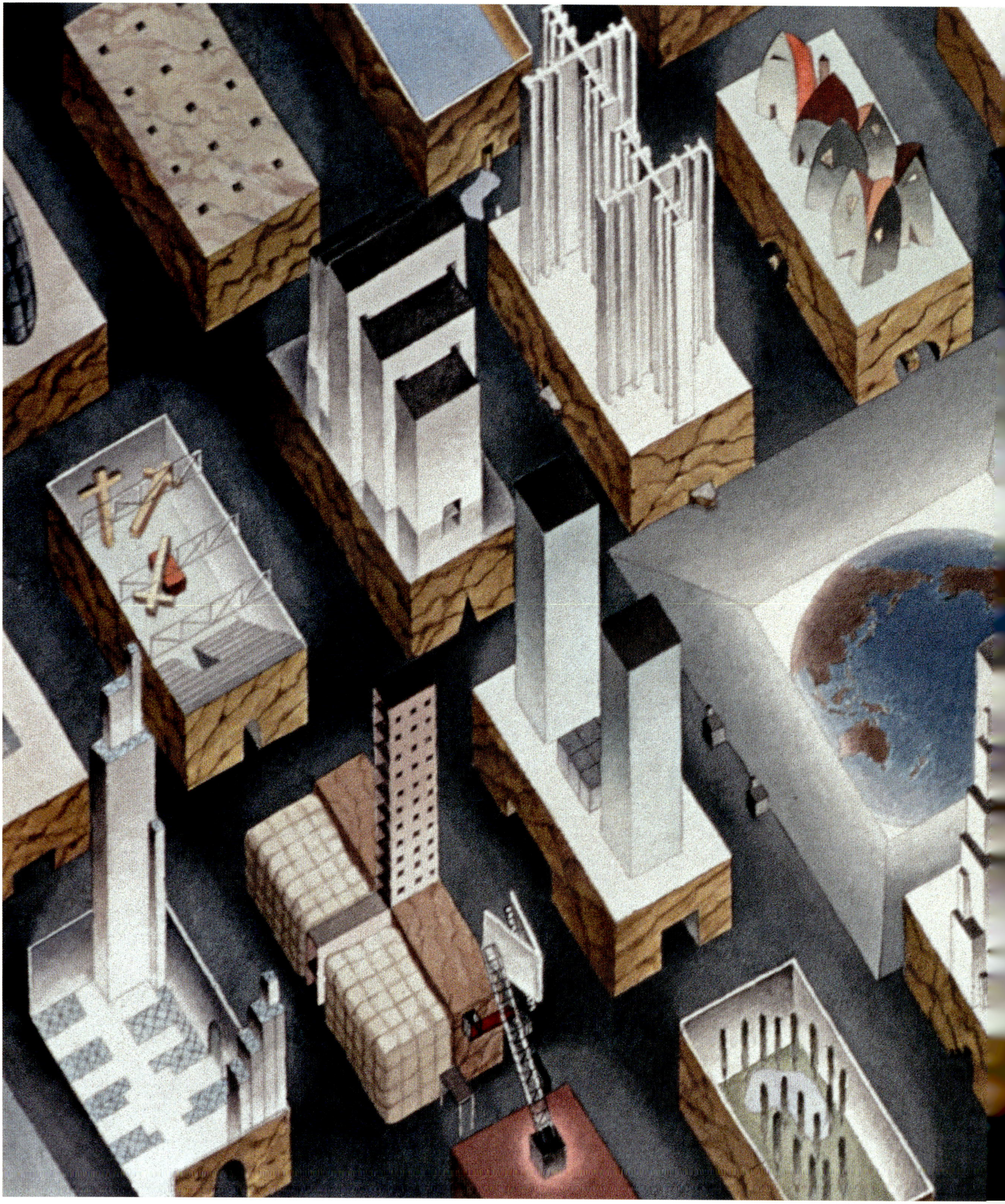

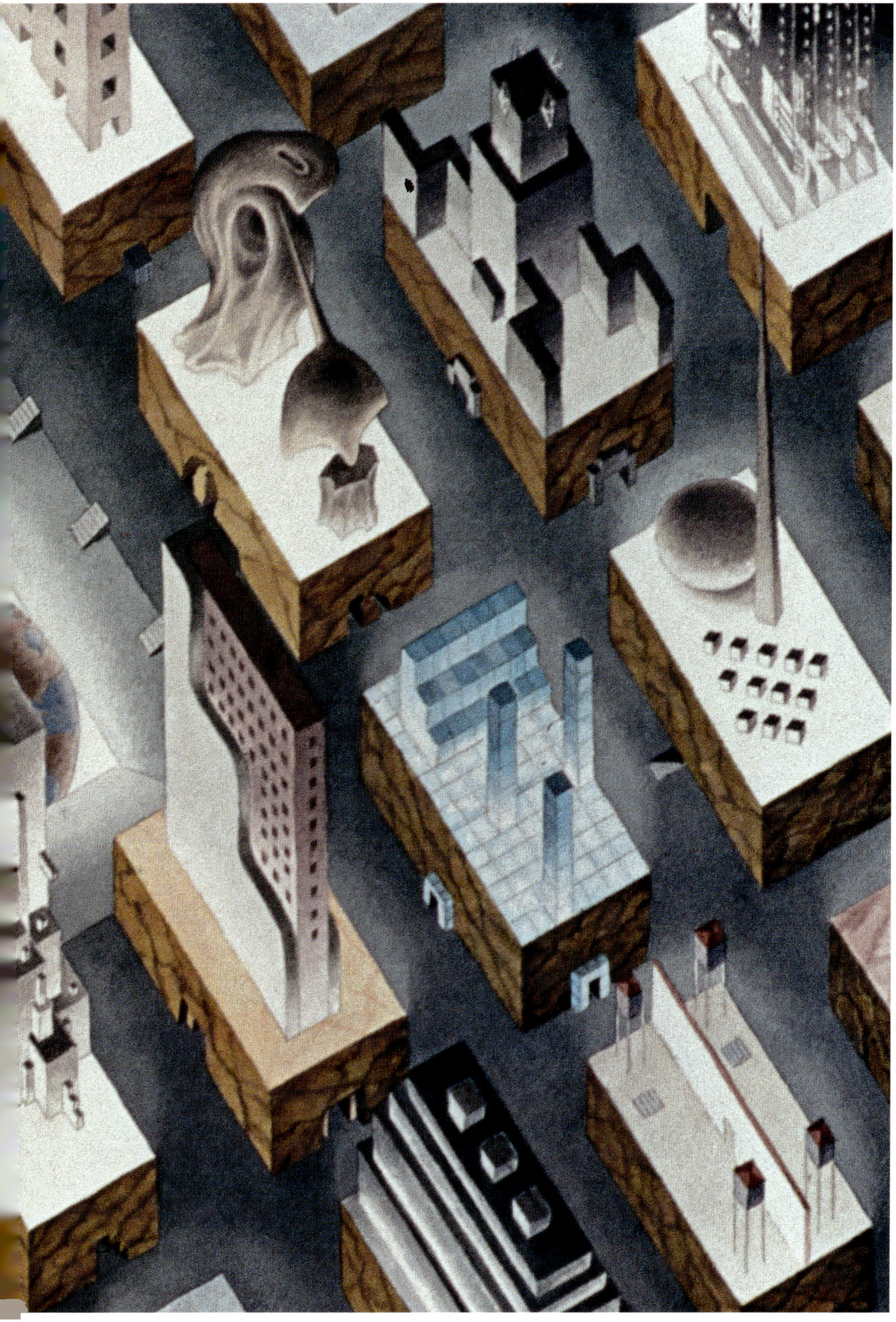

Madelon Vriesendorp • The City of the Captive Globe, Delirious New York
1972

architecture in an attempt to destroy its bolstering up of, to Bataille, socially restrictive structures. Frederick Kiesler and the playwright, theatre director and writer Antonin Artaud are also explored as examples of an alternative architecture of performance, event and space. In the final paragraph, Tschumi states:

> **Just as Bataille believed that architecture was a screening device for crime and sensuality, so too contemporary architectural trends have obscured – and continue to obscure – the existence of a body of work that contradicts the accepted dogmas of a period. For Artaud, the double of reality was madness, the double of art, destruction, and the double of theatre was Artaud's own life. What is the double of architecture?**[20]

Tschumi's preoccupations with the event, the point of view and urban performance would also give him a disregard for the traditional protocols of architectural drawings and provoke him to seek alternative methods of choreographing other architectural experiences in the city.

Meanwhile, and not included for some reason in the *AD*, John Hejduk was starting to draw and partially construct a series of 'Masque' projects situated in many differing city locations. These sought to distil the essence of place, its genius loci and the rituals and day-to-day activities of a city's occupants. This Hejduk would make into a cluster of finely arranged archetypal pavilions. One of the initial projects of the series was the *Thirteen Watchtowers of Cannaregio* (see pages 144–45). Deceptively simple, it possesses a melancholy line of thirteen square-sectioned towers arranged in a campo. The American architect, urbanist and writer Michael Sorkin eloquently describes the project as:

→
John Hejduk
Victims: Sketches of Structures
1984

John Hejduk

Thirteen Watchtowers of Cannaregio

1974–79

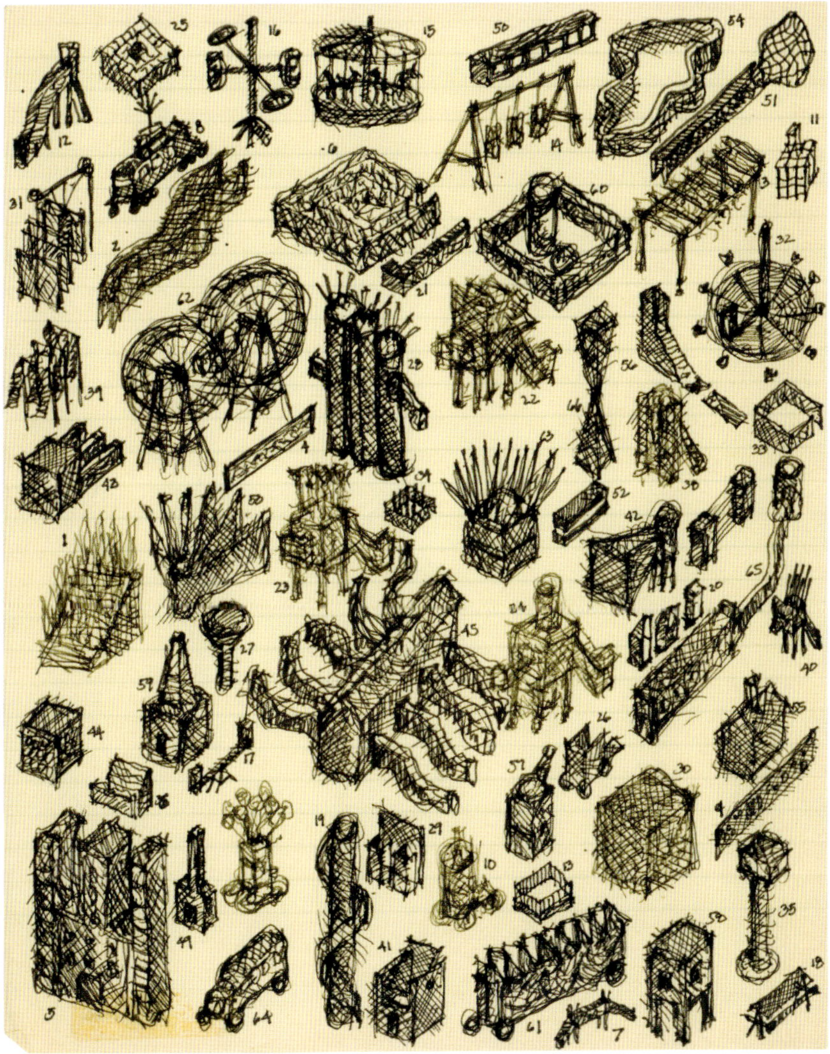

structured around a narrative program which proposes that the city designate a lifetime inhabitant for each of the identical towers, to pass life in monumental, watchful solitude. The program also includes a sort of on-deck house in the campo, where another citizen awaits a vacancy on the death of one of the 13. Elsewhere in the city is a House for the Inhabitant Who Refused to Participate. Working from this outline, Hejduk crafts a lapidary explanation of the dimensions of the distance between this regulated context and a form which artistically redeems its essence. Central to the success of the project is an acute interpretation of the typology of the tower and the historical mesmerizing character of Venice.[21]

Hejduk's 'Masque' projects, of which the *Thirteen Watchtowers* is sometimes credited as the first, sought to describe in microcosm, and with iconic, archetypal simple forms in relation to one another, the lives, memories, occupations and fears of each city's inhabitants.

Simultaneously, Tschumi was producing his Manhattan Transcripts (see pages 146–47), a theoretical project that attempted to delineate the complex workings of the city and to develop notations that might describe them and be more fit for purpose than the disjunctions and anomalies of traditional architectural representations. Tschumi describes his project:

Architecture is not simply about space and form, but also about event, action, and what happens in space. The Manhattan Transcripts differ from most architectural drawings insofar as they are neither real projects nor mere fantasies. Developed in the late '70s, they proposed to transcribe an architectural

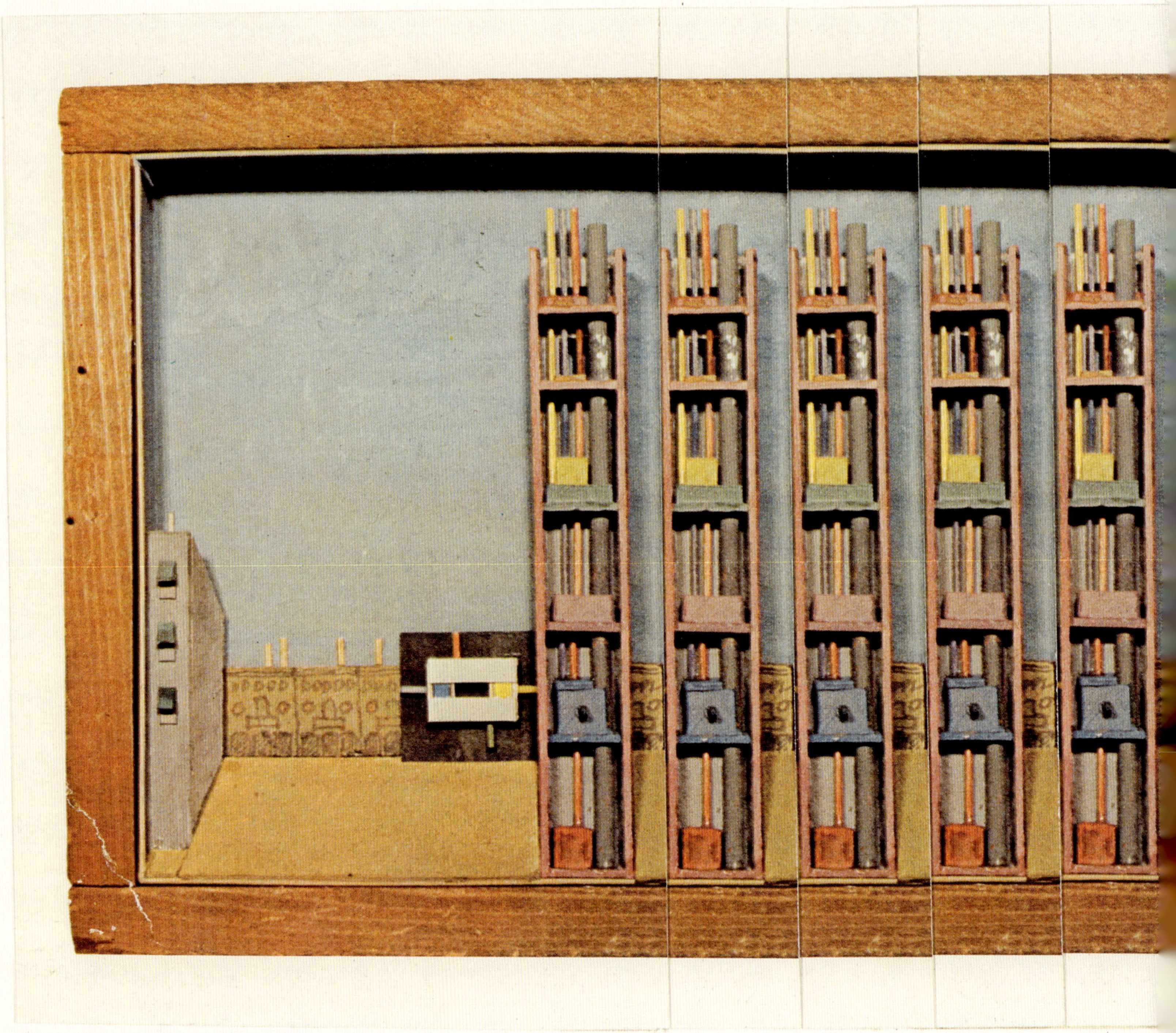

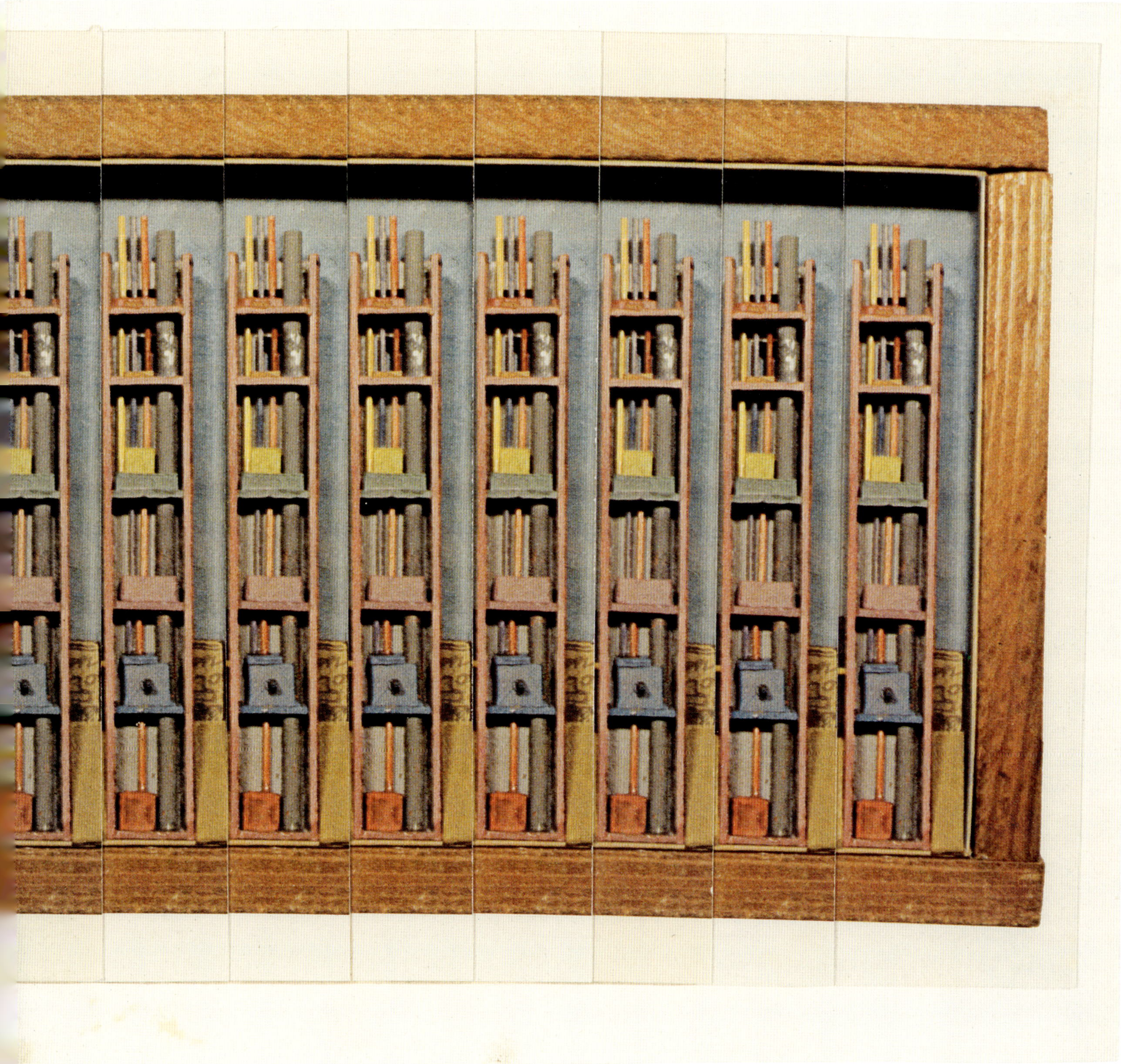

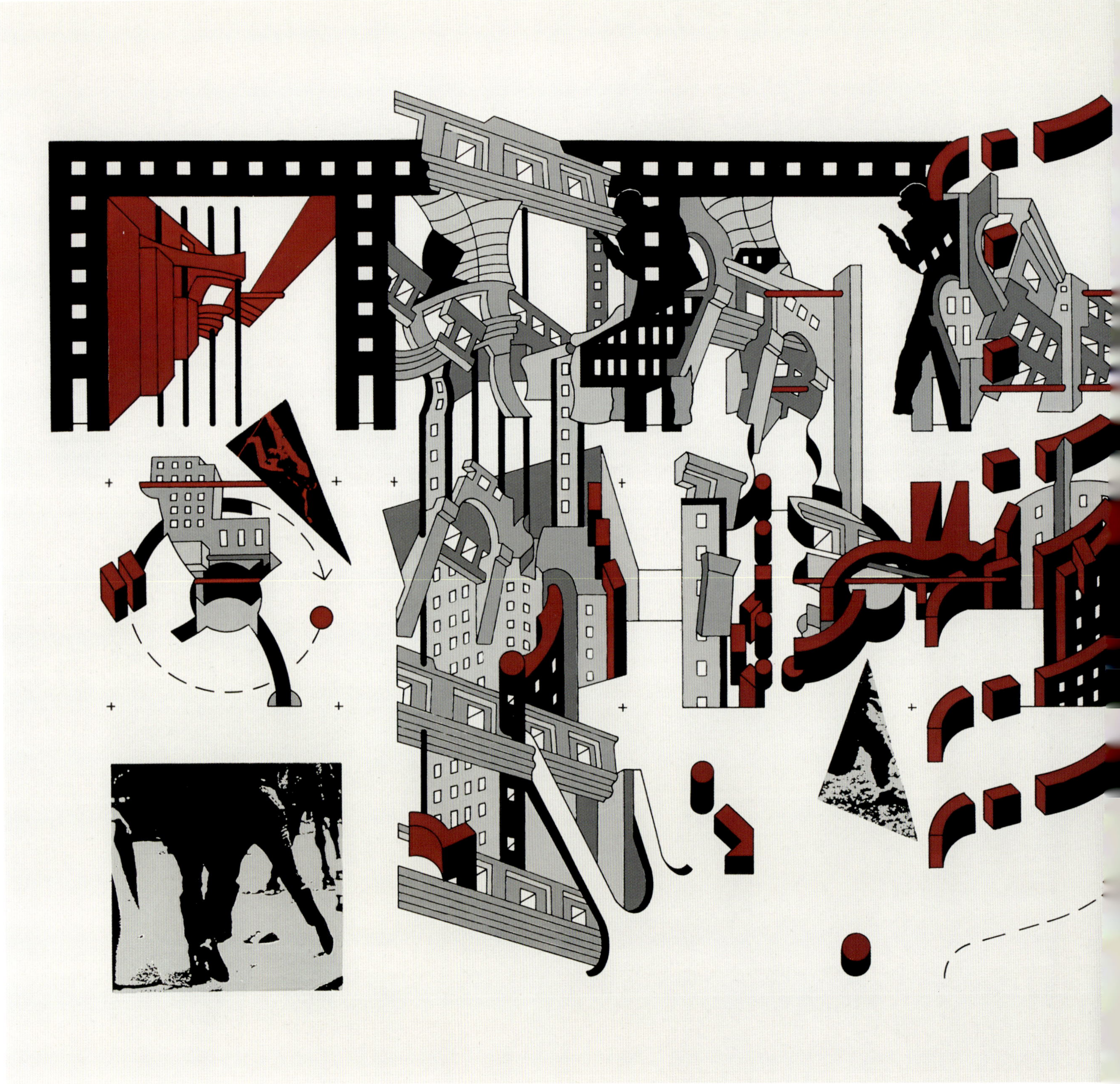

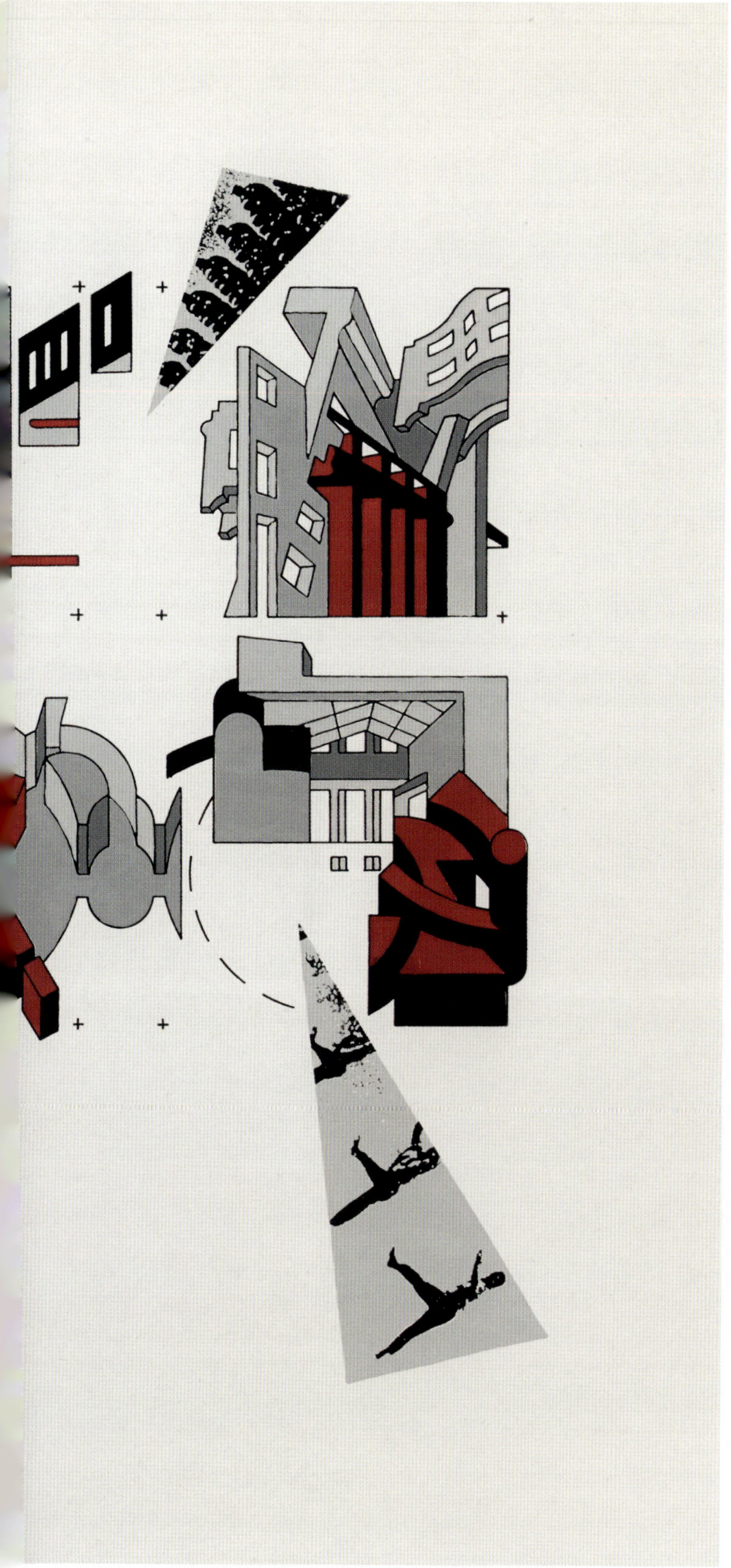

← **Bernard Tschumi**
The Manhattan Transcripts
1976–81

interpretation of reality. To this aim, they employed a particular structure involving photographs that either direct or 'witness' events (some would call them 'functions,' others 'programs'). At the same time, plans, sections, and diagrams outline spaces and indicate the movements of the different protagonists intruding into the architectural 'stage set.' The Transcripts' explicit purpose was to transcribe things normally removed from conventional architectural representation, namely the complex relationship between spaces and their use, between the set and the script, between 'type' and 'program,' between objects and events. Their implicit purpose had to do with the 20th-century city.[22]

The Manhattan Transcripts sought not just to describe but also to develop a means by which one could cinematically direct architectural events in the city. In his Theatre-Museum in his home town of Figueres in Spain (see page 149), Dalí also sought to do the same, not by notation, but by bringing together a cacophony of histories, mythologies and objects to provoke and inspire, and ultimately to expose the modern world and its surreal presence. Inaugurated in 1974 and completed with its extension – the Torre Galatea – in 1983, the Dalí Theatre-Museum is a surreal urban set piece that reaches out around it and insinuates itself into the consciousness.

Dalí decorated the entrance to his Figueres museum with an extraordinary array of Dalínian caryatids that perch on the parapet of the façade. On top of the entrance elevation are a series of white warriors with loaves of bread balanced on their heads, as the writer J. L. Giménez-Frontín describes: 'The artistic use of loaves of bread...dates from the period

→

Salvador Dalí • (clockwise from top left)
Rainy Cadillac, **1941; the central hall, the Mae West room and the central courtyard at the Dalí Theatre-Museum, Figueres, Catalonia, Spain**
1974–83

when Dalí created surrealist objects in Paris at the beginning of the Thirties. According to Dalí, his image of bread had absolutely no function or utilitarian meaning, but was rather a symbol of the gratuity and the excess of free imagination.'[23] Below the bread-burdened warriors are another five bread-headed figures, four of which represent the Fates (a common motif in European polytheism). Each has a gaping hole in its stomach and holds the ultimate Dalínian symbol, the hayfork/crutch. In the centre of this tableau is a mannequin in a diver's suit with a glass bowl on its head. This figure commemorates 'a lecture Dalí tried to give in 1936, jammed into a similar suit, on the occasion of the Surrealist International in London...the diving suit is a symbol of the immersion in the depths of the unconscious proposed by Dalí at the time, when he was most amazed by, and showed greatest faith in, Freud's work'.[24]

The old auditorium of what was once the Municipal Theatre of Figueres, the main space in Dalí's museum, has been topped by an incongruous geodesic dome. Dalí was also a follower of the work and ideas of the American architect and systems theorist Richard Buckminster Fuller and his geodesic domes. It was initially hoped that Buckminster Fuller would design Dalí's dome, but this didn't come to pass and it was instead the creation of the Spaniard Pérez Piñero.

The first port of call within the Figueres museum is the Vestibule, and here Dalí sets out reminders of his respect for other artists including Pablo Picasso and Miró. As one is drawn up the stairs, there is a print from Giovanni Battista Piranesi's *Carceri d'Invenzione (Imaginary Prisons)* series of etchings (1750–61) – another crucial influence. The staircase leads to the fifth level and the Hall of Masterpieces, from which visitors percolate down through the museum. The Hall is a chaotic act of associative curation and includes seminal Dalís as well as some of his personal collection of other artists' works, including Duchamp's *Boîte-en-valise (Box in a Suitcase)* of 1935–41, which features miniature facsimiles of his most influential works. Dalí was a great admirer of Duchamp, and often referenced him in his spatial designs. Indeed, Duchamp was instrumental in designing and coordinating many of the Surrealists' great forays into interior and exhibition design, and Dalí learned much from him in this respect.

Exiting the Hall of Masterpieces, visitors arrive at a corridor. The powerful iconography of the French 'Rue Trajan' street sign here catapults us back in time to one of the greatest, if not the greatest, Surrealist exhibitions, the 'Exposition Internationale du Surréalisme' held at the Galérie Beaux-Arts in Paris from 17 January to 22 February 1938. The signage is also a reference to Surrealist notions of the city, and particularly Paris.

In his book *Displaying the Marvelous* (2001), Lewis Kachur succinctly sums up the myriad of allegories and associations provoked by this boulevard of street signs. According to Kachur, Surrealist artist André Masson underlined the 'emblematic value' of the street signs behind the mannequins. He felt proud to have rue Vivienne, 'a capital of Surrealist myth, important in the *Chants de Maldoror*', and where its author Lautréamont lived. Likewise, the author Gérard de Nerval lived on the evocative rue de la Vieille Lanterne, the sign behind Espinoza's mannequin. Rue Nicolas-Flamel, the first sign on the corridor and an actual street, refers to a medieval alchemist who interested the Surrealists. Perhaps the Porte de Lilas, the sign behind Tanguy's mannequin, alludes to another flea market, or to the well-known literary café Closerie de Lilas. Other blue plaques, such as 'Blood Transfusion' or 'All the Devils' (Seligmann) were clearly fictive and reinforced a macabre mood; whereas Passage des Panoramas is poetically evocative and an appropriate title for the entire row.[25]

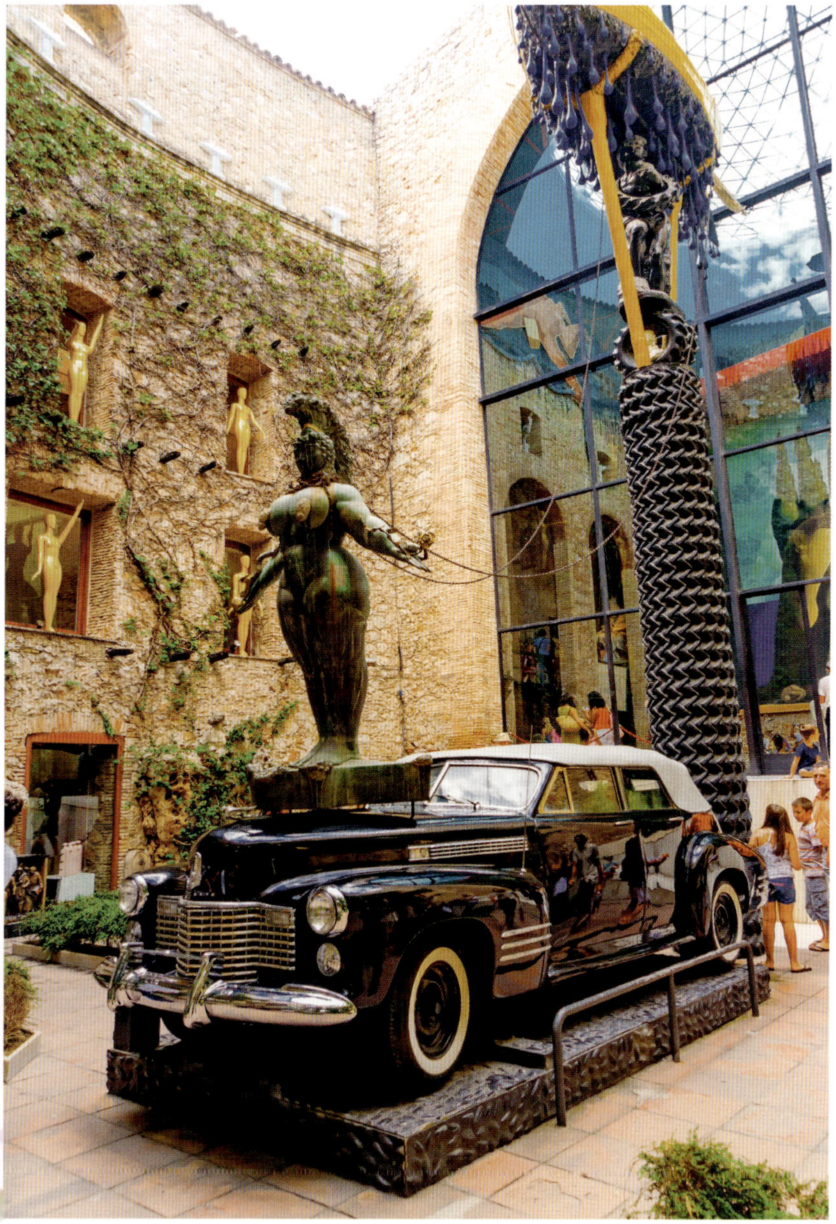
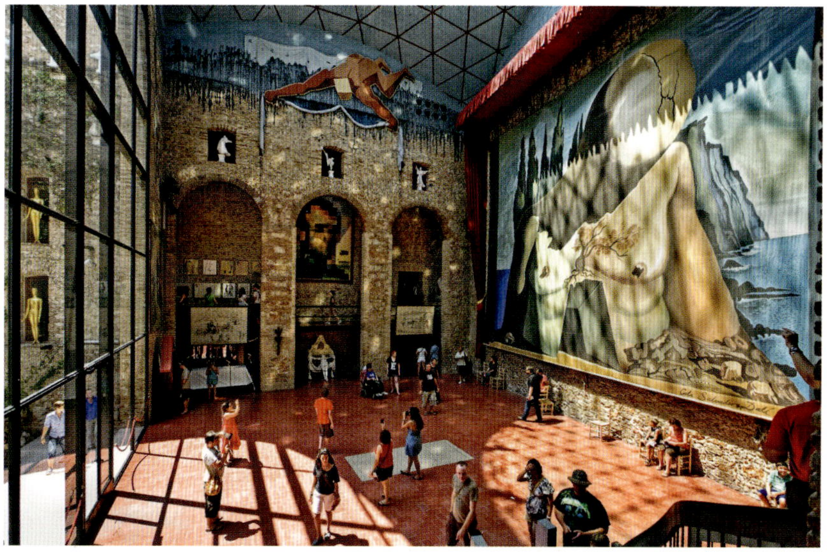
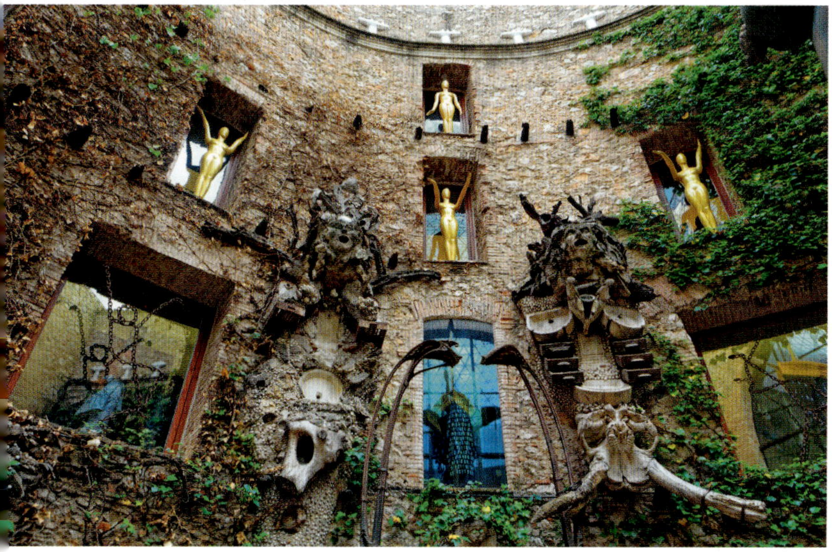
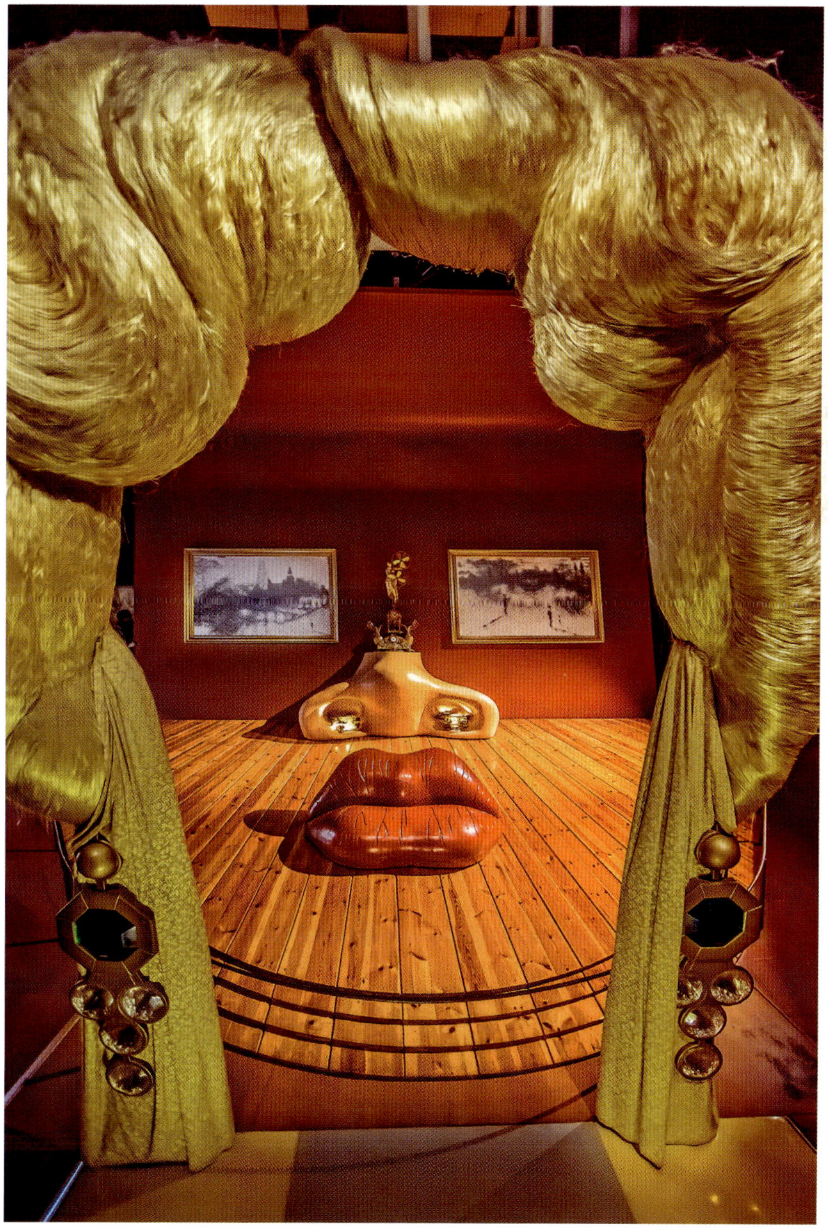

→

C. J. Lim • Par Xien Gou Hai
(Eight Gods Crossing Ocean)
Virtually Venice
2004

At this stage in his career, Dalí was interested in cybernetics, quantum physics, notions of hyperspace, genetics, holograms and much more, gleaned from an awareness of contemporary scientific advances. His work forever pursued the next lateral connection to enable him to expand the envelope of modern art and, vicariously, modern architecture.

On leaving the Figueres museum courtyard, Dalí reminds us again of Surrealism's history. High above the *Rainy Cadillac*, surmounted on a column of thirty-four tractor tyres, is Gala's boat, a sculpture of an upside-down boat hung with large droplets of water and topped by an umbrella. The boat is a reminder, perhaps, of the great depths of the Surrealist ocean.

Dalí is interred under his cupola at the symbolic centre of his museum, another exhibit in his own memory. The final architectural feature is himself.

Virtually Venice, Grimm City, Mechudzu and the Gold Mine

During the 1990s, architects, geographers and urban planners became interested in the new-found ability to harvest large quantities of data from our cities – about demographics, human movement and flows, consumer choices, media habits and so on. This was coupled with the growing need to address the issues arising from the rapidly rising global population, and the Earth's increasing urbanization into megacities, particularly in Southeast Asia. As technologies have become more dexterous, cities and people have become more and more transparent, echoing Breton's calls for a last great quest for the Surrealist group in 1942. This 'transparency' has embraced the virtual, the mixed and the augmented, and is not without its mythologies, which are manifold. It is reflexive in many dimensions; it is disruptive, and it is resilient, ever moving and growing, and held in server farms. Big Data, geographic information systems (GIS), the Web, the Internet of Things and global positioning satellites (GPS) and 3D scanning all contribute to its evolution. While technology and its progress is a complex two-way street, its cultural, political and social effects on architecture and its discourse have been dramatic, much enlivening architecture's surreal potential. Simultaneously, some of the architects who established themselves in the last part of the twentieth century, as well as those now coming to the fore in the early twenty-first century, have shaken off old-school Modernism and instead embraced narrative as a way to describe the non-functional joyous events and symbolic aspects of their designs.

Architect and teacher C. J. Lim, for example, is particularly prodigious in his production of polemic and dexterously surreal architecture and urban plans. In 2004 he was invited to exhibit at the prestigious Venice Architectural Biennale. Virtually Venice, one of his most audacious schemes, takes as its starting point Italo Calvino's *Invisible Cities*, and concentrates on positing a series of transient structures that blossom every summer from their dormant winter states.

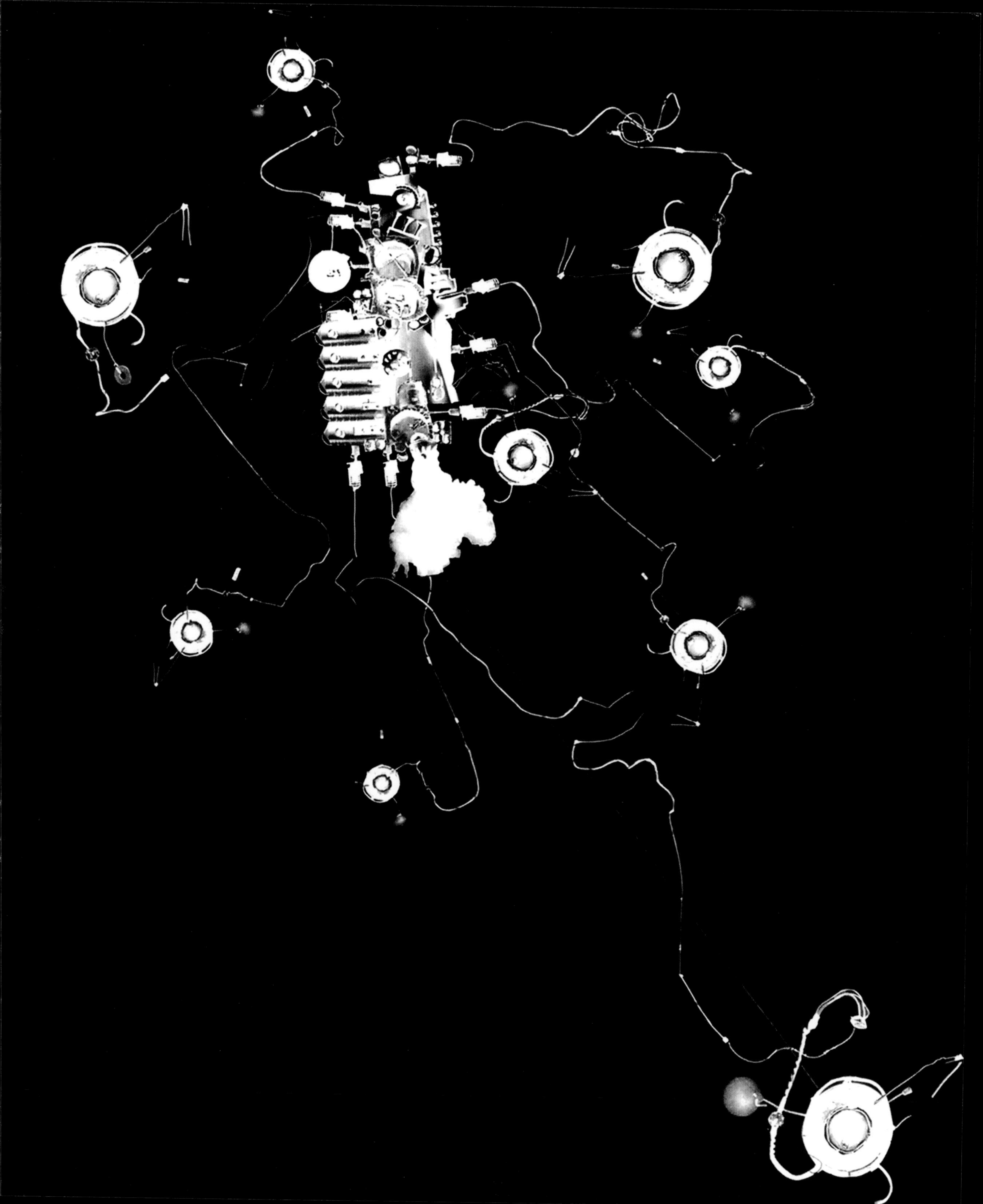

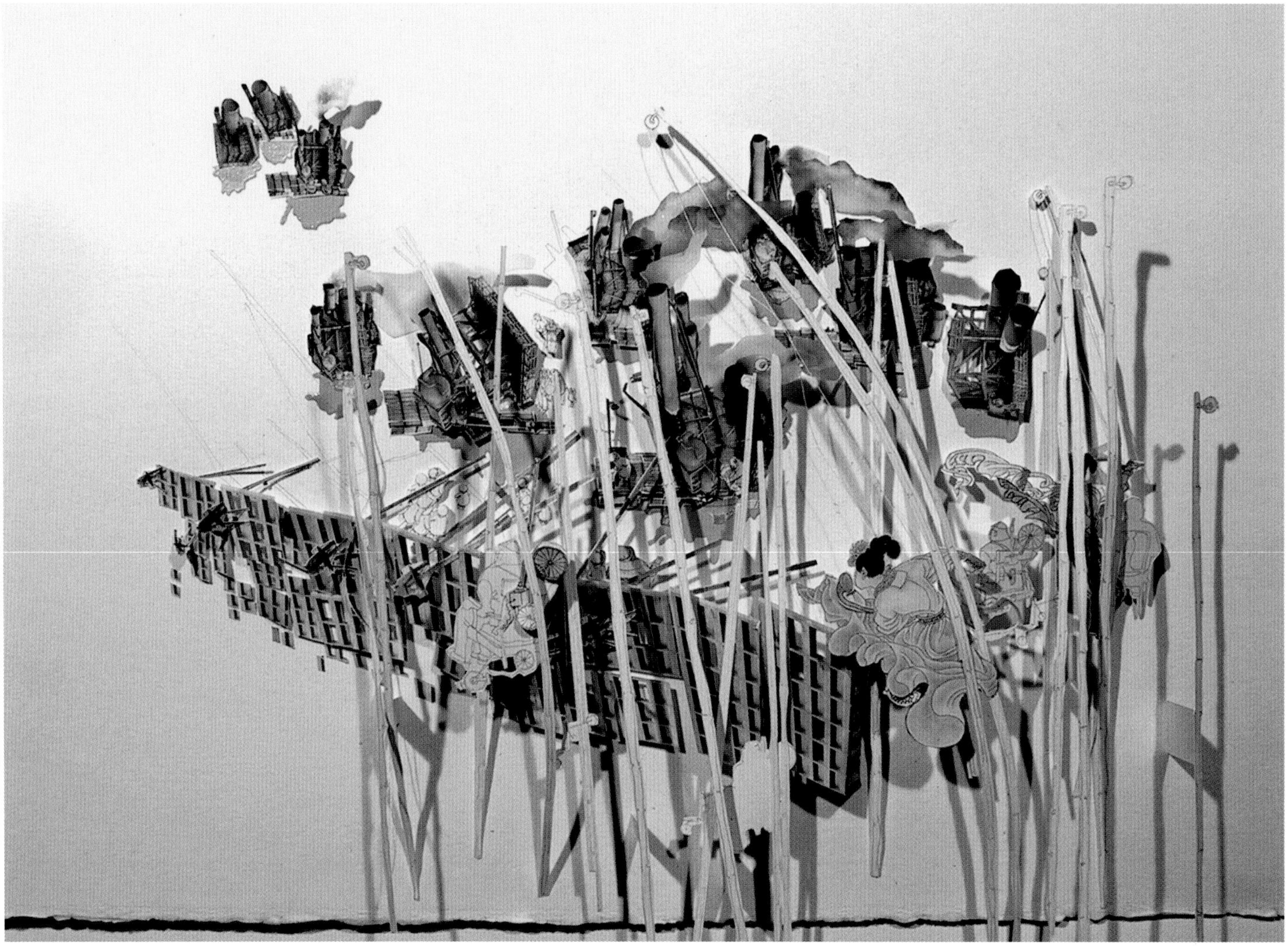

↑ **C. J. Lim** • The Lido
Virtually Venice
2004

→ **C. J. Lim** • The Giardini
Virtually Venice
2004

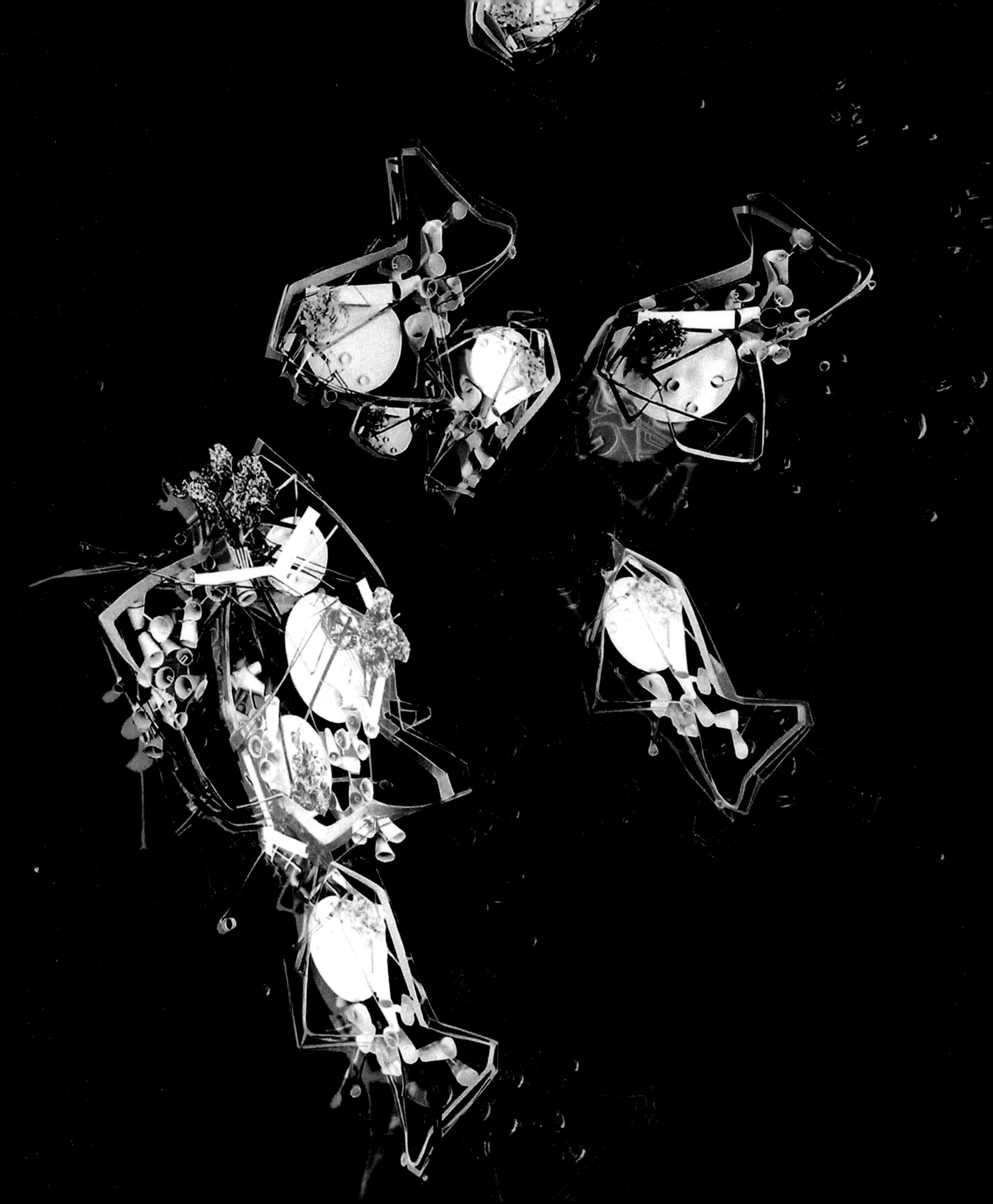

Each piece enlivens, cossets and subverts the symbols, rituals, cuisine and expediencies of Venice, its islands and its Lido and Lagoon. Lim's structures are precarious, fluxing, air- or water-borne light skeins redolent with cross-cultural symbolism exploring the spatial temporality of labyrinthine Venice. In this project, Lim accepts nothing as impossible; his imagination flies unfettered, established architectural materiality is questioned, and its lexicon expanded in the most surreal ways.

As in the theatre, Virtually Venice is structured in six 'acts'. The first, Par Xien Gou Hai (Eight Gods Crossing Ocean), is a kind of watery mechanism that encourages clothes washing and drying, its manifestation and duration conditioned by the time the clothes take to dry. In the Lido: 'For those eager to speak to loved ones at home, or perhaps eavesdrop on conversations, a marvelous set of bendy bamboo fishing rods are provided.'[26] The Giardini is rearticulated into 'a huge matrix of bobbing barrels containing television screens, circlets of lemons and annulets of parchment'.[27] The San Marco Tower is a dining column clad in bird traps that catch pigeons for customers to eat barbecued. The Fontuna Pozzo-Pozza harvests water from around the city. And finally, San Michele is a foot-pampering oasis for tourists who have been on their feet all day sampling Venice's treasures.

Throughout the project, the iconic Lion of Venice manifests itself in leaping cats. Lim shows his Surrealist love of Venice by utilizing similar tactics to Hedjuk. Architect and teacher James Williamson's observations on Hejduk's work are thus equally true of Lim's:

> **In his masque projects, John Hejduk traverses and explores the networks of thought, emotion, and desire. He incorporates the tools of language (sign and narrative) and myth (whether archaic or modern) as the 'physics of poetry' for his pantheism of construction. In so doing, he employs the Surrealists' and alchemists' tenants to transform, reinvent, and rewrite the urban architectural program.[28]**

Practising under the name FleaFollyArchitects, Pascal Bronner and Thomas Hillier, Lim's ex-students, are likewise urban jackdaws and narrative wizards. They collide stories and architectural scales to develop surreal constellations of objects that come together to create miniature cities, but cities of the mind. In their world, cities can fit on tabletops, city plans become necklaces, and fairy tales add dark narratives to their architectural imaginations.

Bronner and Hillier's Grimm City (see pages 159–165) can be seen to take inspiration from both Hejduk and Lim. It is based on the tales of the Brothers Grimm (first published in 1812) that tapped into notions of the uncanny similar to those of the Surrealists. There are dark forests, fearful houses, magical fruits and talking animals, however FleaFolly's city is more machinic, a strange analogue computer composed of elements such as the Morning Star (based on the Grimms' story 'The Seven Ravens'), Grimm City University (based on 'The Old Man and His Grandson'), the Confession Booth ('Our Lady's Child') and the Barometer ('The Three Spinners'). Stories are analysed and are an architectural element for the city is designed from them. Each component represents an analysis of its respective story, becoming an architectural element from which the city is designed. The complex psychological text of the city is therefore rooted in the literature of the Brothers Grimm, their architectures colliding to surreal effect:

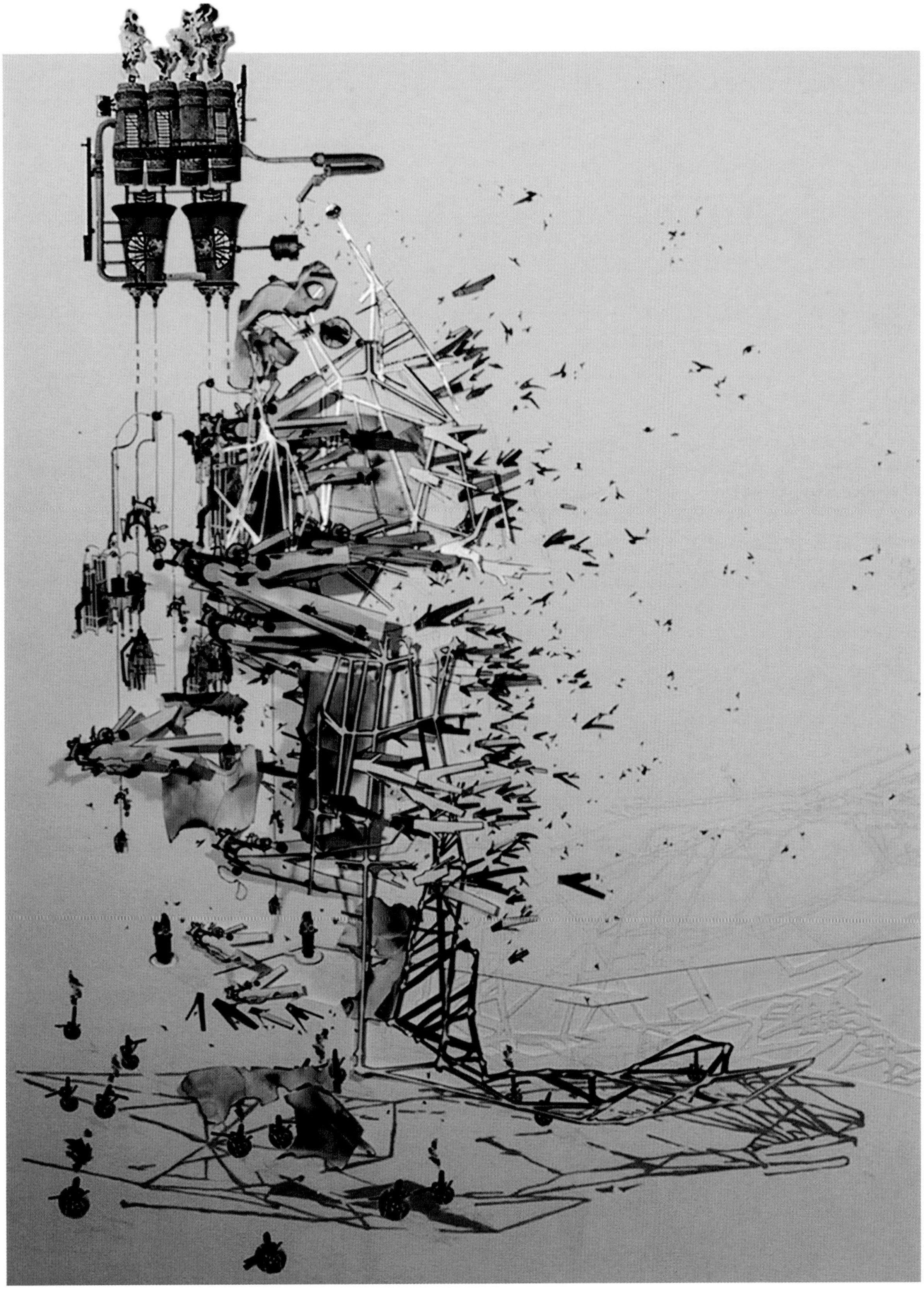

↑ **C. J. Lim** • San Marco Tower

Virtually Venice

2004

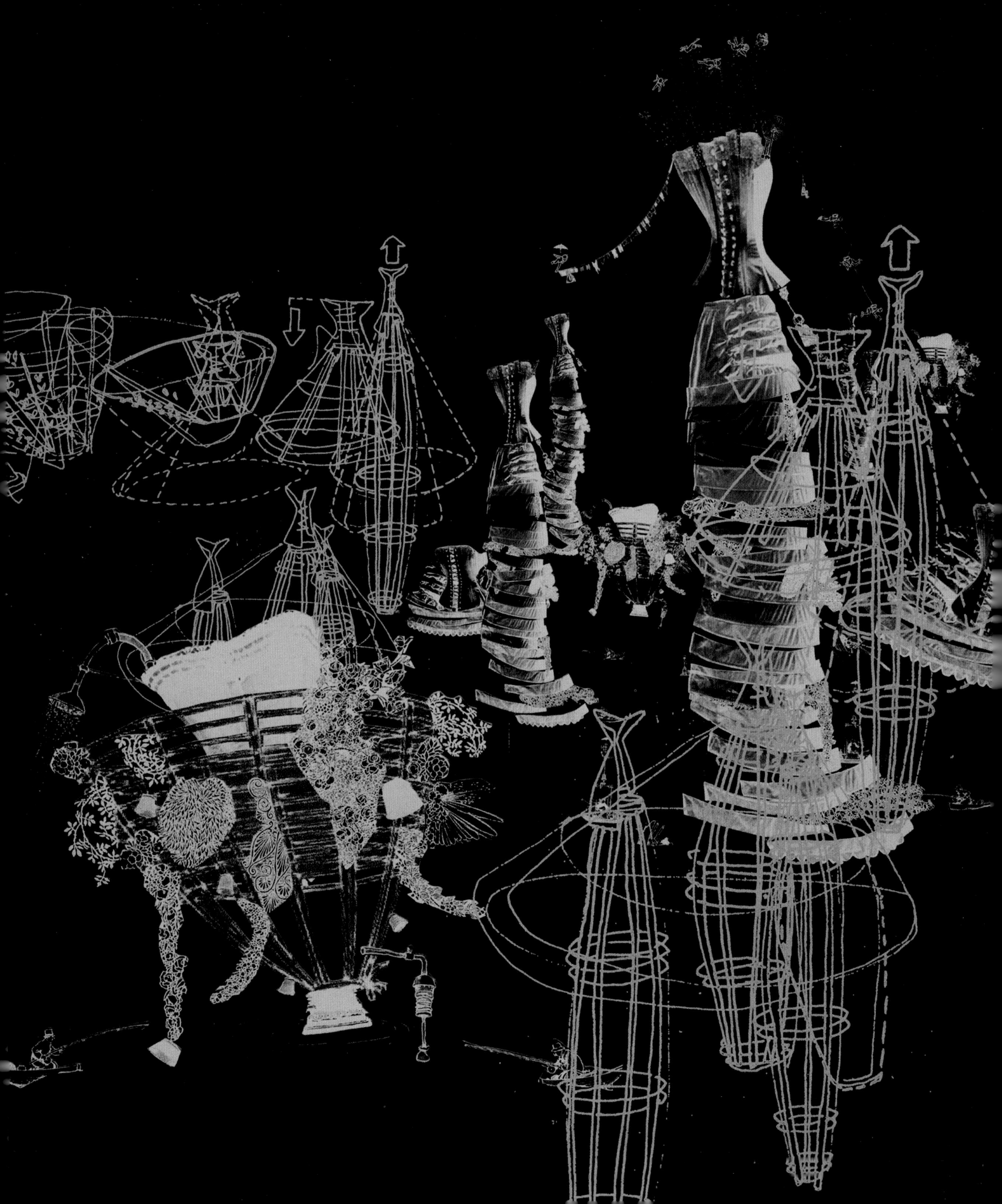

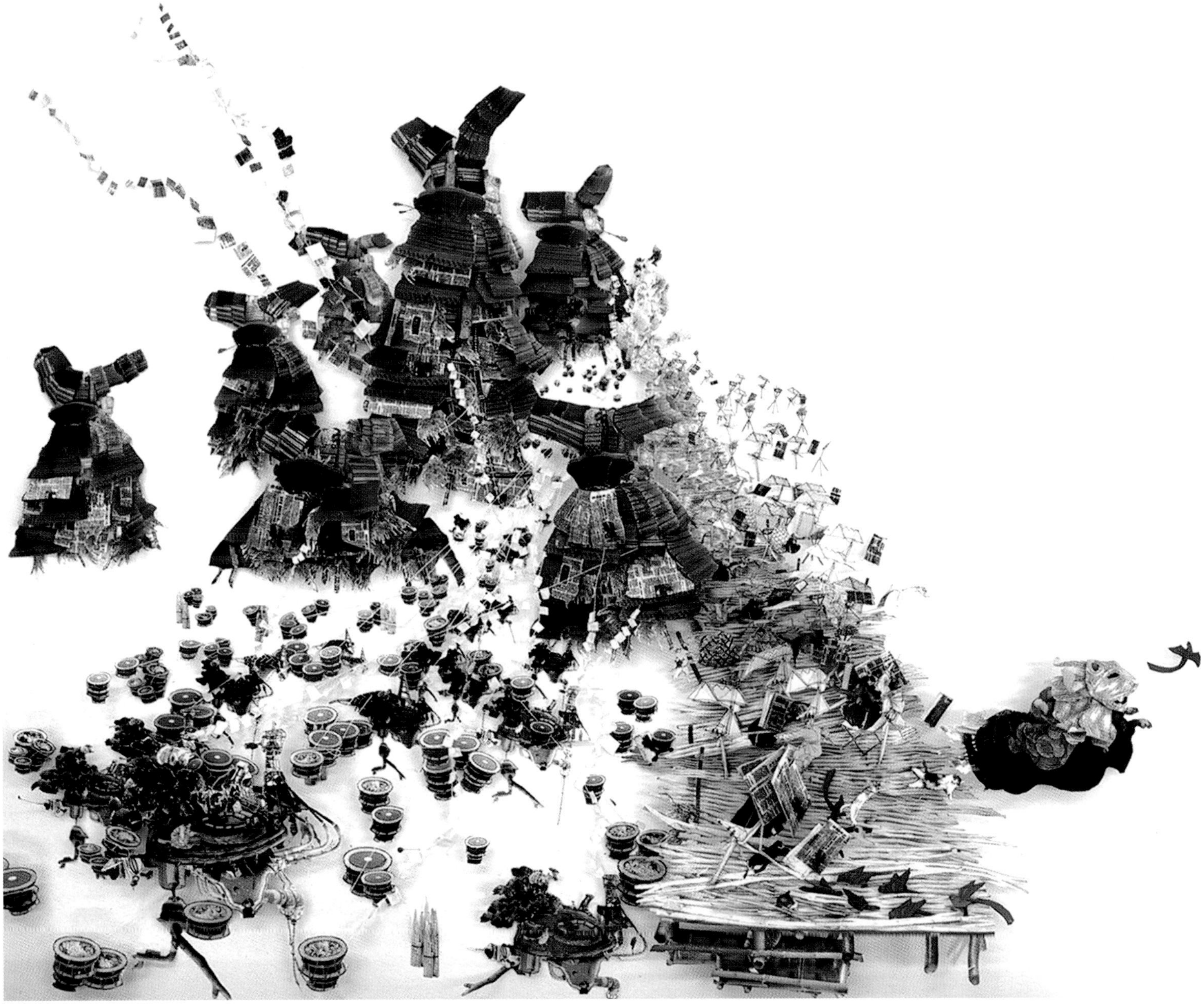

↖ **CJ Lim** • Fontuna Pozzo-Pozza
Virtually Venice
2004

↑ **CJ Lim** • San Michele,
Virtually Venice
2004

At first this city lay dormant hiding all its secrets, but then without warning it began to crawl, dragging its lifeless body across the room, creaking loudly like an old door that won't be closed. With enormous spinning wheels, tower-like limbs and turrets for claws, it began to resemble a machine that had been unjustly woken from its deep slumber. It moved with resolute determination towards the centre of the room until it hovered there above a mirror, a mirror which mysteriously emerged from another place…'Mirror, mirror'.[29]

As the contemporary city awakens to its own metabolism though now being able to mine and analyse its own data, the Bretonian 'Great Transparents' of our era are the invisible waves of data that ebb and flow across and between our cities and our bodies. Architectural designer and teacher Bryan Cantley designs ways to explore these flows and to catch their vicissitudes in his surreal machinery (see pages 167–71. His structures scan, surf and superimpose information. Equally, his architecture is made from the paraphernalia that enables our human web of interconnections and interactions to exchange, classify and store this multidimensional web of digital transactions. Cantley refers to this as 'mechudzu', the digital and mechanical equivalent of its biological counterpart 'kudzu' – a plant that grows fast, penetrates and engulfs and destroys. The Surrealists loved the idea of the unwanted colonization of the urban with the natural. Cantley's virulent, tendril-like propositions are made of the same stuff as the city: steel, cable, sockets, conduits, signage. Like its kudzu namesake, it has no respect for established urban order. Cantley's work is created across the 'reality' spectrum in terms of both its making and its effects, ambiences and urban intentions.

The 'transparent' technologies of our time are often defined by their absence, similar to Nadja at the end of Breton's urban journey, yet they are everywhere and the mechudzu infrastructure is there for the trained eye to see. Cantley husbands these structures, adding to them, making them stronger, and nourishing them; for a farm boy replanted in the city (one of the most surreal – Los Angeles), this seems appropriate. Cantley mashes up architecture, pinning it down, calibrating the damage and drumming along to a new rhythm of form – arced, twisted and deviant though it is. His are high-visibility structures for the invisible. Often he will posit fields of multiple objects, and it is the distortion of other frequencies within these that results in the architecture – transparent digital ghosts in the machine.

These ideas combined with the notion of the 'singularity' where all technologies become sentient and coalesced gives rise to another version of the city, which is very surreal indeed. Conceived by the British architect and teacher Nic Clear, the Gold Mine (see pages 172–75) is a sector of a post-scarcity, post-singularity city of the near future posited where the run-down Canvey Island in the Thames estuary now lies. Named after a nightclub that existed on the island in the 1970s, the Gold Mine is a city at once inspired by Constant's *New Babylon*, a Situationist world city straddling the globe and designed in sectors to achieve different ambiences and 'architectural' conditions. The inhabitants, saved from the tyrannies of work, become 'ludic' players, filling their days with exploration, games and, presumably, sex. As the Surrealist historian Jill Fenton has written concerning Constant's 'city':

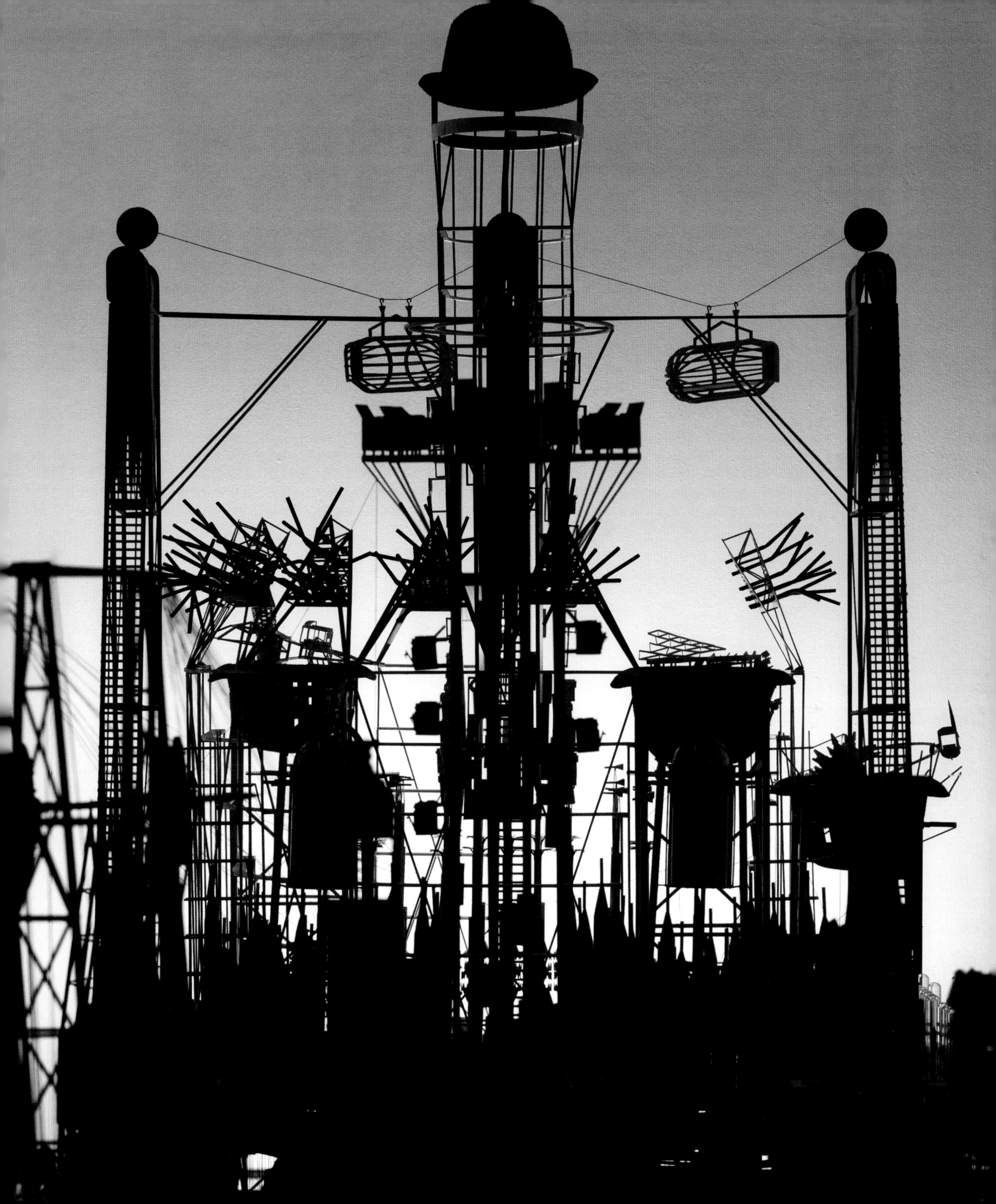

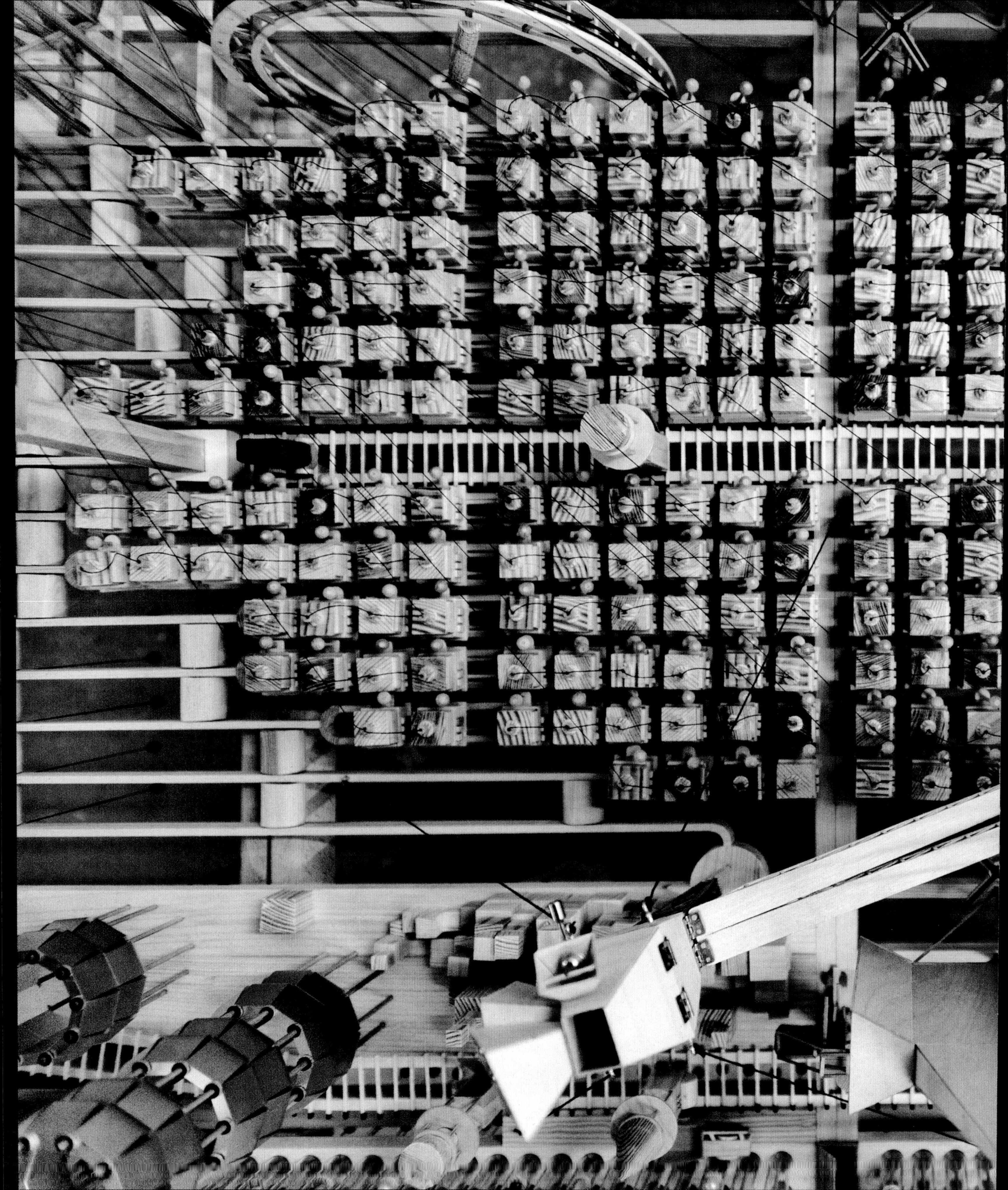

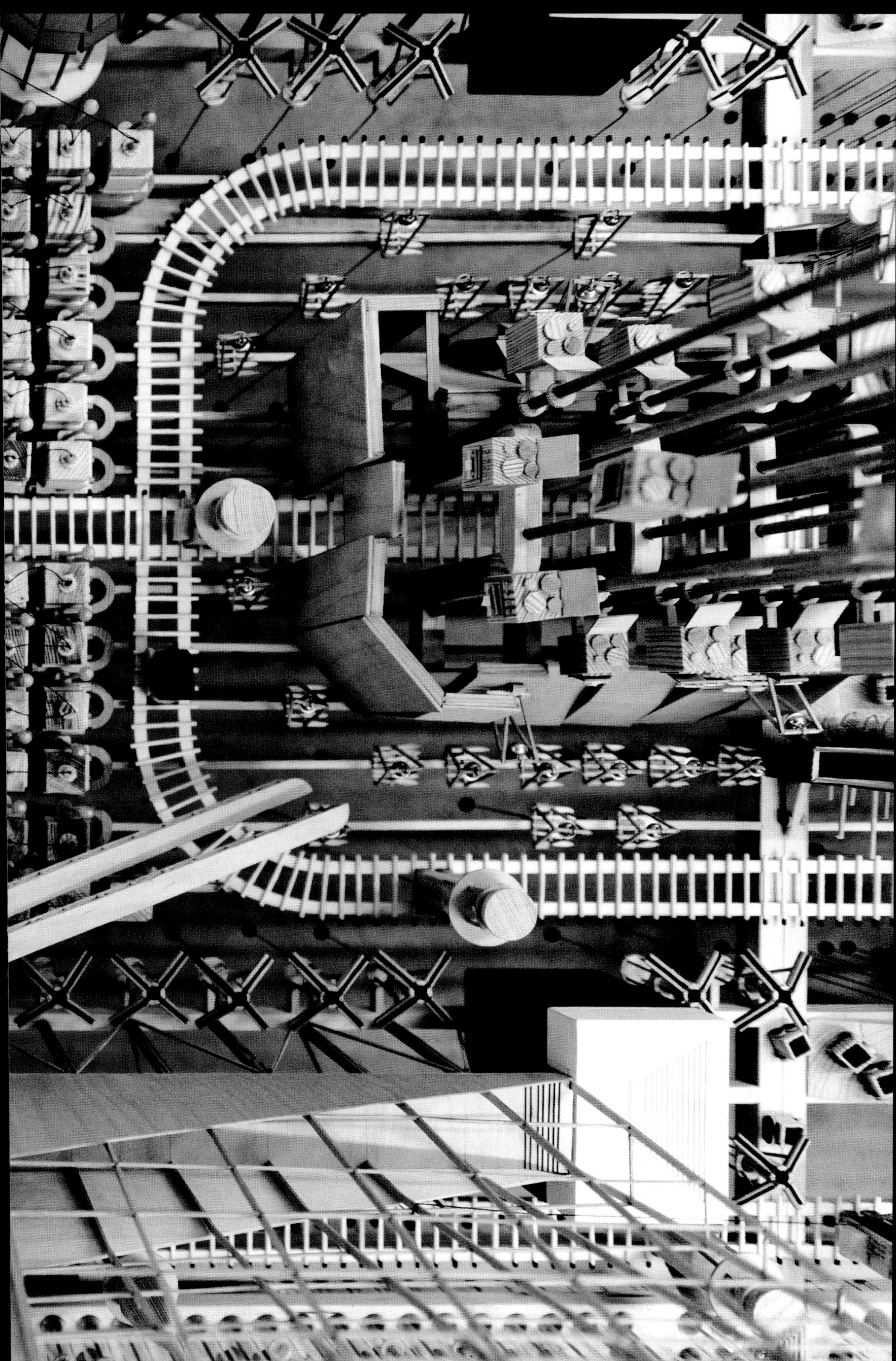

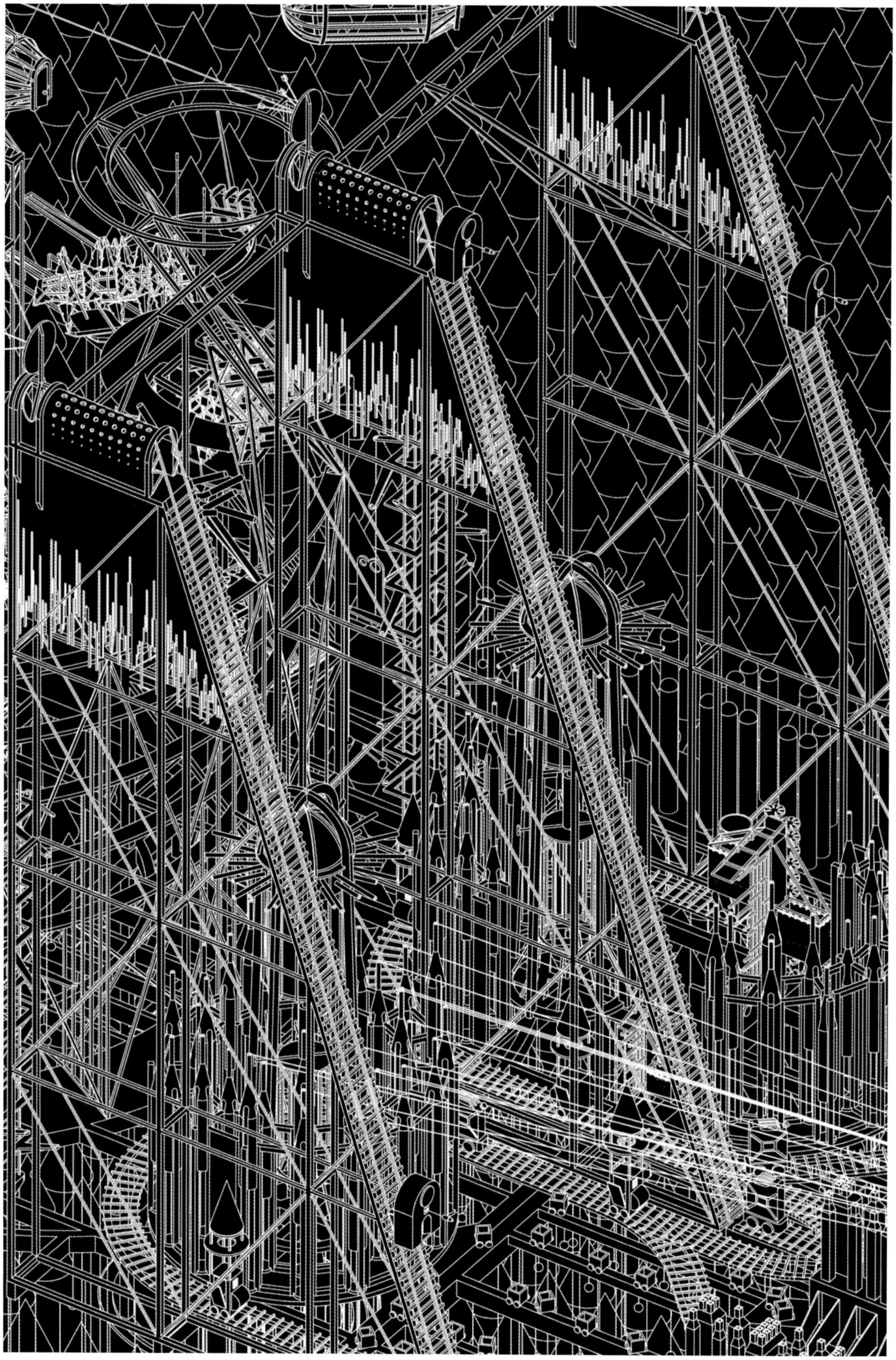

↑→

FleaFollyArchitects • Grimm City

2012

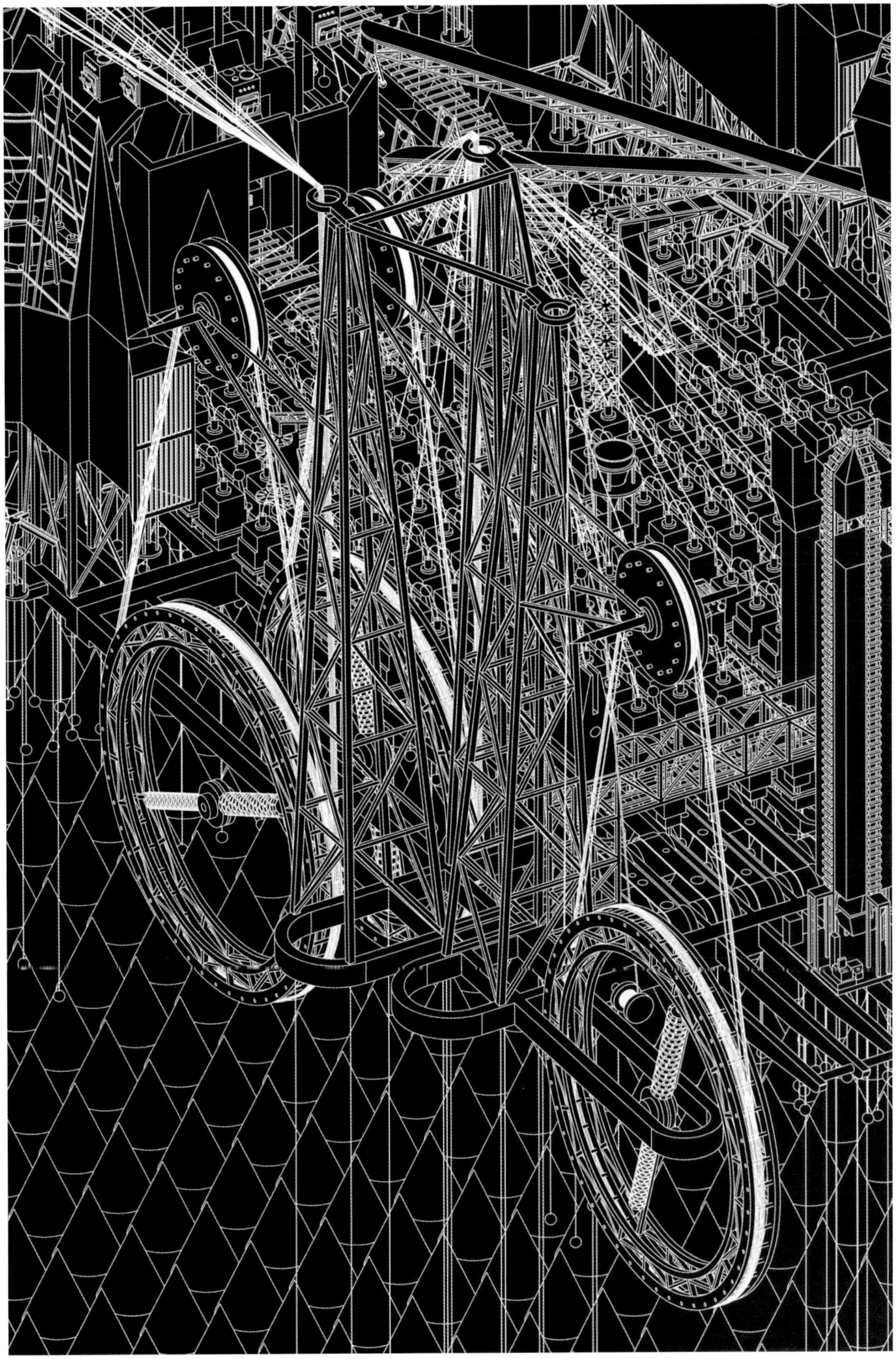

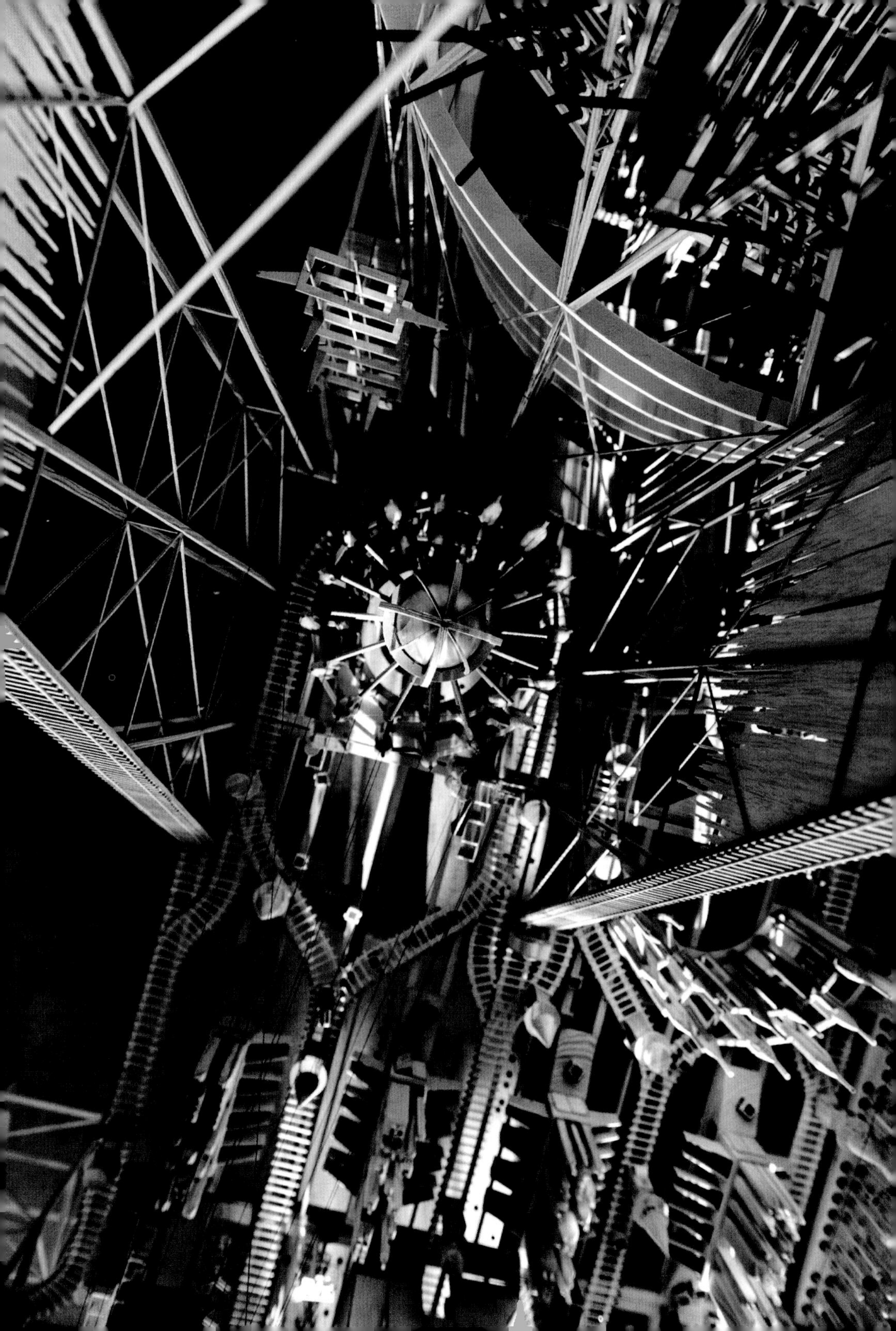

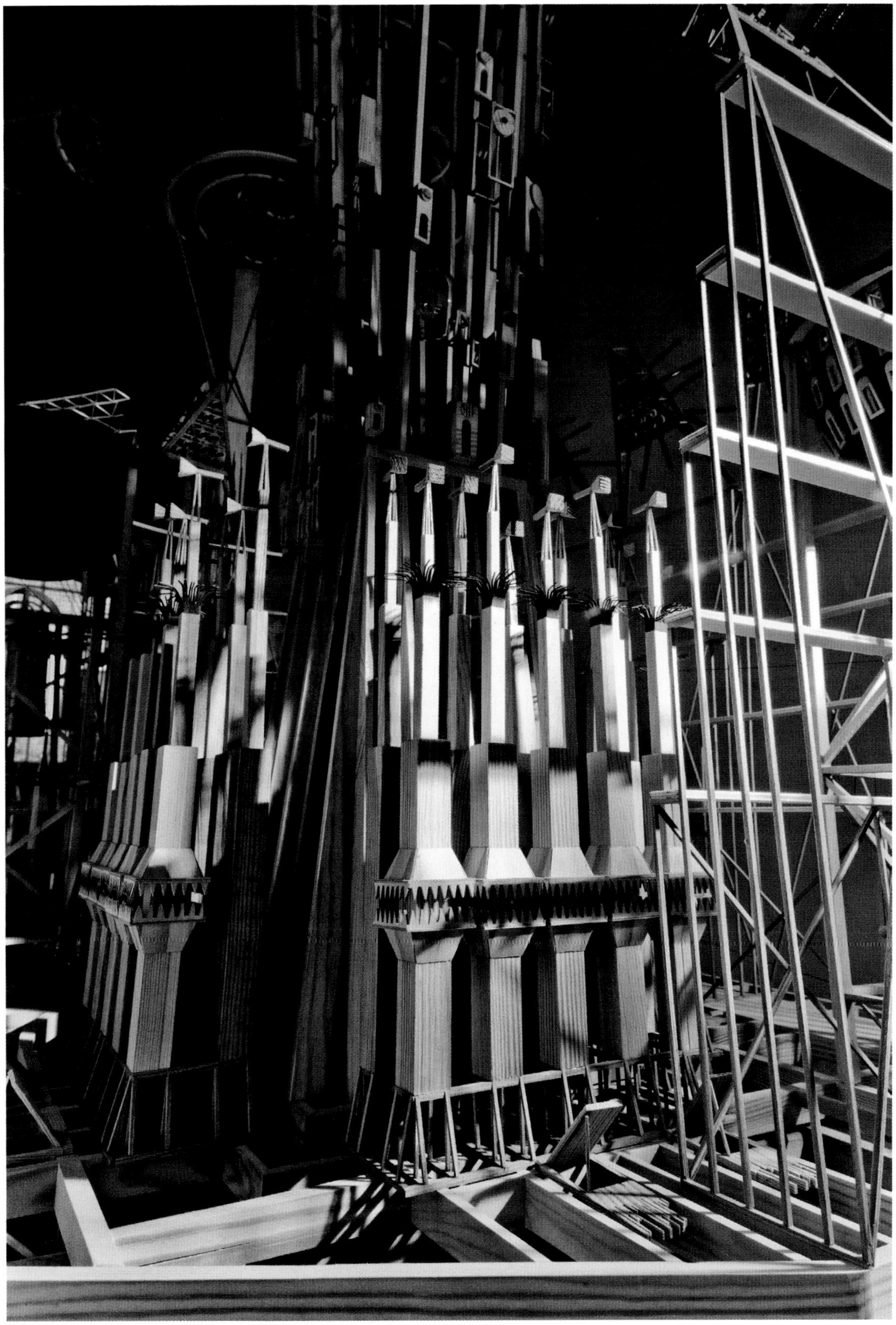

←↑

FleaFollyArchitects • Grimm City

2012

> [It] does not constitute a formal plan or blueprint to be realized in the future, nor a harmonious vision of architecture and space, but desire for a different and better future that seeks to disturb, displace assumptions and to open up ideas on alternative modes of living.[30]

The Gold Mine is also predicated on this desire to provoke debate about the future of the city in the face of advanced technologies. The future in which the Gold Mine is set is one of nanotechnological ubiquity, of hive-mind artificial intelligences, everything sentient in some way: wearable computing, genetic manipulation, virtual and augmented reality everywhere, seamless prosthetic augmentation of the body and boundless potential for creative problem-solving in a world of infinite resources and political conviviality – a society built on mutual benefit. Clear is a science-fiction and film enthusiast, and is very direct about the other key precedent for the project – the *Culture* series of novels by Scottish author Iain Banks, penned from 1987 onwards, which are also set in a universe of abundance and super-intelligent minds.

Home to 3.8 million inhabitants, the Gold Mine has been operational for twenty years, and is often fifty storeys high, though some of its towers can be as tall as two hundred storeys. Clear writes:

> The Gold Mine is constantly being remodelled both by AIs and by human occupants – usually by a combination of both. No architects are involved; the AIs act as expert systems that organise the logistical and structural transformations, while inhabitants can 'sculpt' their own spaces using interactive interfaces. These spaces are usually tested as virtual reality environments that can be modified prior to construction. The spaces of the Gold Mine are multisensory environments.... Virtual reality and augmented reality are extensively used throughout...and sometimes it is possible to differentiate between these and actual space.[31]

Six Surreal Points Reinvigorated

This chapter has described and illustrated the Surrealists' engagement with the city, charted the links of this tradition within architecture, described its reflowering in the late 1970s, and introduced twenty-first-century contemporary technologies and the emergence of narrative within the discourse. In Lim, FleaFolly, Cantley and Clear, Roger Cardinal's six points of the Surrealist city all abound; there is the reading of the poetic text of the city, a love affair with the city, a psychic text, a reading and making of the city's palimpsest, interpreting and contributing to the city of signs – all dreaming of future possibilities, marvellous occurrences and ethereal presences.

However, this is only half the story of the modern city; the other half – its more biological counterpart covered in the final chapter of the book – is the engorged garden or enchanted jungle of Surrealism, where architecture combines with febrile, Art Nouveau twists and twirls, synthetic biology and the manipulation of nature – rarified and surreal indeed.

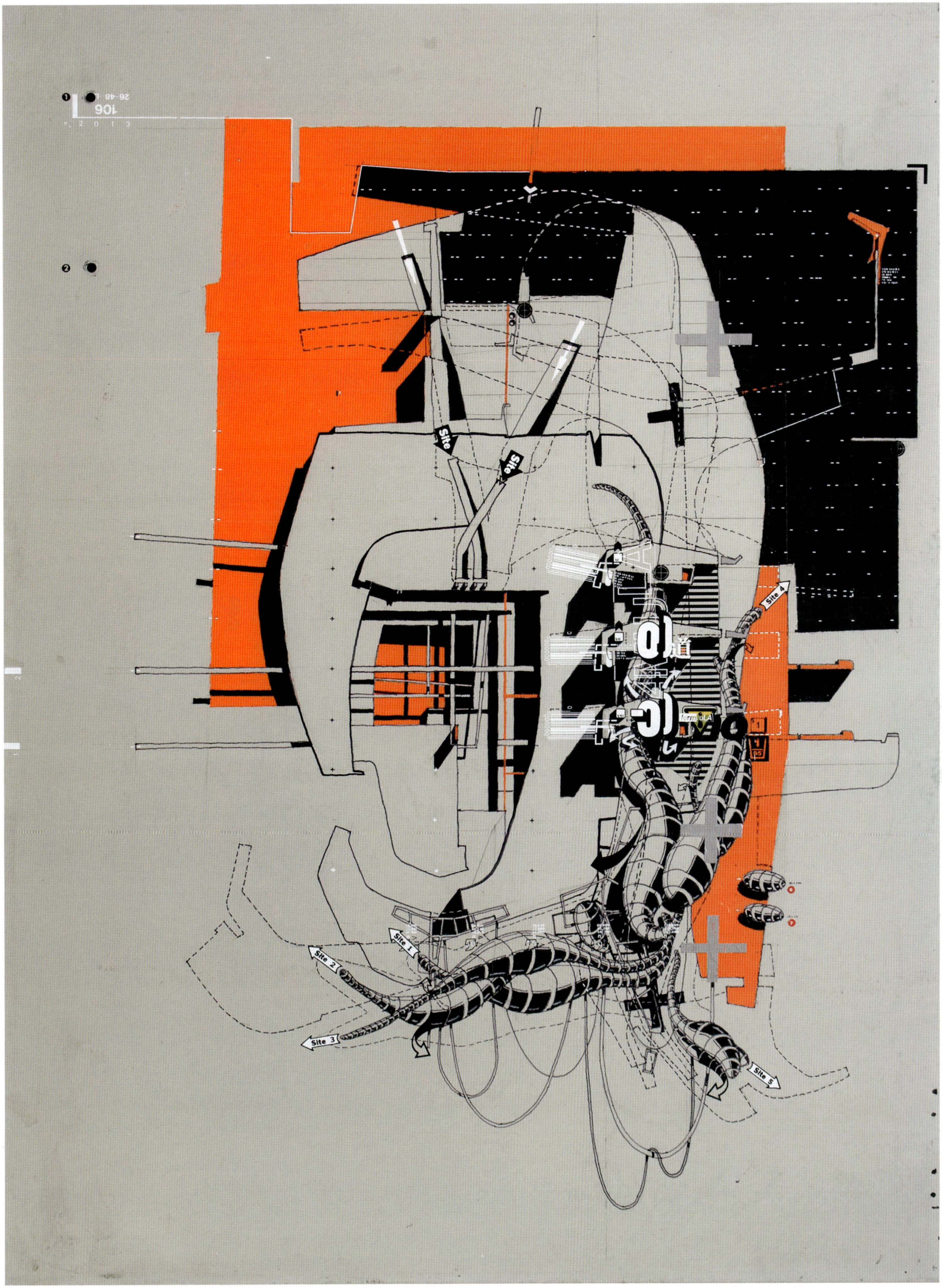
Site
Site
Site 4
Site 1
Site 2
Site 3
Site 5

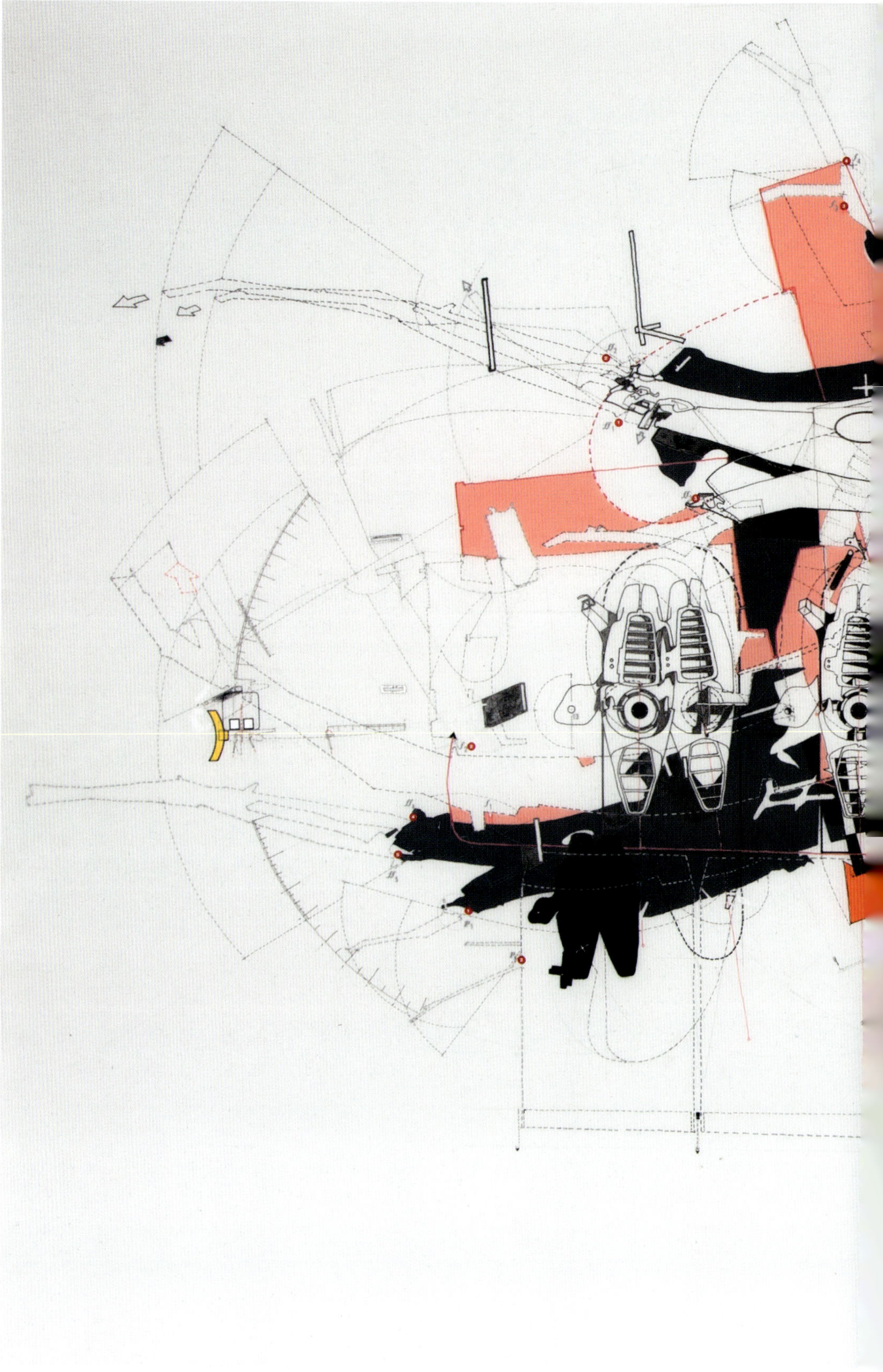

→

Bryan Cantley

Multiplicity Machines

2014

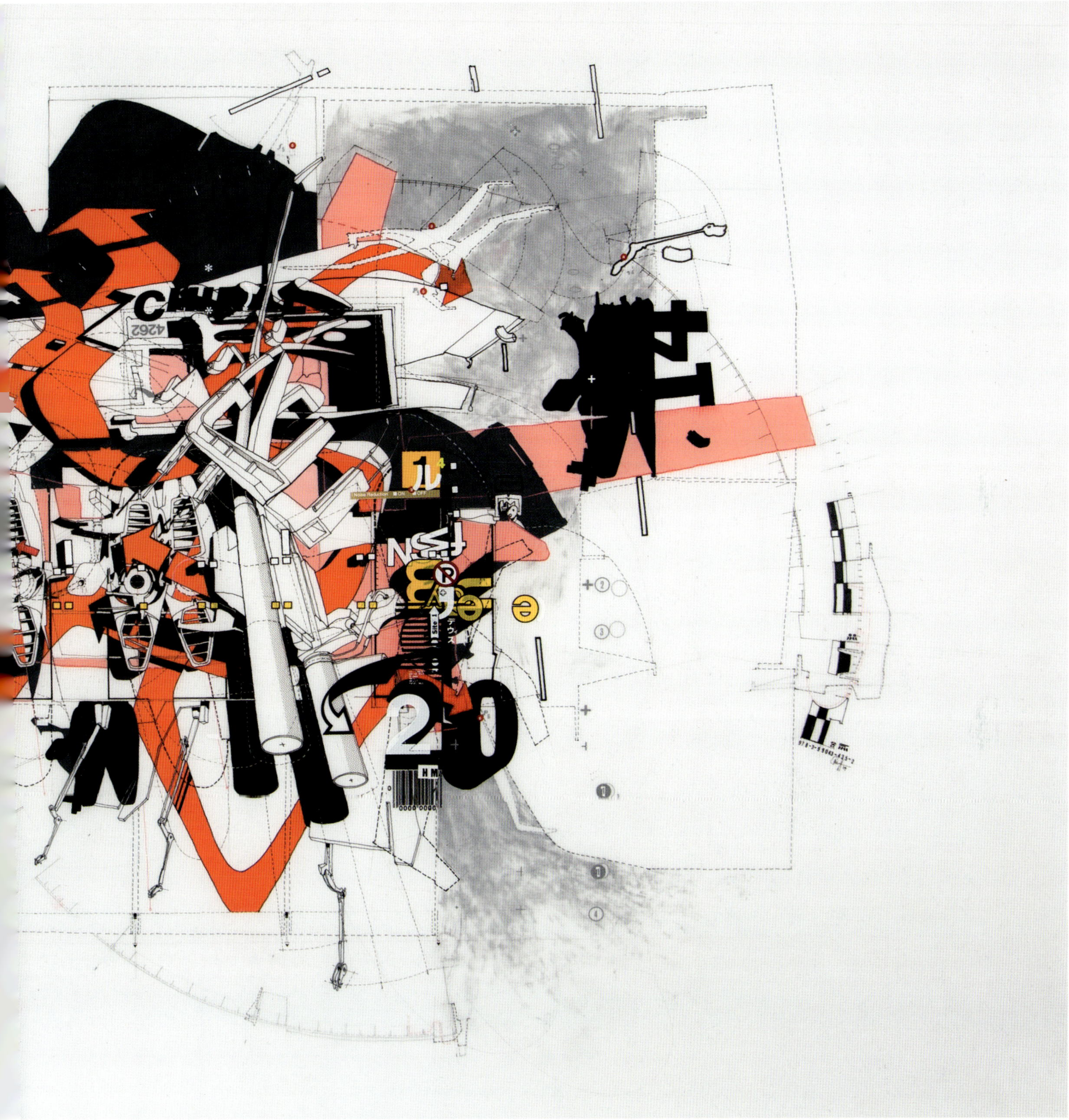

Bryan Cantley

Cosmo-logy Viral Implant

2014

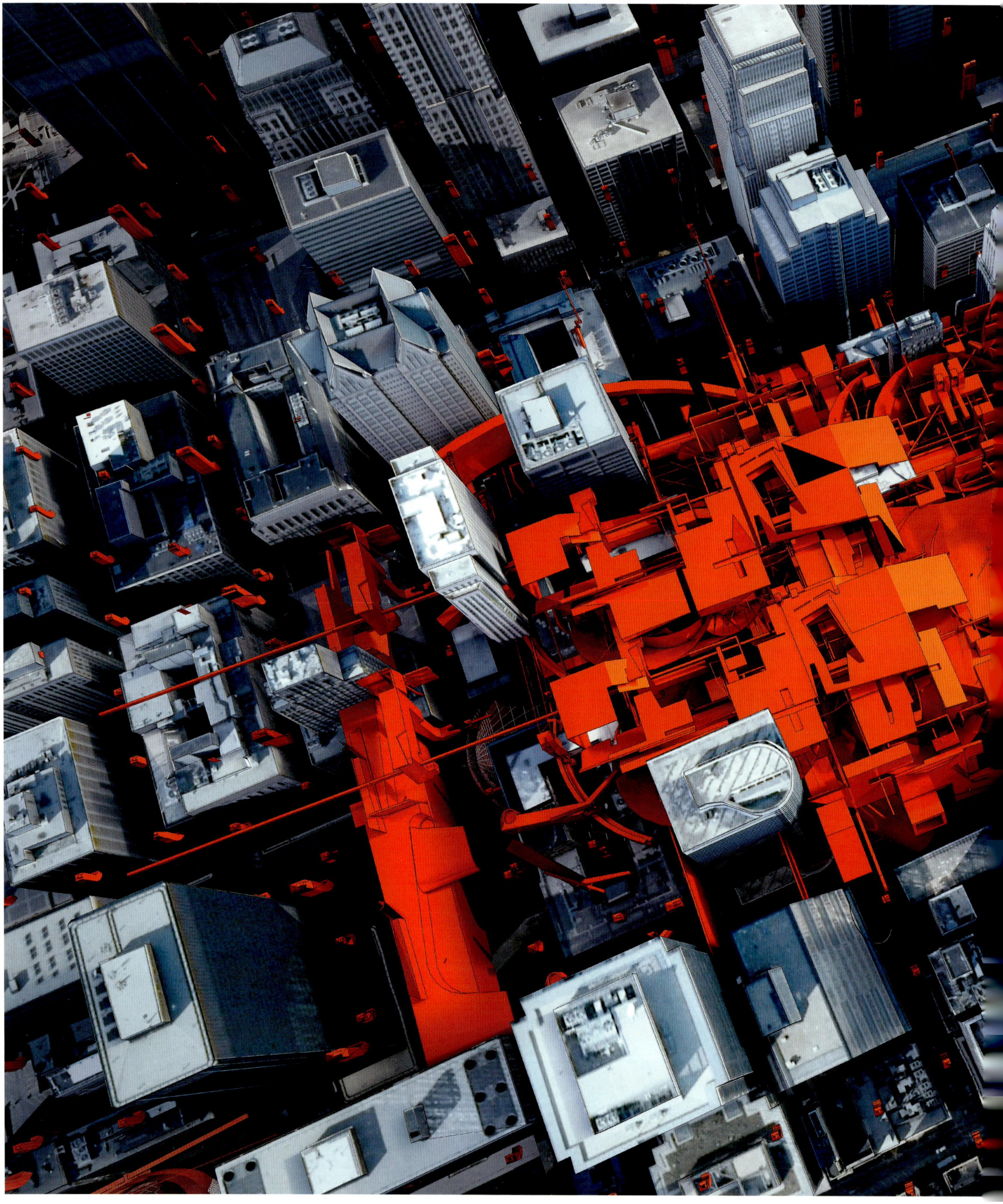

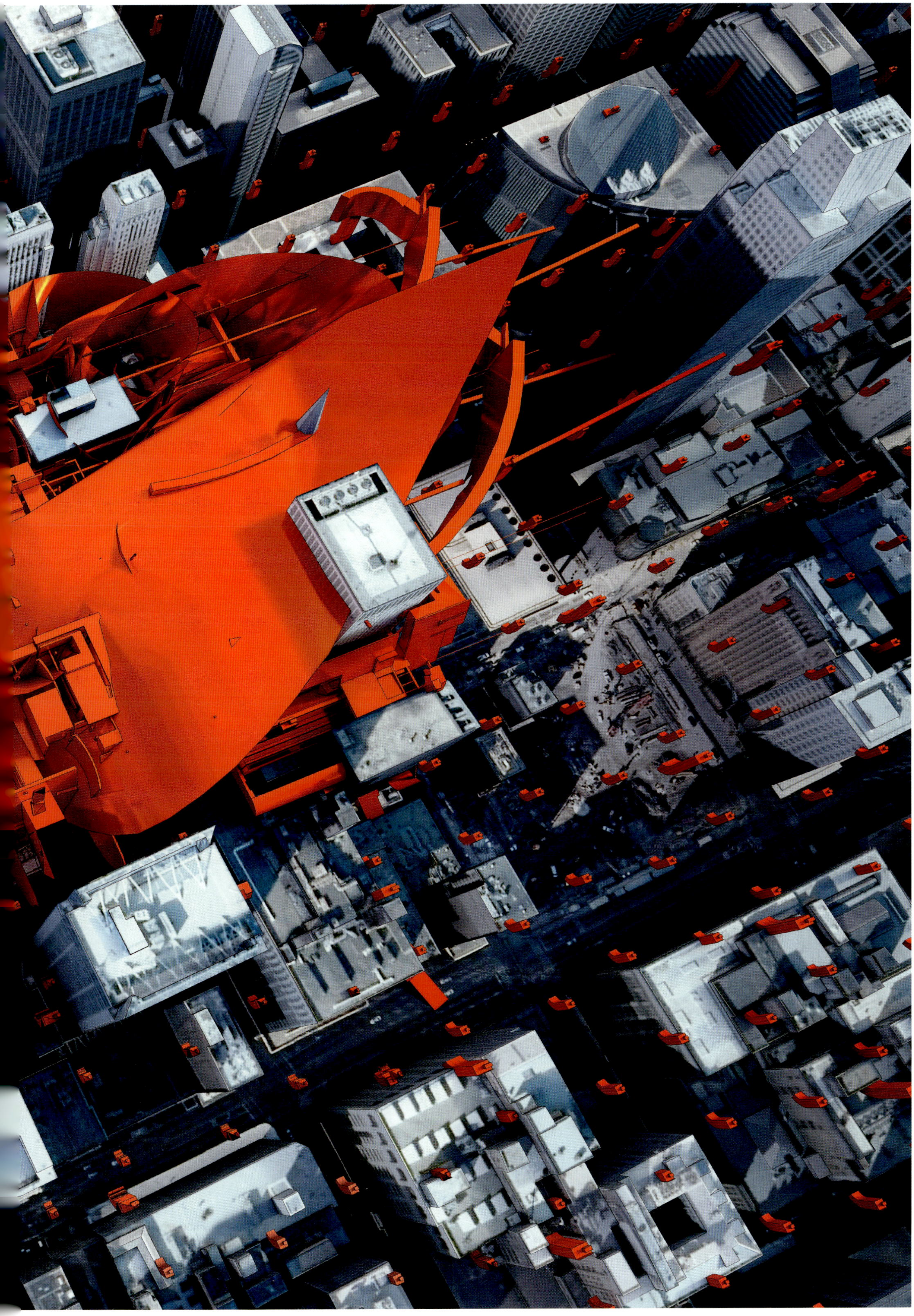

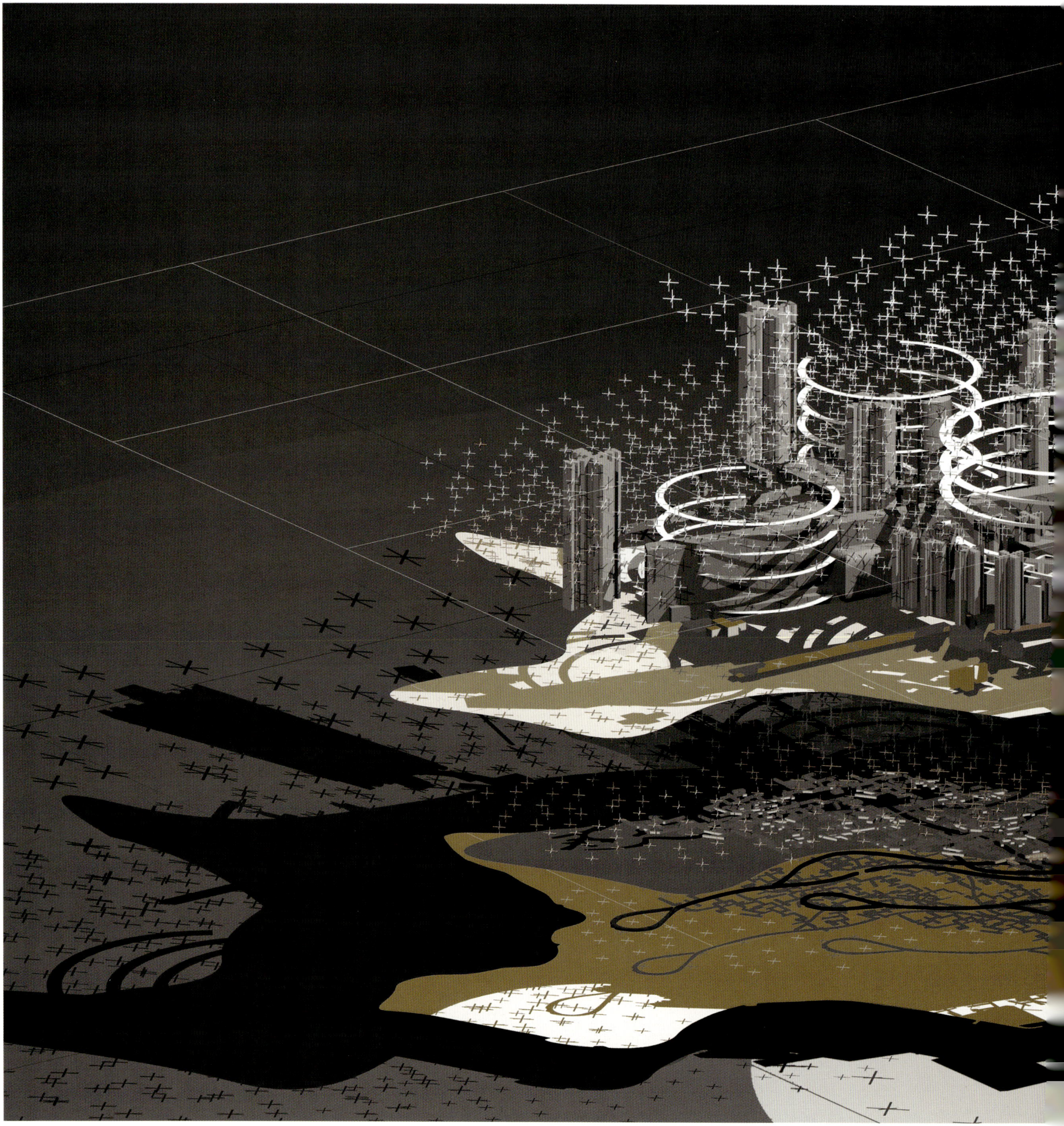

↑

Nic Clear • The Gold Mine **(layered isometric)**

2014

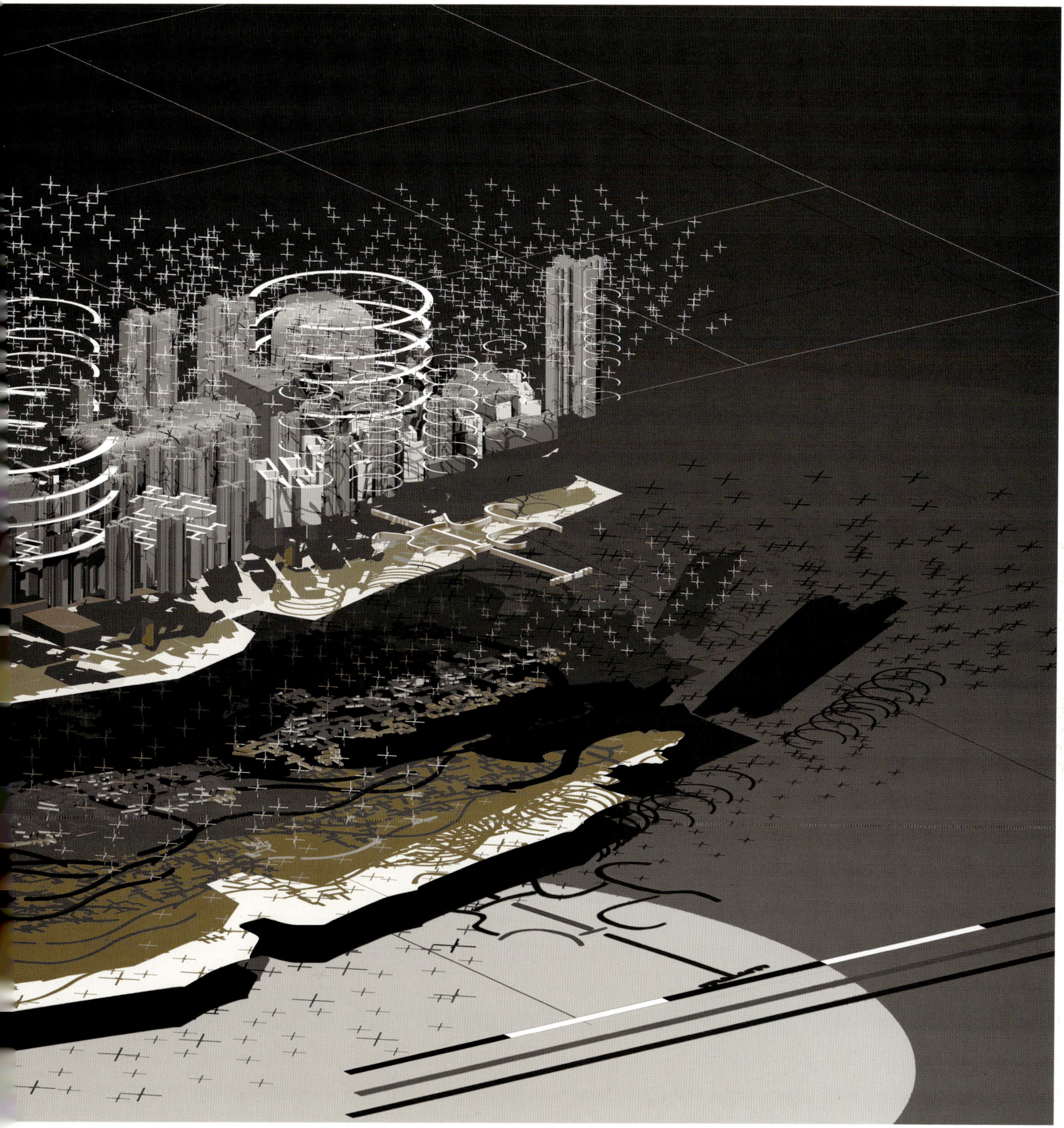

Nic Clear • The Gold Mine **(plan)**

2015

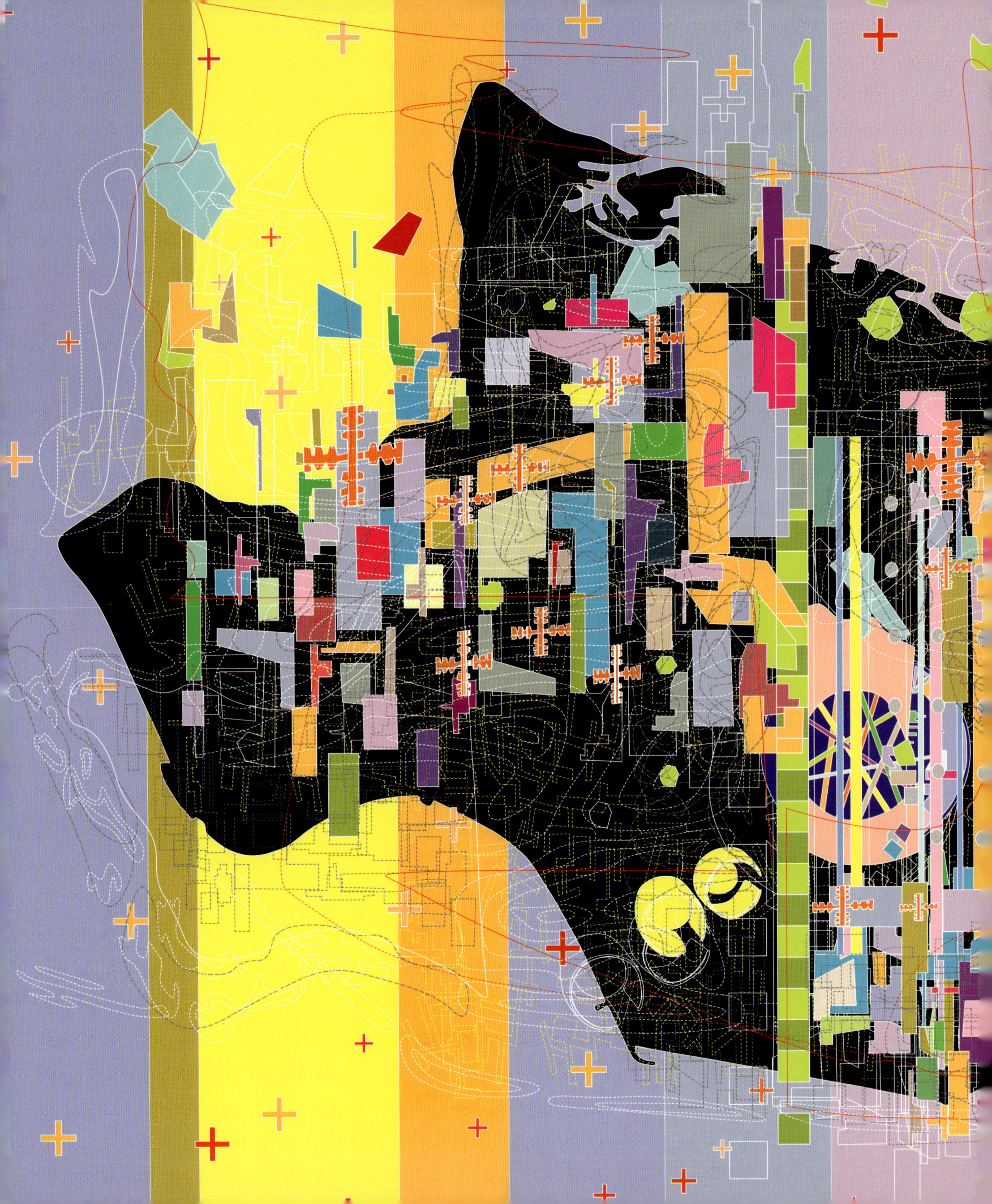

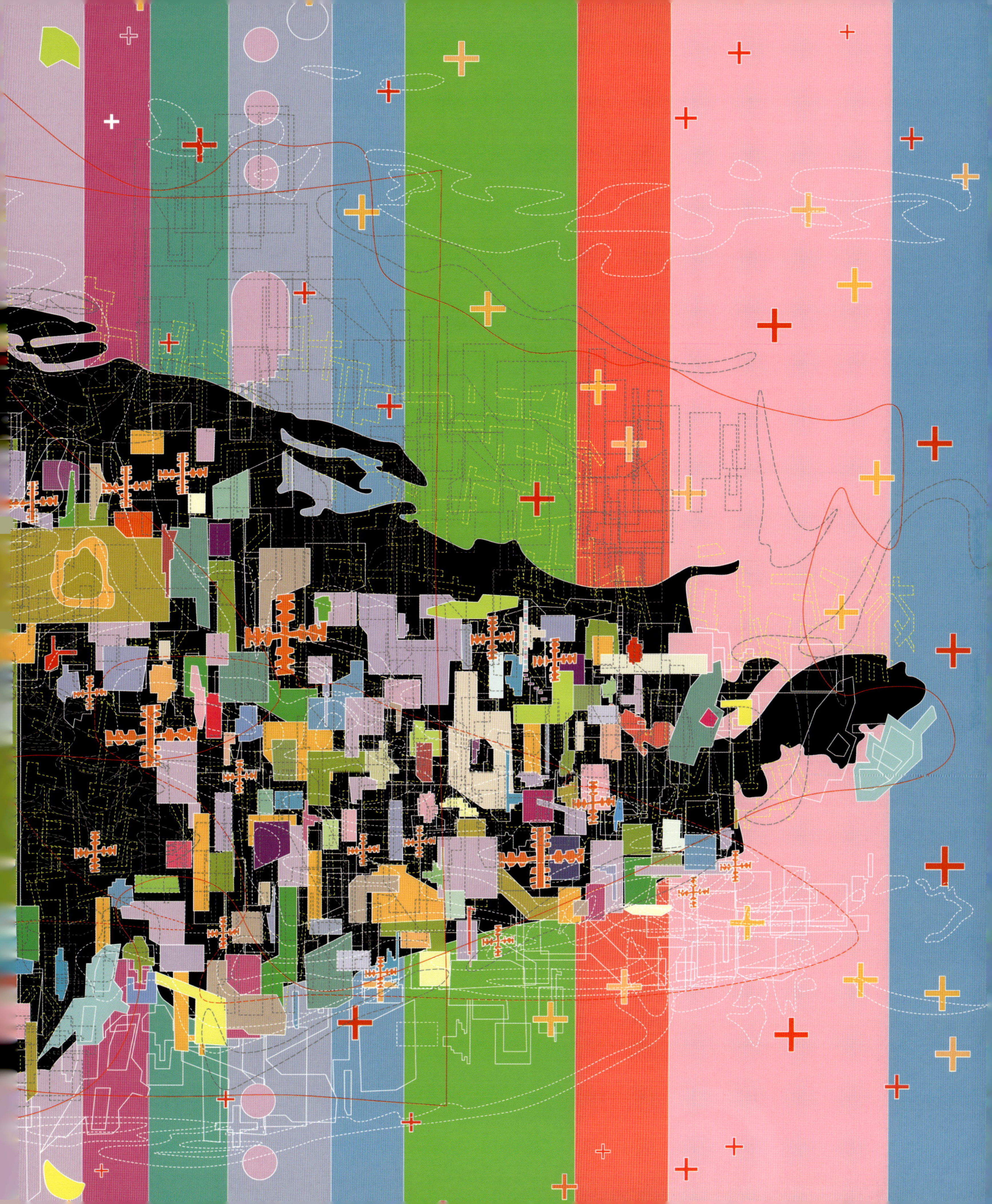

THE SURREAL MEMORY THEATRE OF MIXED REALITY

NEIL SPILLER

'COMMUNICATING VESSELS' | 1998–

WALLED GARDEN FOR LEBBEUS | 2012–14

GIOVANNI BATTISTA PIRANESI
THE GIANT WHEEL, **PLATE IX FROM**
CARCERI D'INVENZIONE
(IMAGINARY PRISONS), 1750–61

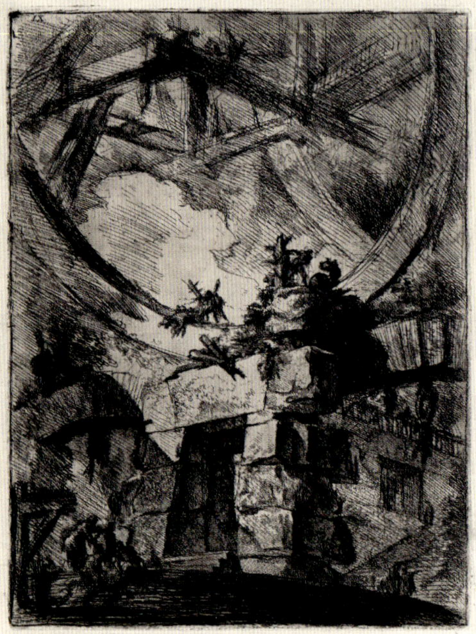

Plate IX was a later addition to the Carceri series – the great window/eye at its centre a fitting inspiration for the upper chamber of the frustum in the Walled Garden for Lebbeus.

'Communicating Vessels' is a self-instigated, drawn and written theoretical architectural design project. The work that is shown and discussed here is part of a larger whole initiated in 1998 that continues onward. The bulk of the project is positioned on an island in Britain's smallest town, Fordwich, just outside Canterbury in England. This is not a traditional architectural site; it is more a psychogeographical place that for the author holds memories of childhood.

The scheme seeks to explore and illustrate the far-reaching effects on architecture of biotechnology, virtuality and nanotechnology, particularly in relation to the old dichotomy between architecture and landscape. Technology is allowing architects to mix and augment real spaces with virtual ones, to question the inertness of materials and, vicariously, architecture, to link and network electronically all manner of spaces and scales of phenomena together, create reflexive spatial relationships between them, and blend the organic and the inorganic. Simultaneously, the aged doctrines of Modernism are being questioned: decoration and Baroque distortion are respectable again. The 'everyday' has proved a fecund breeding ground for new ideas. Narrative is also finding its way into much architectural work. Above all, architecture's relationship with biotechnology is evolving fast.

UNAUGMENTED PLAN, WALLED GARDEN FOR LEBBEUS **2012**

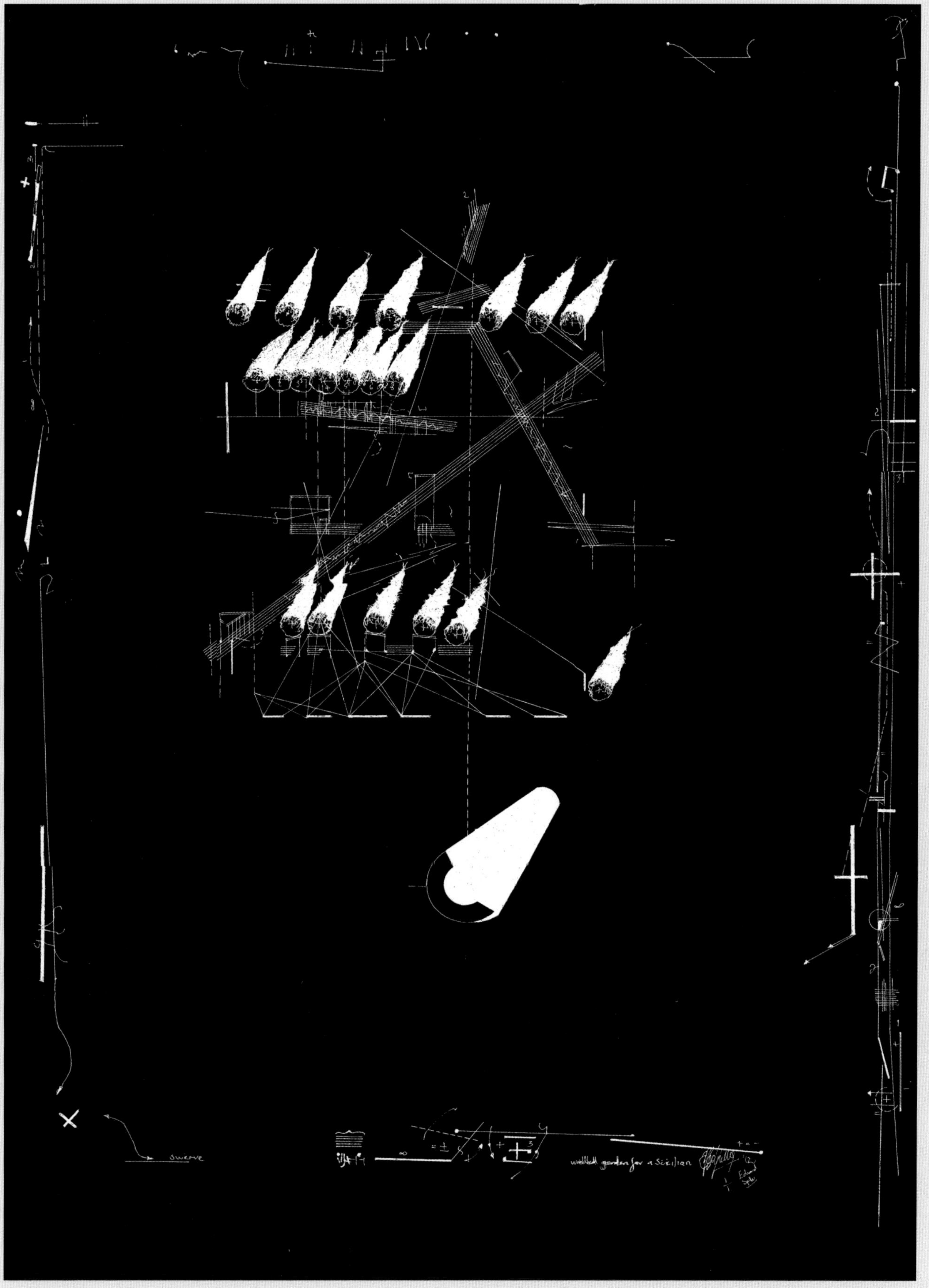

The memorial garden showing the frustum, walls and trees.

The project re-examines traditional paradigms and elements of garden design such as the gazebo, the garden shed, walled garden, bird bath, entrance gates, riverside seats, love seats, vistas, sculptures, fountains, topiary and outside grown rooms among many other objects and spaces. It redesigns them, electronically connects them, explores their virtual and actual materiality, and their cultural and mnemonic importance, and reassesses them in the wake of the impact of advanced technology on the protocols of contemporary architectural design in the twenty-first century. Another preoccupation of the project is that by looking to some of the spatial tactics of the Dadaists, Pataphysicists, Surrealists, Situationists, Oulipo and the Symbolists, we can gain an insight into new spatial arrangements for our architectures that are appropriate for our time. The project now includes more than five hundred drawings and thousands of words of explanation and prose.

Today's spacescapes are a rich mix of the virtual and the actual. The complex clusters of architectural elements and interactions that exist within the 'Communicating Vessels' project are a network of scalar inputs and outputs; some actions impact on actual geographies and some on virtual geographies, and this relationship continues to change as the spaces remix themselves due to chance occurrences.

It is the contention of this architectural project that only a re-evaluation of Surrealism can help us to expand the ambition of our contemporary spacescapes and describe, choreograph and notate their architectural potentials.

One element of 'Communicating Vessels' is the *Walled Garden for Lebbeus*, a remembrance garden that is at once a quiet reflective space, but simultaneously the eye of a virtual storm. Lebbeus Woods, the globally renowned architect and producer of a lifetime of architectural works that rival those of Giovanni Battista Piranesi from the eighteenth century in their dexterity and exploration of architectural space, passed away in 2012 on the night Hurricane Sandy hit New York. In the last phase of his career he had become interested in creating architectural space from fields of vectors, which he manifested in drawings as well as site-specific sculptural interventions.

In reality the *Walled Garden* is a simple enclosure defined by a composition of walls that are not continuous but broken (not ruined) and porous, a few lines of trees, some sculptural pieces and a frustum (truncated cone) – a reference to Aldo Rossi's smokestack memorial at the San Cataldo Cemetery in Modena, Italy (1971; see page 135). Surveying the whole garden is a sculpture of a De Chirico-like woman; the plaque on her plinth says 'Electra'. Electra has no back to her head:

> *Now the boy pushed his face into the hollowed void in the back of the statue's head, and feeling her cold caress around his face and her clayey cold kiss on his lips he opened his eyes wide, seeing through her eyes. Immediately the garden went dark and was filled with a foreboding.... A clap of thunder, deafening, in his ears, he felt the statue shudder with its force.*[1]

This is an augmented-reality storm, a storm of memory, of icons, of raining vectors and virtual snowdrifting that rages and, eventually, abates, returning to calmness as it disappears. Some of the drawings show this time-based fury and ultimate abatement. Traditional architectural drawings would fail to show such a tumult. Here, however, the charting of time, shifting algorithms, the interrelationships between virtual and actual terrains and mnemonic references requires the drawings to have a shifting status that treads the fine line between traditional architectural drawing and Surrealist tactics and protocols of representation.

Other *Walled Garden* drawings explore the architectural anatomy and events that take place in the upper and lower chambers of the frustum as the storm passes overhead. The top space of the cone takes its inspiration from two key references: Plate IX for the second edition of Piranesi's *Carceri d'Invenzione (Imaginary Prisons;* 1750–61), his epic suite of unbuildable etchings, musing on prisons, but really essays in the mutability of the potential of architectural space – a Dalínian favourite – and Alberto Giacometti's *The Palace at 4 a.m.* (1932–33; see pages 78–79). As the 'eye' of the storm traverses over the top of the 'eye' of the frustum, the upper chamber becomes progressively darker, and the light-sensitive figure of a woman retreats in the sheltering niche built into its curved walls. She is attached in the larger, lower chamber to a huge meat hook from which is suspended a mannequin. As the woman above repeatedly goes in and out of her shelter, the meat hook/mannequin moves backwards and forwards in a rocking motion.

Initially, the lower chamber is also filled with the black 'grease', a biomechanical fluid that powers all of the Communicating Vessels on the island. The more the storm is activated, the more the rocking in the lower chamber and the more the grease is powered to nanotechnologically make the other half of the tableau – an artificial swan. Once the process is complete, this surreal Leda and the Swan is revealed. In this story from Greek mythology (so important to the Surrealists and particularly to Salvador Dalí, who often painted his wife/muse Gala as Leda) Zeus, who, like the 'grease' and Surrealism itself, is a metamorphic entity, takes the form of a swan and seduces or rapes Leda. Depictions of the myth have a continuity through time, from the fifteenth and sixteenth centuries in the works of great artists such as Leonardo da Vinci and Michelangelo, and more contemporary pieces by, for example, the American painter Cy Twombley, and in the twentieth-century literary references of the Irish poet William Butler Yeats and American novelist Sylvia Plath. Even Hilda Doolittle, Freud's patient latterly, wrote of this bestial act in romantic terms. It therefore seemed appropriate that the nuances of these other free thinkers who made their own creative universes should also feature in the design of the Garden for Lebbeus.

BALLAD OF CRAFTY JACK **2013**
↓

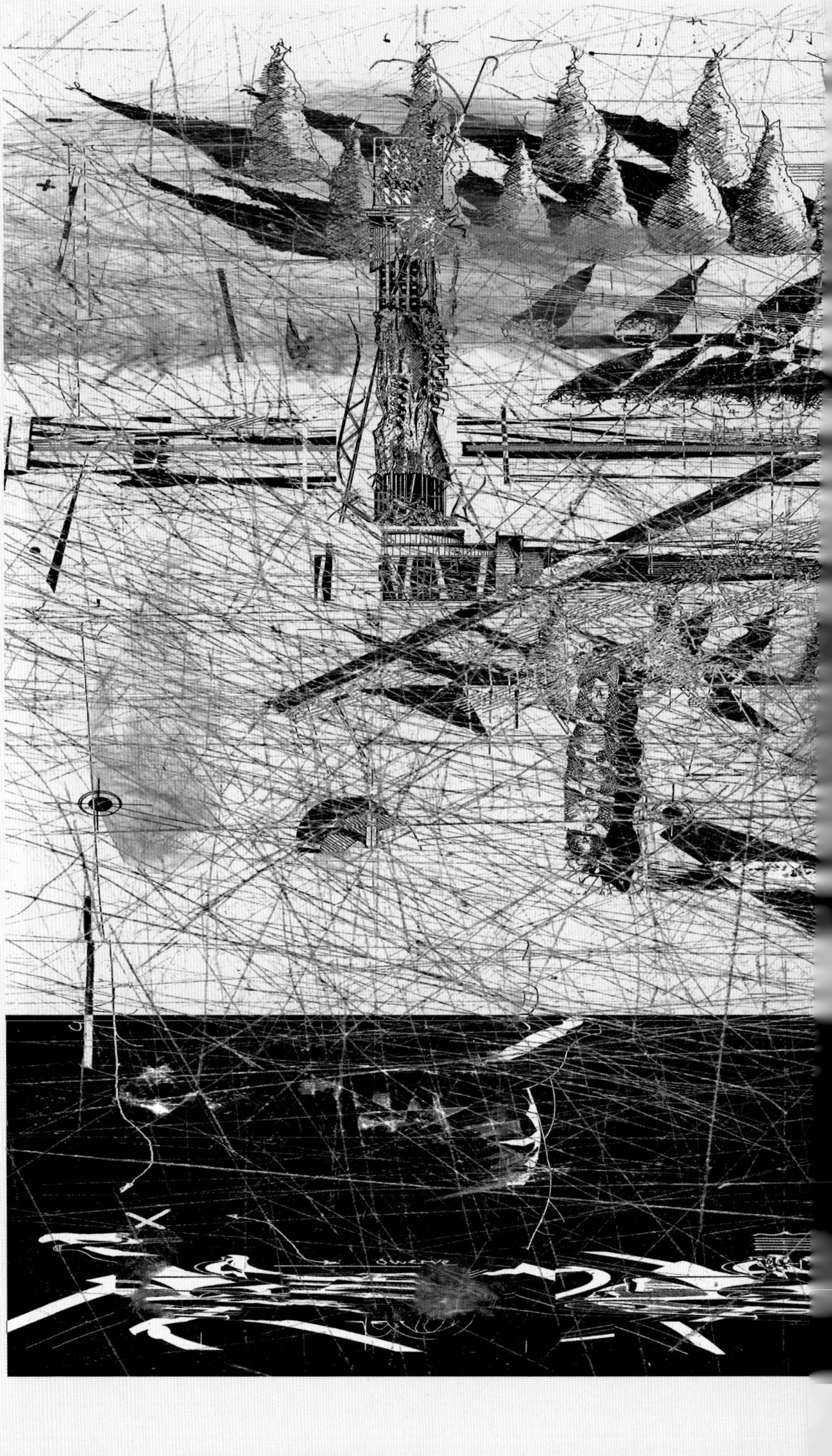

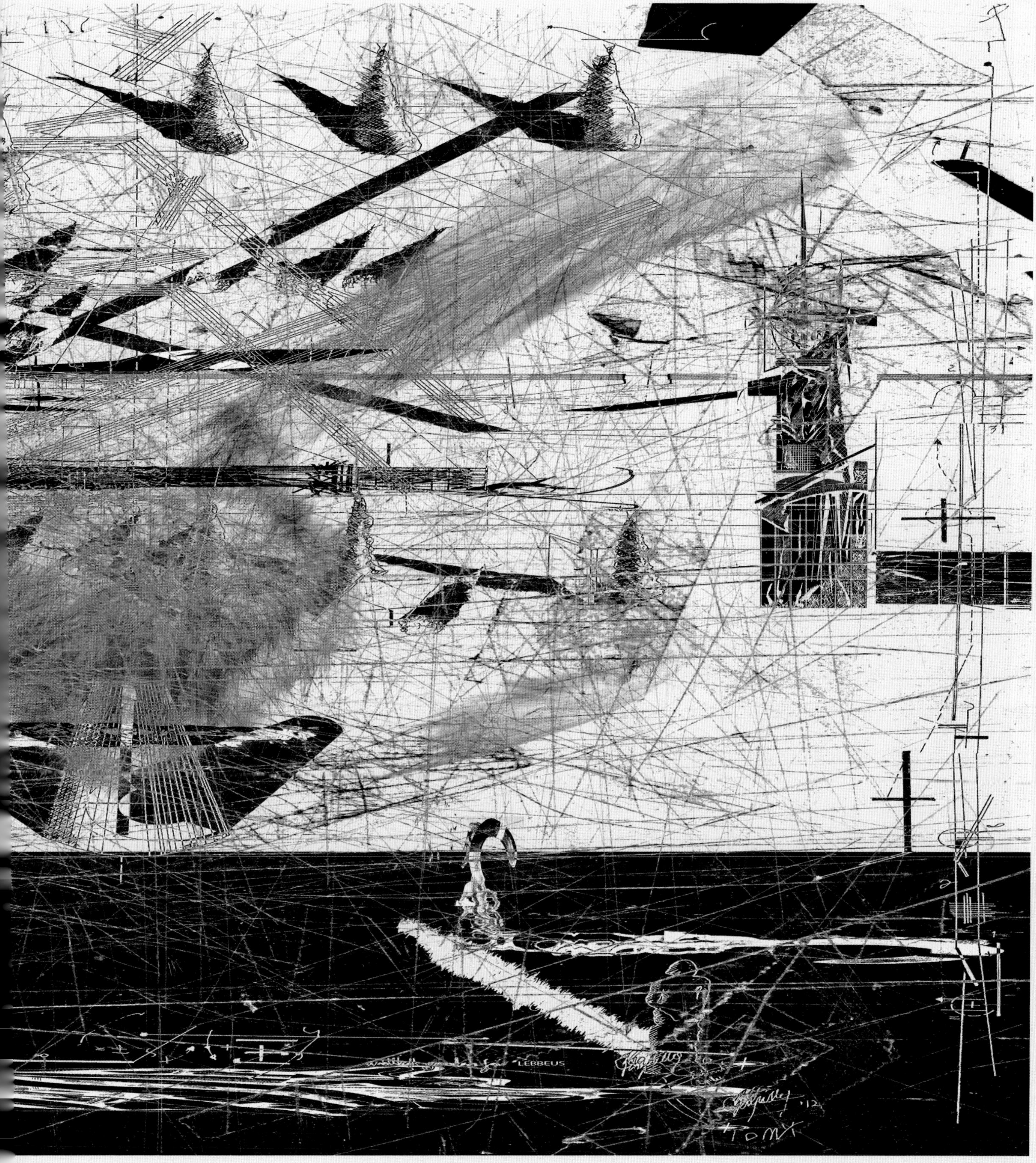

↑
The storm with virtual ghosts and actual landscape.

↓

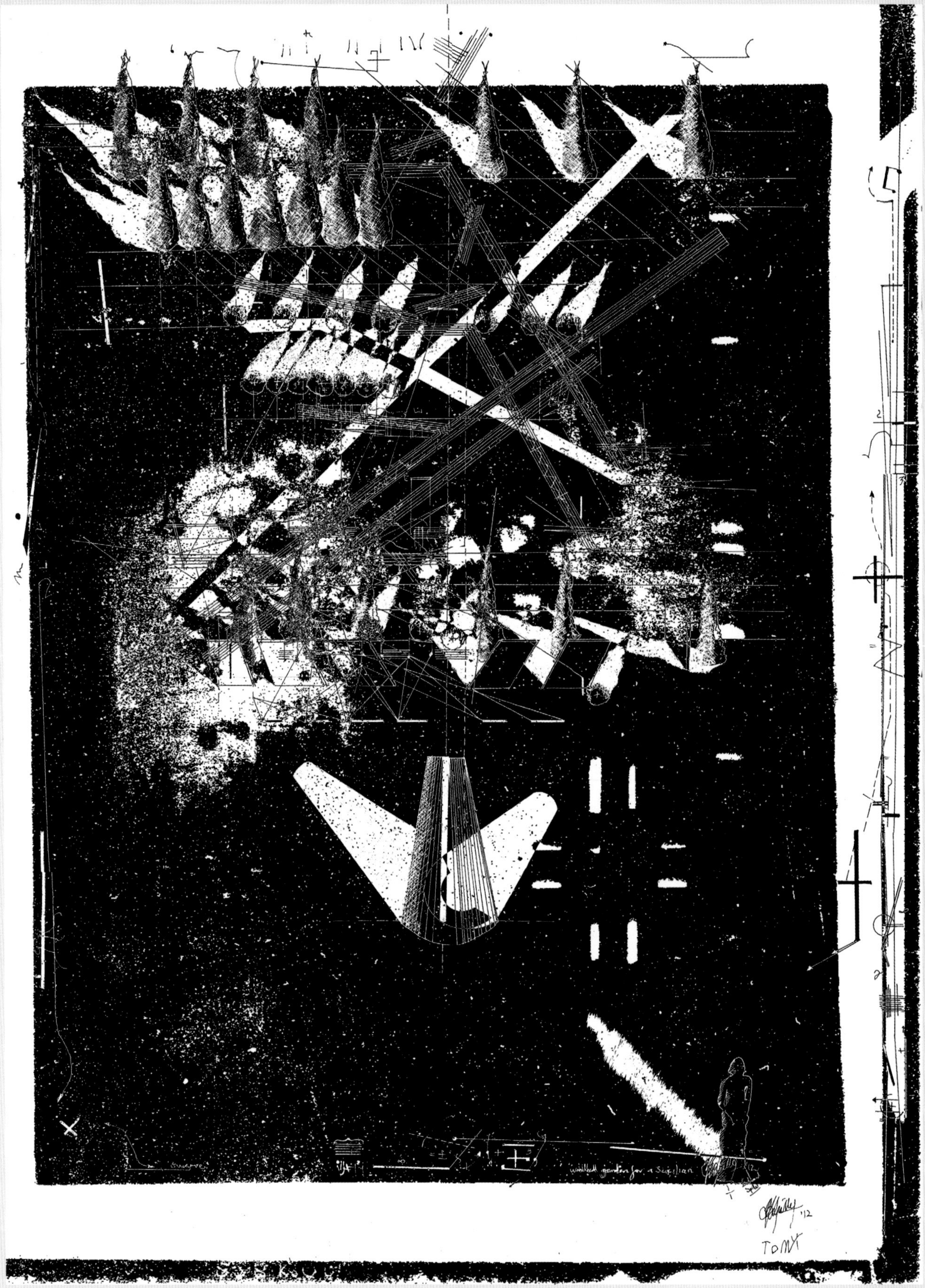

↑

The genesis of the augmented-reality storm.

↓

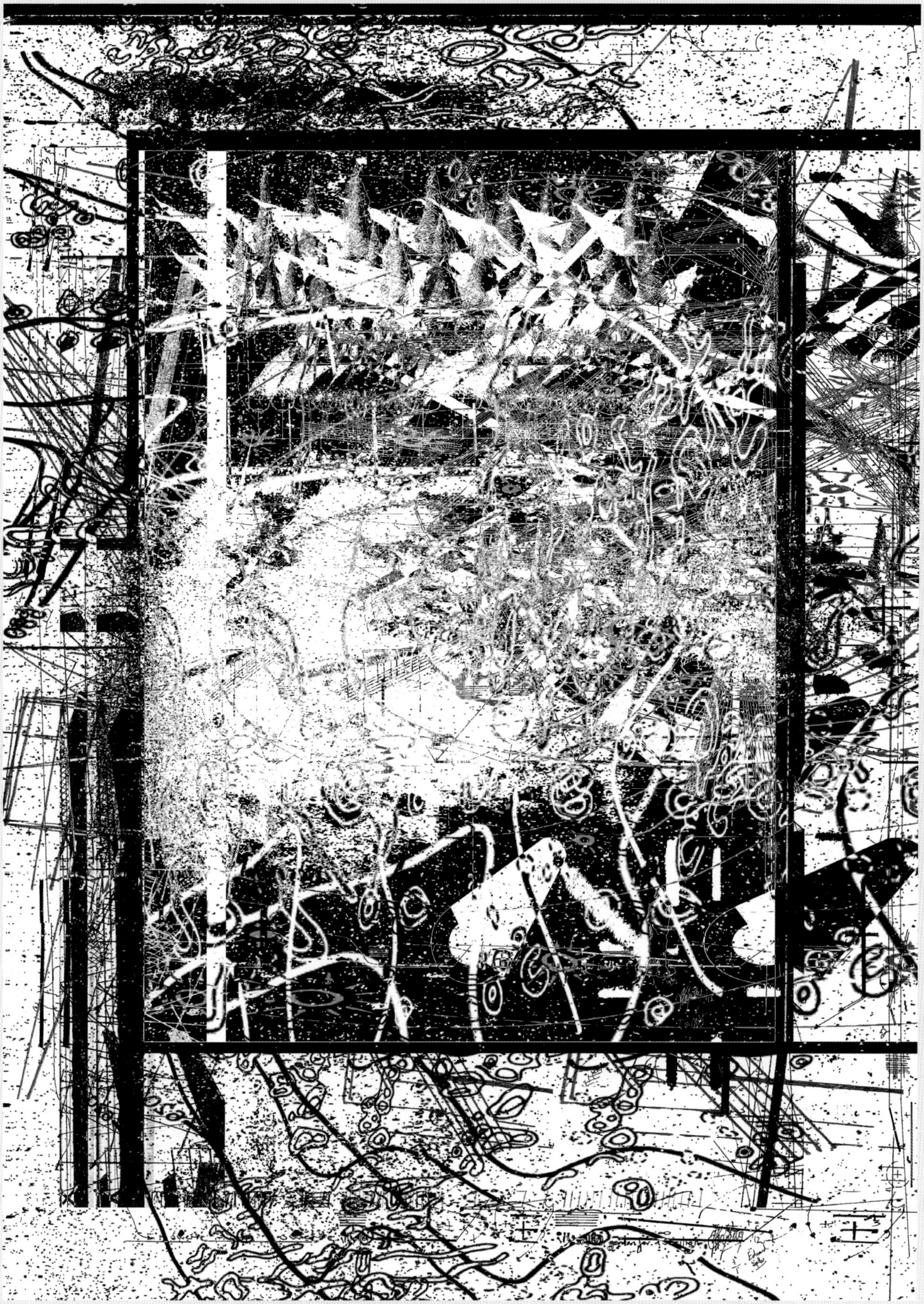

↑

The zenith of the storm showing the virtual snowdrifts.

GOLD STORM **2013**
↓

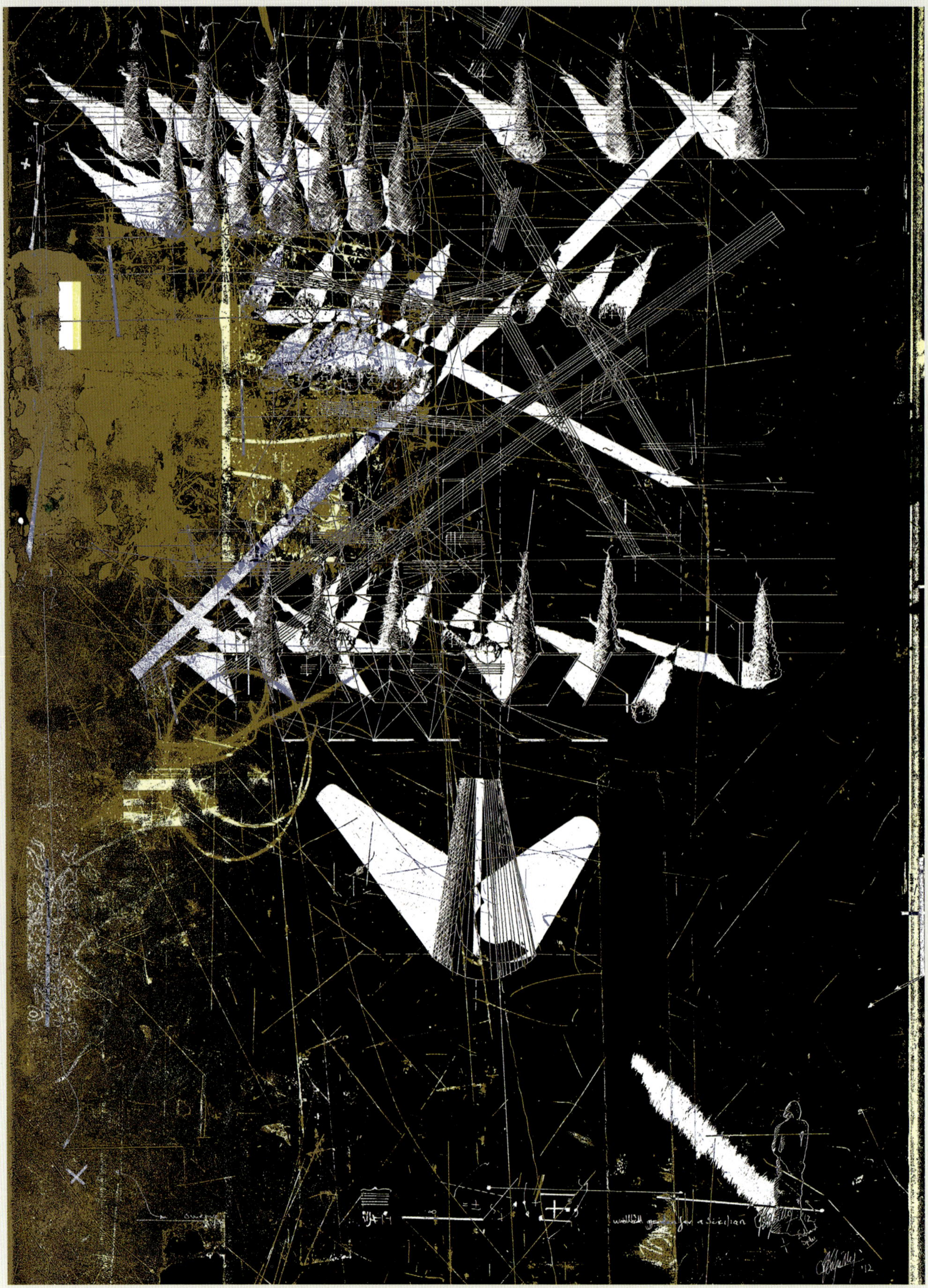

↑
The Garden does not always simulate real storms, and might on occasion teem with gold or other effects.

STORM OVER FRUSTUM (UPPER CHAMBER) **2014**

↓

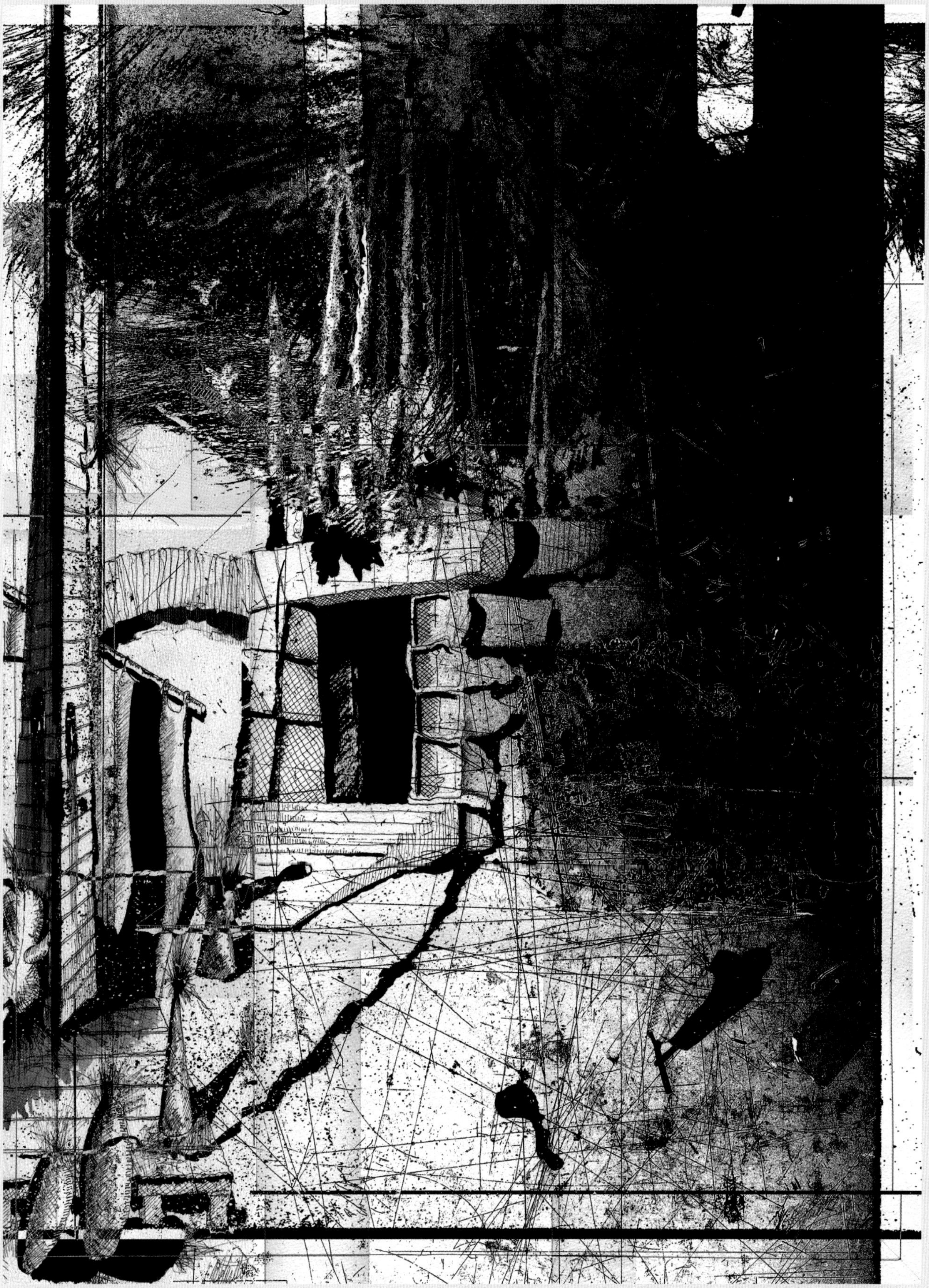

↑

The storm passes over the open top of the frustum, creating darkness.

LEDA AND THE SWAN WITH GREASE RESIDUE **2014**

↓

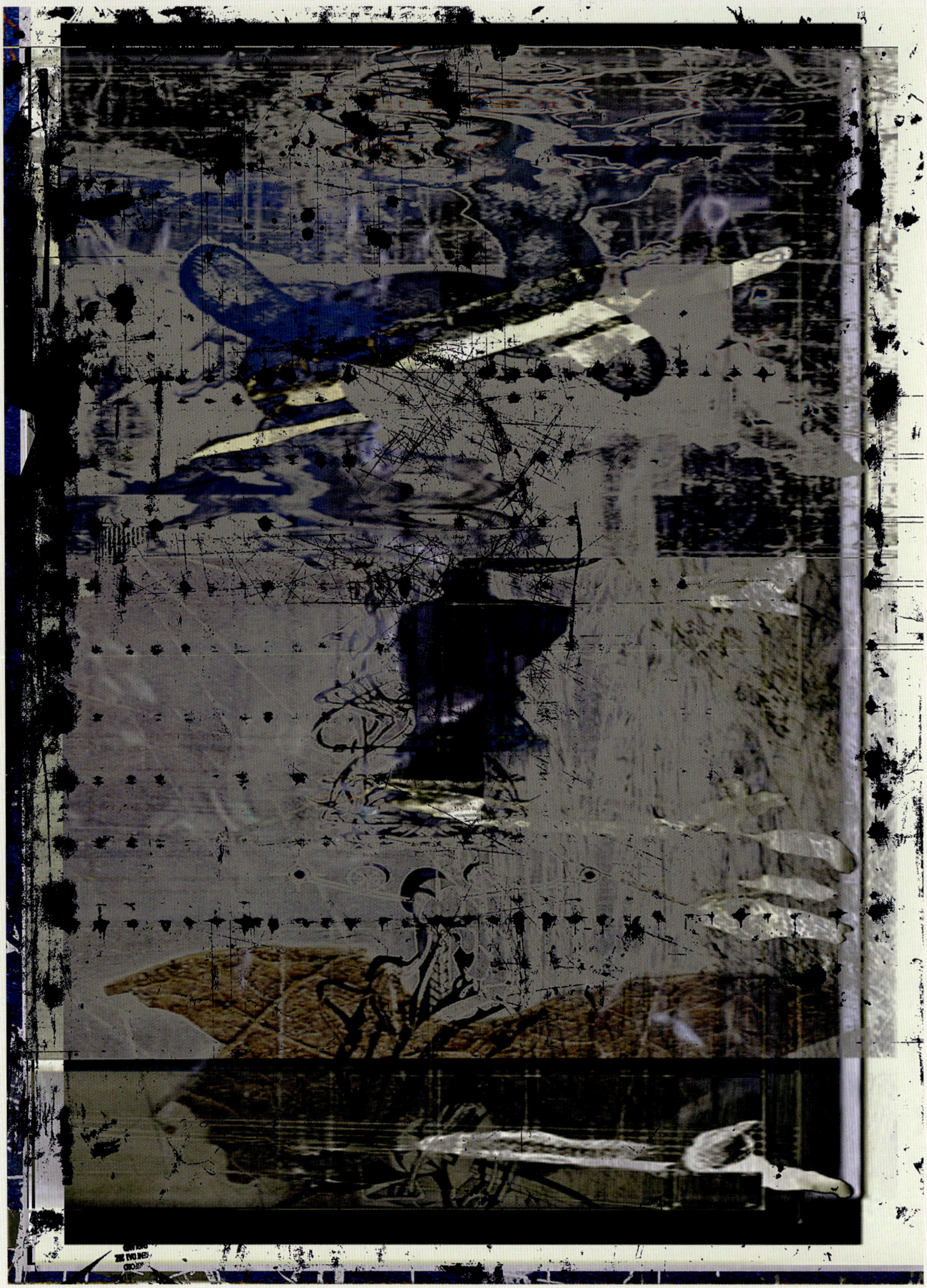

↑

The grease from which the tableau is formed slowly disappears.

LEDA AND THE SWAN COMPLETE **2014**

↓

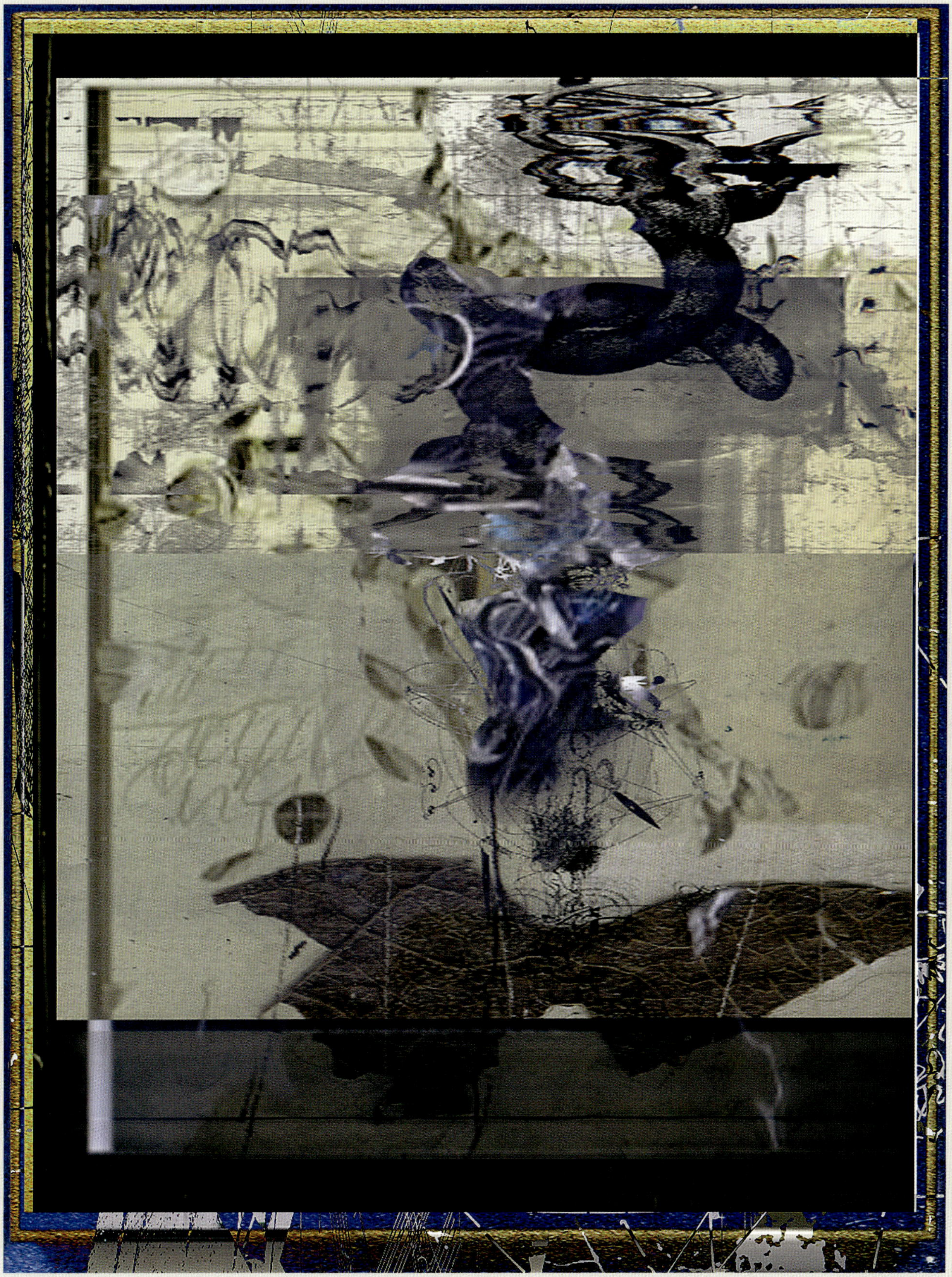

↑

The final tableau is revealed.

[These organisms] whose physical being is sometimes flabby and sometimes porous, at other times osseous but fragile, breaking open to display huge colonies of seeds or bulbs which grow and ferment in the blind hope of some vital metamorphosis, that seem to struggle against a soft impenetrable skin – these abnormal creatures with pointed or horny protuberances, or petticoats, skirts and fringes of fibrils and pistils, articulations that are sometimes mucous and sometimes cartilaginous, might well belong to one of the great families of jungle flora, ambiguous, savage, and fascinating in their monstrous way.

Leo Lionni, 'Parallel Botany', 1977[1]

The Art Nouveau decorative objects disclose to us, in the most tangible way, the persistence of dream through reality, because, submitted to a painstaking examination, these objects offer us the most striking oneiric element.... In the hideous street, gnawed on all sides, by the perpetual torment of a corrosive reality with its appalling quality, in the hideous street, the delirious and completely beautiful ornamentation of the Art Nouveau mouths of the [Paris-Guimard] Métro.

Salvador Dalí, 'Surtout l'art ornemental', 1931[2]

THE ENGORGED GARDEN

CHAPTER IV

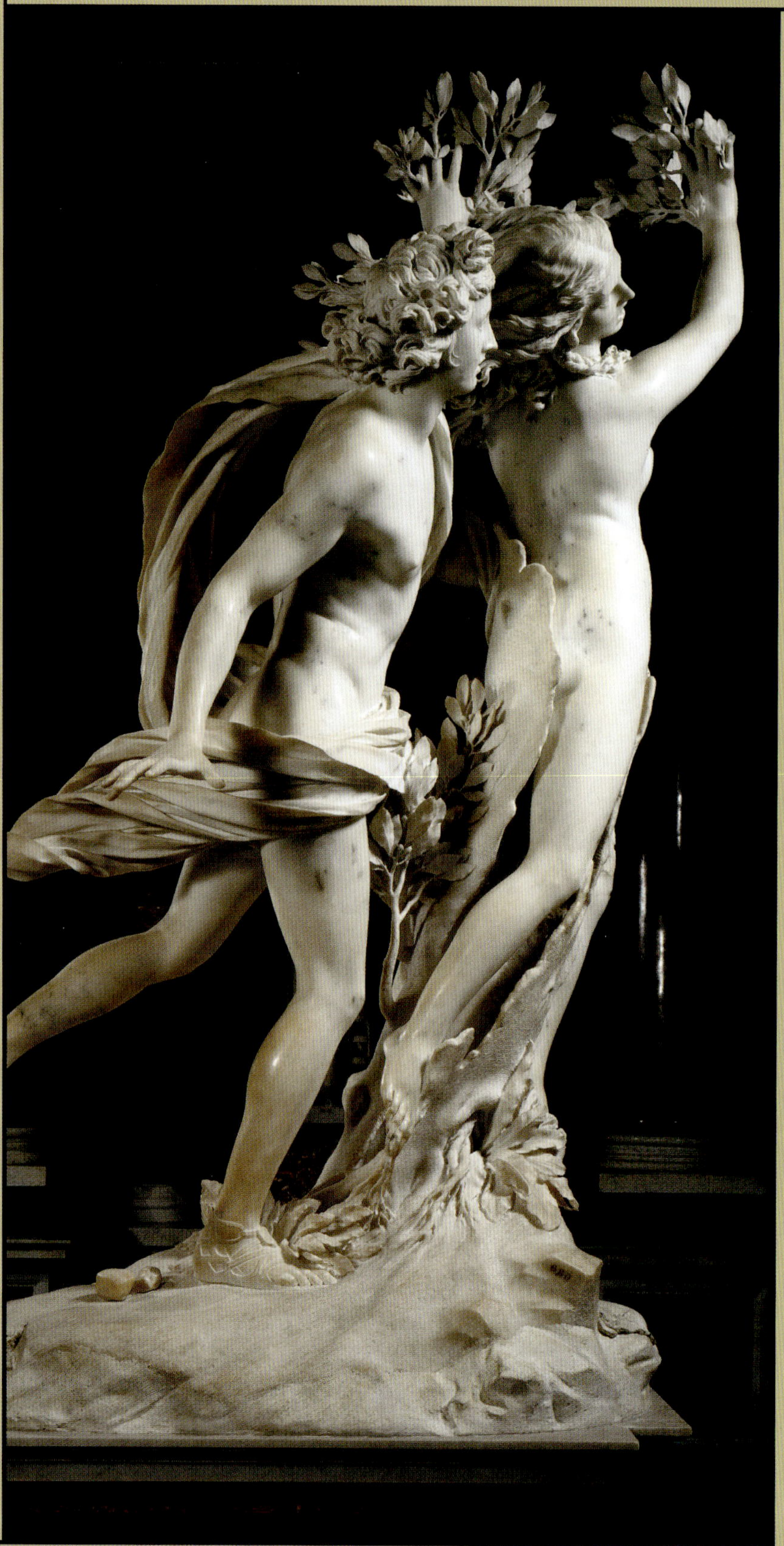

←

Gian Lorenzo Bernini • Apollo and Daphne

1622–25

For millennia, architecture has been imbued with forms derived from nature. The tree/column, the forest canopy/roof and the acanthus leaf/capital – there are endless examples. Likewise, natural landscape features have often been prone to animistic interpretations: river nymphs, mountain gods and dark forest demons. Our mythologies and our architectures of the past and the future are dependent on these points of crossover between alive and dead, the organic and inorganic. What interested the Surrealists is the moment of transition and its potential for all manner of hysterical interpretation and creative power. Especially beguiling for them were the opportunities of combining the mechanistic with the organic. This chapter is about both the moment of metamorphosis, where simultaneity is at its strongest, and the architectural synthesis of the biological with human agency.

Semiotic Metamorphosis

Salvador Dalí in particular was drawn to the myth of Apollo and Daphne and the way in which it defines this moment of metamorphosis. In both Greek and Roman versions, the myth tells the story of the river nymph, Daphne, who ignites the ardour of the god Apollo. To escape his desirous embrace and carnal attentions, Daphne turns herself into a tree. The subject of much art over the centuries, one sculpture stands out above anything else: the Italian sculptor Gian Lorenzo Bernini's *Apollo and Daphne*, housed in the Galleria Borghese in Rome. Bernini's great work catches the couple right at that moment of change, of betweenness, where one thing becomes another. Daphne's fingers are growing leaves and branches, her feet are starting to become roots, and her torso starting to be engulfed in bark. She represents the momentary multiple dualities of tree/woman, desire/chastity and animate/inanimate.

This point of inflection was a source of marvellous beauty for the Surrealists and is at the heart of their creative discourse – beauty through transgression. It also often involves the subversion or violent disregard of the ordered geometries of the garden with its parterres and topiary in favour of the bloody, moist, fecundity of the jungle – where fear meets beauty. Henri Rousseau's jungle paintings reflect these associations (see pages 18–19), and fanned the Surrealists' primordial fears of the jungle, its strangeness, its teetering on the edge of chaos and death where life is cheap and dispatched without emotion:

> **It is not, in the end, the inauthenticity of Rousseau's Jungles as such that counts for me here; it is what they could do for their spectators (at least momentarily) from a scientifically ordered world (the world for which the Museum stood as a dominant scientific institution in progressive Third Republic France), and they could de-familiarize the worlds of distant flora and fauna made familiar by the popular culture of the exotic under colonialism.**[3]

This defamiliarization of the familiar can also reveal the moment of betweenness. The divergence or swerve from the logical, the established and the epistemologically already defined is embodied in Alfred Jarry's 'clinamen' (the principle of deviance). As we have seen (see page 13), the clinamen is a 'pataphysical concept, but in Jarry's *Exploits and Opinions of Doctor Faustroll, 'Pataphysician* (1911) it is given physical form and a caretaker – Jarry's friend, Rousseau. The Clinamen in the book is a painting machine, a kind of

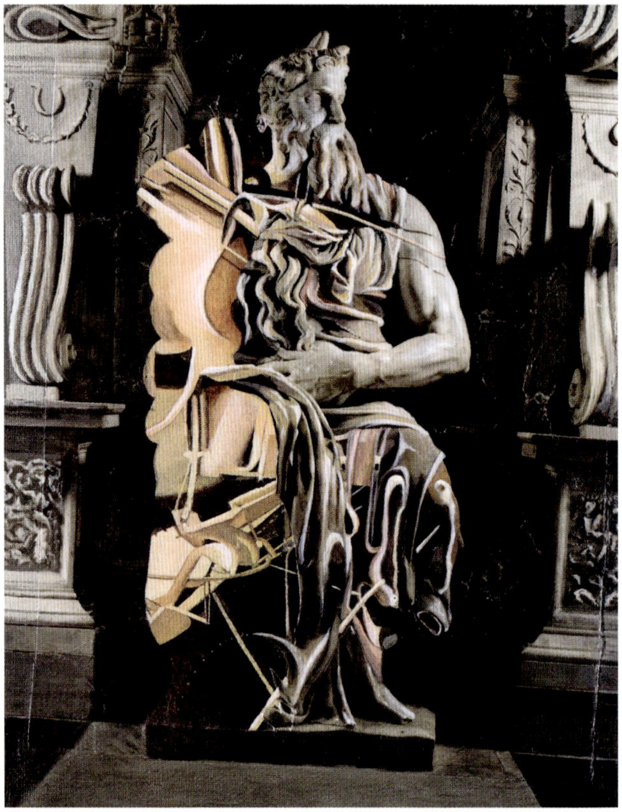

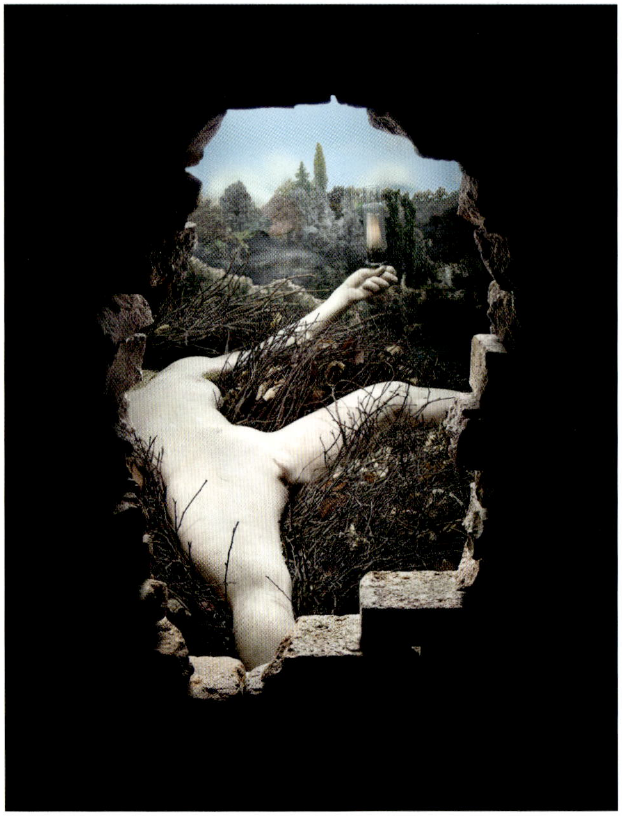

sprawling, irreverent, spurting, incontinent automaton monster. Its job is to choreograph chance in the desecration of the defined epistemologies of painting (one should remember that when *Faustroll* was written, abstraction in art was starting to take hold and to threaten the artistic establishment). It is almost inconceivable that Marcel Duchamp (with his liking for Jarry's work) did not take some inspiration from the Clinamen during his development of some of the components of the *The Bride Stripped Bare by Her Bachelors, Even (The Large Glass*; see page 45). The Clinamen represents again the idea of 'betweenness' – a transition, a fleeting point of possibility and transgression. Jarry describes his wilful creation as follows:

> **Meanwhile, after there was no one left in the world, the painting Machine, animated inside by a system of weightless springs, revolved in azimuth in the iron hall of the Palace of Machines, the only monument standing in a deserted and razed Paris. Like a spinning top, it dashed itself against the pillars, swayed and veered in infinitely varied directions. It followed its own whim in blowing on to the wall's canvas the succession of primary colours ranged according to the tubes of its stomach, like a pousse-l'amour in a bar, the higher colours nearer the surface In the sealed palace which alone ruffled this dead smoothness, this modern deluge of the universal Seine, the unforeseen beast Clinamen ejaculated onto the walls of its universe.[4]**

The Clinamen has influenced a whole strand of painting and drawing machines in modern art and architecture, including the 'Métamatics' series by the Swiss artist Jean Tinguely in the mid-1950s, and the British architect and teacher Nat Chard's series of surreal 'Drawing Instruments' (see page 212).

In his study of Michelangelo's *Moses* (*c.* 1513–15), Sigmund Freud also recognizes in the sculpture this moment of the possible bifurcation of events. He sees three emotional

←

Natalija Subotincic

Interpretation of Rooms, Freud's fascination with the unconscious of Michelangelo's Moses

2009

↙

Marcel Duchamp

Étant donnés: 1. La chute d'eau, 2. Le gaz d'éclairage (Given: 1. The Waterfall, 2. The Illuminating Gas

Philadelphia Museum of Art

1946–66

states portrayed at once in this depiction of Moses just having witnessed the Jews worshipping a pagan icon: immediate anger (prompting the possibility of springing into violent action), pity and stoicism, a renewed determination to change his tribe's unpious ways according to the Ten Commandments on his Tablets of Stone, handed down by God:

> As our eyes travel down it the figure exhibits three distinct emotional strata. The lines of the face reflect the feelings, which have won the ascendancy; the middle of the figure shows the traces of suppressed movement; and the foot still retains the attitude of the projected action. It is as though the controlling influence had proceeded downwards from above. No mention has been made so far of the left arm, and it seems to claim a share in our interpretation. The hand is laid in the lap in a mild gesture and holds as though in a caress the end of the flowing beard. It seems as if it is meant to counteract the violence with which the other hand had misused the beard a few moments ago.[5]

Natalija Subotincic has noted in her studies of Freud (see pages 13–17) that this simultaneity and temporal extension is also present in the *Large Glass*, its initial conception on the Jura to Paris road in 1913, and Duchamp's last great work, *Étant donnés*. She explains her preoccupation with this space of duration in both Duchamp and Michelangelo:

> I know lots of people talk about Freud as a dualist but I have a very different reading of him based on my knowledge of what is going on in these [consulting] rooms from a number of perspectives.... I think he is most fascinated with what gets caught between....My investigation of Duchamp revealed to me that the *Étant donnés* was equally pungent with potential for an 'act' which is either about to happen, has already happened, or is in the process of happening, or all three but in the end remains not fully known. One can only speculate, as Freud was doing with Moses.... The *Étant donnés* located Duchamp's fascinations somewhere within the aftermath of the consummation of the *Bride and Bachelor*, and the beginning of the gestation of what I came to refer to as the 'headlight child' (Duchamp's words). Essentially I think Duchamp completed in the *Étant donnés* what he left incomplete in the *Large Glass*. For me they are a single work that exists in a duration...and the *Étant donnés* blows things wide open with potential....This is why I think I included Duchamp with Moses...because I was trying to get at Freud's Moses and the question of potential and being caught between.[6]

The 'headlight child', conceived in Duchamp's notes on his journey to Jura, describe it as the arbiter between dimensions, as having an extended duration and form – similar to André Breton's conceptions of the 'Great Transparents' of nearly thirty years later – and possibly not totally intelligible to human beings.

Surreal works 'blossom' with potential, they are machines of simultaneity, dimensionally extended, hybrid, unfamiliar and metamorphic in ways that transgress perceived natural boundaries. This is what makes them convulsively marvellous, and is what Dalí saw in Art Nouveau architecture. Nothing is sacred, particularly biology.

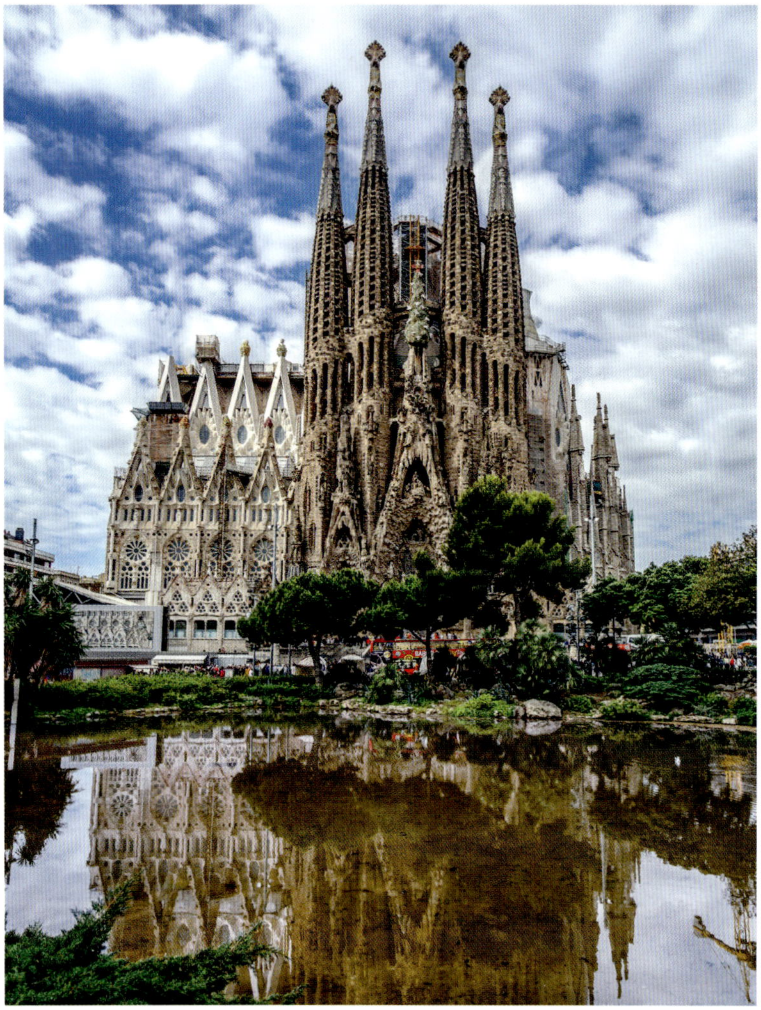
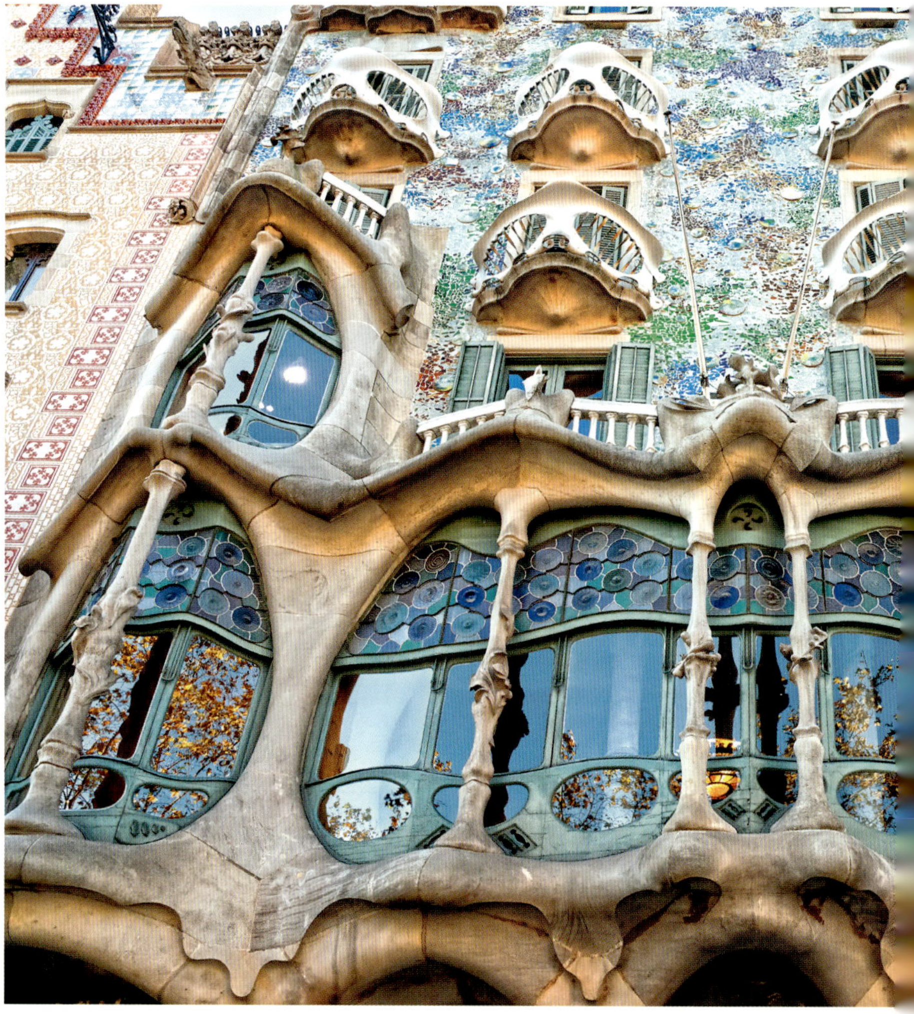
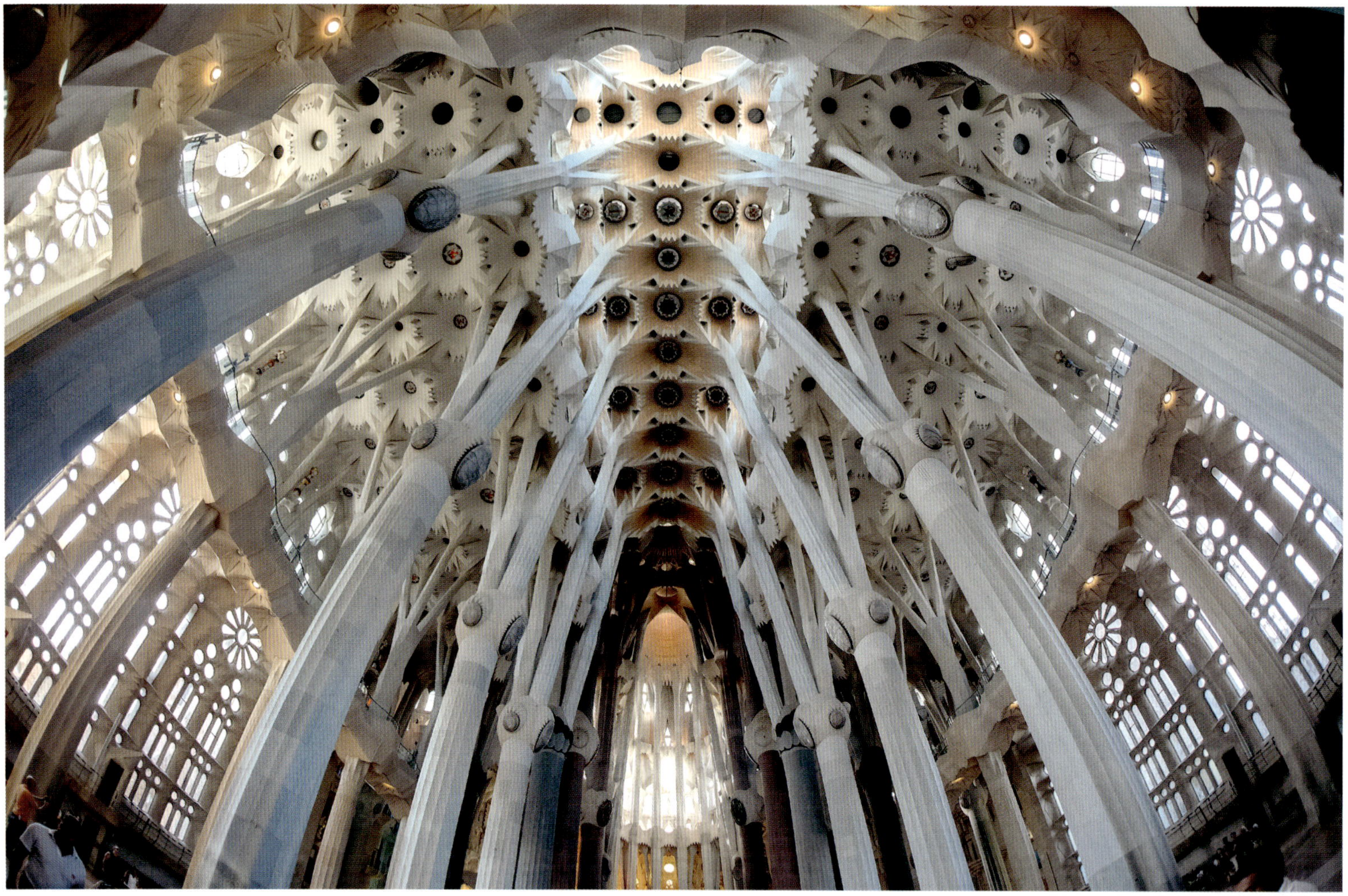
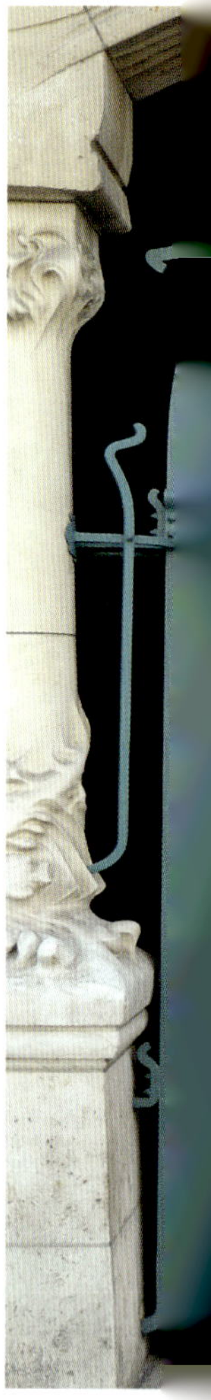

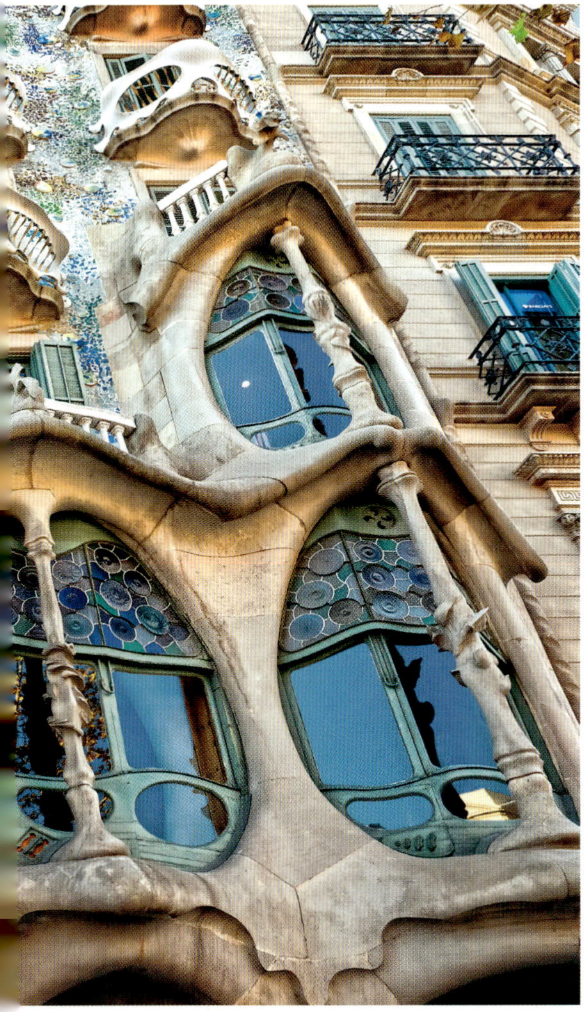

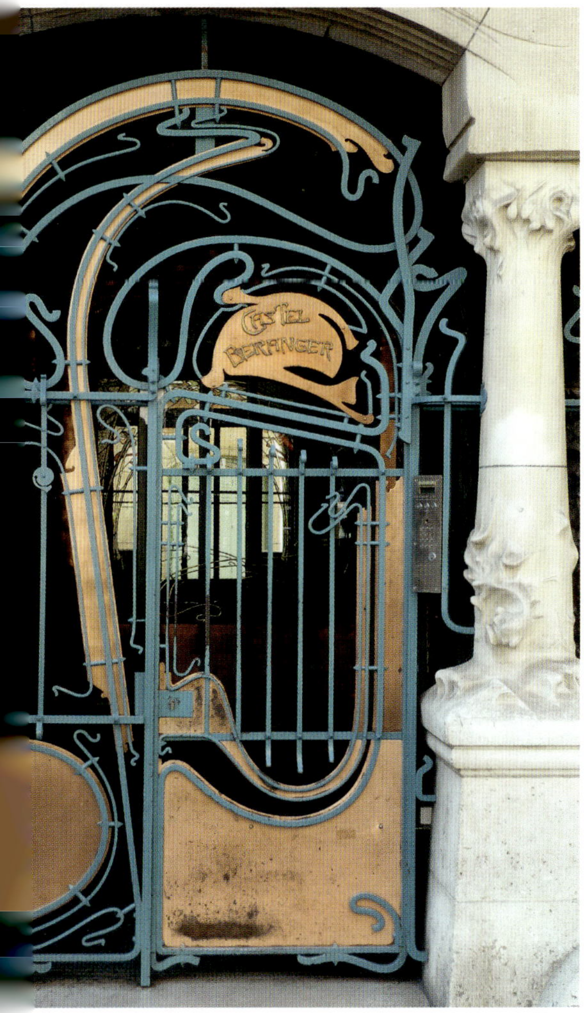

Edible Beauty and Metallic Nature

Dalí is the artist who did the most to bring architecture into Surrealist discourse, but first he had to find an architectural style at odds with the cleanliness and functionalist piety of Le Corbusier's Modernism to champion. Art Nouveau fitted the bill perfectly, especially the versions by Hector Guimard and Antoni Gaudí. At the end of 1933, the Surrealist journal *Minotaure* published Dalí's essay 'Concerning the Terrifying and Edible Beauty of Art Nouveau Architecture'. In this text Dalí portrays Art Nouveau architecture as a kind of creative 'grinding' machine that is again caught between an architectural language of potential capable of continuous metamorphosis and the ability to construct unimaginable architectural combinations:

> With Art Nouveau, architectural elements of the past, in addition to being submitted to a frequent and complete convulsive-formal grinding that will give birth to a new stylization, will be summoned to life again and called to survive under their real original aspect, so that, combined with one another, being merged within one another (in spite of their most irreconcilable and implacable intellectual antagonism), they are going to attain the highest degree of aesthetic depreciation, exhibiting in their relations the kind of terrible impurity that knows no equivalent or equal other than the immaculate purity of oneiric intertwinings.[7]

↖ **Antoni Gaudí**
← **La Sagrada Família**
(far left, top and bottom)
Barcelona
1982–

↖ **Antoni Gaudí • Casa Batlló**
(House of Bones; above left)
Barcelona
1904
← **Hector Guimard**
Entry gate, Castel Béranger,
Paris (bottom left)
1887

Dalí's interpretation of Art Nouveau is delirious, hysterical, ecstatic and, fundamentally, an oral, ultimately cannibalistic, experience. 'Eat Me!… Me Too' he drools over pictures of Art Nouveau details of a gate, column bases and railings used to illustrate the article. He evokes the architecture of Gaudí as proof that he is not fantasizing, but dealing with real buildings that according to him are the built manifestation of clouds reflected in water – dreamy and erotic:

> Erotic desire is the downfall of intellectual aesthetics. There where Venus of Logic fades away, there the Venus of 'bad taste', the 'Venus in Furs' is heralded under the sign of the unique beauty of real ferment that is vital and materialist…. Beauty is none other than the sum total of the consciousness of our perversion…. Breton said 'Beauty will be convulsive or will cease to be.' The new Surrealist age of 'cannibalism of objects' equally justifies the following conclusion: Beauty will be edible or will cease to be.[8]

In 1932, Dalí began to paint his wife/muse Gala with branches sprouting from her head. This 'Daphne' motif that he returned to time and time again throughout his life provided an important concept around which his fixation with his paranoiac-critical method, bodies, architecture and vegetative petrification and fecundity could condense. In Art Nouveau he also found Guimard's Paris Métro entrance light design (1910–12), which he associated with the praying mantis – a significant Surrealist reference at this time – and included as one of the illustrations for his *Minotaure* essay accompanied by the caption, 'It has moreover to do with the metal atavism of Millet's *L'Angelus*' – an observation provoked by its bowed head/bulb and stooped demeanour.

By 1938, these influences could be seen in his *Rainy Taxi* (see page 50) at the 'Exposition Internationale du Surréalisme' in Paris, where nature invaded the static vehicle, its lights on – perhaps a reference to the then recently published notes in Duchamp's *Green Box* of 1934 that describe some of the inspirations for the *Large Glass* and include mention of the Jura-Paris trip and the 'headlight child'. In fact, the exhibition's main gallery space, entered after the boulevard of mannequins, is itself an essay in nature's invasion of architectural space/interiors; its darkness, braziers, coal sacks hanging from the ceiling, leaves on the ground and beds another interpretation of the hybridized scene illustrated in Jarry's *Ubu Roi* backdrop (see page 12) some forty years previously. Nature's invasion of where it should not be manifests again in the reprise of Dalí's *Rainy Taxi* in his Dream of Venus pavilion building at the 1939 World's Fair in New York (see pages 130–32), and also in the exterior of the pavilion with its Daphne-like petrified skyline. In his Theatre-Museum in Figueres (see pages 148–49), we can again see the importance for Dalí of the confluence of these ideas about ongoing metamorphosis and the artistic potential of hybridizing the organic and the inorganic. Leaving his courtyard, which features the *Rainy Cadillac* (see pages 149–50), visitors pass through a doorway framed by two guardian-like forms, Guimard's Métro lamps hovering mantis-like above.

Twenty Years After the Tide and Rain

The French Surrealist painter Yves Tanguy also predicated his work on an interest in biomorphic forms. The former sailor started to paint, it is said, having experienced a sudden epiphany on seeing a De Chirico painting in 1922. By 1924 he had been inducted into the Paris Surrealist group under the auspices of Breton. Tanguy's work provokes an uncanny sensation in the viewer of having seen these forms before, yet we haven't – they are at once alien and familiar. Throughout his life Tanguy, on the face of it, explored a very limited artistic lexicon, yet it could always excite and he developed some of the most extraordinary works of Surrealism. Many of his canvases featured bleak 'beaches' thrown into deep perspective with distant horizons. Agglomerations of objects create little, carefully constructed constellations of forms, as if composed and deserted by a retreating tide. The structures seem to have no function and no external support, and in so doing often imply biological typologies: abstracted slugs, beans, shells, horns, transparent anemones and diaphanous membranes. But they are also architectural, intimating an architectural future of biological elements, an architecture that is soft, wet and has new geometric rules.

From 1940 to 1942, Max Ernst worked on what is reputed by some to be his masterpiece, *Europe After the Rain II* (see pages 198–99). It is a further comment on the theme of a previous piece of work he produced in 1933. A desolate map/landscape of Europe, no national boundaries are visible, just the same ubiquitous sludge, dark shadows and hot spots of bloodlike stains. Like Dalí's *Soft Construction with Boiled Beans (Premonition of Civil War*; see page 51) it betrays its author's sense of foreboding; particularly, as a liberal German, of the events and, perhaps, speculative fearful outcome of the Second World War should Fascism triumph. *Europe After the Rain II* abandons the plan form in favour of a perspective. The painting shows a landscape of desolation, not without a scary beauty, but silent, petrified and twisted. Two figures give the scene its scale; they might be statues or ragged fighters. The colours are a mixture of rust, algae-green and yellowing-orange carboniferous deposits. But it is the forms

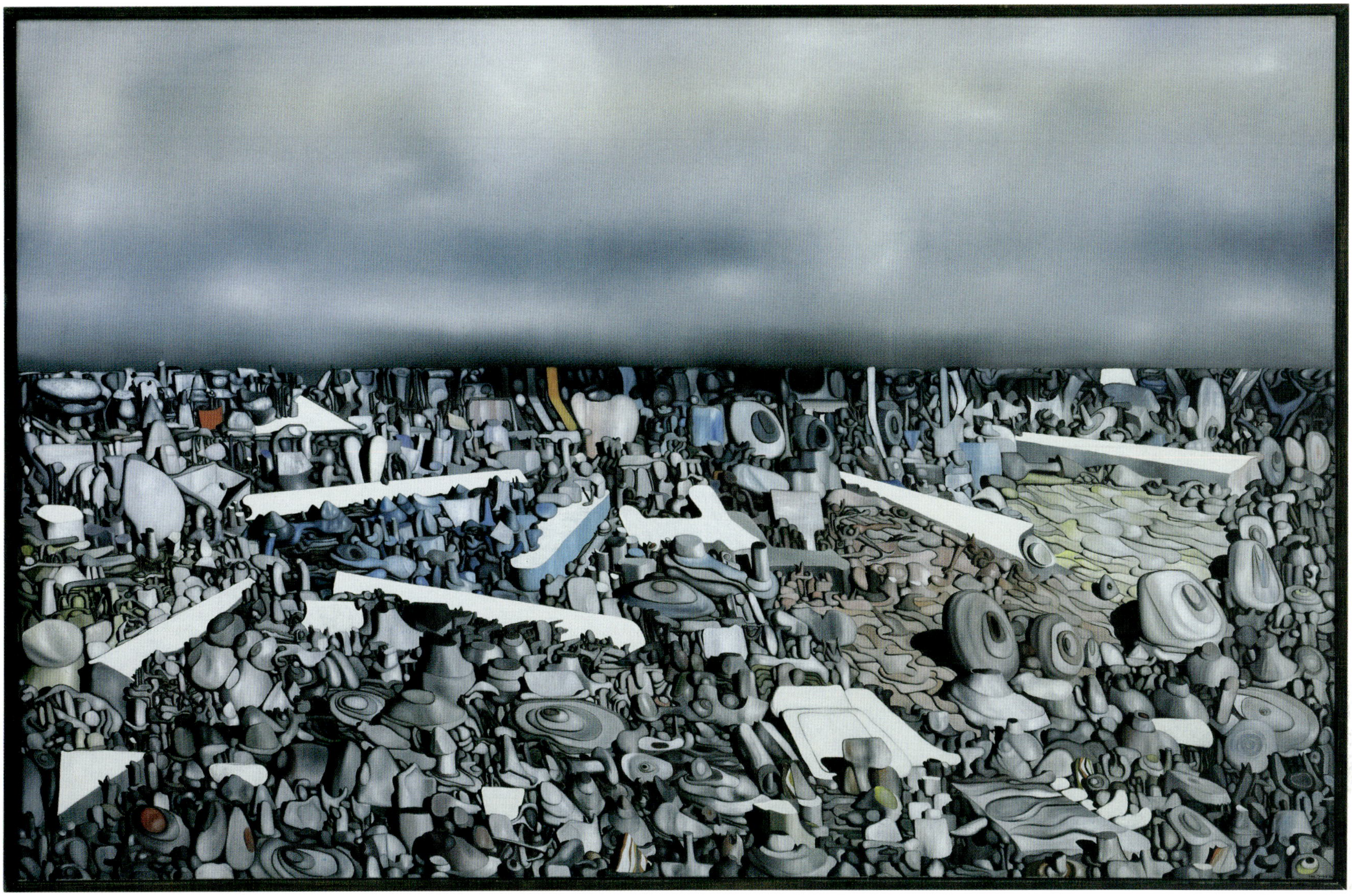

↑

Yves Tanguy

Multiplication of the Arcs

1954

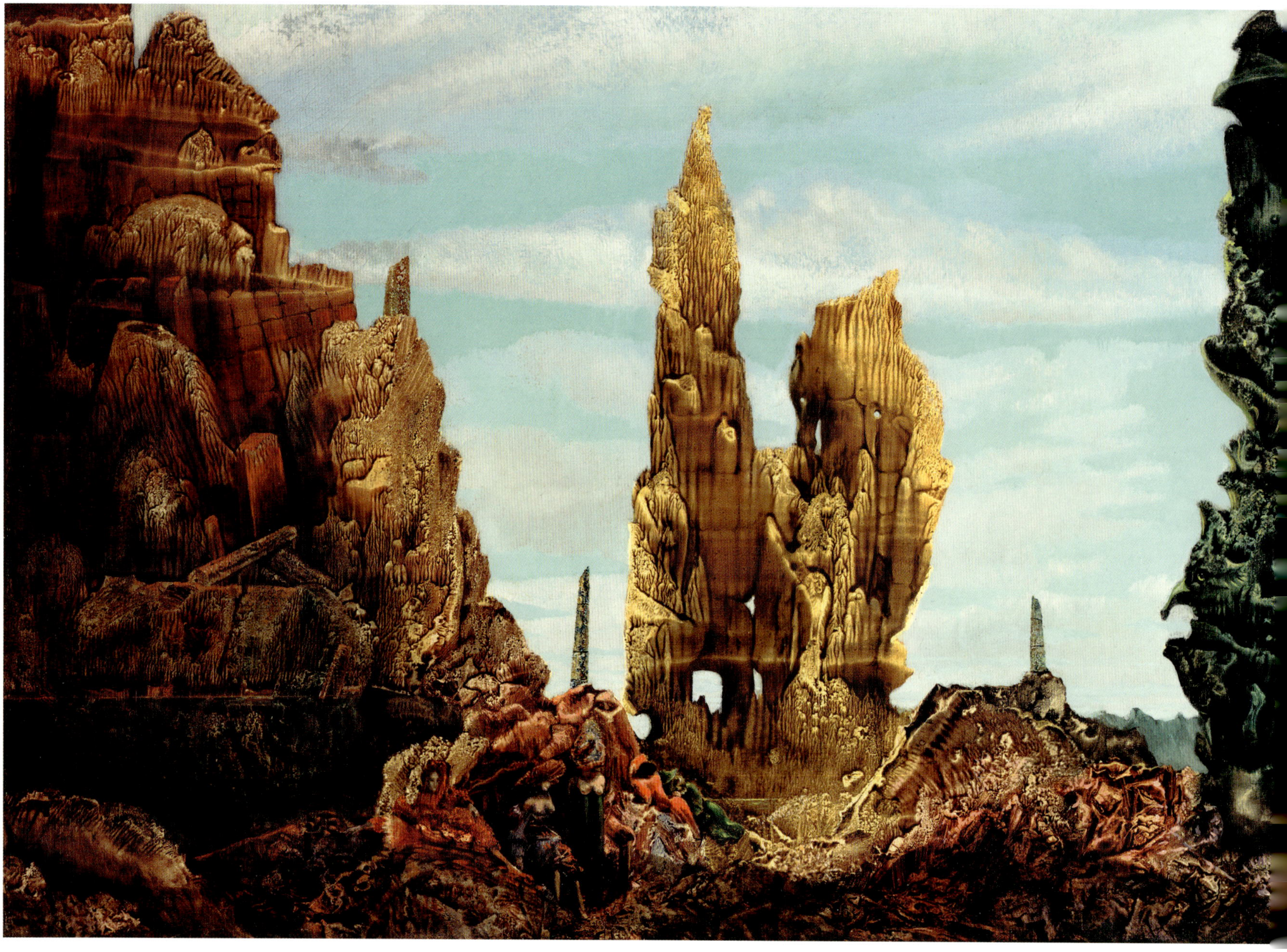

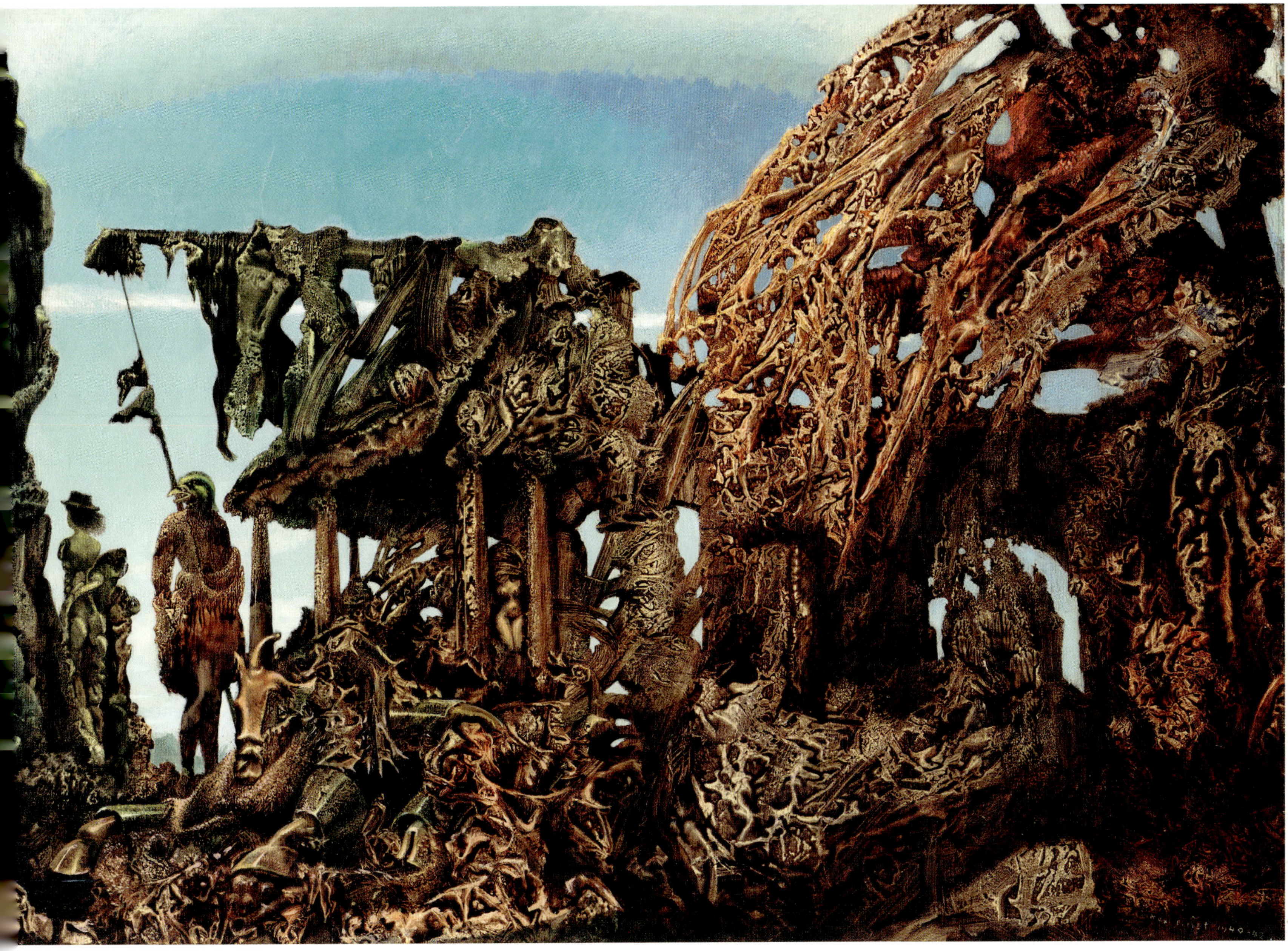

↑
Max Ernst • Europe After the Rain II

1940–42

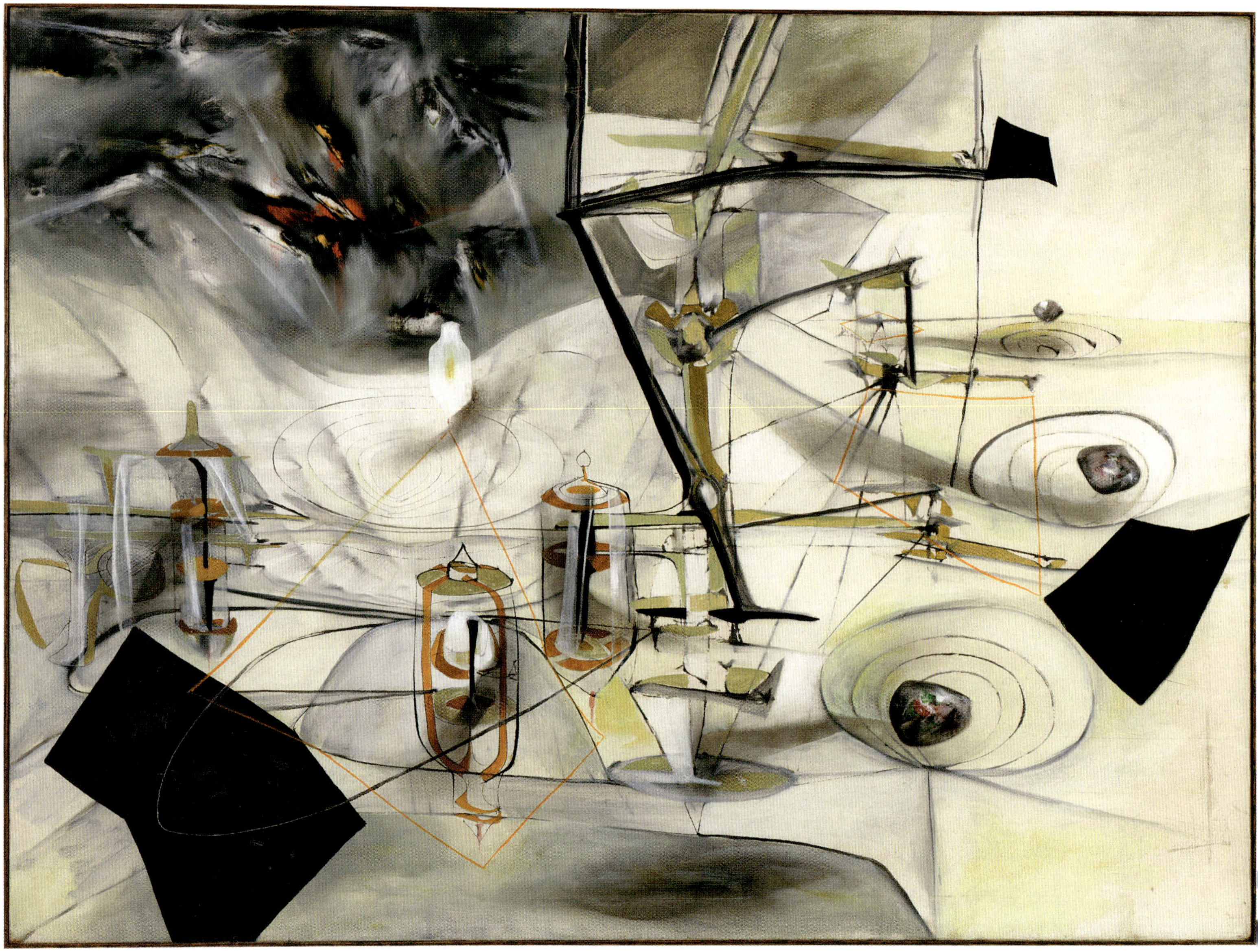

↙ **Roberto Matta**
The Bachelors Twenty Years After
1943

that are the most remarkable, achieved by Ernst's use of the process of decalcomania (transferring designs from prepared glass, paper or timber onto canvas to create a mottled and uneven 'metamorphic' effect). These are architectures of ruins, of deposition, patination, colonization and even contagion, all caught in a calcified and clogged wreckage – a landscape not of human making, but one abandoned and given over to the small, the chemical and the single celled.

Inspired by Tanguy and Ernst, and armed with his training in architecture and internship at Le Corbusier's atelier, Roberto Matta also started to paint canvases that speculated on biomorphic form. His works eloquently spoke of higher spatial dimensions, psychological space and landscape, one even speculating on the future of established Surrealist precedents. In his 1943 painting *The Bachelors Twenty Years Later*, now in the Philadelphia Museum of Modern Art:

> Matta admired Duchamp's explorations of science and eroticism and he gave these themes new energy in an explosion of nebulous vapors that swirl in a vision of primal chaos. In the context of Surrealism, Matta's lamp-like bachelors conjure up the unseen, supernatural entities called 'Great Transparents,' conceived by André Breton, who was also a Surrealist, as modern mythological beings.... Twenty years later, the bachelors are energized by the Chilean artist's infinite space and incisive linear markings, recalling the symmetrical cracks in the original work, which occurred when the two sheets of glass were accidentally smashed. The sexual tension that permeates the *Large Glass* is translated into an explosive electromagnetic force field, as the excitement of the transparent, lamp-like bachelors generates an illuminating gas that mixes with other nebulous vapors to produce a vision of primary chaos, with slivers of stormy crystalline light.[9]

These three artists did much to define the Surrealist lexicon in terms of architectures of biological forms and processes (Tanguy and Ernst), higher and virtual spatial dimensions (Matta), vegetative substrates (Tanguy and Ernst) and galaxies of gravity gradients (Matta). And all of these notions have taken on renewed importance in the twenty-first century with its synthetic biologies, mixed virtual and actual spaces and understanding of the relativity of time.

At the end of 1958, as the Surrealists were grappling to reconcile themselves with Pop Art and the evolving scientific understanding of space and reality, Dalí published his *Anti-Matter Manifesto* in the catalogue for an exhibition at the Carstairs Gallery, New York:

> If the physicists are producing anti-matter, let it be allowed to the painters, already specialists in angels, to paint it.... Today the exterior world – that of physics – has transcended the one of psychology. My father today is Dr Heisenberg.... It is with pi-mesons and the most gelatinous and indeterminate neutrinos that I want to paint the beauty of the angels and of reality. I will very soon succeed in doing so.[10]

By 1970, probably utilizing his paranoiac-critical method, Dalí had pulled off a unique synthesis of the geometries of Art Nouveau architecture and the evolving science of genetics armed only with a cylinder, a toothbrush and some spaghetti, in his mind proving that Guimard's work was a forerunner of all future architecture to come:

> Proof: his aesthetic is governed by cylindrical anamorphosis, and the cylinder is generated by the sphere. Into the universe of a transparent cylinder that I ask you to take in your left hand, drop a toothbrush of the same length that I ask you to drop into the interior with your right hand; you will observe the helical principle that precedes the double helix of deoxyribonucleic acid of Crick and Watson. Now, instead of a toothbrush, drop in boiled spaghetti and you will see born – always under the monarchy of the sphere, which

→

Leo Lionni

(left) drawing for the book Parallel Botany,

showing a composition of key parallel plants

(centre and right)

Tubolara **and** Sigurya barbulata,

illustrations from Parallel Botany

1977

rises and falls in the cylinder – all the sublime 'Spaghetti Style' of Guimard and now, pay attention – the best of all is about to be announced: the ornamentation of Guimard is nothing but the cylindrical anamorphosis of hereditary symmetries.[11]

Another act of supreme surreal imagination that further integrates the biology of botany, the magical and hints of technologies to come was the Italian author, artist and illustrator Leo Lionni's book *Parallel Botany* (1977). With a sustained conceit, the book introduces us to imaginary, intrepid botanists, numerous fictional species of parallel plants and the strange cultures (human and vegetal) in which they grew. His 'parallel plants' were named as such so that when they were discovered, the existing taxonomy of 'normal' plants did not have to be changed. Parallel plants have many qualities that are non-existent in the usual botanical world. They disintegrate when touched, they consist of a dark, light-sucking material and they have no organs – they question our sense of reality:

Thus, the discovery of this unusual and disquieting botany was bound to upset the illusory consistency of our previous notions of reality. 'So much so,' writes Dulieu [invented botanist] 'that it is from these very notions that its plants, mysteriously alienated from the events of growth and decay which struggle for the domination of the biosphere, appear to draw their vital juices, and thereby emerge, perennially immune, outside the sphere of normal perceptions and the links and associations of the memory, in a fashion quite "other", ambiguous, perverse and beyond our ken. We are unable to grasp it because of the long-consecrated notion of reality which clings so obstinately, like a twining and perhaps poisonous ivy, to our logic.'[12]

The book describes numerous types of parallel plants, including the 'woodland tweezers' whose arrangement on the forest floor resembles the moves in a game of 'Go'. Another example is the '*Siguria barbulata*' with its distinctive cephalocarpus – irregular protruding fruit. We are also told of the '*Tubolara*', a plant which:

represents the coexistence in time and space of the feminine and masculine principles. It is lingam (male organ) and yoni (vulva), and as the physical union of man and woman it symbolizes the essence of created things.... In the jungles of Tampur in northern Rajastan there is a variety of Tubolara considerably smaller than that of Talistan. For the local inhabitants it is taboo. Ramesh Sashtra [another invention] thinks that this taboo originated in the belief that the darkness inside the plants represents the dark night of death, populated by white bats which seize the bodies of the dead in order to devour their intestines.[13]

Lionni's book does much to illustrate the potential of Surrealism's intersection with botany, technology and architecture.

Between Zero and Infinity

Such breaking of confirmed epistemologies and the introduction of alien ideas into established ontologies are a standard technique of the Surrealists. Architecture is always a discipline that is slightly behind the arc of technology, politics and artistic subversion. However, in a few short years in the late 1970s and early 1980s, the Polish-American architect Daniel Libeskind developed a series of theoretical projects (see pages 204–11) that accelerated the slow, conservative, progression of architectural discourse beyond the comfort zone of many into surreal territory. These works explored semiotics, vectorial space, notation, choreography of chance and the viral and biological contagion of cities, announcing the growing importance of biology to architecture, and appeared first in his book *Between Zero and Infinity* in 1981.[14]

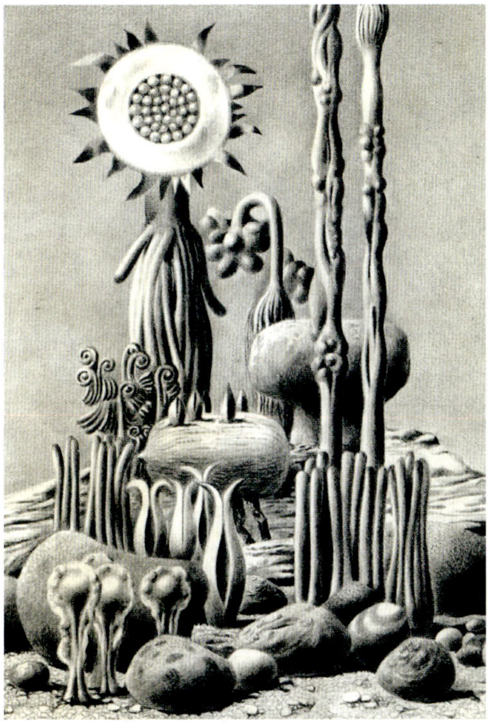

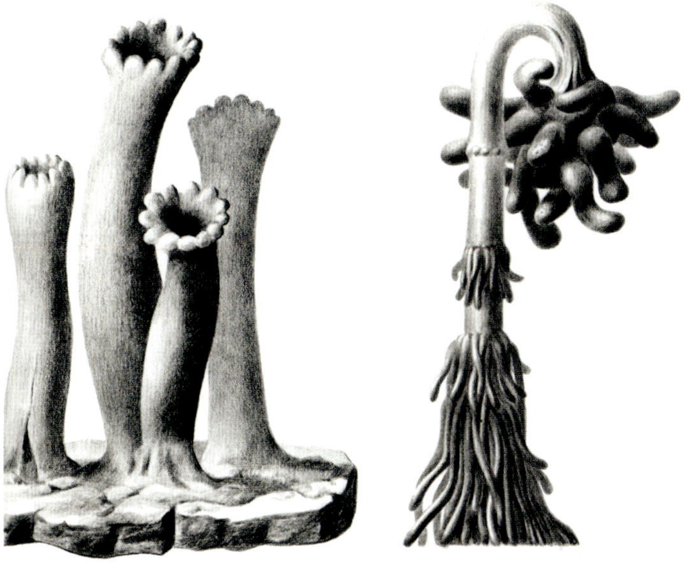

The book shows the progression of Libeskind's thoughts on architecture and the speed at which they occurred. Ensconced at the Cranbrook Academy of Art, near Detroit in Michigan, with a small bunch of dedicated students, Libeskind had started to make work that expanded the notions of what might constitute architecture. A reference point for this group and the architect himself were the old avant-garde movements in art and architecture – the surreal metaphysics of De Chirico, the Futurists and the Constructivists, the work of Le Corbusier and many others, channelled to construct a heady mix of potential architectures. An initial series of collages, made in Toronto in 1978, have nuances of both De Chirico and Ernst; featuring surreal combinations of cakes, hands, fruit, shoes and breads, they set out Libeskind's preoccupations and precedents at this time, with homages to both De Chirico and Gaudí.

The following year Libeskind, now at Cranbrook, drew his first iconic, seminal project: *Micromegas* (1979; named after a satirical story by Voltaire). These highly complex drawings oscillate between architecture, notation and vectors. In flouting every architectural representational protocol, they make us unsure whether we are looking at plan, section or perspective, or all three simultaneously, yet we know they are architectural. Libeskind's important contribution to architectural theory thus lies in showing us that the boundaries of architecture are very wide indeed, as he tightropes around some of them. Still, a few clues to his inspirations are left for us to decipher within this cacophony of finely executed lines, boundaries and prisms reminiscent of Piranesi's unbuildable fantasy *Carceri* (see pages 176–78). For example, in one of the *Micromegas* drawings, *Maldoror's Equation* (see page 205), is it an umbrella that we can see within?

By 1981, Libeskind was producing immaculately detailed pencil drawings –much looser and less abstracted than the *Micromegas* – that intricately collaged architectural fragments such as cornices, walls and doors with notations and swirling material in works such as *Ossification* (see page 206) – biological material-like tree trunks. Two years later, in 1983, he published and exhibited *Chamber Works: Architectural Meditations on Themes from Heraclitus*.[15] In this suite of drawings, Libeskind pushed the envelope of what might be considered architecture even further. The drawings are constellations of lines of various thickness, vectors and potentialities, each plate determined by different aspect ratios for compositional purposes. Michael Moorcock's description of the geometry of the city, quoted at the beginning of the previous chapter, resonates here.

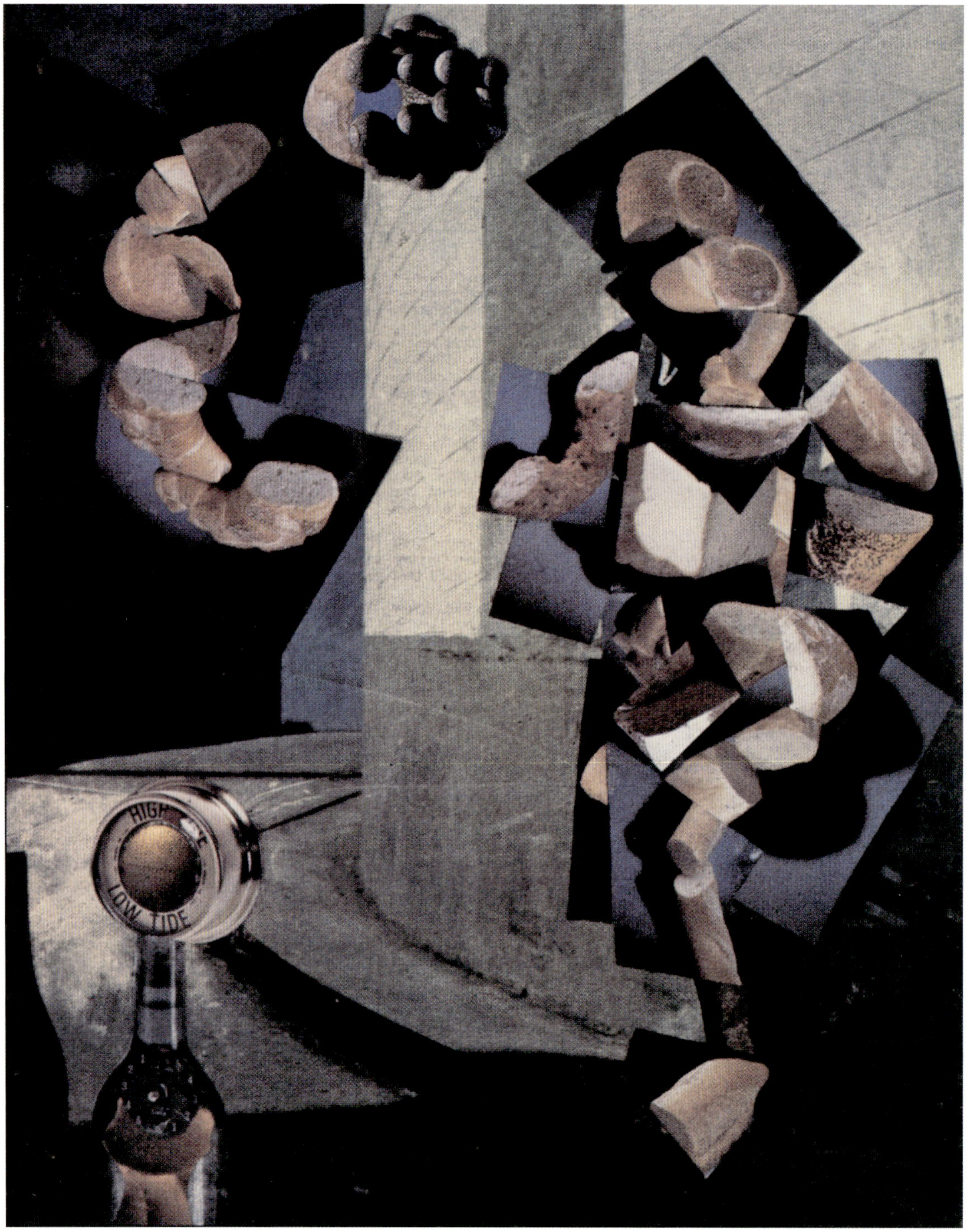

↑

Daniel Libeskind • Gaudi at Mid-Tide

from The Other Side: Ikon and Idea

1978

↓

Daniel Libeskind

Maldoror's Equation

from Micromegas

1979

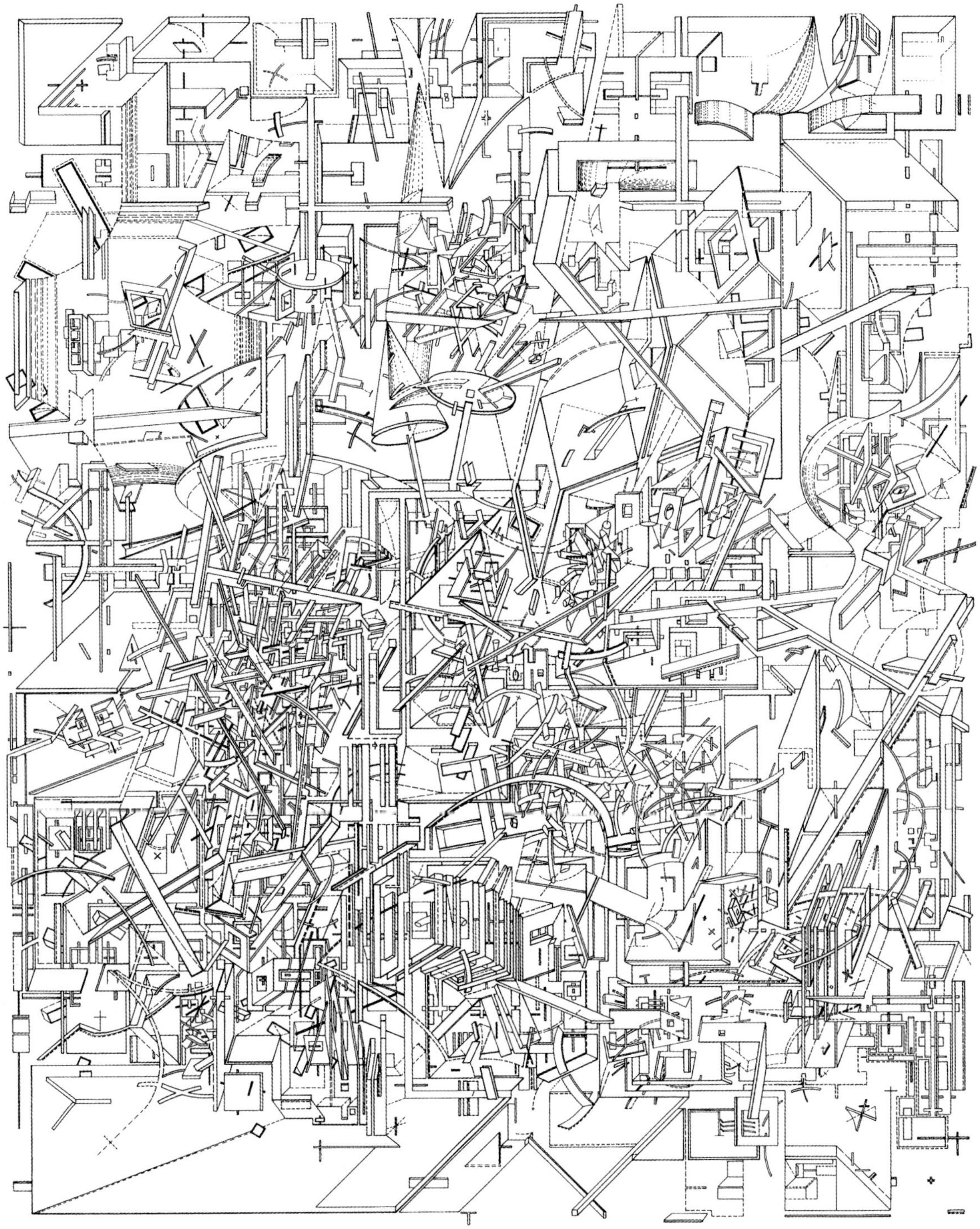

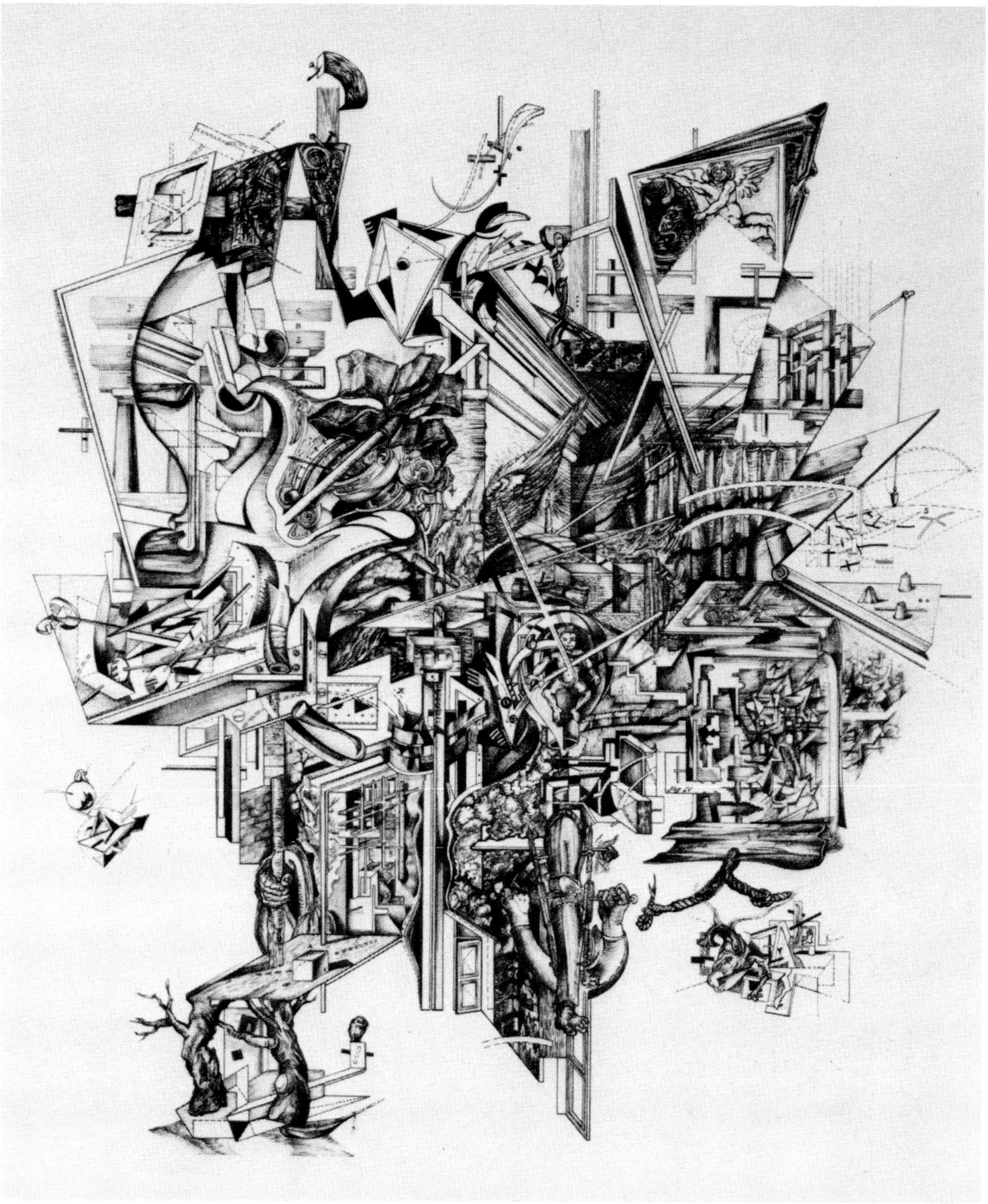

↑

Daniel Libeskind • Ossification

from Anatomy's Melancholy

1981

→

Daniel Libeskind • Chamber Works:

Architectural Meditations

on Themes from Heraclitus

1983

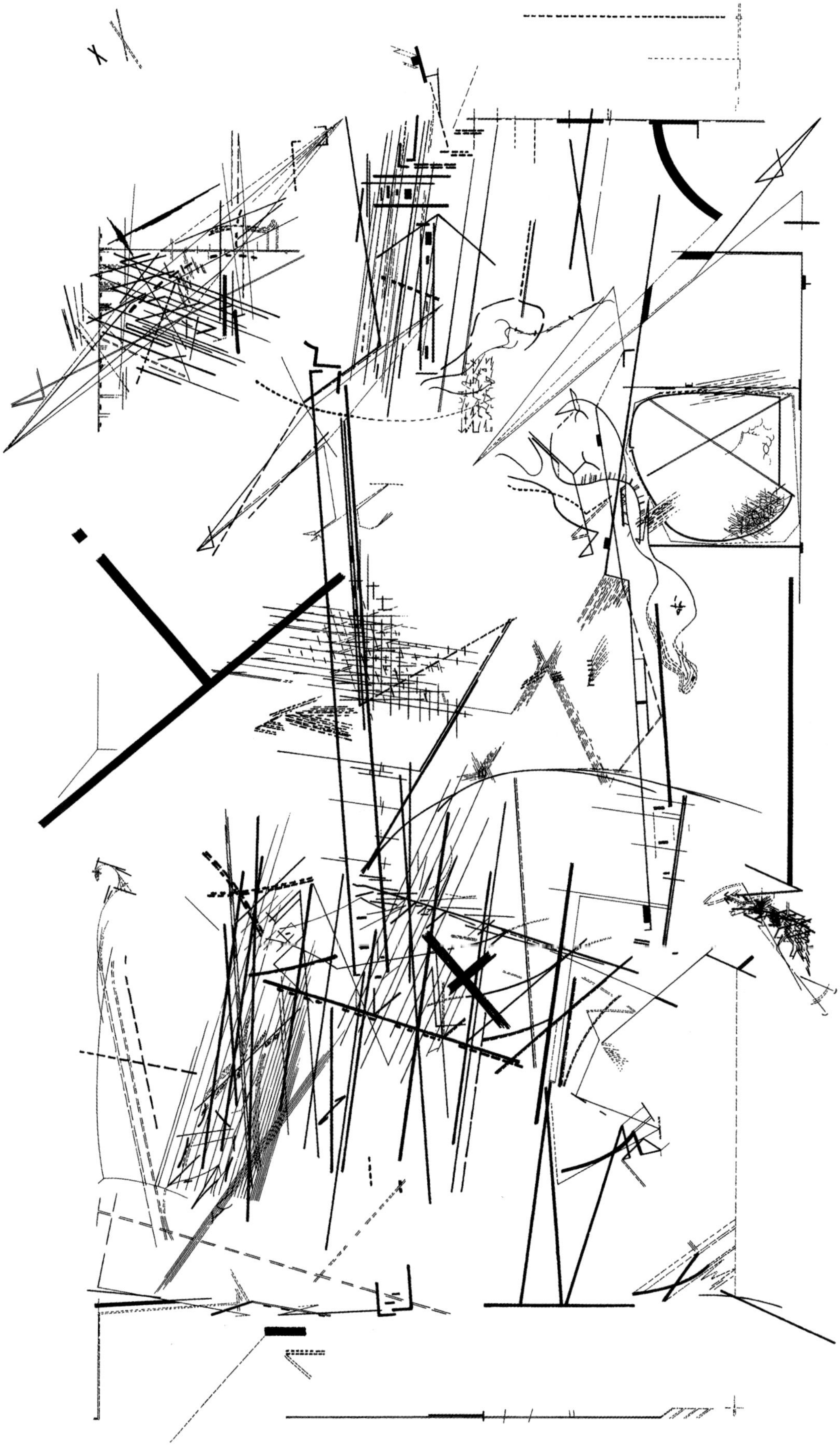

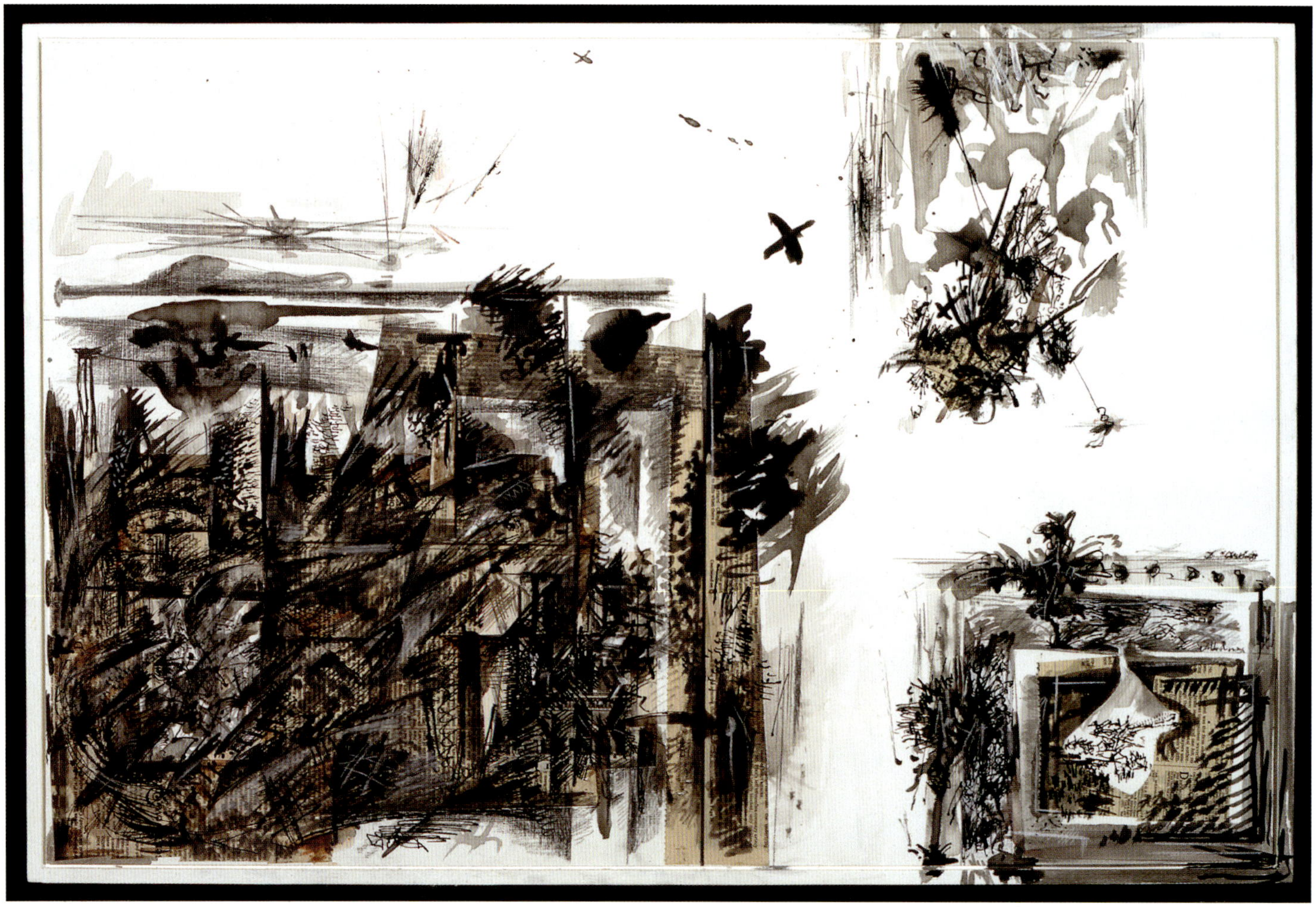

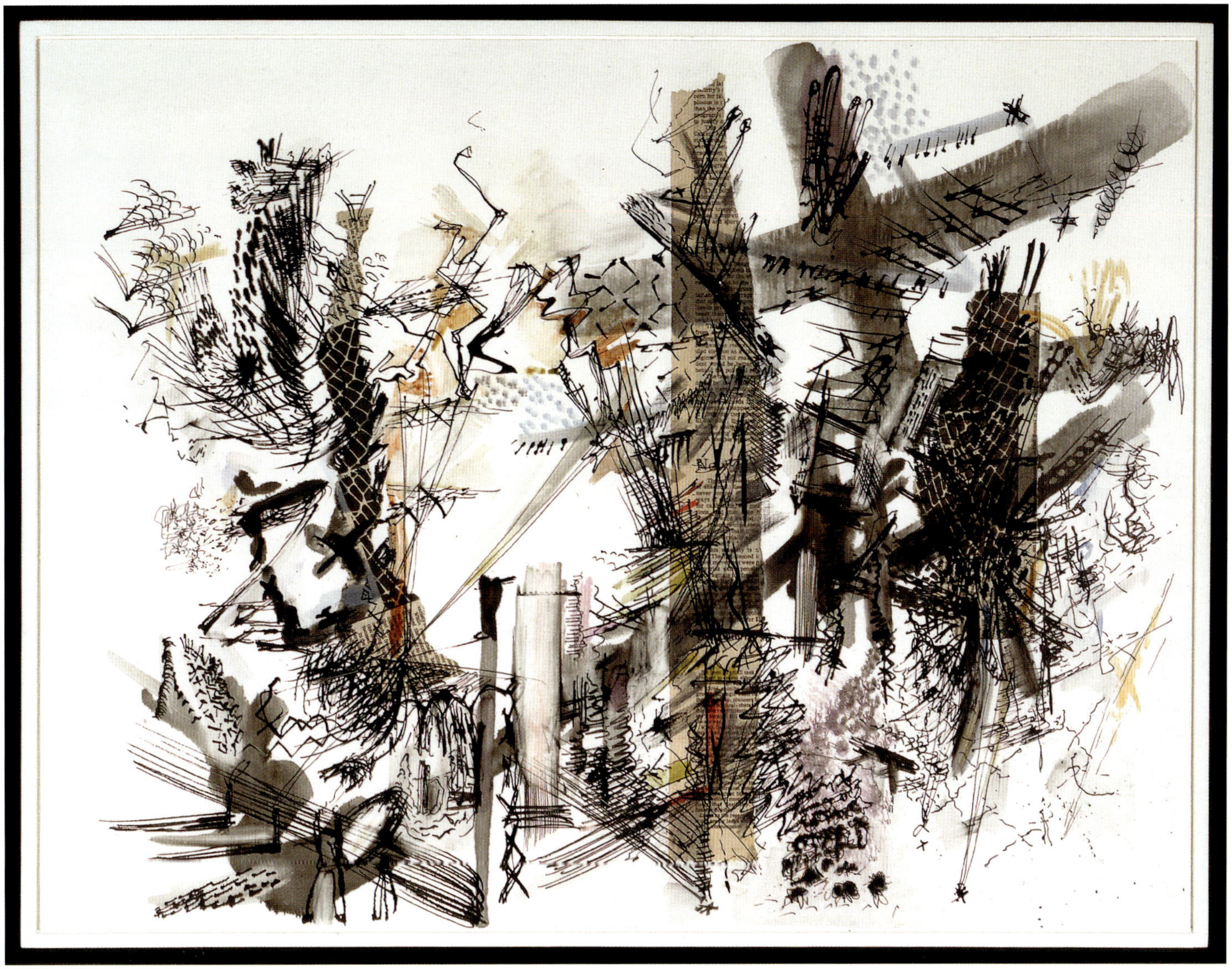

↖↑

Daniel Libeskind • Theatrum Mundi

1985

↓→

Daniel Libeskind • Theatrum Mundi

1985

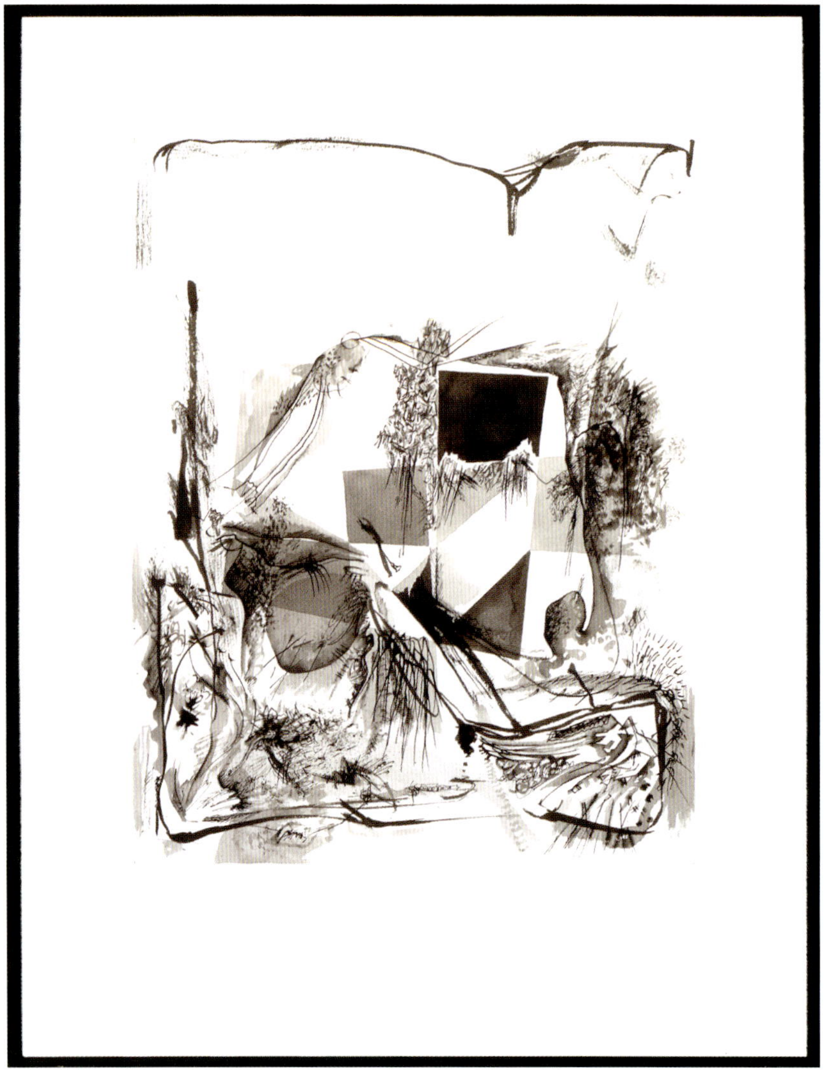

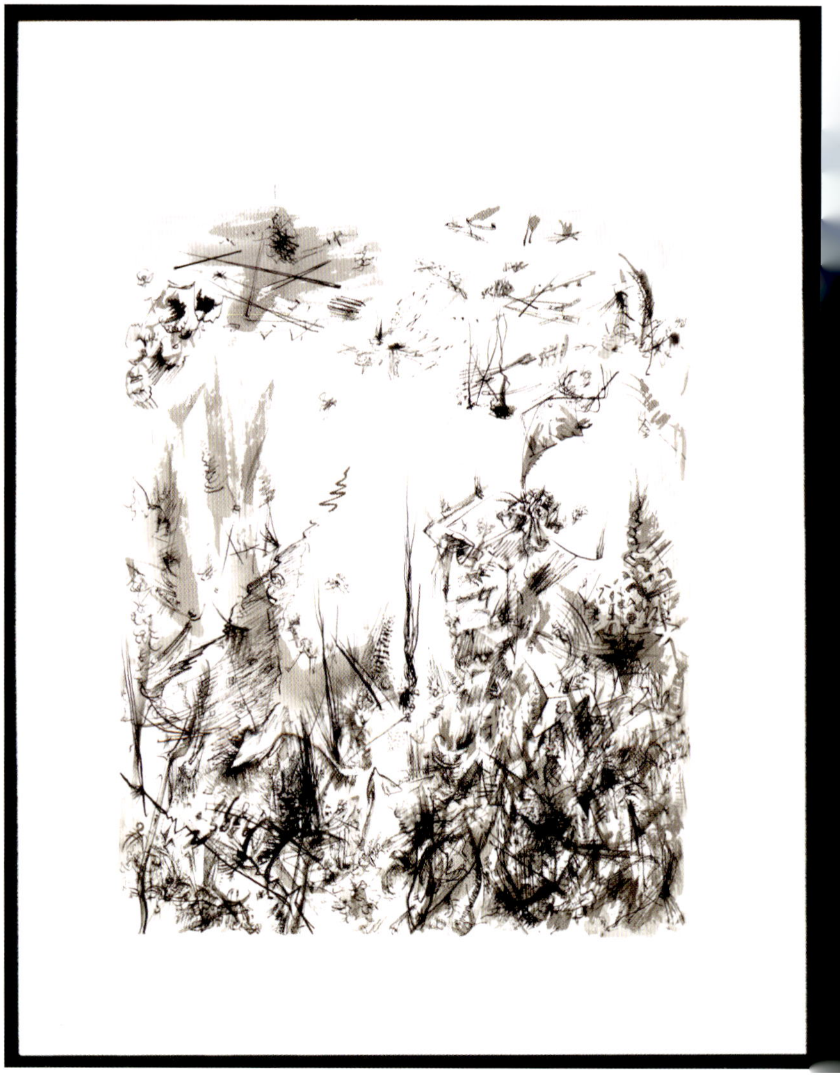

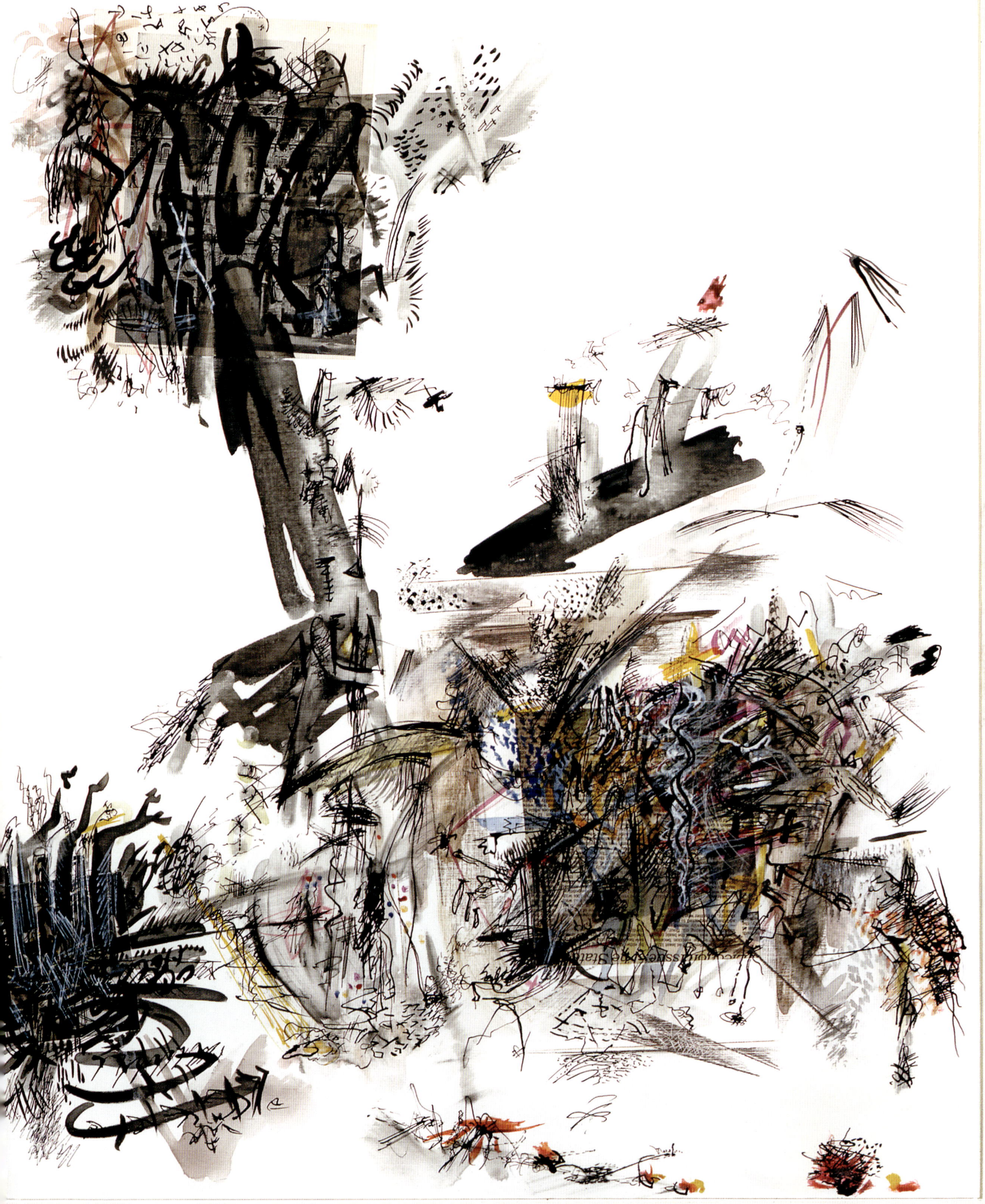

Another two years and Libeskind was exhibiting at the Architectural Association in London, which published his *Theatrum Mundi: Through the Green Membranes of Space*,[16] demonstrating that his architectural trajectory had rapidly evolved. Gone was the tight discipline of T-square and set square and the exactitude of precise angles and pristine junctioning, all replaced by quick, sketched nervous lines and splurges of colour quickly applied. The overall effect is one of thickets of intensity, smeared and smudged – colonies of contagion. Nanotechnologists call this exponential expansion of bacterial reproduction the 'grey-goo' problem, which they use to describe the scenario of their self-replicating molecular machines suddenly going out of control, whereby in a matter of hours the whole Earth is covered in grey-goo. Are these drawings a premonition of such a problem for architecture, or a postcard to architects calling for them to wake up to these new paradigms of architectural practice? Libeskind's own words are ambiguous:

> The premonition of the future – in the sense of Theatrum Mundi – is presented here in the form of a city besieged by an unknown infection, an action taking place within the nucleic medium that flows in the bloodstream of architectural thought.... To deal with the urban seems an impudence, which takes the most biological, private and hidden form of existence possible today, and turns this reality into collective fiction. The space of the City is closed because it is transparent.[17]

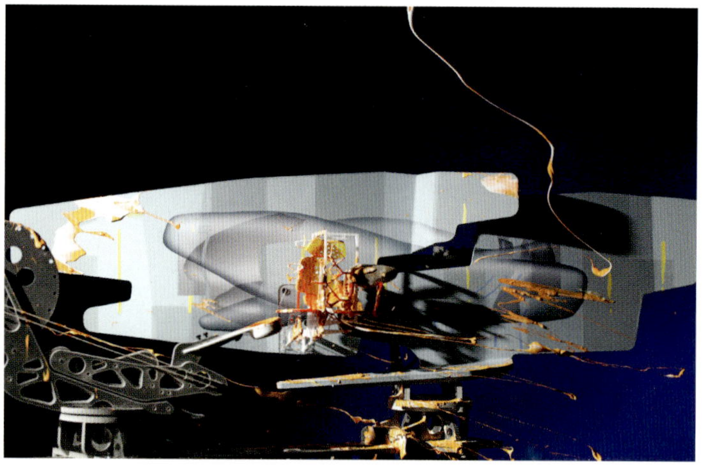

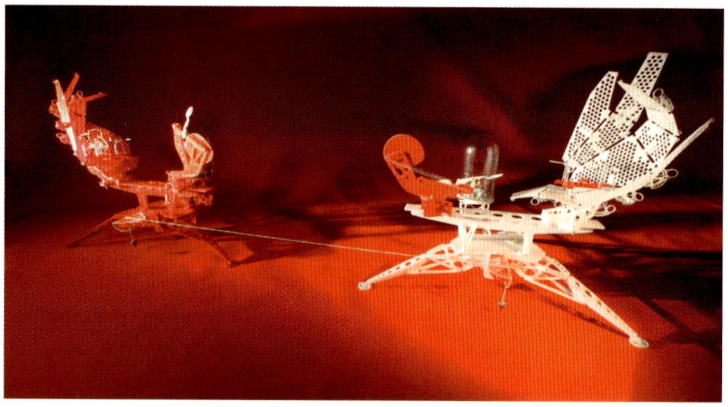

'Between Zero and Infinity' is a quote from the last two sentences of Jarry's *Doctor Faustroll*: 'GOD IS THE TANGENTIAL POINT BETWEEN ZERO AND INFINITY. 'Pataphysics is the science.'[18] In these few short years, Libeskind negotiated pushing architecture to almost nothing yet at the same time opening up its infinite nature, welcoming us into its surreal jungle just as Lionni had done.

At the end of the second decade of the twenty-first century, technology has moved on and humanity's dominion and understanding of nature and its processes is much advanced.

Contamination, Cutlery and Mutation in the Grotesque Jungle

Perry Kulper is a creator of modern jungles; he draughts them, collages them, and computer models and manipulates them. None of these techniques are separated from one another. In the modern architectural world, the distinction between the virtual and the actual is as non-existent in the microcosm of the drawing as it is in the macrocosm of the building/landscape. Theoretical dwellings in desert landscapes, metazoos, 'fast twitches' and bird motels and blooms are Kulper's stock in trade. For him, everything is worth hybridizing, scaling up or down, placing in alien landscapes, changing from vertical to horizontal or making the non-aerial fly. In this respect, his work can be seen as mandalic, representing the modern architectural condition in its field-like quality.

The jungle that we have created, a jungle of multiple visceral and digital connections, fast interchangeability and interoperability makes the modern world one of diverse, shifting field conditions, and Kulper's work can be read in this context. His drawings are never meant to be static; they simply catch a metamorphic system at a moment in time. Perry Kulper has collaborated in recent years with Nat Chard, bringing Kulper's interests in surreal cartography together with Chard's drawing machine engines of chance. We can imagine these ecological machinic and biological zones as bubbling, expanding and disappearing like boiling water. In much the same way as Matta's work of the early to mid-1940s

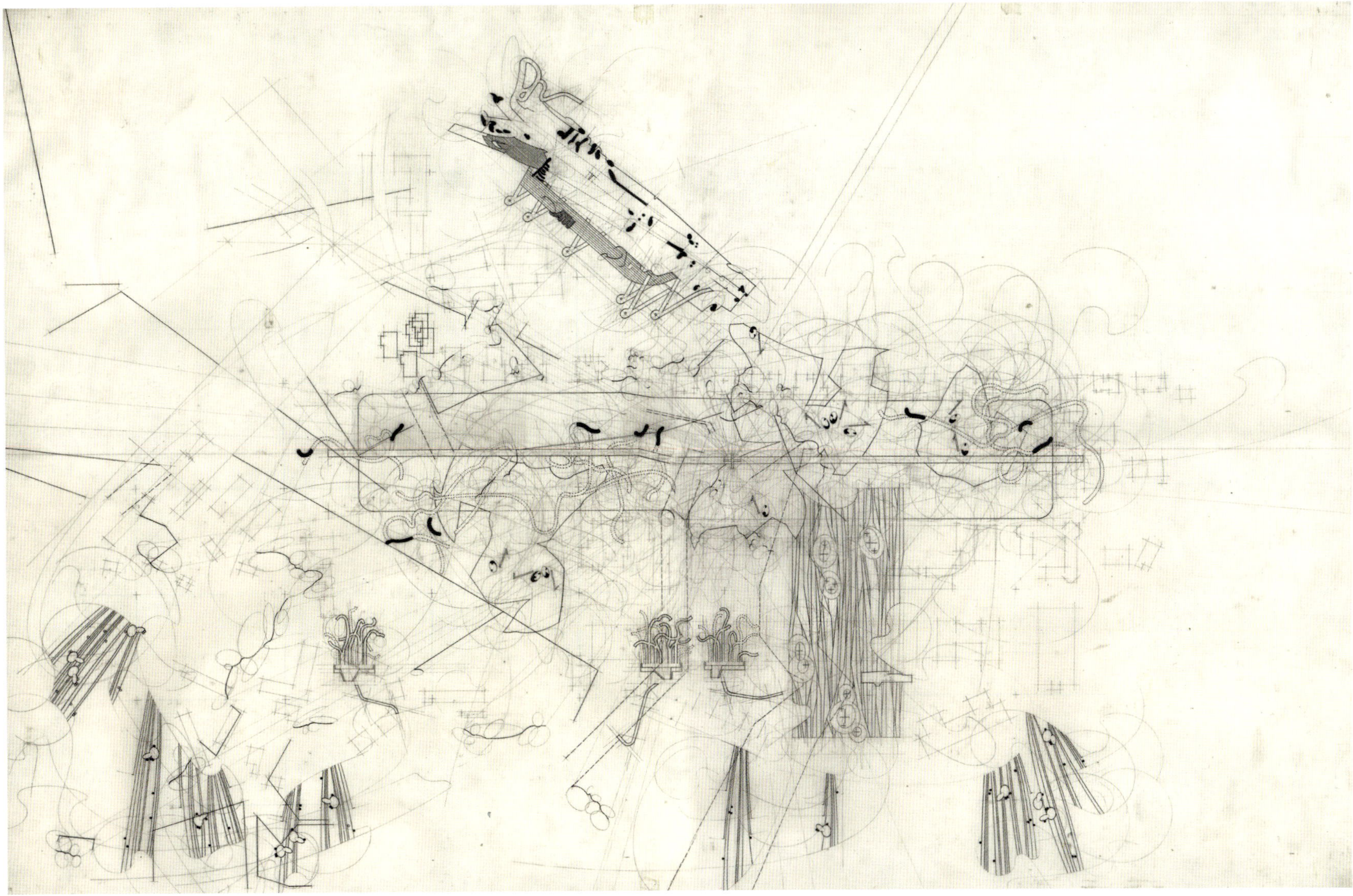

↖ **Nat Chard**
(in collaboration with Perry Kulper)
Drawing Instrument Eight in Action
2013

↖ **Nat Chard**
(in collaboration with Perry Kulper)
Two versions of Drawing Instrument Five
2010

↑
Perry Kulper • David's Island
New Rochelle, New York
1997

↷
Perry Kulper
Central California History Museum
2010

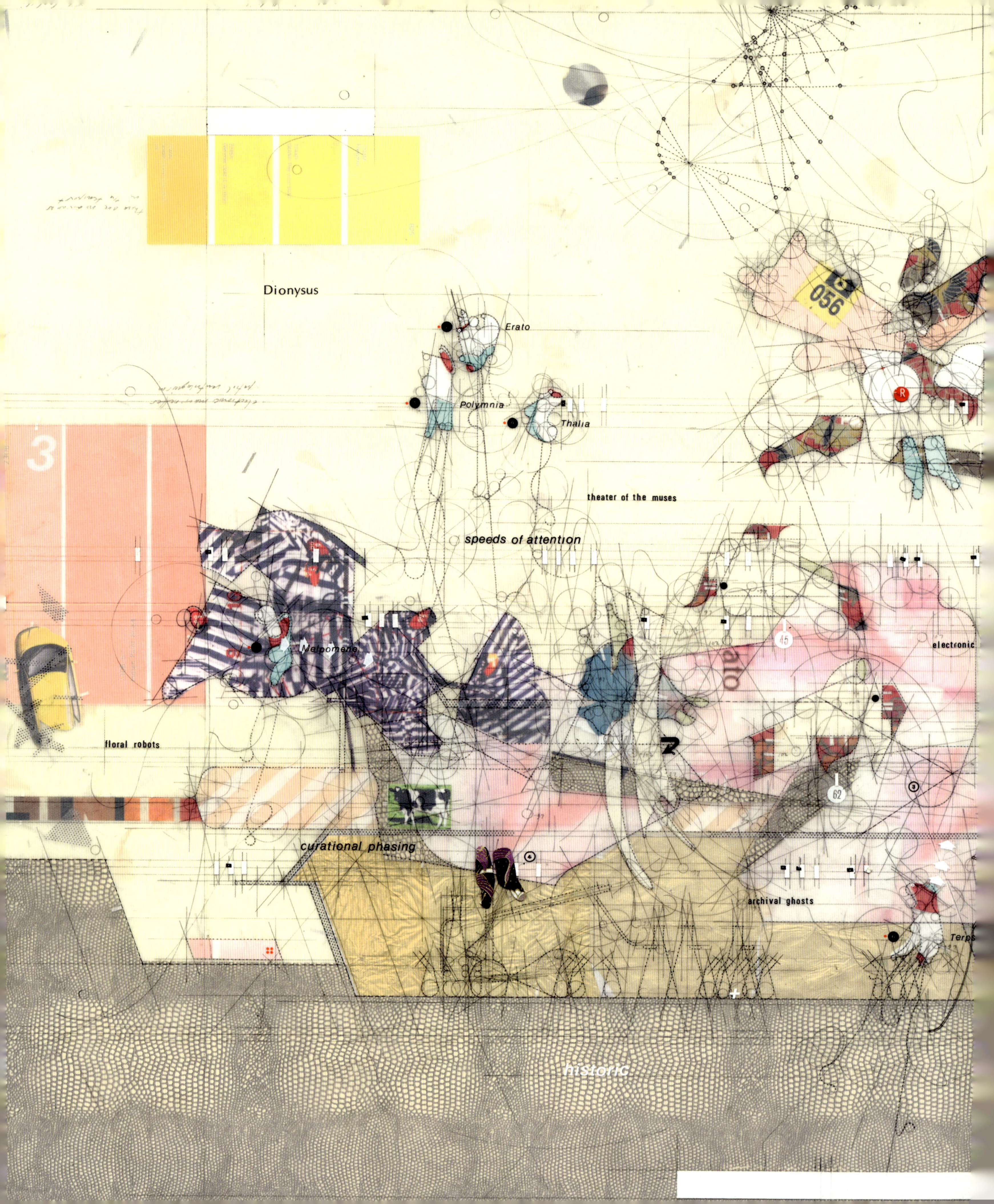
Dionysus
Erato
Polymnia
Thalia
theater of the muses
speeds of attention
Melpomene
electronic
floral robots
curational phasing
archival ghosts
Terps
historic

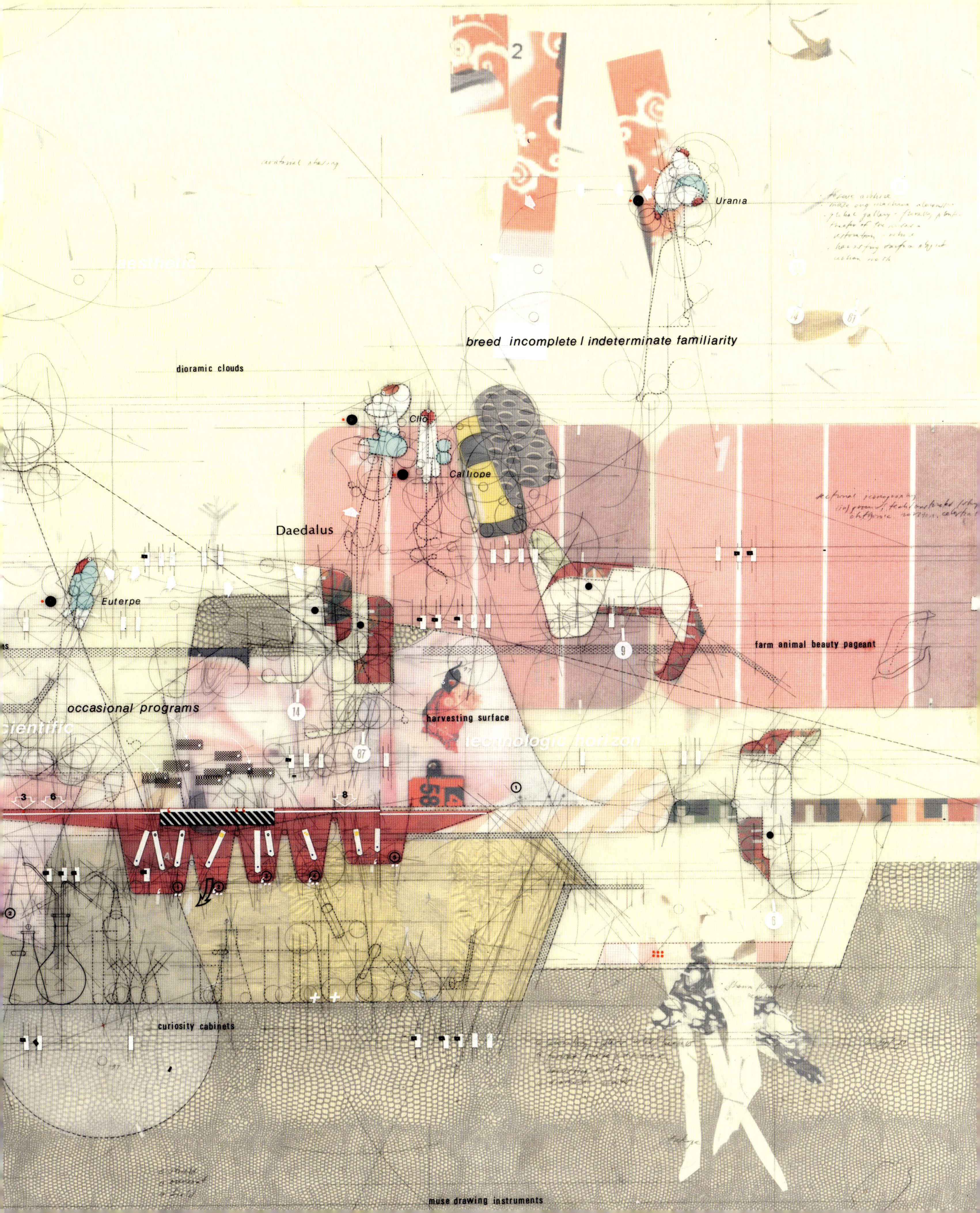

Urania
breed incomplete / indeterminate familiarity
dioramic clouds
Clio
Calliope
Daedalus
Euterpe
farm animal beauty pageant
occasional programs
harvesting surface
curiosity cabinets
muse drawing instruments

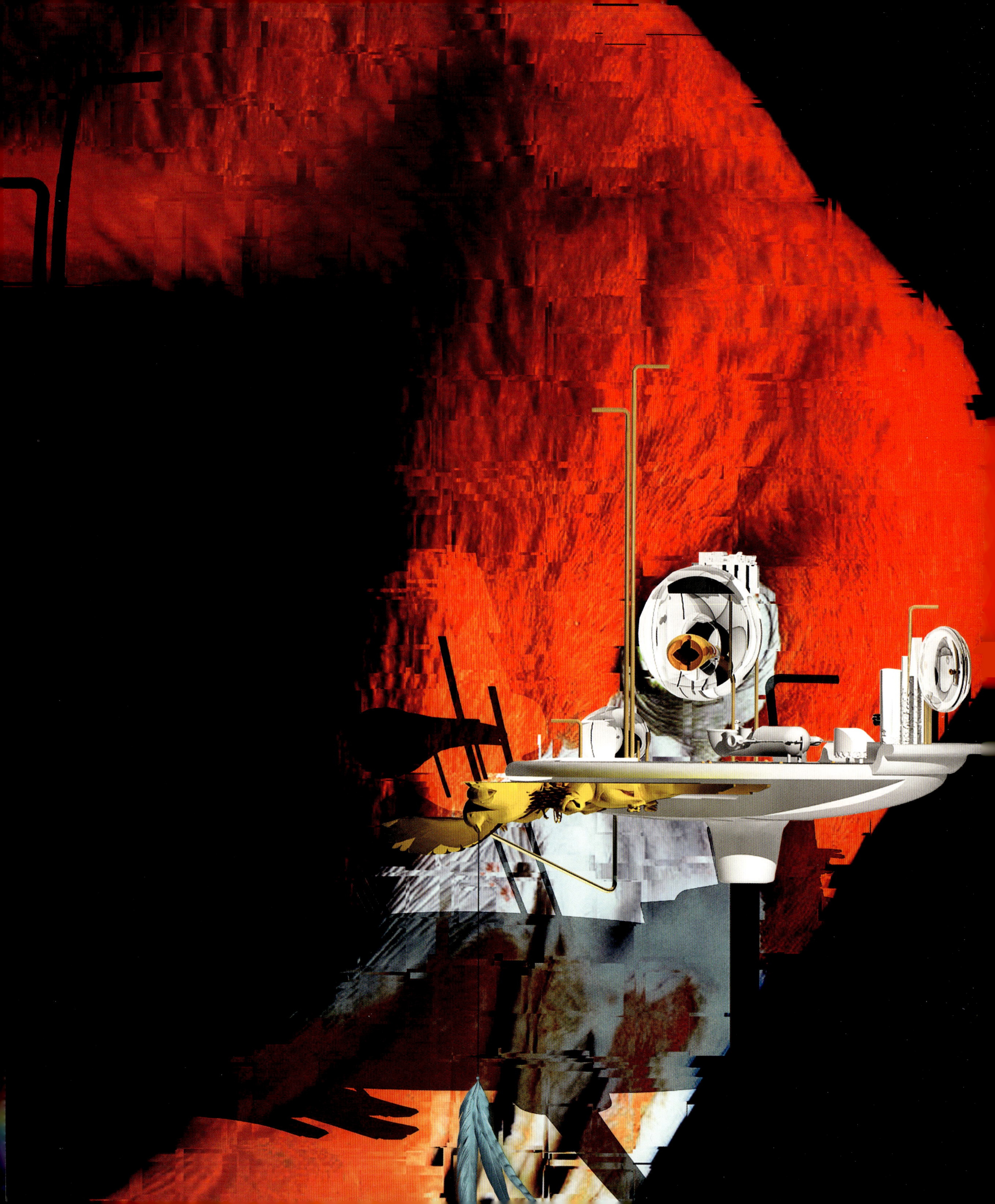

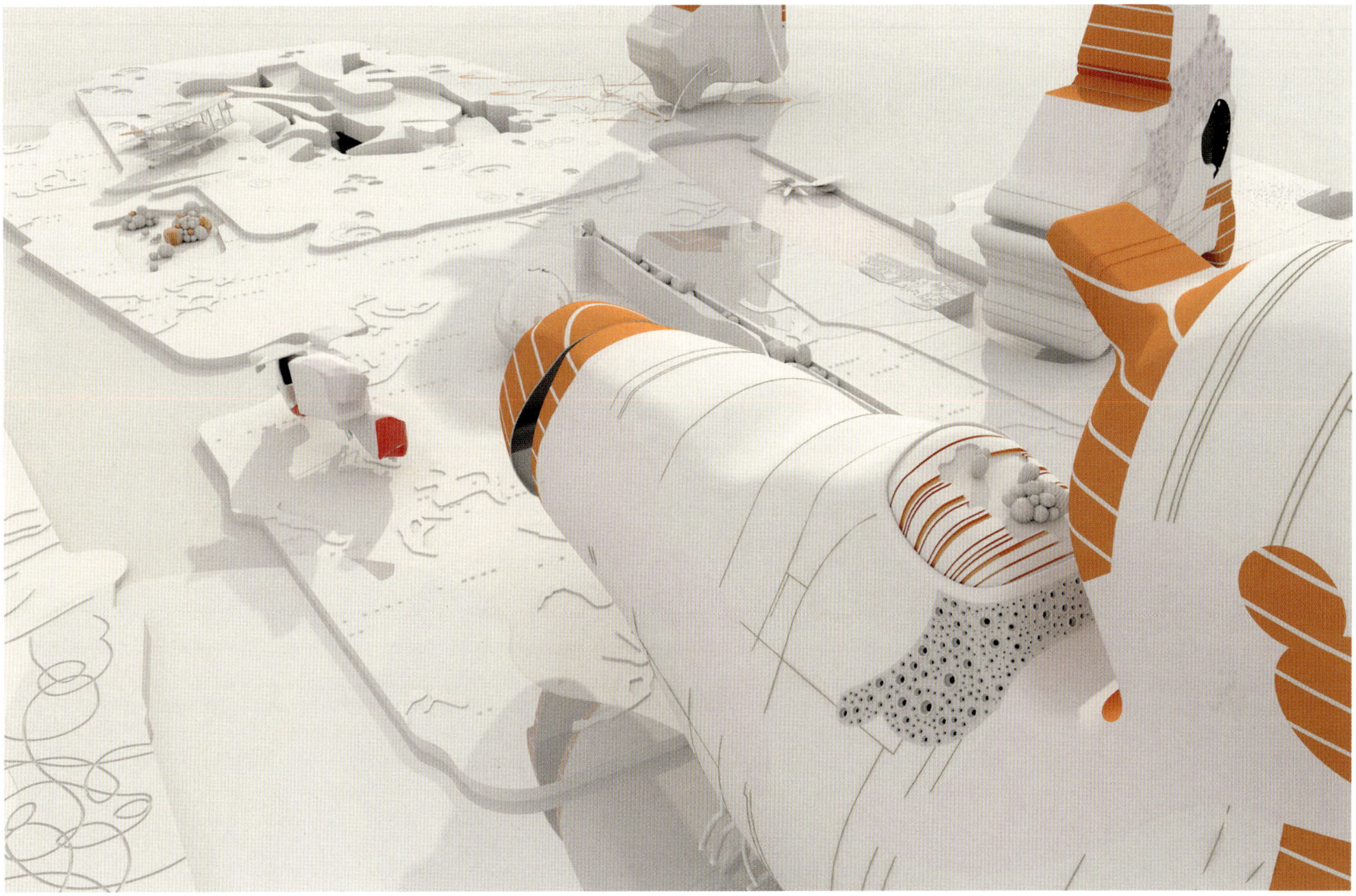

↑

Perry Kulper (digital modelling by Sen Liu) • Top of Lozenge, Fast Twitch: Speculative Desert Dwelling

2015

←

Perry Kulper with Omar Ali, Sam Seeger and Mark Keller • Flamingo v.02, Flights O' Fancy Bird Motel: in a sky – somewhere, Migrant Garden

2015

suggests wormholes in space and time, so does Kulper's. Our technologically enhanced jungles use the wet and the dry; the digital and the blooded in a metamorphic mix always trying to achieve ubiquity. This jungle is growing and becoming wilder around the world: red in digital tooth and claw.

The Argentinian architect and teacher Hernan Diaz Alonso is also not immune to evoking Art Nouveau forms and Dalínian polemic in his architectural investigations into the digital (see pages 219–20). Diaz Alonso once worked for the Catalan architect Enric Miralles (also a fan of Dalí's), who was renowned for his own arresting architecture and original thought patterns. We can thus perceive in Diaz Alonso's work a Catalan genealogy of Dalí, Gaudí and Miralles as well as an American avant-garde sensibility that picks up East and West Coast digital preoccupations of the recent past. Diaz Alonso is not an architect who accepts compromise; he has a surreal imagination and a techno-romantic eye reminiscent of the Art Nouveau movement and its Dalínian cylindrical monarchy. In his own words:

> [A] big part of the transformation in architecture of the last 20 years has been aesthetics. The idea of aesthetics mutates the tradition of composition and order, acting as an agent to study the paradigm shift towards formal excesses as opposed to the ubiquitous platform of types. If types are traditionally viewed as categories of standardisation and symbolic expressions of form, then formal mutation/rituals/techno-romanticism are the malleable entities that are in constant metamorphosis. As such, adaptation and mutation represent the main characteristics of current discourse. A shifting aesthetic paradigm – butchery, grotesque etc. – requires a lineage in order to be acknowledged as such. Indeed, a type also needs a lineage to become such, but a mutant sense of aesthetics has more freedom because it can mutate.[19]

In his 2010 design for silverware cutlery and plates for Alessi, entitled Instruments of Manner, Diaz Alonso created an essay in the curlicues and whirligigs of Art Nouveau. The set is beautiful – almost unusable – yet has the potential to subvert the established manners and etiquette of dining. In a nutshell, this is what he does with his building designs. His propositions always contain constellations of formal mutations: bubbles expand and are punctured, splines are lofted, urban strangeness is engaged not with deference, but with a devil-may-care attitude. Through these projects, the jungle and the abattoir meet and are introduced to even the most staid cities, like Helsinki. For Diaz Alonso, architecture is made with cinematic effect, advanced digital fabrication techniques and computer visualization – he pulls both digital and actual material to the limits of its integrity:

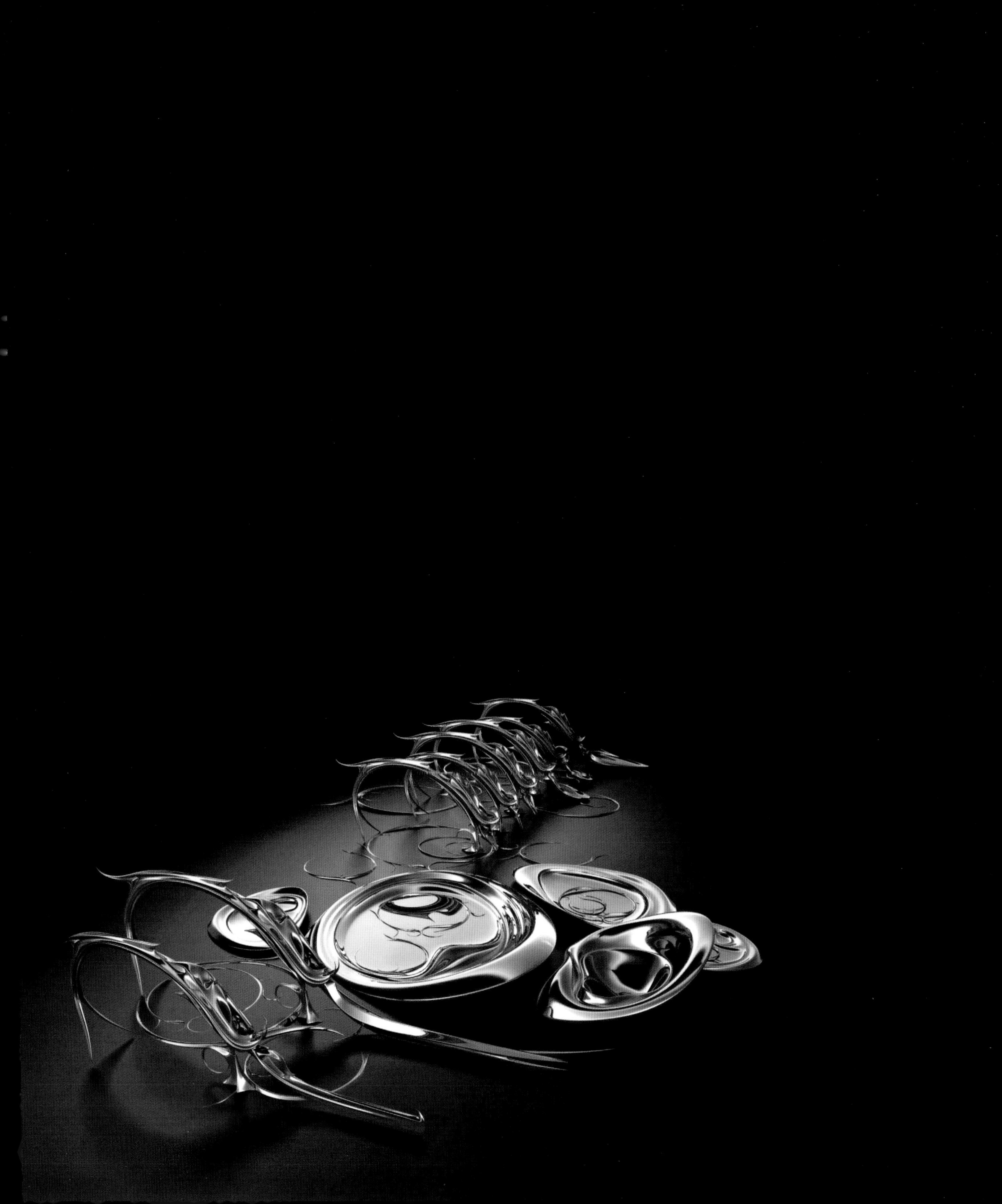

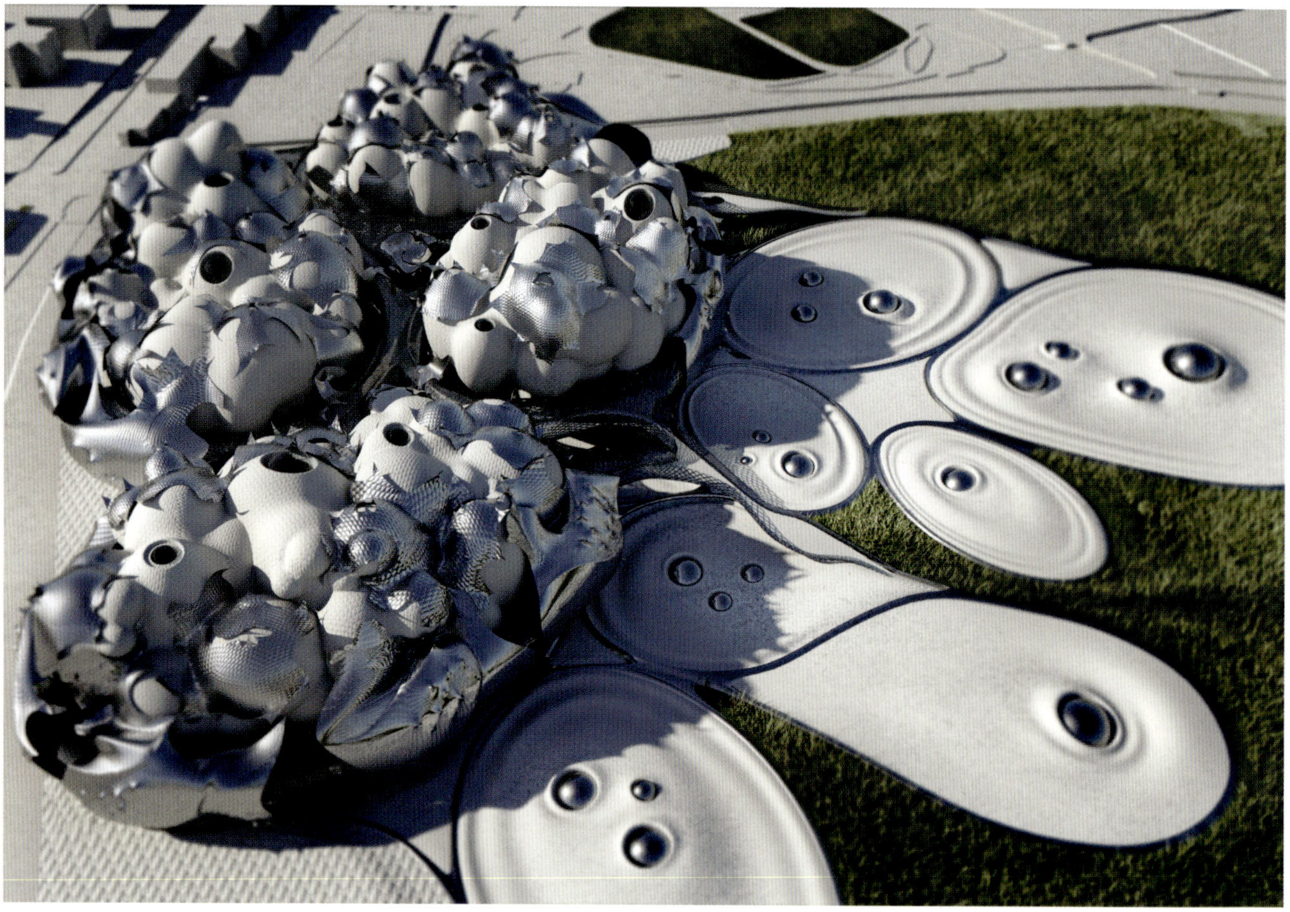

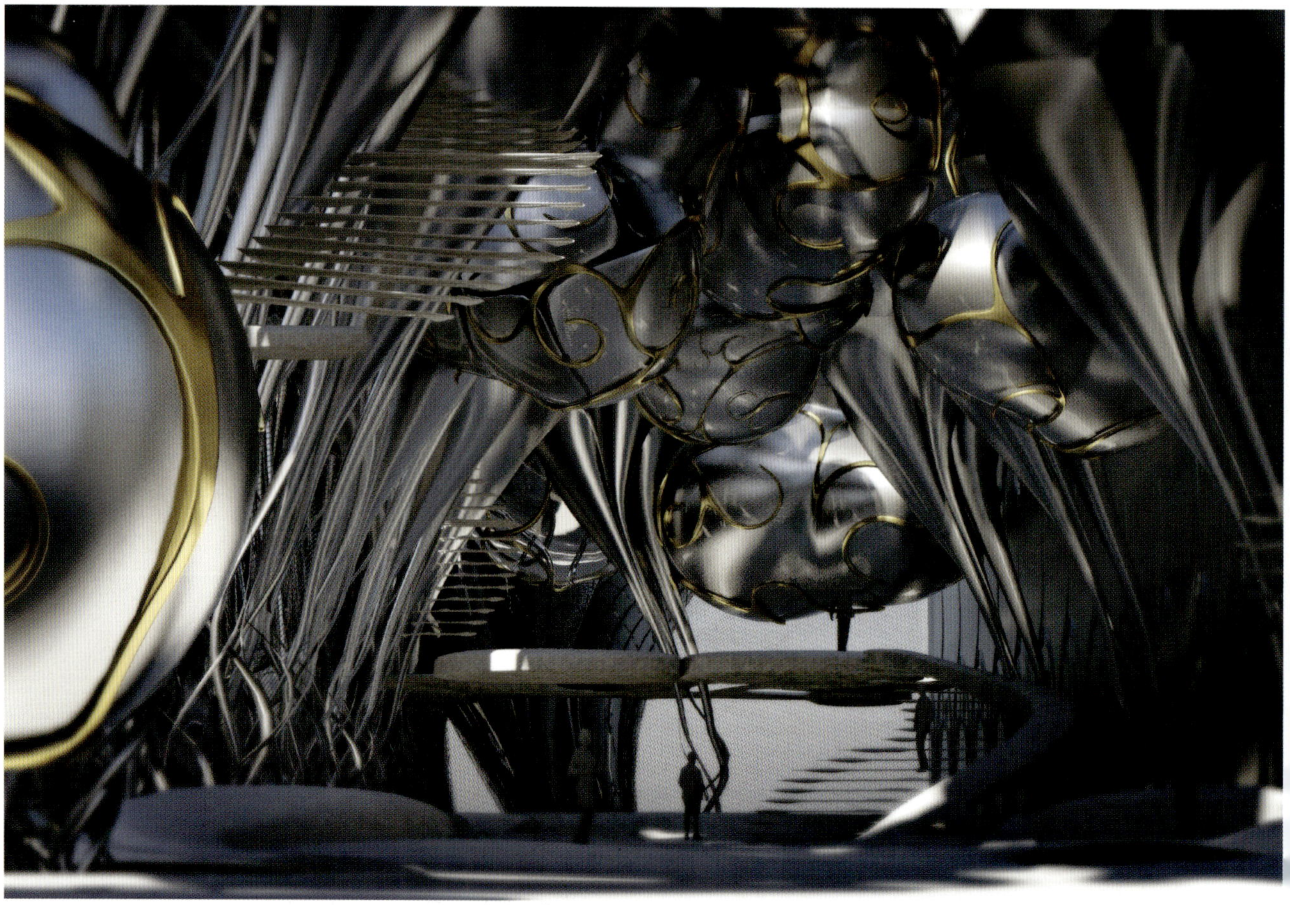

← Xefirotarch/Hernan Diaz Alonso
New National Gallery
and Ludwig Museum
International Competition, Budapest
2014

↙ Xefirotarch/Hernan Diaz Alonso
Helsinki Central Library
Competition, Helsinki
2012

> There is beauty in mess, contamination, putrefaction, all of which must be approached with passion. If one doesn't have passion for something, one shouldn't be doing it in the first place. How can something be moved forward if there is no confrontation? We need to strive for the equilibrium necessary to create the perfect ideal of imagination, innovation and originality. We should believe in the integrity of the pursuit – and the obsessions. In the end, the sole purpose of architecture is to imagine and challenge the culture of the discipline from every possible angle.[20]

Corsets and Dada Wetness in the Jungle and the Lagoon

The Surrealists enjoyed the evidence around them of the power of nature to subsume humanity's technological hubris. In 2006–7, architect and artist Christian Kerrigan, then a student, started to use this natural imperative not to subvert architecture, but to create it, the result of which is a stunning proposition, at once construction site, farm, factory, ship dry-dock and jungle (see pages 222–26).

Conceptually, his A Ship Carving Its Own Obelisk is predicated on the notion that, with the use of large-scale bonsai techniques, the positioning of steel corsets movable over time (to create denser growing timbers) and some judicious nanotechnology applied to a forest over the space of two hundred years, one could grow a timber ship. A subsequent study recognized that over such a long construction period the brief might change, and so all of the machinery and partly made maritime constructions would need to mutate themselves, using the same techniques, to construct a new product – an obelisk. These new emergent technologies could be used with other imperatives, husbanding methods or phenomena to create/grow architectures and objects.

From 2007 to 2014, myself, medical doctor Rachel Armstrong and protocell chemist Martin Hanczyc developed a series of experiments, drawings, texts and concepts on how to deploy protocells to create architectural environments. The team chose to investigate protocells that have no molecularly engineered organelles (cell organs), but are merely oil droplets that are dynamic, can be chemically charged and simply programmed to have simple aspirations such as attraction to light:

> Protocells do not operate within the realms of biological processes that are associated with living systems, but are driven by primordial organising forces – the laws of physics and chemistry. Yet protocells can be regarded as 'native' terrestrial entities that can operate in a much wider solution space of possibility than biology does. So while DNA produces biology as a result of its proliferating cellular processes, populations of protocells create completely different forms, functions and landscapes from their materials.[21]

Such notions and the resulting shifting, time-based forms that could be created with technologies such as this question the very basis of architecture, its dogmas and doctrines, and posit a surreal world where nothing is stable. The team was thus prompted to readdress Dada polemic expressions in the light of this potential cataclysmic metamorphosis in architectural thought. Our 'Manifesto for Protocell Architecture: Against Biological Formalism', which took Dada polemics and rearticulated them, was published in the *Architectural Design (AD) Protocell Architecture* issue guest-edited by myself and Rachel Armstrong in 2011. The manifesto headings were as follows:

> We want to change the world with almost nothing.
> What we call protocell architecture is, at root, a piece of Dadaist and Surrealist research, in which all the lofty questions have become involved.
> Architecture is dead, long live architecture.
> Protocell architecture swallows contrast and all contradictions including the grotesquery and illogicality of life.
> What is generally termed life is really a frothy nothing that merely connects.

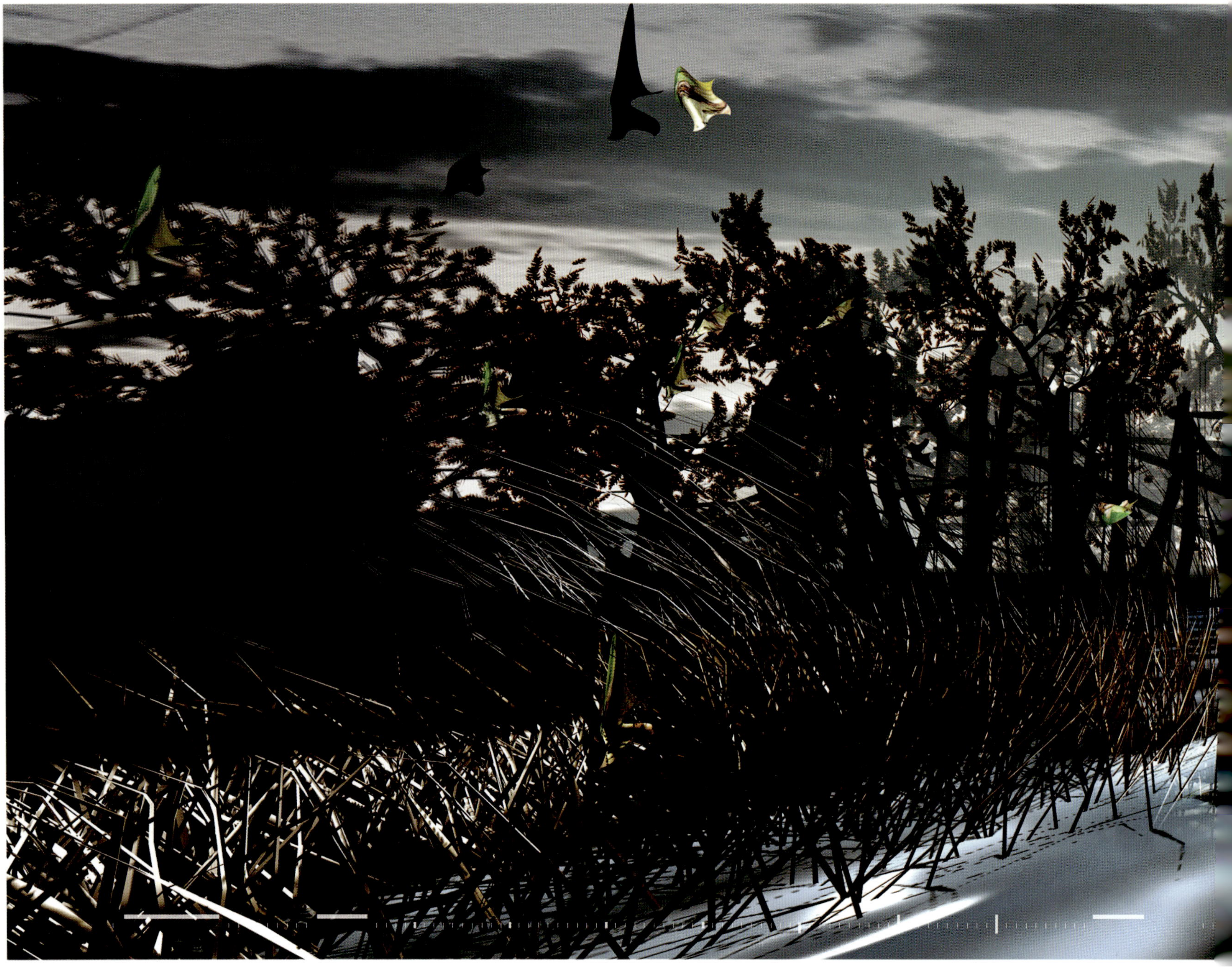

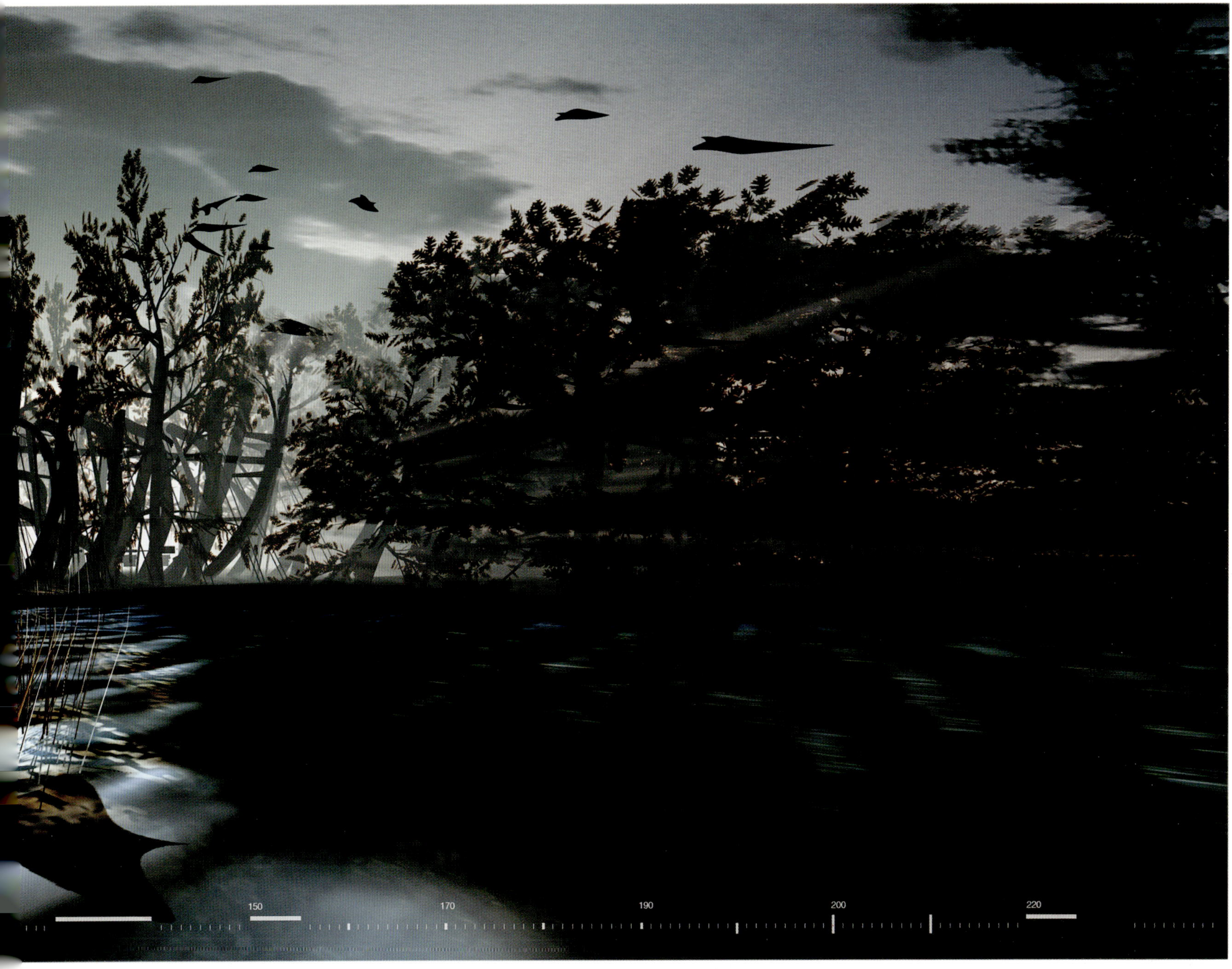

↑

Christian Kerrigan • Growing a Hidden Architecture: Ship's Silhouette

2006

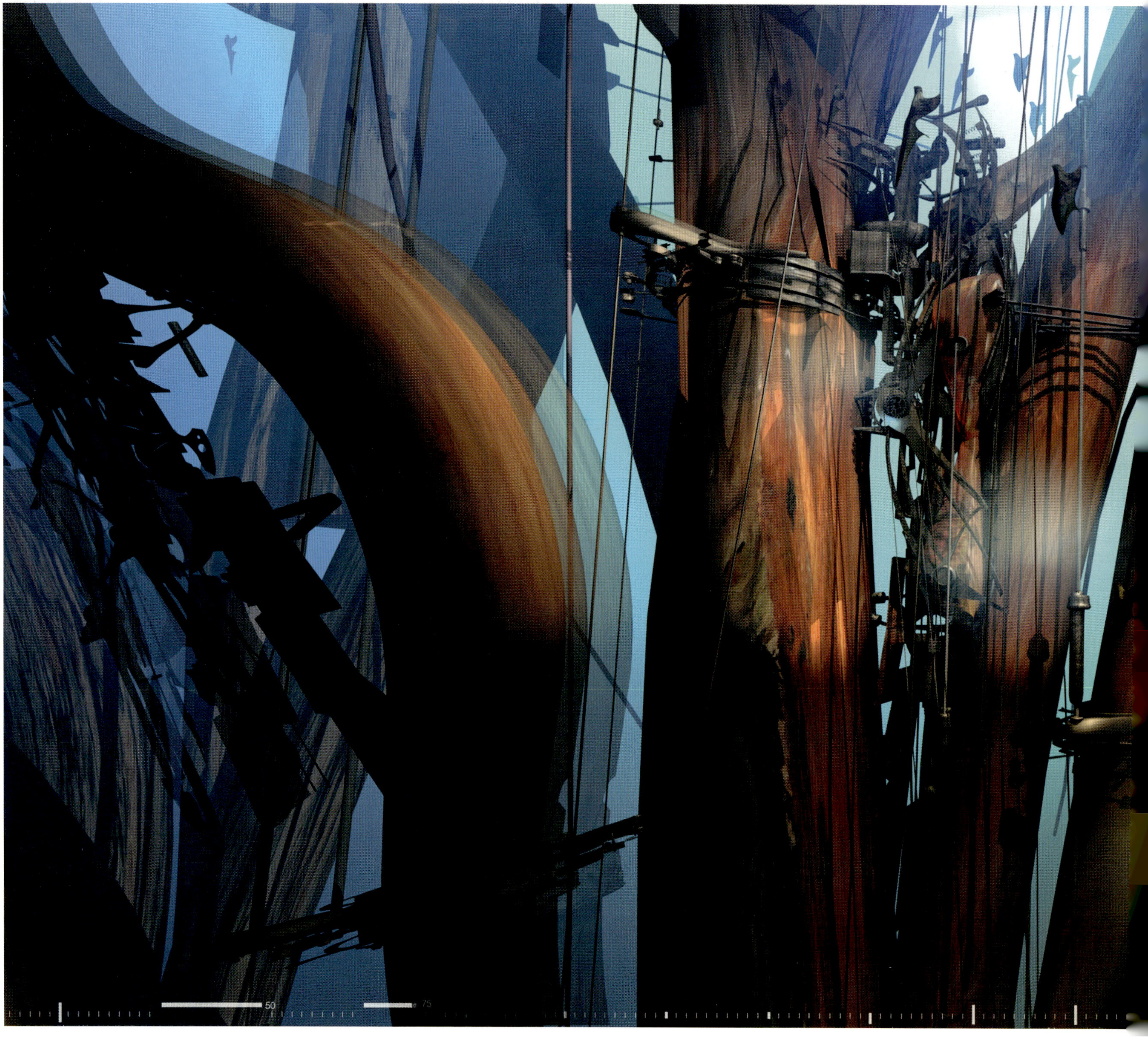
50
75

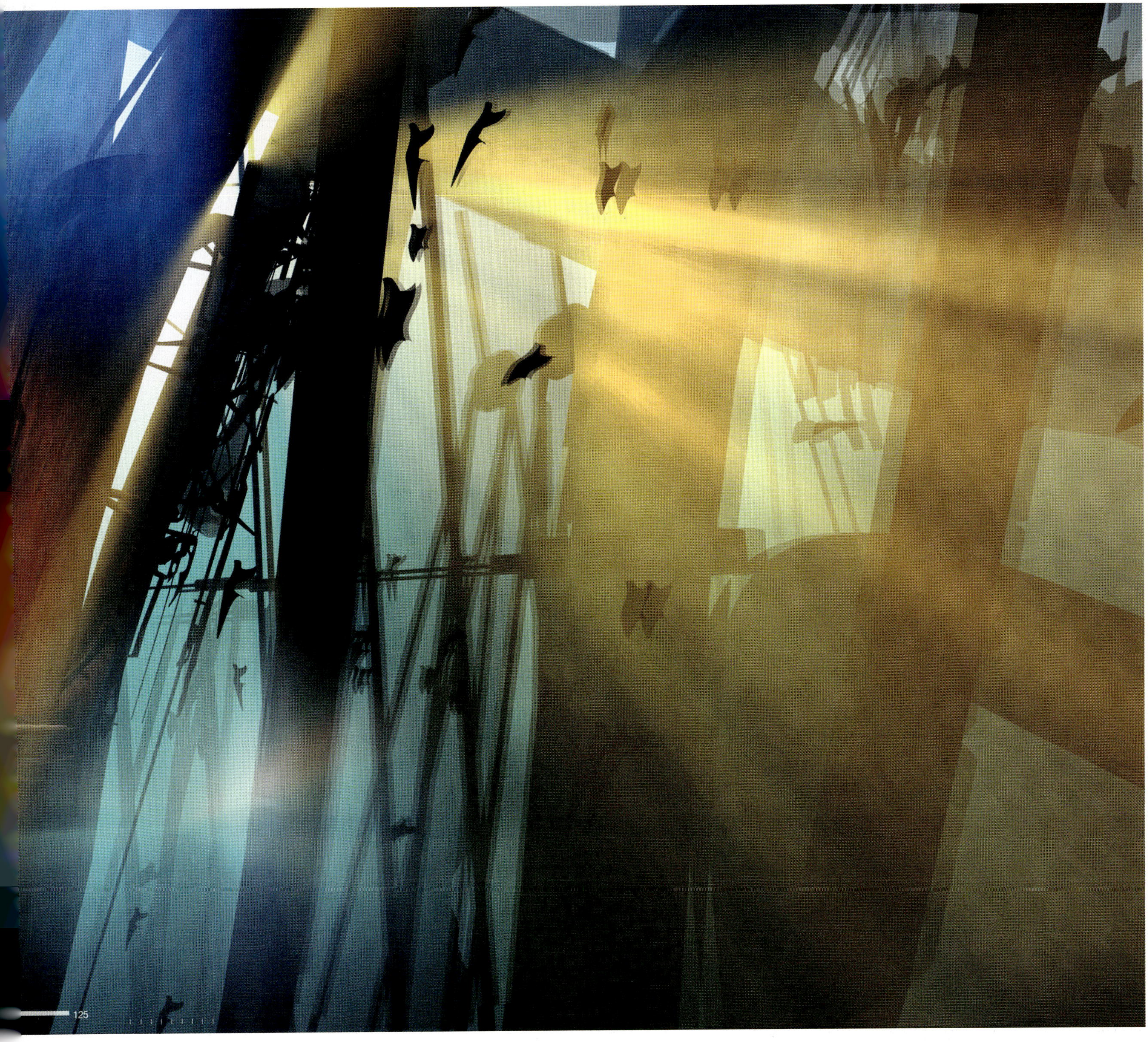

↑

Christian Kerrigan • Growing a Hidden Architecture: Amber Forest After 200 Years

2006

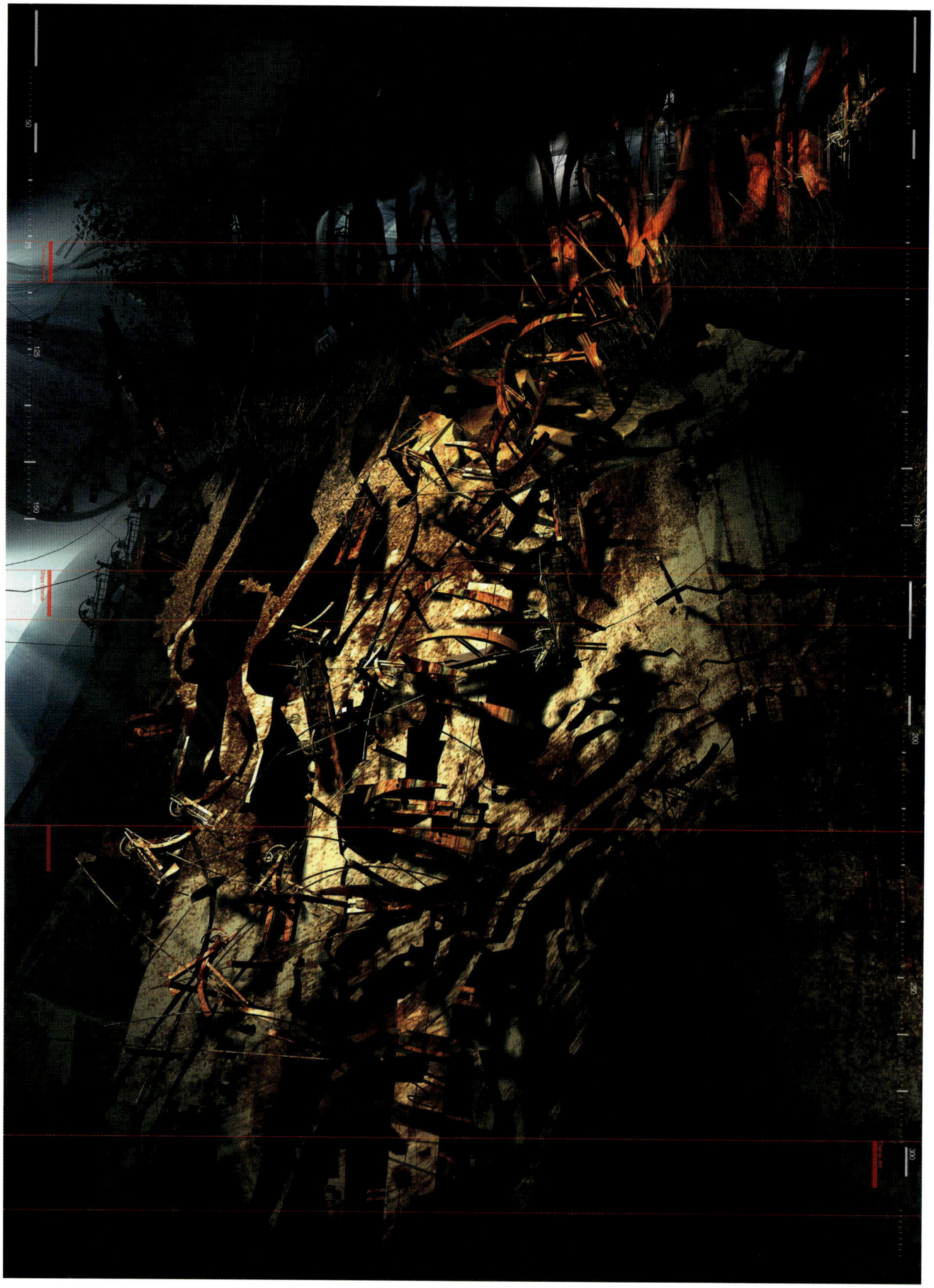

←

Christian Kerrigan • A Ship Carving Its Own Obelisk: General Arrangement Plan

2007

> **We do not wish to imitate nature, we do not wish to reproduce nature, we want to produce architecture in the way a plant produces its fruit. We do not want to depict, we want to produce directly, not indirectly, since there is no trace of abstraction. We call it protocell architecture.**
> **We want to collage effective organic machinery that composes itself according to the drivers of biological design.**
> **We want over and over again, movement and connection; we see peace only in dynamism.**
> **The head is round, so thoughts can revolve. The head of architecture is green, robust, synthesized, and exists everywhere simultaneously, whether it is large or very, very small.**
> **We wish to blur the firm boundaries that self-certain people delineate around all we can achieve.**
> **We tell you the tricks of today are the truths of tomorrow.**
> **We will work with things that we do not want to design, things that already have systematic existence.**
> **You know as well as we do that architecture is nothing more than rhythms and connections.**
> **We will construct exquisite corpses, not dead but alive and useful.**
> **We deal in a second aesthetic, one that initiates beginnings and moulds with natural forces.**[22]

In 2010, architect Dan Slavinsky, then a student and influenced by our protocell research, sought to create a language of architecture that was a juxtaposition of the wet and moving and the solid and dry. The project, In Arcadia at the End of Time (see pages 228–29), had an edibility to it in Dalínian terms:

> **The proposal speculates upon the possibility of a flexible architecture being achieved using Living Technology, and seeks to establish a new lexicon of ornament based on this new approach. The premise being, that we are moving towards a model of complex and systems-based architecture that celebrates the use of hybrid technologies to better integrate our buildings into Nature. The drawings depict an Arcadia frozen at the End of Time – an ambiguous garden of symbolism, referencing the architectural movement of Art Nouveau, in which this new code of 'Soft Ornament' is expressed.**
> **As part of the series, I have tested these ideas by applying them to the design of interior of the Bride of Denmark bar, the private pub in the basement of No. 9 Queen Anne's Gate, London, under the former offices of the AR, which has been closed for several decades.**
> **I have sought to re-instate this exclusive drinking establishment as an Absinthe Bar. The well-proportioned Georgian interior provides the setting for exploring how 'ordered' and 'vagrant' geometries could co-exist.**[23]

Christian Kerrigan was also part of a team (along with myself, Rachel Armstrong and Martin Hanczyc) brought together to propose a synthetic biological theoretical solution to the problem of Venice sinking, for which Kerrigan created the arresting visualizations. The 2009–10 Future Venice project (see pages 230–33) offers an alternative to a huge, expensive top-down engineering project, and posits a bottom-up emergent possible solution to Venice's instability.

Protocells can be made to transverse along chemical gradients in aqueous solutions (chemotaxis), can be attracted to or repulsed from light (phototaxis) and can be made to shed skins. In the Future Venice proposition, harmless

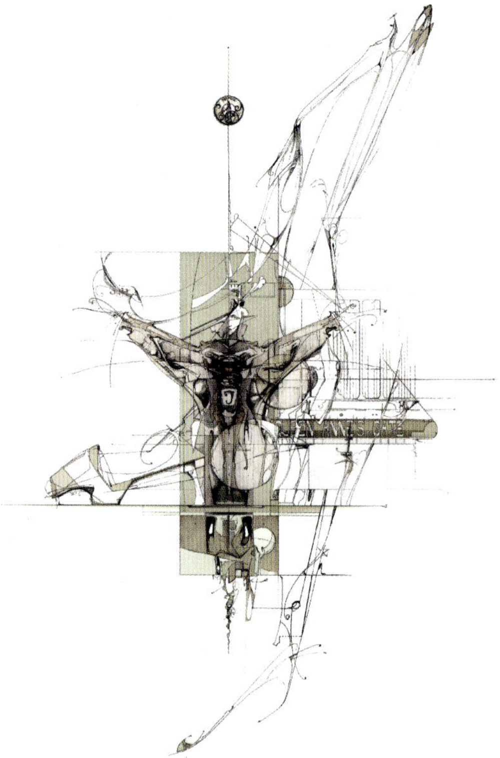

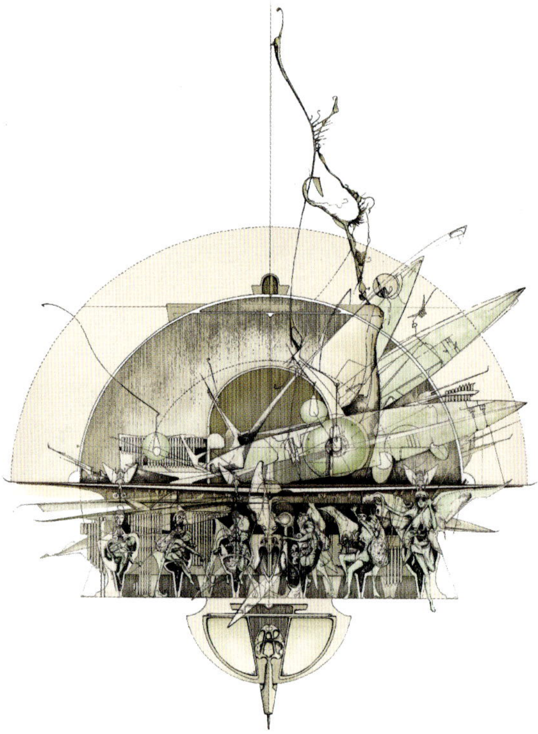

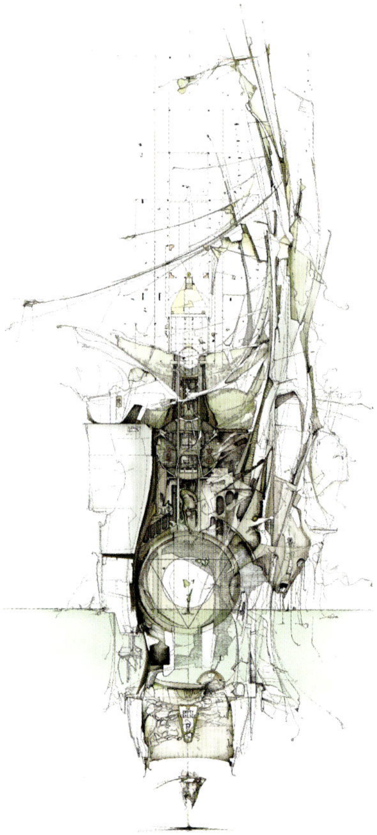

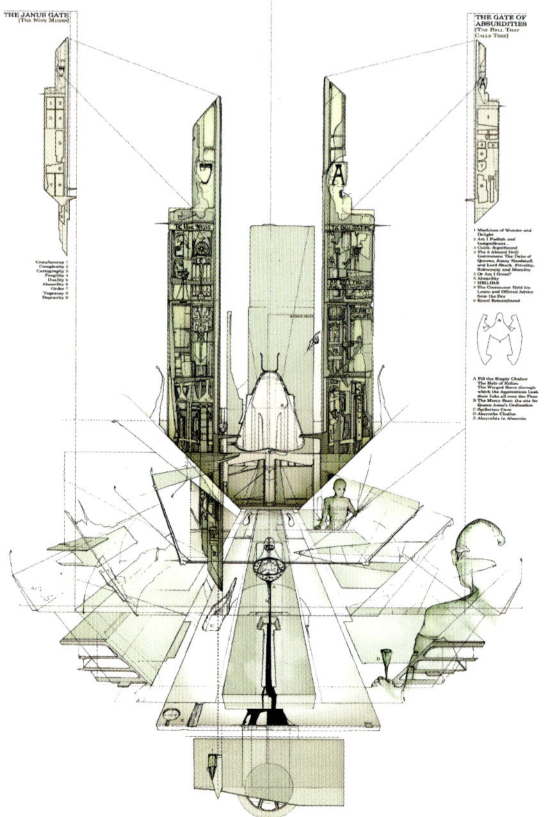
THE JANUS GATE
[The Nine Muses]
THE GATE OF ABSURDITIES
[The Bell That Calls Time]

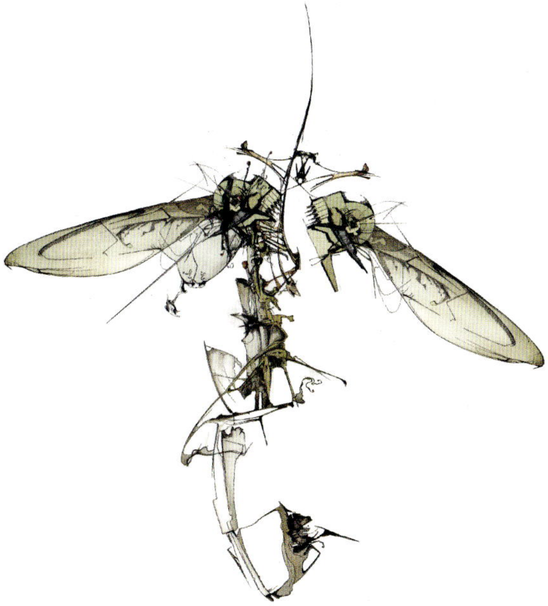

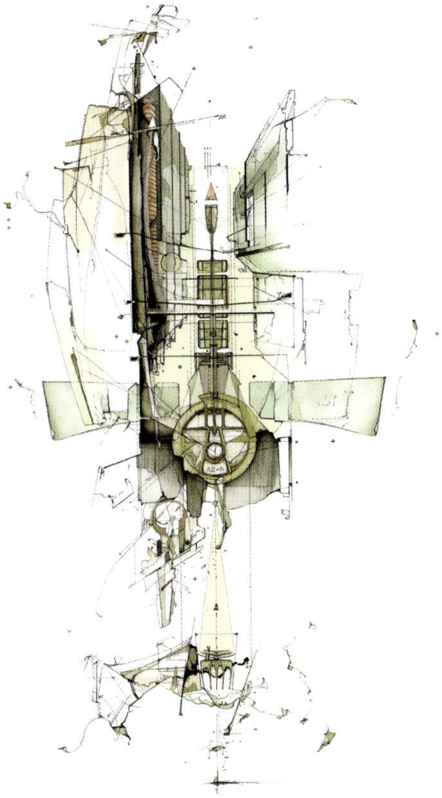

← **Dan Slavinsky • (clockwise from top left)**
The Bride of Denmark Bar – Janus Gate;
The Bride of Denmark Bar – Elevation;
Soft Ornament No. 27;
Soft Ornament No. 41;
On the Possibilities of an Interior;
Soft Ornament No. 40, **all from** In Arcadia at the End of Time
2010

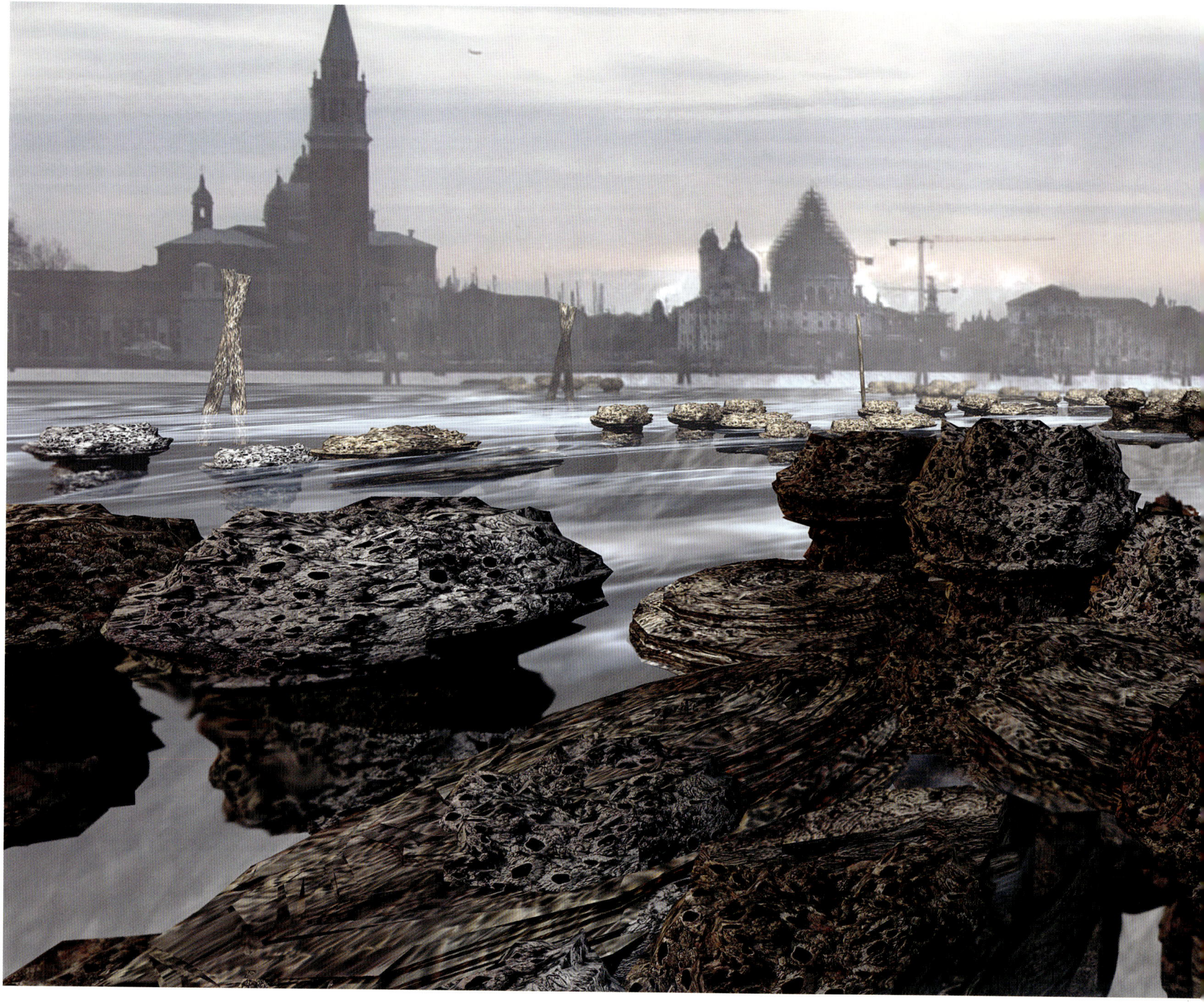

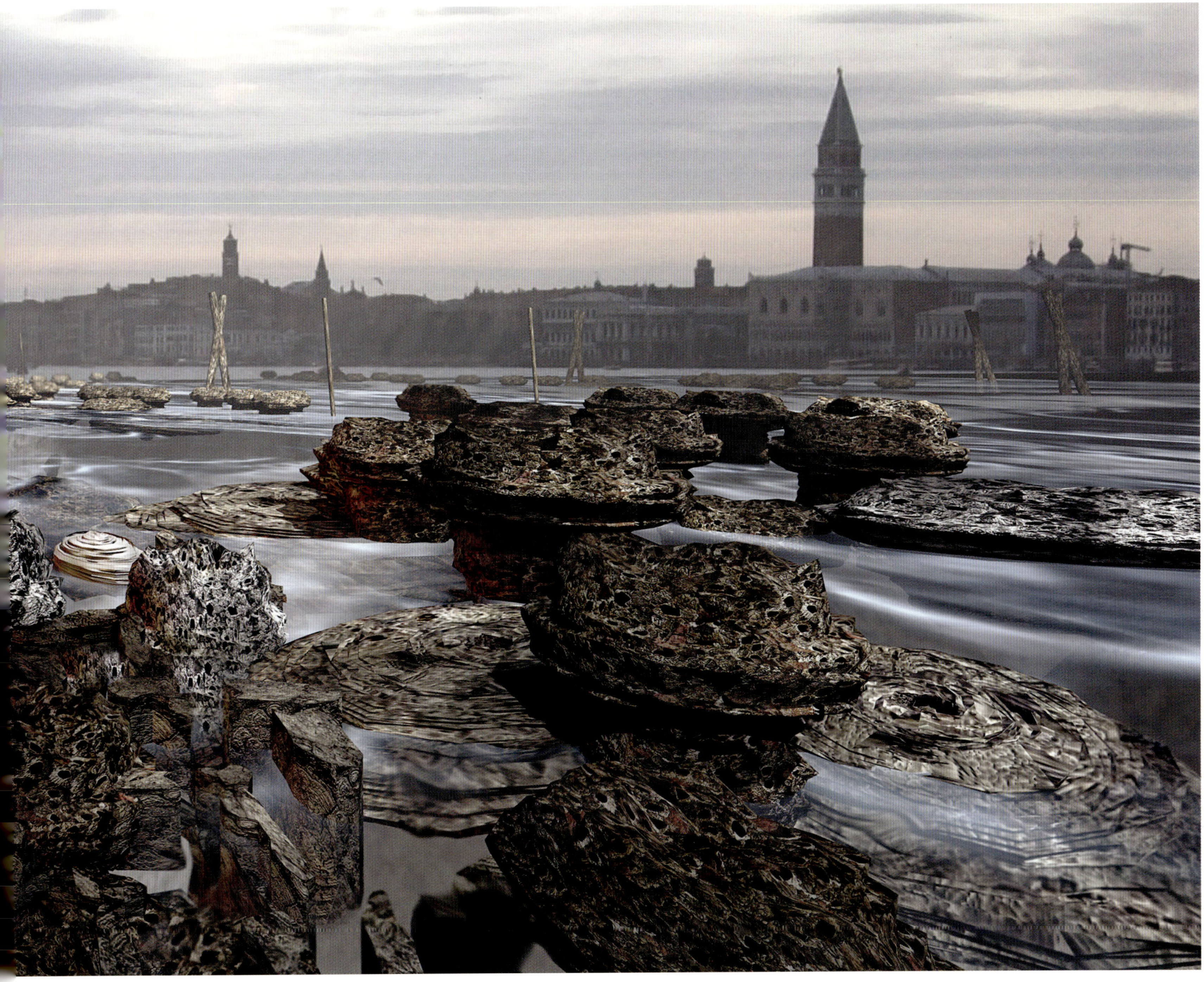

↑

Neil Spiller, Rachel Armstrong and Martin Hanczyc (AVATAR) • Future Venice (visualizations by Christian Kerrigan)

2009

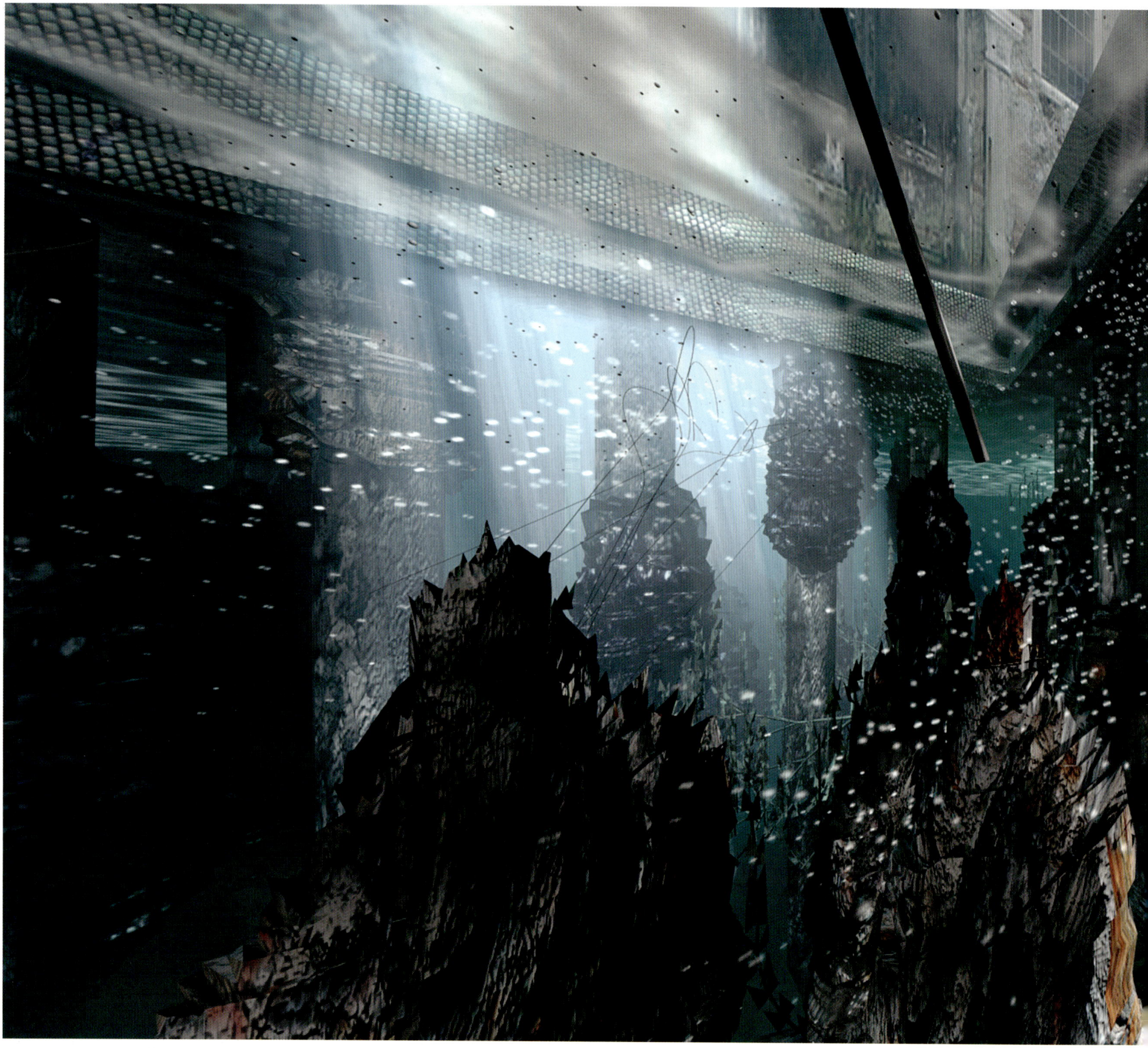

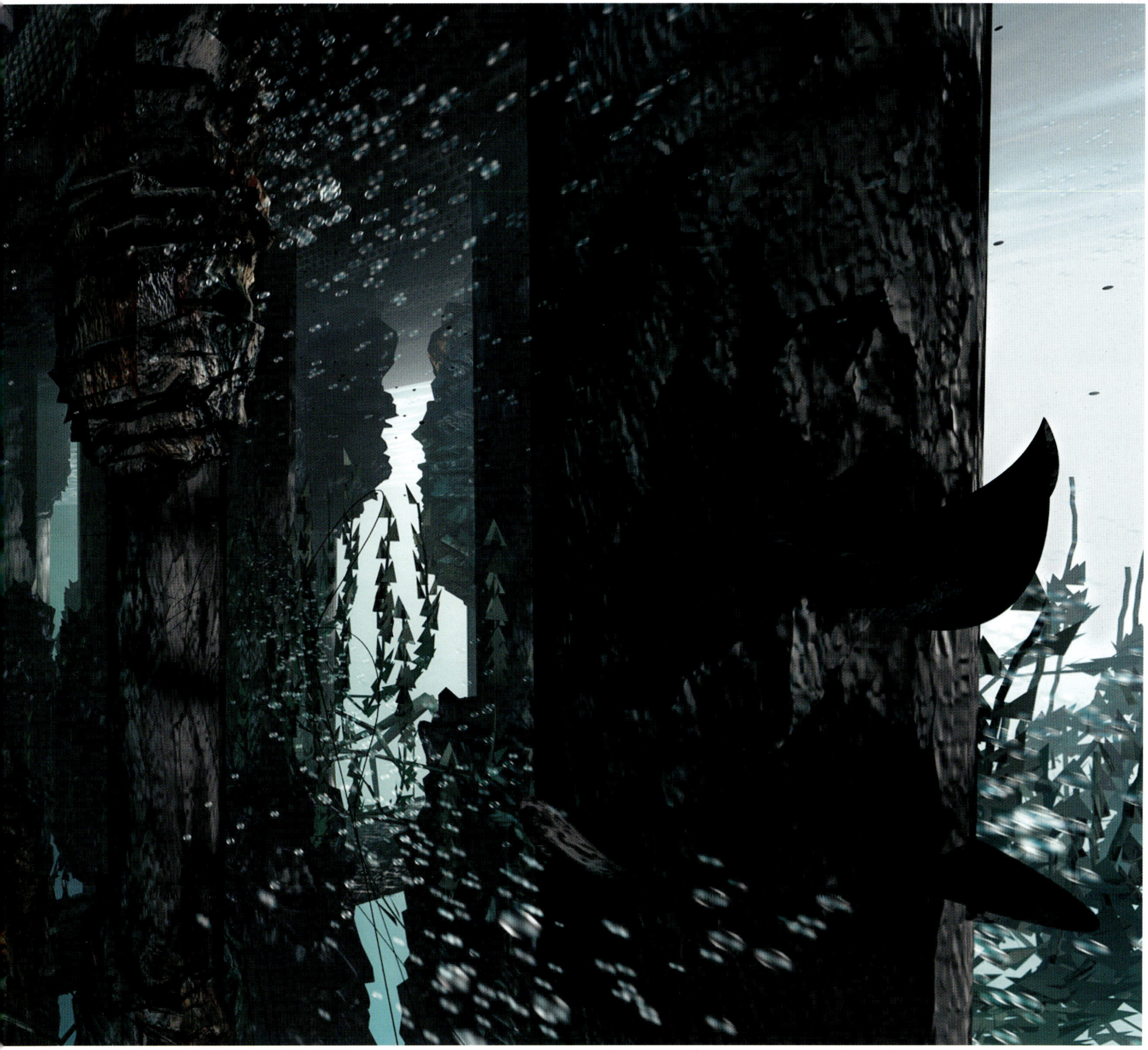

↑

Neil Spiller, Rachel Armstrong and Martin Hanczyc (AVATAR) • Future Venice (visualizations by Christian Kerrigan)

2009

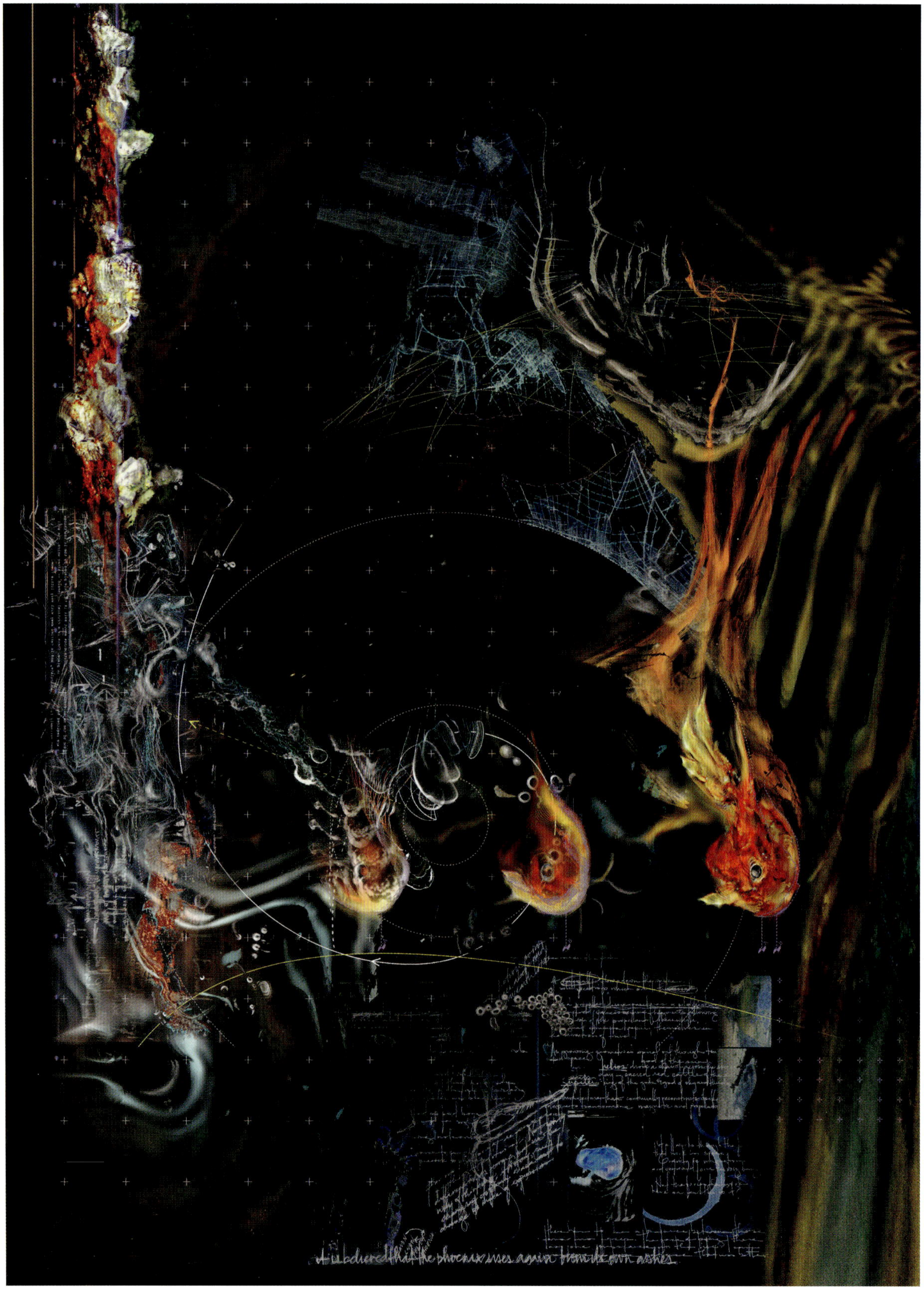
it is believed that the phoenix rises again from its own ashes

←

Elizabeth Anne Williams and Phil Watson • Expansion of Neptune's Schism

2013

protocells are released into the city's canals and lagoon, they seek out and congregate in the dark areas around Venice's timber piled foundations, shed deposits of limestone and start to create reefs under its buildings to solidify and enhance the load-bearing capacity of its foundations.

Protocell and synthetic biological processes might also be key to how we could colonize other planets, and to space travel generally. We might 'seed' spaceships with emergent materials that, in the decades or hundreds of years to get to where they are going, start to change and respond to their environments, creating evolving ecologies of landscapes and objects. The surreal potential of these technologies is endless. Architect Elizabeth Anne Williams has made initial graphic forays into what these landscapes might look like at certain points early in their history. This is an architecture not immediately recognized as such, but conceived of time, metabolic pathways, viscosity, gravity and fleeting association. It is an architecture that makes no distinction between the organic and the inorganic, or the natural and the artificial.

Sexy Knowledge

What is interesting for the surrealist is the connection that can be made between the exchange of information in wet, unconventional computers and the sexual act of desire and the mixing of information. There is much precedent for such notions. Duchamp was very adept at these sorts of analogies and epistemologies. His *Large Glass* is conceptually activated by gas, water and electromagnetic forces to create a tableau of desire, auto-erotics and barely maintained equilibrium.[24]

This understanding of the dynamic nature of our world and our need to relinquish our demands for architectural inertness, ecological stasis and bodily sanctity and instead rejoice in simultaneities, is now becoming more common among architects. As we have seen, in not denying us our desires, urges, ability to conflate groups of diverse images, experience fear, and create and interact with the psychic texts of our lives and environments, the Surrealist lexicon of thought has mapped out some of the possibilities of future bodies, houses, cities and their inherent landscapes. In so doing, Surrealism, its protocols and tactics continue to be highly valuable for architectural progress and discourse, and will become more so in the future as a yardstick with which to assimilate and theorize new technologies (both biological and virtual) while not forgetting we are human and prone to all manner of marvellous subversion; this is, after all, the greatest asset of humanity's jungle of blood. Surrealism 'outs' this subversion and makes it visible, and it is through this visibility that architecture can become enlivened and invigorated for a new century.

SAFE HOUSES FOR WET ANGELS

Mark West

Projects From a Career in Surrealist Praxis

1985–2015

The American architect and teacher Mark West's career spans almost four decades, and as such has transversed or intersected with a variety of technological, political and, indeed, architectural changes. He is fully committed to the notion that good, thoughtful architecture can change society in both the global north and south, and continues to work in a variety of media conjuring the three- and four-dimensional from the two-dimensional. Models, beautiful pencil drawings, collages, photographs and concrete casts created using fabric formwork represent his architectures. They are always surreal, and through such projects West has engaged with all four central themes of this book: the body, the house, the city and the biomechanical landscape.

West talks of his own body as an organ of assimilation of architectural fashion and taste, politics and paranoia – we are what we eat – and along the way makes architecture that has convulsive beauty, an architecture of mastication:

> *As we all eat and metabolize bits of the world, the fragments from this particular body are examined... primarily as evidence of changes in our collective cultural-technical ecology more than as evidence of changes in a particular imagination.*[1]

We are products of the world we make and the barriers we imagine we perceive. In 1985, West designed the Safehouse project – a comment on Cold War paranoia and boundary infringement mediated by televisual and electronic sentinels. The house is an impenetrable bunker-like mass, bristling with antennas – a response to the many remembered 'duck and cover' exercises in school yards, under school desks and in government information films as a method of personal protection against the effects of a nuclear attack. All manner of surveillance paraphernalia is part of the project:

> *These devices were catalogued and deployed in four categories: Early Warning Systems, Sensors, Decoys, and Lawn Furniture. The house itself was entirely sealed; it had no entry or exit. Its windows were inward-facing TV monitors (cathode ray tubes) displaying video feeds from outside and/or inside, as determined and controlled by the inhabitants.*
>
> *Though made as a dark cynical critique, its parts were meticulously crafted and it gave off a surprising, uncanny, and strange beauty. Rather than becoming the intended diabolical experiment or cautionary tale, it turned into pure seduction. Now it is only a memory, having been trashed decades ago.*[2]

Combined with this international danger of 'mutually assured destruction' was the internal danger of the feral city. Cities like New York were decaying and in recession in the 1970s and early 1980s, the popular conception in Middle America that they housed a 'cancer' of immorality, decadence, un-American activities (crime, left-wing politics and sexual deviance) and subversion – all to be protected from. Welcome to the jungle baby!

The ideal paranoid domestic dwelling of the 1980s Cold War – a cross between bunker, spy station and House Beautiful.

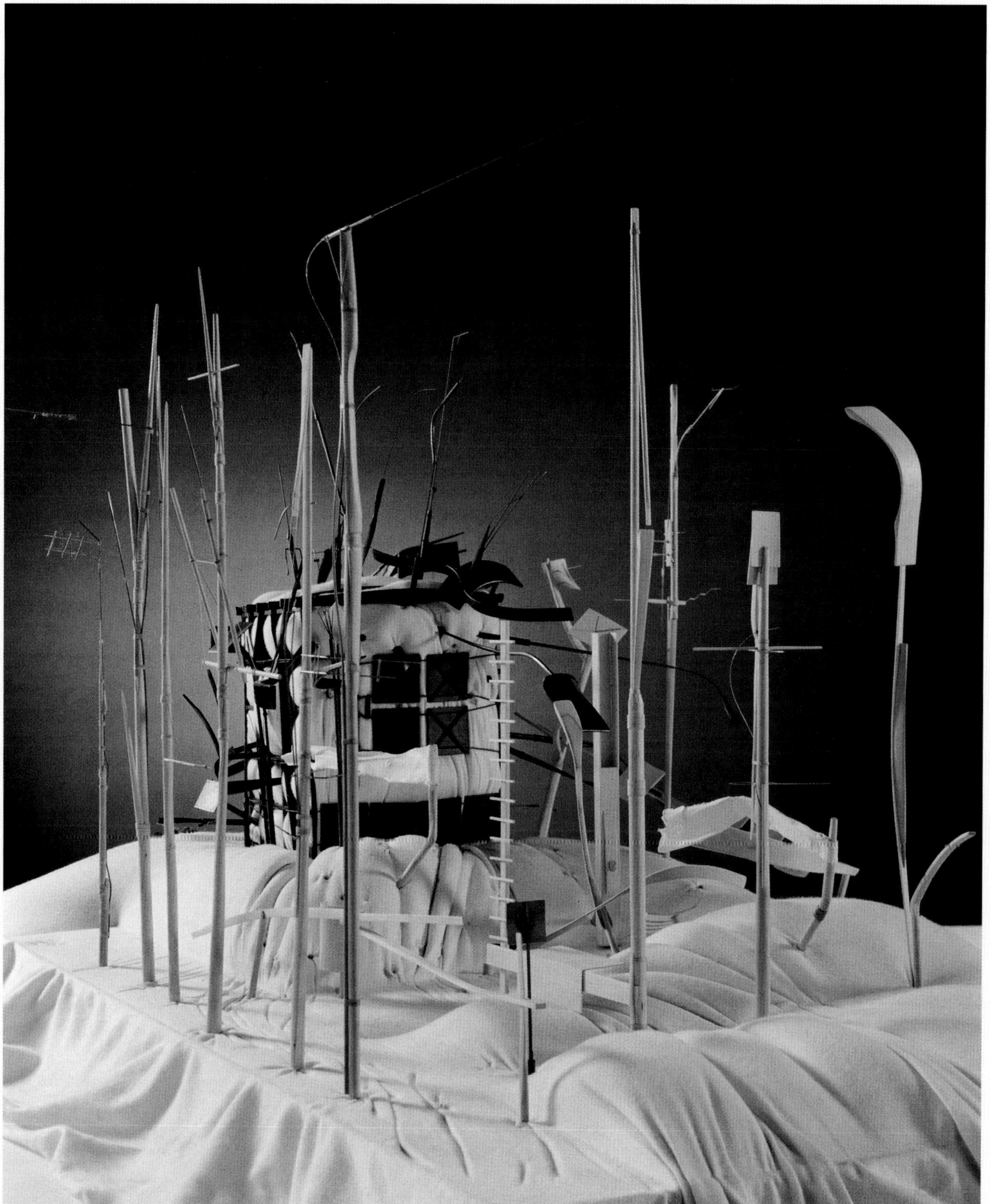

HOTEL EDWARD HOPPER **2007**

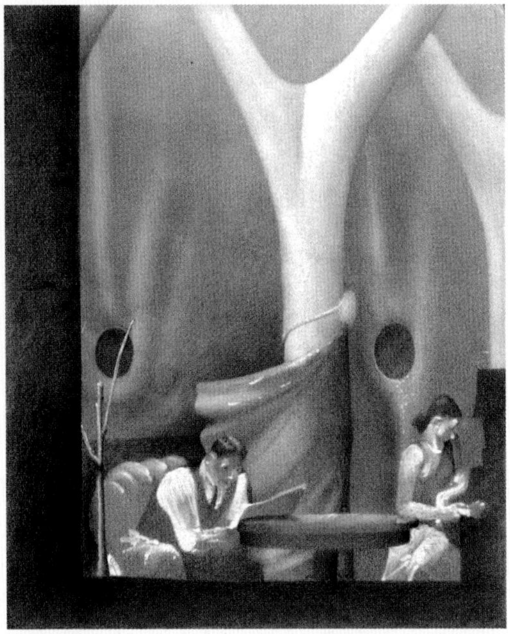

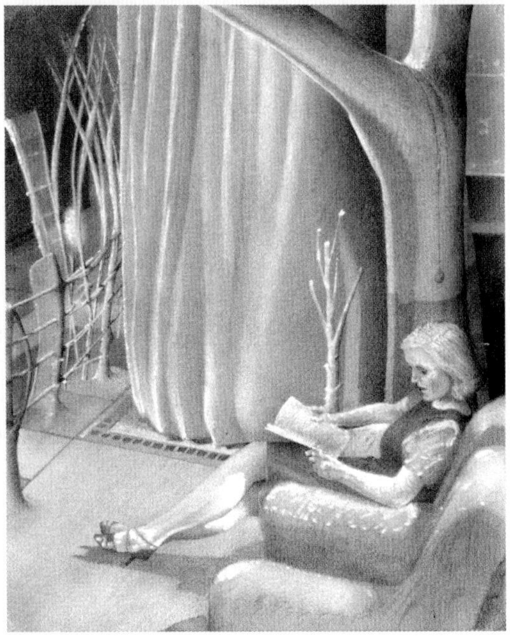

The drawings speculate not only on individual architectural spaces of the Hotel but also on the possibility of their fabric formed concrete construction.

In 1990, a year after the Berlin Wall came down and the Eastern Bloc had been thrust into disarray, the Storefront for Art and Architecture gallery in Manhattan exhibited a project by West and Natalija Subotincic entitled *Project Atlas*. In a world breathing a short sigh of relief in the belief that all would be well after this interim period of readjustment, they asked what and where the new dangers were. They imagined that the jungle had merged with the mechanistic city and conjoined to create *The Beauties*, a series of biomechanical, toxic, military yet uncontrollable contagions – soldiers from a biotechnical future:

> *These graphite portraits are built, collage-like, from projected, imagined, and hallucinated parts. They mean to seduce, even while they repulse. Their method of construction owes much to a long series of previous 'blackout' collage/drawings from the mid-eighties that also mashed up bio and mechanical image fragments using a hallucinatory method of visual finding/construction.*[3]

West is not solely a 'paper architect', however. He has an almost unique ability to combine the conceptually 'out there' with the wherewithal to construct his visions. Nowhere is this truer than in his proposition for *Hotel Edward Hopper*. He has researched the construction of fabric-formed concrete and developed some very simple tying methods that create extraordinary shapes once the concrete has set within these fabric formworks. This gives his work a surreality and pragmatism way beyond standard structural engineering textbooks. It has the same, but different, semiotic and multivalent aspirations as Gaudí – it tells stories and implies something 'other', something to do with desire. West's forms are blousy; they billow, and they are voluptuous, often with a hint of corset, or seductively part-revealing the soft and curvaceous forms below. Hotel Edward Hopper negotiates the tightrope between visionary architecture and concrete-cast practicality to create a surreal series of architectural spaces, inspired by the characters depicted in Hopper's paintings of American life:

THE BEAUTIES 2 AND THE BEAUTIES 3,
PROJECT ATLAS **1990**

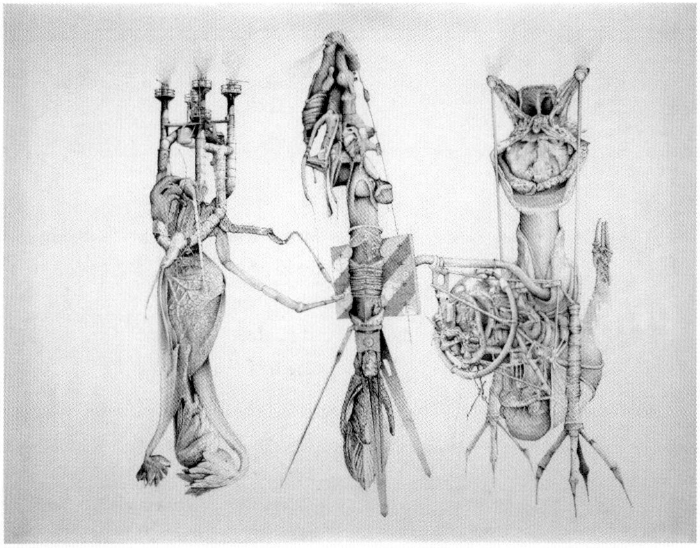

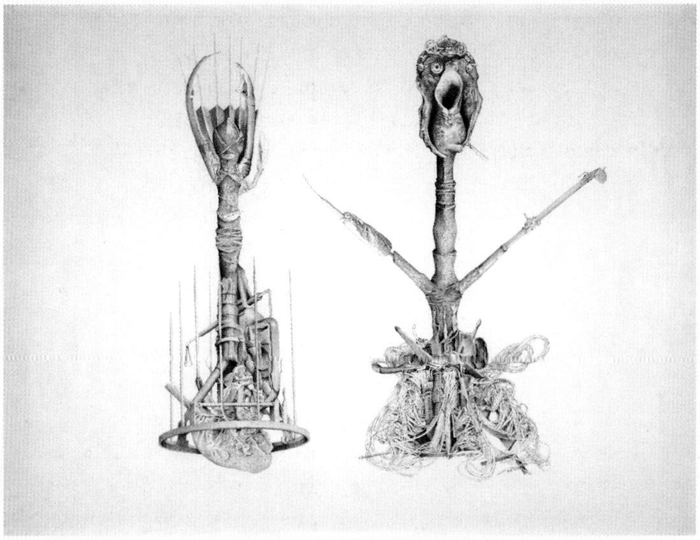

The devices concocted for the competition were amalgams of military hardware, industry and biological life.

> *The 'hotel' itself was found after clothing these figures/characters in spaces composed from several very real technical inventions involving quasi self-forming architectural components (fabric-formed concrete walls, panels, columns, shells, and so forth). As each drawing envisioned another space, the 'Hotel' took form not just as visual images or spatial propositions, but as reasoned technical proposals with substantially clarified wall sections backed-up by thoroughly worked out material fabrication and erection procedures.*[4]

In his *Tangled City* series of collages – musings on the interchangeability of urban biological structures and their mechanistic counterparts – West reveals the further potential of hybridity to enhance our understanding of the new technological terrain of the city.

West's interest is in the jungle of the city with its great transparent virtual technologies, in the jungle of the Developing World (where he hopes his simple fabric formwork construction methods will help alleviate some suffering, providing much needed cheap and easy-to-make shelter), and in the surreal jungle of biomechanical architecture. And it is between these three jungles that contemporary architecture must operate in the twenty-first century. While technology, politics and architectural fashions have changed over West's career, his artistic concern with explorations of hybrid forms of the biological and mechanical has remained constant, as demonstrated by the series of excavations/hallucinations worked into photo-collages that he produced in 2015. These images (*Wet Angels*, *Emblem of the Forest Floor* and *Construction Site*; see pages 242–43) are harbingers of a surreal architectural future. To quote West: 'Together they form a kind of coloured dream of a disturbed yet beautiful world.'[5]

TANGLED CITY (DETAIL) **2012**

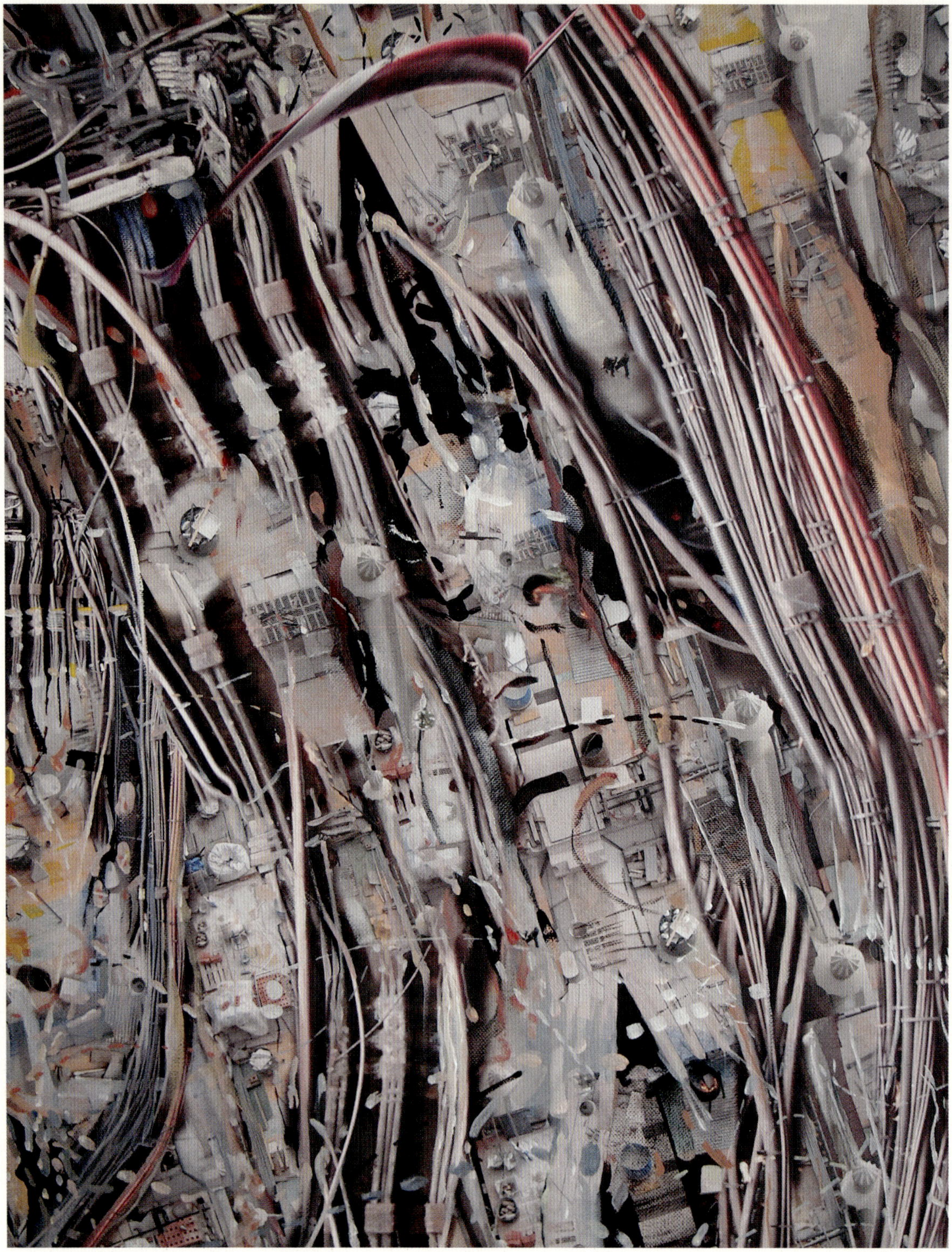

TANGLED CITY (DETAIL) **2012**

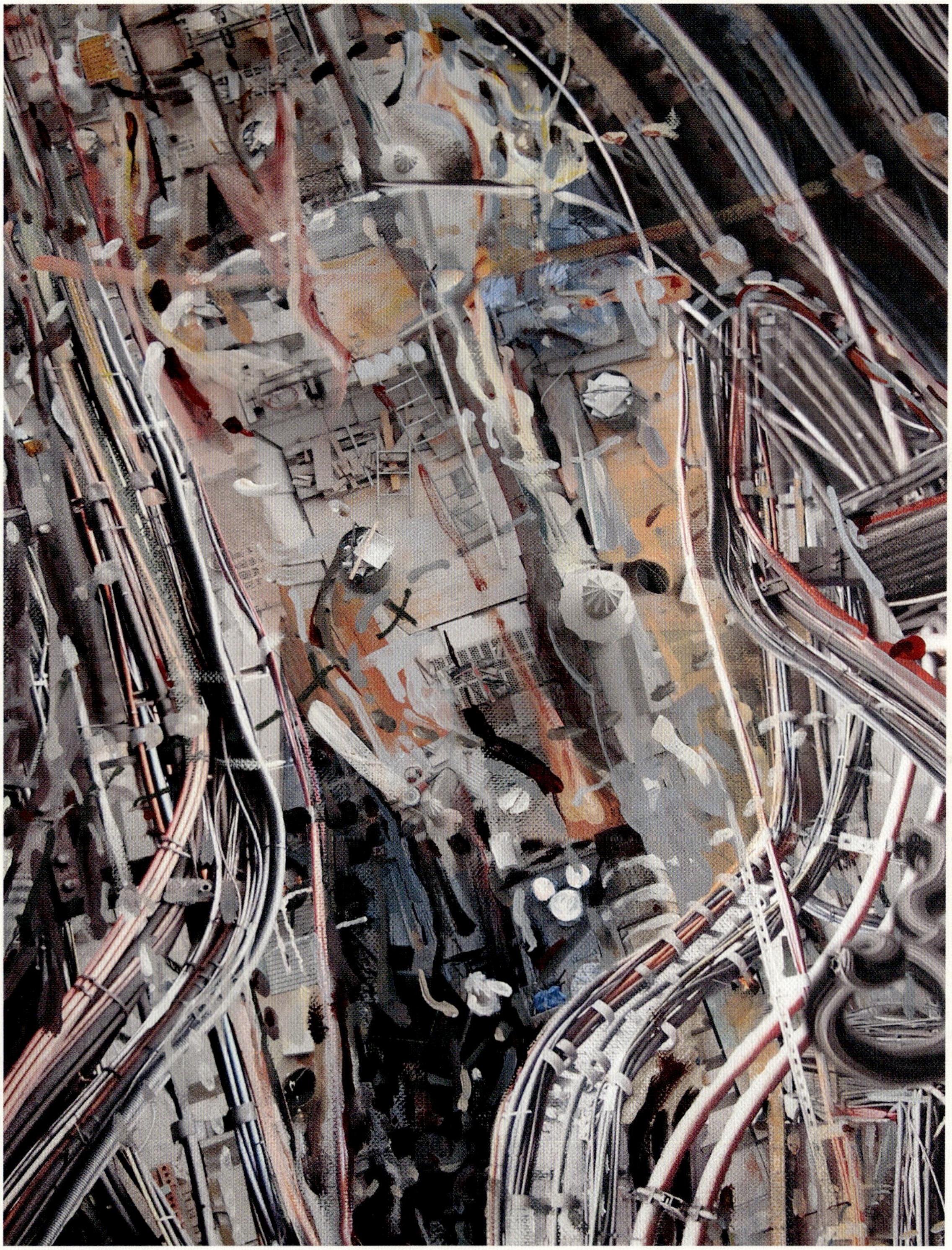

←→
Explorations in photo-collage and paint of the hybrid biological and mechanical structures of the city.

WET ANGELS, CONSTRUCTION SITE (DETAIL) **2015**

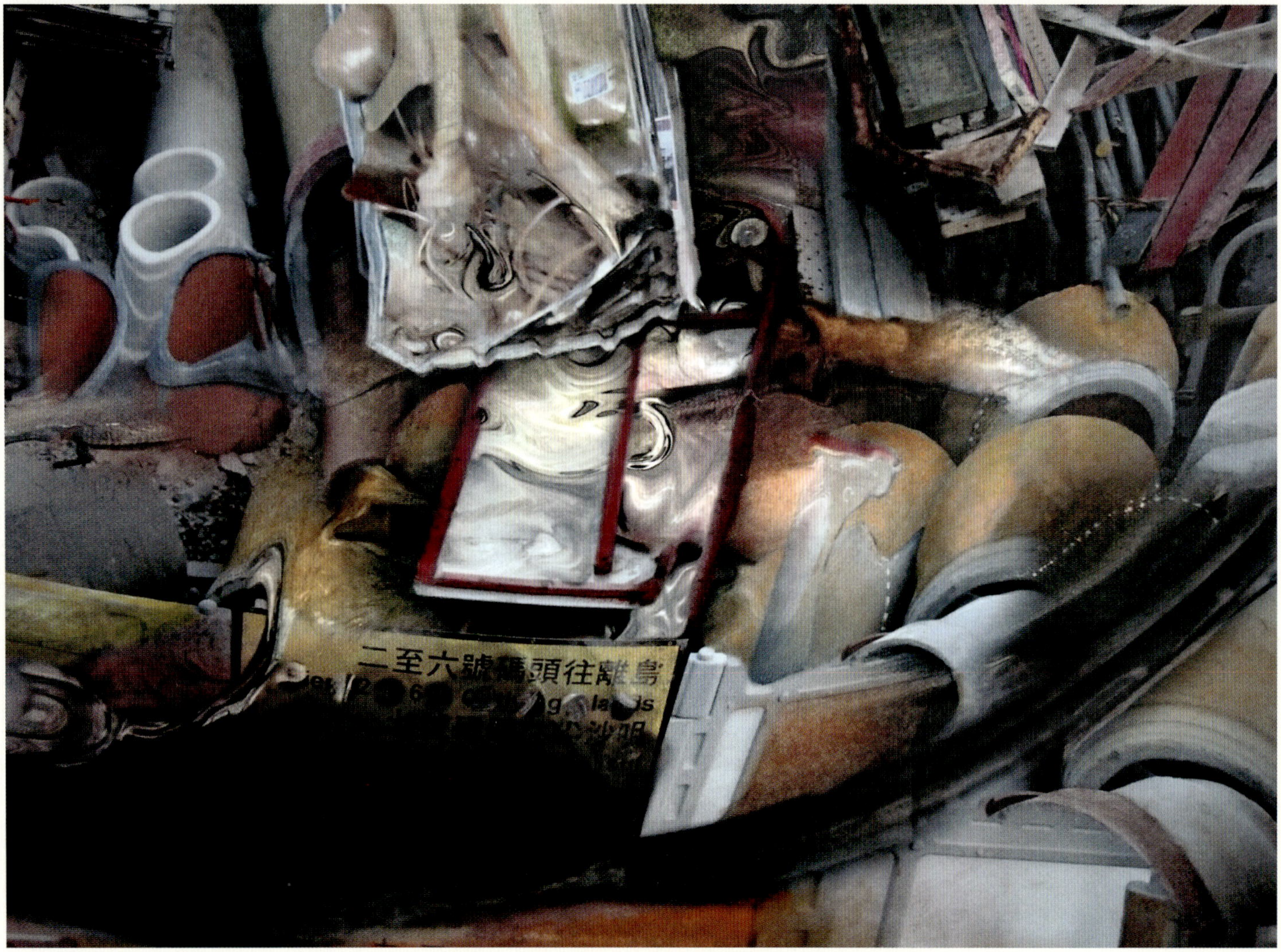

WET ANGELS, EMBLEM OF THE FOREST (DETAIL) **2015**

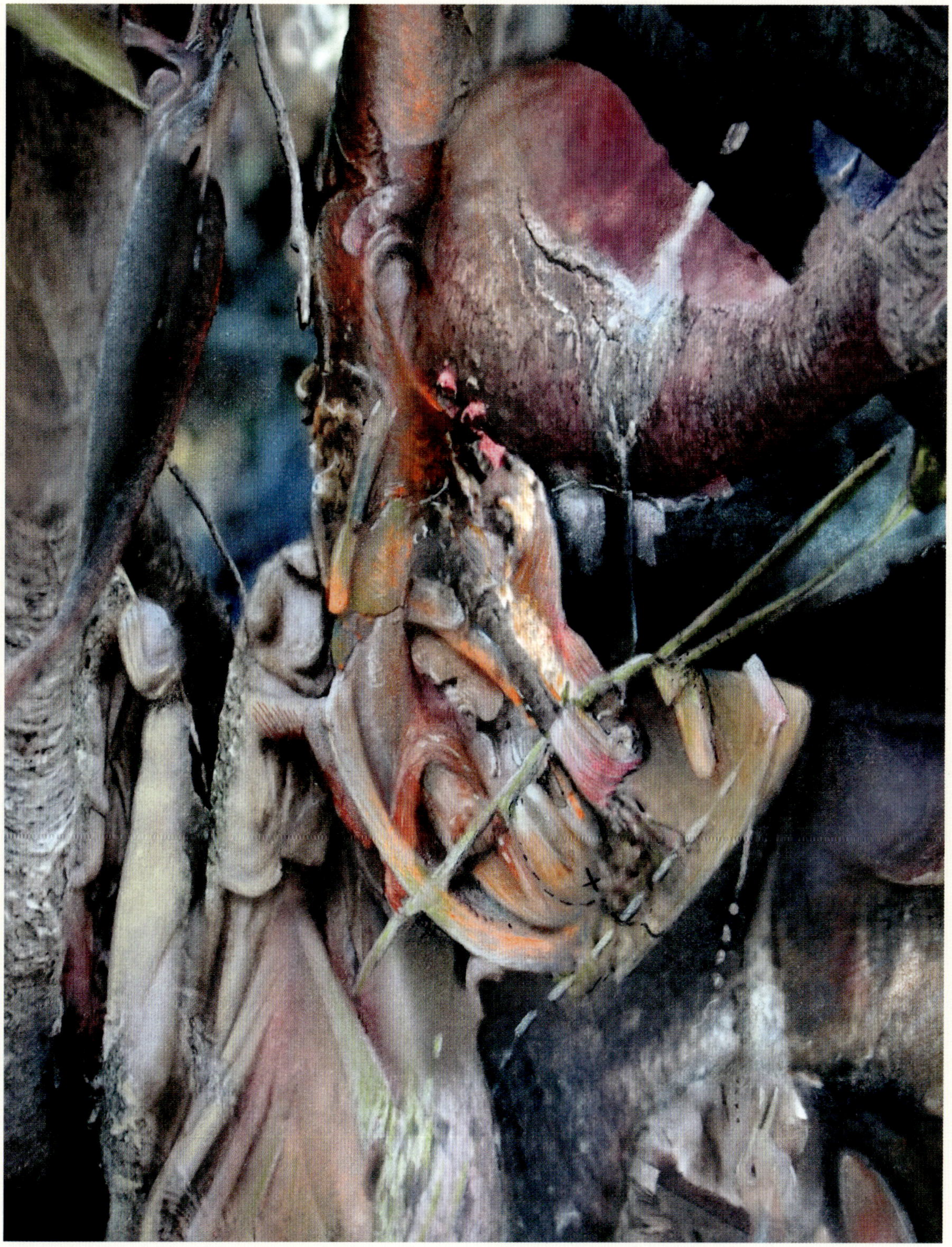

←→

The hybridization of the biomechanical further explored as spaces of myth, dark forest and wet fabrication.

Author Biography

Neil Spiller is Hawksmoor Chair of Architecture and Landscape at the University of Greenwich, London. He is the author of *Visionary Architecture and Digital Architecture Now*, both published by Thames & Hudson. His architectural design work and research have been widely published and exhibited worldwide.

Acknowledgments

This book has benefited from the goodwill of many people. First, the collections, museums and estates of deceased artists and architects and, second, those living architects who have given their work so generously – this is deeply appreciated and I take this opportunity to thank you all publicly.

I thank Lucas Dietrich, at Thames & Hudson, whose wise editorial counsel and friendship is always spot on. Above all I would like to thank Caroline Ellerby, for managing the whole project and me, securing permissions, editing my texts, extracting captions and asking me difficult questions – I couldn't have done it without her.

Photo Acknowledgments

Key
Images acknowledged by page number
a = above, b = below, c = centre
l = left, r = right

1 © Photo Library/Photographer/Archive;
8, **14a**, **14b**, **15**, **16**, **17**, **192a** © Natalija Subotincic. Natalija Subotincic. is the sole author of all the photographic images, paintings, models and construction of the chicken bone dining table and the Sigmund Freud Cabinet study. Natalija Subotincic would like to thank the generous support of: The University of Manitoba, Canada (Creative Works Grant and RGP Research Grant), The Department of Architecture, University of Manitoba, Canada, The Freud Museum in London, U.K., The Sigmund Freud Museum in Vienna, Austria;
10 © Collection Palais Idéal - Emmanuel Georges;
12 © Alastair Brotchie;
13 © Freud Museum London;
18 © National Portrait Gallery, London;
19 © The Norton Simon Foundation, Pasadena, CA;
21 Photo The Philadelphia Museum of Art/Art Resource/Scala, Florence. © DACS 2016;
22 Photo The Philadelphia Museum of Art/Art Resource/Scala, Florence. © Succession Marcel Duchamp/ADAGP, Paris and DACS, London 2016;
24 © ADAGP, Paris and DACS, London 2016;
25 Photo Moderna Museet, Stockholm, Sweden/Bridgeman Images. © ADAGP, Paris and DACS, London 2016;
26 Photo Scala, Florence/bpk, Bildagentur fuer Kunst, Kultur und Geschichte, Berlin. © DACS 2016;
32, **33**, **34l**, **34r**, **35a**, **35b**, **36**, **37** © Natalie Gall;
40 © Yorgos Loizos;
42 © Photo Scala, Florence;
43 Photo Yale University Art Gallery. © DACS 2016;
44 © The estate of Sir Jacob Epstein;
45 Photo The Philadelphia Museum of Art/Art Resource/Scala, Florence. © Succession Marcel Duchamp/ADAGP, Paris and DACS, London 2016;
47l © University of Applied Arts Vienna, Oskar Kokoschka-Center/ faksimile digital. © Fondation Oskar Kokoschka/DACS 2016;
47r Denise Bellon, 1938 © les films de l'équinoxe-fonds photographique Denise Bellon. © Salvador Dalí, Fundació Gala-Salvador Dalí, DACS, 2016;
48a, **48b** Photo Centre Pompidou, MNAM-CCI/Philippe Migeat/Dist. RMN-GP. © ADAGP, Paris and DACS, London 2016;
49 Digital image, The Museum of Modern Art, New York/Scala, Florence. © ADAGP, Paris and DACS, London 2016;
51 Photo The Philadelphia Museum of Art/Art Resource/Scala, Florence. © Salvador Dalí, Fundació Gala-Salvador Dalí, DACS, 2016;
52 © Tate, London;

53 Photo Centre Pompidou, MNAM-CCI, Dist Philippe Migeat/RMN-Grand Palais. © ADAGP, Paris and DACS, London 2016;
55a Photo Simon Hunter © Stelarc;
55b Photo Takatoshi Shinoda © Stelarc;
56–57, 58–59, 60, 61 © Lucas Che Tizard;
62l, 62r, 63 © Neil Spiller;
65a, 65b © Bastian Glaessner;
66 Photo Scala, Florence/bpk, Bildagentur fuer Kunst, Kultur und Geschichte, Berlin. © ADAGP, Paris and DACS, London 2016;
67 © HR Giger 1973. Courtesy HR Giger Museum, Gruyère, Switzerland;
68 Public Domain – G B Piranesi, *Pianta di Roma*, 1762, Rome: Marcellus Theatre and Pantheon plan;
69 © 2015 Andy Davies/HR Giger Museum, Gruyère, Switzerland;
70a, 70b © HR Giger 1975. Courtesy HR Giger Museum, Gruyère, Switzerland;
71 © HR Giger 1981. Courtesy HR Giger Museum, Gruyère, Switzerland;
72 © HR Giger 1983. Courtesy HR Giger Museum, Gruyère, Switzerland;
73 © HR Giger 1987. Courtesy HR Giger Museum, Gruyère, Switzerland;
76 © Tom Cartledge;
78l Digital image, The Museum of Modern Art, New York/Scala, Florence. © ADAGP, Paris and DACS, London 2016;
78r Photo Fine Art Images/Heritage Images/Scala, Florence. © ADAGP, Paris and DACS, London 2016;
79a Photo Digital image, The Museum of Modern Art, New York/Scala, Florence. © The Estate of Alberto Giacometti (Fondation Giacometti, Paris and ADAGP, Paris), licensed in the UK by ACS and DACS, London 2016;
79b © DeAgostini Picture Library/Scala, Florence;
80–81 © FLC/ADAGP, Paris and DACS, London 2016;
82 Photo Collection of Gale and Ira Drukier. © ADAGP, Paris and DACS, London 2016;
84a, 84bl 84br © FAT Architecture (Kevin Rhowbotham, Clive Sall, Sean Griffiths, Adrian Friend and Paul Kiera);
86–87 © Austrian Frederick and Lillian Kiesler Private Foundation, photographer unknown;
88 © Austrian Frederick and Lillian Kiesler Private Foundation;
89 Photo G. Barrows © Austrian Frederick and Lillian Kiesler Private Foundation;
90–91 © Austrian Frederick and Lillian Kiesler Private Foundation;
93 Digital image, The Museum of Modern Art, New York/Scala, Florence. © Succession Marcel Duchamp/ADAGP, Paris and DACS, London 2016;
95al, 95ar, 95b, 96, 97 © Estate of Lebbeus Woods;
99l, 99r © Tom Cartledge;
102 © Collection Canadian Centre for Architecture, Montreal;
104 Photo Hélène Binet. Courtesy Collection Canadian Centre for Architecture, Montreal;
106, 107al, 107ar, 107bl, 107br © 2015. Digital image, The Museum of Modern Art, New York/Scala, Florence. Images used by permission from the Douglas Darden Estate, courtesy of Allison Collins;
108a, 108b © Keiichi Matsuda 2010;
110a, 110b, 111, 112 © Lenastina Andersson;
113a, 113c, 113b © Images courtesy Greg Lynn FORM;
115, 116, 118, 120, 121 © The Capp Street Project Archive at California College of the Arts Libraries, San Francisco, California;
124 © FleaFolly Architects;
126 Photo Musée d'Orsay, Dist. Patrice Schmidt/RMN-Grand Palais;
128–29 © Neil Spiller;
130, 131 Photo Eric Schaal © Fundació Gala-Salvador Dalí Figueres, 2016;
133, 134 © Eredi Aldo Rossi;
137 138–39, 140–41 © Image by Madelon Vriesendorp; courtesy of OMA;
143, 144–45 © Collection Canadian Centre for Architecture, Montreal;
146 © Bernard Tschumi;
149al, © imagIN.gr photography/Shutterstock.com;
149ar, © Vladimir Sazonov/Shutterstock.com
149bl, © Roka/Shutterstock.com;
149br, © Kiev.Victor/Shutterstock.com;
151, 152, 153, 155, 156, 157 © C. J. Lim;
159, 160–61, 162, 163, 164, 165 © FleaFolly Architects;
167, 168–69 Photos Matt Gusyh © Bryan Cantley;
170–71 © Bryan Cantley, rendering by Mike Amaya;
172–73, 174–75 © Photos Nic Clear;
176 The Arthur Ross Collection of European Prints, Yale University Art Gallery;
177, 180–81, 182, 183, 184, 185, 186, 187 © Neil Spiller;
190 © Photo Scala, Florence. Courtesy the Ministero Beni e Att. Culturali;
192b Photo The Philadelphia Museum of Art. © Succession Marcel Duchamp/ADAGP, Paris and DACS, London 2016;
194al © KarSol/Shutterstock.com;
194ar © Luciano Mortula/Shutterstock.com;
194bl © Semen Lixodeev/Shutterstock.com;
194br © 2011 Stephen Silverman;
197 Digital image, The Museum of Modern Art, New York/Scala, Florence. © ARS, NY and DACS, London 2016;
198–99 Photo Allen Phillips/Wadsworth Atheneum. © ADAGP, Paris and DACS, London 2016;
200 Photo The Philadelphia Museum of Art/Art Resource/Scala, Florence. © ADAGP, Paris and DACS, London 2016;
203l, 203c, 203r © 1977 by Leo Lionni, © renewed 2005 by Nora Lionni and Louis Mannie Lionni;
204, 205, 206, 207, 208, 209, 210l, 210r, 211 © Daniel Libeskind;
212a, 212b © Nat Chard;
213, 214–15, 216, 217 © Perry Kulper;
219, 220a, 220b © Xefirotarch/Hernan Diaz Alonso;
222–23, 224–25, 226 © Christian Kerrigan;
228al, 228ar, 228bl, 228br, 229a, 229b © Dan Slavinsky;
230–31, 232–33 © Christian Kerrigan;
234 © Elizabeth Anne Williams;
237, 238a, 238b, 239a, 239b, 240, 241, 242, 243 © Mark West.

Selected Bibliography

Sarane Alexandrian,
Surrealist Art,
London and New York,
1970

André Breton,
Manifestoes of Surrealism,
trans. Richard Seaver and Helen R. Lane,
Ann Arbor, MI,
1972

Italo Calvino,
Invisible Cities **[1972],**
trans. William Weaver,
San Diego, New York, London,
1974

Nan Ellin (ed.),
Architecture of Fear,
New York,
1997

Haim Finkelstein (ed. and trans.),
The Collected Writings of Salvador Dalí,
Cambridge,
1998

Arie Graafland,
Architectural Bodies,
ed. Michael Speaks,
Rotterdam,
1996

Lewis Kachur,
Displaying the Marvelous,
Cambridge, MA,
2001

George Melly,
Paris and the Surrealists,
London,
1991

Thomas Mical (ed.),
Surrealism and Architecture,
London and New York,
2004

Jennifer Mundy (ed.),
Surrealism: Desire Unbound,
London,
2001

Aldo Rossi,
The Architecture of the City **[1966],**
trans. Diane Ghirado and Joan Ockman
(revised edn by Aldo Rossi and
Peter Eisenman from the original
published in Padua in 1966),
Cambridge, MA, and London,
1982

Colin Rowe and Fred Koetter,
Collage City,
Cambridge, MA, and London,
1978

Robert Venturi,
Complexity and Contradiction in Architecture,
New York,
1966

Anthony Vidler,
The Architectural Uncanny:
Essays in the Modern Unhomely,
Cambridge, MA,
1992

References

Introduction

1 Natalija Subotincic, 'Incarnate Tendencies: An Architecture of Culinary Refuse', in Jamie Horwitz and Paulette Singley (eds), *Eating Architecture*, Cambridge, MA, 2004 (quote is from the unpaginated 'Gallery of Recipes' section located between pp. 36 and 37).

2 'He is fair as the retractility of the claws of birds of prey, or again as the uncertainty of the muscular movements in wounds in the soft parts of the lower cervical region, or rather, as that perpetual rattrap always reset by the trapped animal, which by itself can catch rodents indefinitely and work even when hidden under straw; and above all, as the chance meeting on a dissecting table of a sewing machine and an umbrella!', Comte de Lautrémont, The Songs of Maldoror [1868–69], in *Maldoror and the Complete Works of the Comte de Lautrémont*, 1994, p. 193.

3 Guillaume Apollinaire, programme note to *Parade*, 18 May 1917.

4 'Comte de Lautréamont, *The Songs of Maldoror* [1868–9], in *Maldoror and the Complete Works of the Comte de Lautréamont*, 1994.

5 André Breton, 'Manifesto of Surrealism', pp. 26–27.

6 Andre Breton, 'Second Manifesto of Surrealism' [1930], in *Manifestoes of Surrealism*, pp. 123–24.

7 Christian Bök, *'Pataphysics: The Poetics of an Imaginary Science*, Evanston, IL, 2002, p. 18.

8 Natalija Subotincic, 'A Holding Environment: Drawing Out and Constructing Sigmund Freud's Psychical Terrain', in Eduardo Aquino, Kelley Beaverford and Marcella Eaton (eds), *Dead on Arrival*, Winnipeg, 2009, p. 76.

9 Natalija Subotincic, *Never Speak With Your Mouth Full*, Winnipeg, 2008, booklet 2, 'With Your', p. 24.

10 André Breton, 'Manifesto of Surrealism', p. 14.

11 Dagmar Motycka Weston, 'The Situational Space of André Breton's Atelier and Personal Museum in Paris', in Soumyen Bandyopadhyay, Jane Lomholt, Nicholas Temple and Renée Tobe (eds), *The Humanities in Architectural Design*, London, 2010, p. 208.

12 Anthony Vidler, *The Architectural Uncanny: Essays in the Modern Unhomely*, Cambridge, MA, 1992, p. 7.

13 Ibid., p. 7.

14 Giorgio de Chirico, 'Mystery and Creation', in Herschel B. Chipp (ed.), *Theories of Modern Art: A Source Book by Artists and Critics*, Berkeley and Los Angeles, CA, 1969, p. 402.

15 Tristan Tzara, 'Manifeste Dada', *Dada 3*, Zurich, 1918.

16 Louis Aragon, *Paris Peasant*, trans. Simon Watson Taylor, London, 1987, pp. 36–37.

17 George Melly, *Paris and the Surrealists*, London, 1991, p. 110.

18 Roger Cardinal, 'The Soluble City: The Surrealist Perception of Paris', in Dalibor Vesely (ed.), *Architectural Design*, *Surrealism and Architecture*, 48, 2–3, 1978, pp. 143–49.

Cooking With Chance In The Cauldron Of Creativity

1 Oulipo stands for *Ouvroir de littérature potentielle* and is a loose confederacy of writers searching for new ways to introduce creative constraints into their work as a method to conceive of previously unimagined combinations of words and letters to produce poetry and prose.

2 Natalie Gall, unpublished, untitled, document sent to the author 27 June 2015.

3 Leonora Carrington, *The Hearing Trumpet*, New York, 1976, pp. 136–39.

4 Natalie Gall, document sent to the author.

Chapter I: Surreal Bodies

1 Alfred Jarry, *Exploits and Opinions of Doctor Faustroll, 'Pataphysician* [1911], in Alfred Jarry, *Three Early Novels: Collected Works II*, trans. Alastair Brotchie et al., London, 2006, p. 134.

2 Xavière Gauthier, *Surréalisme et sexualité*, Paris, 1971, p. 211, quoted in Arie Graafland, *Architectural Bodies*, ed. Michael Speaks, Rotterdam, 1996, p. 53.

3 Linda Harris, *The Secret Heresy of Hieronymous Bosch*, Edinburgh, 1995.

4 Sigmund Freud, 'The Uncanny' [1919], in *The Standard Edition of the Complete Psychological Works of Sigmund Freud*, trans. James Strachey, London, 1955.

5 Raymond Roussel, *Impressions of Africa* [1910], trans. Lindy Foord and Rayner Heppenstall, London, 2001, p. 10.

6 Duchamp, interviewed by James Johnson Sweeney, 1946, quoted in Linda Dalrymple Henderson, *Duchamp in Context*, Princeton, NJ, and Oxford, 1998, p. 51.

7 Marcel Duchamp, 'Note in the Green Box' [1912], in *From the Green Box*, trans. George Heard Hamilton, New Haven, CT, 1957, unpaginated.

8 Dalrymple Henderson, *Duchamp in Context*, p. 49.

10 Jennifer Mundy, *Duchamp, Man Ray, Picabia*, London, 2008, p. 10.

11 Dietmar Elger and Uta Grosenick (eds), *Dadaism*, Los Angeles, 2004, p. 38.

12 André Breton, 'Manifesto of Surrealism' [1924], in André Breton, *Manifestoes of Surrealism*, trans. Richard Seaver and Helen R. Lane, Ann Arbor, MI, 1972, p. 16.

13 Sue Taylor explores Bellmer's motivations and preoccupations in some detail in her book *Hans Bellmer: The Anatomy of Anxiety*, Cambridge, MA, and London, 2000.

14 Ibid., p. 24.

15 Hans Bellmer, 'Notes on the Subject of the Ball Joint' [1938], reprinted in the Hans Bellmer special issue of *Obliques*, Paris, 1938, pp. 82–91.

16 Lewis Kachur, *Displaying the Marvelous*, Cambridge, MA, 2001, p. 40.

17 Jean Baudrillard, *Fatal Strategies: Crystal Revenge*, trans. Philip Beitchman and W. G. J. Niesluchowski, ed. Jim Fleming, New York, 1990, p. 80.

18 John McHale, 'The Expendable Ikon', *Architectural Design*, February 1959, pp. 82–83.

19 See: http://stelarc.org/_.swf.
20 William Burroughs, *Naked Lunch*, New York, 1959, p. 9.
21 Donna Haraway, 'A Cyborg Manifesto: Science, Technology and Socialist-Feminism in the 1980s', *Simians, Cyborgs, and Women*, New York, 1989, p. 150.
22 William Gibson, *Neuromancer*, London, 1993, p. 67.
23 Scott Bukatman, *Terminal Identity: The Virtual Subject in Postmodern Science Fiction*, Durham, NC, and London, 1993, p. 296.
24 Neil Spiller, 'Deformology: The Poetics of Cybridised Architecture', *Junk Jet*, 2, 2008, pp. 22–29.
25 *The Gospel of Thomas*, 22.

The Architecture Of Biomechanical Chimeras

1 Neil Cox, in Jennifer Mundy (ed.), *Surrealism: Desire Unbound*, London, 2001, p. 232.

Chapter II: The Surreal House

1 John Hejduk, 'Sentences on the House and other Sentences', *Pewter Wings, Golden Horns, Silver Veils*, New York, 1997, pp. 214–19.
2 Giorgio de Chirico, 'Statues, Furniture and Generals', *Hebdomeros* [1929], Cambridge, MA, 1992, p. 246.
3 Salvador Dalí, 'Concerning the Terrifying and Edible Beauty of Art Nouveau Architecture', *Minotaure*, 3–4, December 1933, pp. 69–76, quoted in Haim Finkelstein (ed. and trans.), *The Collected Writings of Salvador Dalí*, Cambridge, 1998, pp. 194–95.
4 Ibid.
5 Anne Troutman, 'Inside Fear: Secret Places and Hidden Spaces in Dwelling', in Nan Ellin (ed.), *Architecture of Fear*, New York, 1997, p. 143.
6 Tristan Tzara, 'D'un certain automatisme du Gout', *Minotaure*, 3–4, December 1933, p. 847.
7 Roberto Matta (adapted by Georges Hugnet), 'Mathématique sensible – architecture du temps' ('Sensible Mathematics – Architecture of Time'), *Minotaure*, 11, May 1938, p. 43.
8 Stephen Phillips, 'Frederick Kiesler and his Dream Machine', in Thomas Mical (ed.), *Surrealism and Architecture*, London and New York, 2005, p. 150.
9 FAT, 'Anti-Oedipal House', *AD Architecture and the Horizon*, Profile 122, July/August 1996, p. 72.
10 Frances Yates, *The Art of Memory*, Chicago, IL, 1966.
11 Charles Henri Ford (ed.), *View: The Marcel Duchamp Special Issue*, no. 5, vol. 1, March 1945, p. 24.
12 James Joyce, *Finnegans Wake,* New York, 1965, p. 183.
13 Lebbeus Woods, 'Measuring Light', 30 April 2012: https://lebbeuswoods.wordpress.com.
14 Lebbeus Woods, 'Solo House @ 20', 1 December 2008: https://lebbeuswoods.wordpress.com.
15 Neil Spiller, 'Digital Solipsism and the Paradox of the Great "Forgetting"', in Rivka Oxman and Robert Oxman (eds), *AD The New Structuralism*, July/August 2010, pp. 130–34.
16 Anne Troutman, 'Inside Fear', p. 143.
17 Le Corbusier, '5D *Fusion* (Red)', *Le Poeme de l'angle droit* (The Poem of the Right Angle), Paris, 1955.
18 Walter Benjamin, 'Passagen-Werk', *Gesammelte Schriften*, 5, 1982, p. 573.
19 John Hejduk, 'Cemetery for the Ashes of the Still Life Painter', *Adjusting Foundations*, ed. Kim Shkapich, New York, 1995.
20 Canadian Centre for Architecture, 'John Hejduk: House of the Suicide and The House of the Mother of the Suicide': www.cca.qc.ca.
21 Peter Schneider, 'The House at the End of Time: Douglas Darden's Oxygen House', *PART 7: Technology & the Home, Journal of CUNY PhD Program in Art History*, New York, 2001, see: http://part-archive.finitude.org/part7/practice/schnei.html.
22 Ibid.
23 Raymond Roussel, *Locus Solus* [1970], trans. Rupert Copeland Cuningham, London, 2003, p. 120.

Juiceless Cyborgs – Invisible in White Light

1 Greg Bear, *Blood Music*, New York, 1985, p. 188.
2 Anthony Vidler, *The Architectural Uncanny: Essays in the Modern Unhomely*, Cambridge, MA, 1992, p. 161.
3 The 'dissecting-table' is from the famous line coined by the Comte de Lautréamont in his Proto-Surrealist novel *Chants de Maldoror* (1868–69) to describe the beauty of a young boy 'beautiful as the chance meeting on a dissecting-table of a sewing machine and an umbrella' – an expression often quoted by Surrealists.

Chapter III: The Great Transparent City

1 Italo Calvino, *Invisible Cities* [1972], trans. William Weaver, San Diego, New York, London, 1974, p. 12.
2 Michael Moorcock, *Mother London*, London, 1988, p. 7.
3 Howard Eiland and William W. Jennings (eds), *Walter Benjamin: Selected Writings, Vol 4, 1938–40*, Cambridge, MA, 2003, p. 19.
4 Louis Aragon, *Paris Peasant*, trans. Simon Watson Taylor, Boston, MA, 1994.
5 Fernando Magallanes, 'Landscape Surrealism', in Thomas Mical (ed.), *Surrealism and Architecture*, London and New York, 2005, p. 222.
6 André Breton, *Nadja* [1928], trans. R. Howard, New York, 1962.
7 Roger Cardinal, 'The Soluble City: The Surrealist Perception of Paris', in Dalibor Vesely (ed.), *AD Surrealism and Architecture*, 48, 2–3, 1978, pp. 143–49.
8 Italo Calvino, *Invisible Cities*, p. 5 (preface).
9 Sarane Alexandrian, *Surrealist Art*, London and New York, 1970, p. 100.
10 Rem Koolhaas, 'Biuer! Ai bring ou surrealism aulredi meni pipoul in niu york jove bin infected bai zi laifquiving and marvelous sors of surrealism', in *AD Surrealism and Architecture*, p. 153.
11 Ibid., p. 159.
12 Salvador Dalí quoted in Ingrid Schaffner, *Salvador Dalí's Dream of Venus: The Surrealist Funhouse from the 1939 World's Fair*, New York, 2002, p. 10.

13 André Breton, 'Prolegomena to a Third Surrealist Manifesto or Not' [1942], in André Breton, *Manifestoes of Surrealism*, trans. Richard Seaver and Helen R. Lane, Ann Arbor, MI, 1972, p. 293.
14 Aldo Rossi, *The Architecture of the City* [1966], trans. Diane Ghirado and Joan Ockman (revised edn by Aldo Rossi and Peter Eisenman from the original published in Padua in 1966), Cambridge, MA, and London, 1982, p. 65.
15 Robert Venturi, *Complexity and Contradiction in Architecture*, New York, 1966, p. 16.
16 Italo Calvino, *Invisible Cities*, p. 140.
17 Robert Venturi, Denise Scott Brown and Steven Izenour, *Learning from Las Vegas*, Cambridge, MA, and London, 1972, p. 13.
18 Colin Rowe and Fred Koetter, *Collage City*, Cambridge, MA, and London, 1978, p. 119.
19 *AD Surrealism and Architecture*, pp. 153–64.
20 Bernard Tschumi, 'Architecture and Its Double', in *AD Surrealism and Architecture*, p. 116.
21 Michael Sorkin, *Exquisite Corpse: Writing on Buildings*, New York, 1991, p. 183.
22 See www.tschumi.com/projects/18/.
23 J. L. Giménez-Frontín, *Teatre-Museu Dalí*, Barcelona and Madrid, 1999, p. 19.
24 Ibid., p. 21.
25 Lewis Kachur, *Displaying the Marvelous*, Cambridge, MA, and London, 2001, p. 51.
26 C. J. Lim, *Virtually Venice*, London, 2006, p. 33.
27 Ibid.
28 James Williamson, 'Acropolis Now!', in Thomas Mical, *Surrealism and Architecture*, p. 326.
29 Pascal Bronner and Thomas Hillier, *Grimm City: An Architectural Fairy Tale* (self-published), unpaginated, 2012.
30 Jill Fenton, 'Re-enchanting the City', in Thomas Mical, *Surrealism and Architecture*, p. 210.
31 Nic Clear, 'The Gold Mine: A Ludic Architecture', in Mark Garcia (ed.), *AD Future Details of Architecture*, July/August 2014, p. 132.

The Surreal Memory Theatre

1 Neil Spiller, 'Detailing the Walled Garden for Lebbeus', in Mark Garcia (ed.), *AD Future Details of Architecture*, July/August 2014, p. 126.

Chapter IV: The Engorged Garden

1 Leo Lionni, *Parallel Botany*, New York, 1977, p. 5.
2 Salvador Dalí, *Surtout l'art ornemental*, exh. cat., Galerie Pierre Colle, Paris, 1931.
3 Christopher Green, 'Souvenirs of the Jardín des Plantes: Making the Exotic Strange Again', *Jungles in Paris: The Paintings of Henri Rousseau*, exh. cat., Tate, London, 2005, pp. 39–40.
4 Alfred Jarry, *Exploits and Opinions of Doctor Faustroll, 'Pataphysician* [1911], in Alfred Jarry, *Three Early Novels: Collected Works II*, trans. Alastair Brotchie et al., London, 2006, pp. 195–96.
5 Sigmund Freud, 'The Moses of Michelangelo', *The Standard Edition of the Complete Psychological Works of Sigmund Freud: Volume XIII (1913–1914) Totem and Taboo and Other Works*, trans. James Strachey, London, 1st edn, 1955, p. 230.
6 Natalija Subotincic, email to the author, 5 July 2015.
7 Salvador Dalí, 'Concerning the Terrifying and Edible Beauty of Art Nouveau Architecture', *Minotaure* 3–4, December 1933, pp. 69–76, quoted in Haim Finkelstein (ed. and trans.), *The Collected Writings of Salvador Dalí*, Cambridge, 1998, pp. 194–95.
8 Ibid., p. 200
9 See: www.philamuseum.org/collections/permanent/85338.html.
10 Salvador Dalí, *Anti-Matter Manifesto*, exh. cat., Carstairs Gallery, New York, 1958.
11 Salvador Dalí, *The Cylindrical Monarchy of Guimard* [1968], trans. Albert Field, *Arts Magazine*, March 1970, pp. 42–43.
12 Leo Lionni, *Parallel Botany*, p. 7.
13 Ibid., p. 79.
14 Daniel Libeskind, *Between Zero and Infinity*, New York, 1981.
15 Daniel Libeskind, *Chamber Works: Architectural Meditations on Themes from Heraclitus*, London, 1983.
16 Daniel Libeskind, *Theatrum Mundi: Through the Green Membranes of Space*, inside back cover, London, 1985, unpaginated.
17 Ibid.
18 Alfred Jarry, *Exploits and Opinions of Doctor Faustroll, 'Pataphysician*, p. 218.
19 Hernan Diaz Alonso, 'Pretentious and Incoherent Thoughts on Architecture – Right Now', in Neil Spiller and Nic Clear (eds), *Educating Architects: How Tomorrow's Practitioners Will Learn Today*, London, 2014, p. 264.
20. Ibid., p. 268.
21 Neil Spiller and Rachel Armstrong, 'It's a Brand New Morning', in Neil Spiller and Rachel Armstrong (eds), *AD Protocell Architecture*, March/April 2011, p. 21.
22 Neil Spiller, Rachel Armstrong and Martin Hanczyc, 'A Manifesto for Protocell Architecture: Against Biological Formalism', in ibid., pp. 24–25.
23 Daniel Slavinsky, unpublished notes for his In Arcadia at the End of Time project.
24 Neil Spiller, 'Protocells: the Universal Solvent', in Spiller and Armstrong (eds), *AD Protocell Architecture*, p. 67.

Safe Houses for Wet Angels

1 Mark West, 'Out of Our Hands: Three Architectural Fantasies for Strange and Sad Ecologies', in Shaun Murray (ed.), *Design Ecologies 2.2: A Sentient Relic*, Bristol, 2012, pp. 214–35.
2 Ibid., p. 216.
3 Ibid., p. 218.
4 Ibid., p. 224.
5 Ibid., p. 231.

Index

Page numbers in *italic* refer to illustrations